**05**

TORONTO

Where to Stay and Eat
for All Budgets

Must-See Sights
and Local Secrets

Ratings You Can Trust

Fodor's Travel Publications   New York, Toronto, London, Sydney, Auckland
www.fodors.com

FODOR'S TORONTO 2005
Editor: Sarah Sper

Editorial Production: Jacinta O'Halloran
Editorial Contributors: Ashley Anderson, Bruce Bishop, Collin Campbell, Lisa Dunford, Satu Hummasti, Hannah James, Ilona Kauremszky, Shannon Kelly, Jack Kohane, Kirsten McKenzie, Vernon O'Reilly-Ramesar, Sara Waxman
Maps: David Lindroth, *cartographer;* Bob Blake and Rebecca Baer, *map editors*
Design: Fabrizio La Rocca, *creative director;* Guido Caroti, *art director;* Melanie Marin, *senior picture editor*
Production/Manufacturing: Robert B. Shields
Cover Photo (Nathan Phillips Square): Walter Bibikow/Viesti Associates

ISBN 1–4000–1470–0

ISSN 1044-6133

SPECIAL SALES
This book is available for special discounts for bulk purchases for sales promotions or premiums. Special editions, including personalized covers, excerpts of existing books, and corporate imprints, can be created in large quantities for special needs. For more information, write to Special Markets/Premium Sales, 1745 Broadway, MD 6-2, New York, NY 10019 or e-mail specialmarkets@randomhouse.com.

AN IMPORTANT TIP & AN INVITATION
Although all prices, opening times, and other details in this book are based on information supplied to us at press time, changes occur all the time in the travel world, and Fodor's cannot accept responsibility for facts that become outdated or for inadvertent errors or omissions. So **always confirm information when it matters,** especially if you're making a detour to visit a specific place. Your experiences—positive and negative—matter to us. If we have missed or misstated something, **please write to us.** We follow up on all suggestions. Contact the Toronto editor at editors@fodors.com or c/o Fodor's at 1745 Broadway, New York, New York 10019.

PRINTED IN THE UNITED STATES OF AMERICA

10 9 8 7 6 5 4 3 2 1

DESTINATION TORONTO

Torontonians are chagrined that outsiders often compare their home-town to New York City. True, it's their nation's cultural and com-munications capital. The downtown bustles, and there are skyscrapers. In fact, the city stands in for Manhattan in many a Holly-wood blockbuster. Toronto's population is ethnically diverse, encom-passing more than 100 ethnic groups speaking more than 100 languages. The city is dynamic and exciting. Yet when you stand on the glass floor of the CN Tower observation deck, 1,122 feet above the street, you see not only the urban maze below but also acres of green reaching out toward the horizon and Lake Ontario stretching blue toward the U.S. border. Yorkville, where the well-heeled dine and shop for their little luxuries, is low-key, and a sense of pleasant ease crops up again and again as you make your way around town, from the St. Lawrence Market to the Harbourfront. Relax, and enjoy the scene.

Tim Jarrell, Publisher

CONTENTS

Maps

CloseUps

ABOUT THIS BOOK

The best source for travel advice is a like-minded friend who's just been where you're headed. But with or without that friend, you'll be in great shape to find your way around your destination once you learn to find your way around your Fodor's guide.

SELECTION

Our goal is to cover the best properties, sights, and activities in their category, as well as the most interesting communities to visit. You can go on the assumption that everything in this book is recommended wholeheartedly by our writers and editors. Flip to **On the Road with Fodor's** to learn more about who they are. It goes without saying that no property pays to be included.

RATINGS

Orange stars ★ denote sights and properties that our editors and writers consider the very best in the area covered by the entire book. These, the best of the best, are listed in the **Fodor's Choice** section in the front of the book. Black stars ★ highlight the sights and properties we deem **Highly Recommended**, the don't-miss sights within any region. In Toronto, sights pinpointed with numbered map bullets ❶ in the margins tend to be more important than those without bullets.

SPECIAL SPOTS

Pleasures & Pastimes and text on chapter title pages focus on experiences that reveal the spirit of the destination. Also watch for **Off the Beaten Path** sights. Some are out of the way, some are quirky, and all are worthwhile. When the munchies hit, look for **Need a Break?** suggestions.

TIME IT RIGHT

Check **On the Calendar** up front and chapters' **Timing** sections for weather and crowd overviews and best days and times to visit.

SEE IT ALL

Use Fodor's exclusive **Great Itineraries** as a model for your trip. **Good Walks** guide you to important sights in each Toronto neighborhood; ▶ indicates the starting points of walks and itineraries in the text and on the map.

BUDGET WELL

Hotel and restaurant price categories from ¢ to $$$$ are defined in the opening pages of each chapter—expect to find a balanced selection for every budget. For attractions, we always give standard adult admission fees; reductions are usually available for children, students, and senior citizens. Want to pay with plastic? **AE, D, DC, MC, V** following restaurant and hotel listings indicate whether American Express, Discover, Diner's Club, MasterCard, or Visa are accepted.

BASIC INFO

Smart Travel Tips lists travel essentials for the entire area covered by the book; city- and region-specific basics can also be found in the side-trips chapter. To find the best way to get around, see the transportation section; see individual modes of travel for details.

ON THE MAPS

Maps throughout the book show you what's where and help you find your way around. Black and orange numbered bullets ❶❶ in the text correlate to bullets on maps.

BACKGROUND	We give background information within the chapters in the course of explaining sights as well as in **CloseUp** boxes.
FIND IT FAST	Within the Exploring Toronto chapter, sights are grouped by neighborhood. Where to Eat and Where to Stay are also organized by neighborhood—Where to Eat is further divided by cuisine type. The Nightlife & the Arts and Sports & the Outdoors chapters are arranged alphabetically by entertainment type. Within Shopping, a description of the city's main shopping districts is followed by a list of specialty shops grouped according to their focus. Side Trips is divided into small regions; attractive routes and interesting places between towns are flagged as **En Route**. Heads at the top of each page help you find what you need within a chapter.
DON'T FORGET	**Restaurants** are open for lunch and dinner daily unless we state otherwise; we mention dress only when there's a specific requirement and reservations only when they're essential or not accepted—it's always best to book ahead. **Hotels** have private baths, phone, TVs, and air-conditioning and operate on the European Plan (a.k.a. EP, meaning without meals, unless otherwise noted). We always list facilities but not whether you'll be charged extra to use them, so when pricing accommodations, find out what's included.
SYMBOLS	

Many Listings
- ★ Fodor's Choice
- ★ Highly recommended
- ⊠ Physical address
- ✦ Directions
- ⌂ Mailing address
- ☎ Telephone
- 🗏 Fax
- ⊕ On the Web
- ✎ E-mail
- 🎫 Admission fee
- ⊙ Open/closed times
- ► Start of walk/itinerary
- Ⓜ Metro stations
- ⊟ Credit cards

Outdoors
- ⅄ Golf
- ⚠ Camping

Hotels & Restaurants
- 🏨 Hotel
- ⬐ Number of rooms
- ⌂ Facilities
- ⍩ Meal plans
- ✗ Restaurant
- ⍐ Reservations
- 🏛 Dress code
- ⍀ Smoking
- ⍾ BYOB
- ✗🏨 Hotel with restaurant that warrants a visit

Other
- ☺ Family-friendly
- 🛈 Contact information
- ⇨ See also
- ⊠ Branch address
- ☞ Take note

ON THE ROAD WITH FODOR'S

A trip takes you out of yourself. Concerns of life at home completely disappear, driven away by more immediate thoughts—about, say, what marvels will beguile the next day, or where you'll have dinner. That's where Fodor's comes in. We make sure that you know all your options, so that you don't miss something that's around the next bend just because you didn't know it was there. Because the best memories of your trip might well have nothing to do with what you came to Toronto to see, we guide you to sights large and small all over the city. You might set out for a SkyDome game, but back at home you find yourself unable to forget the dim sum you ate at Lai Wah Heen. With Fodor's at your side, serendipitous discoveries are never far away.

Our success in showing you every corner of Toronto is a credit to our extraordinary writers. Although there's no substitute for travel advice from a good friend who knows your style, our contributors are the next best thing—the kind of people you would poll for travel advice if you knew them.

Ashley Anderson, who updated and expanded the Toronto shopping chapter, is a freelance journalist based in Toronto who has written for *Toronto Life Magazine* and the *Toronto Star,* among other publications. She particularly enjoys the field research involved in writing about shopping.

Bruce Bishop, who updated the Smart Travel Tips, Exploring, and Side Trips chapters, is the former president of the Travel Media Association of Canada. Based in Toronto, he is a freelance travel writer and has written for the *Globe and Mail* and the *Toronto Star,* among others.

Hannah James, who updated the Nightlife & the Arts chapter, is a freelance writer who lives in Toronto and regularly paints the town red. She's written about arts and entertainment for *NOW Magazine, Canadian Art, WHERE Toronto,* and *The Varsity,* the University of Toronto's newspaper. One of Hannah's favorite things about Toronto is its multicultural flavor.

Enthusiastic day tripper **Ilona Kauremszky** updated the North of Toronto portion of the Side Trips chapter. She is the founding president of the Travel Media Association of Canada's Ontario Chapter and an active member of the Society of American Travel Writers. She writes a weekly travel column for the *Toronto Sun,* edits ⊕ www.mycompass.ca, and contributes to the *Globe and Mail* and the *National Post* among other publications.

Jack Kohane, who updated the Where to Stay chapter, relished searching out dazzling new hotels and quaint, century-plus bed-and-breakfast homes. As an award-winning freelance travel and business journalist, he has written features for *North American Country Inns, Innspire Magazine, Spa Life, The National Post,* and the *Toronto Sun,* focusing on Ontario and Canadian vacation getaway destinations. He's unabashedly proud of his hometown, and considers it one of the friendliest and safest cities on the planet. Though he's traveled far and wide, he insists there's really no place like home.

Native Torontonian **Kirsten McKenzie** has spent the last three years skiing, running, and biking everywhere while completing her master's degree in health science. Before she hit the books and the Toronto outdoors, she spent three years trekking the Himalayas and traversing the Indian subcontinent solo. Her adventurous and sporty spirit helped her to update the Sports & the Outdoors chapter.

Irish-born Side Trips updater **Vernon O'Reilly-Ramesar** is a writer and broadcaster who divides his time between Canada and the Caribbean. He considers Toronto his home and loves its seamless blend of big city excitement and small town friendliness.

Sara Waxman, who wrote the Dining chapter and the Side Trips chapter restaurant listings, is the restaurant critic for the *Toronto Sun.* She also writes occasional travel stories for *Flare, Enroute, Elle,* the *Globe and Mail,* and *The National Post.*

Old Toronto

The first settlements have mostly been obliterated in this earliest part of town, just north of the waterfront, but several public buildings from the 19th century remain. A visually exciting streetscape results from the mix of old buildings, new buildings, and old buildings restored for new uses. The area's draws include the Hockey Hall of Fame and Museum, the lively St. Lawrence Market, and the Hummingbird and St. Lawrence cultural centers.

The Financial District

Canada's financial and legal power is focused on Bay Street, west of Old Toronto. It's home to imposing skyscrapers in various early- and late-20th-century styles and most of the major theaters. In the 1990s, TEDA (Toronto Entertainment District Association) was formed by neighborhood theaters, hotels, and restaurants to better publicize its attractions. Cinemas, dance clubs, comedy clubs, 250 restaurants, and many of the big hotels and boutique lodgings are all within this Entertainment District.

The Harbourfront

Toronto is bordered by Lake Ontario, and after decades of neglect the city has turned its waterfro nt into a major asset. This most southerly area of the city includes lots of opportunities for outdoor activities and amusements, making it ideal for visitors with children. Among the attractions along the waterfront are Ontario Place, CN Tower, SkyDome, Fort York, and Harbourfront Centre, a cultural and recreation center. Just a 15-minute ferryboat ride across Toronto Bay is the best-kept secret of them all, the Toronto Islands.

Dundas and Queen Streets

The north-central core area of Dundas and Queen Streets is interesting for the vibrant street life of Kensington Market, Chinatown, and Nathan Phillips Square (the park in front of City Hall). Cultural interests can be filled by the Art Gallery of Ontario, the Ontario College of Art Design, many commercial galleries, and two restored historic homes. Shoppers flock to the mammoth Eaton Centre and fashionable Queen Street West with its trendsetting habitués.

Around Queen's Park

Just west of the Dundas and Queen streets area, the Ontario provincial legislature and the main campus of the University of Toronto occupy prime central real estate. The area is liberally scattered with parks and lawns as well as libraries and museums, including the city's most famous, the Royal Ontario Museum. (Several of its galleries are open, but it remains under massive refurbishment until 2006.) On the northern edge of this area is Yorkville, filled with restaurants and elegant, upscale stores and boutiques, and The Annex, an artsy neighborhood. To the west is Little Italy, with restaurants and cafés along College Street that have made it one of the coolest scenes in town. The Church–Wellesley area to the east is a tightly knit gay community which hosts Pride Week in June, attracting over a million people.

Cabbagetown

This architecturally diverse area on the eastern edge of the central core, once the home of poor WASPs, has been restored by middle-class home owners. The streets hold some of the city's loveliest homes from the late 19th and early 20th centuries. The term Cabbagetown, though originally applied to an area farther south, comes from the fact that many of the poor residents grew cabbages on their lawns to feed the family or to sell in hopes of earning a few pennies.

Greater Toronto

Head north on Yonge Street from Bloor Street to reach residential Midtown, a hotbed of trendy restaurants and upscale shopping northwest of downtown. Many smaller neighborhoods compose this area, including Eglinton, Summerhill, Rosedale, St. Clair, and Davisville. Casa Loma, in the Midtown neighborhood of Forest Hills, is surrounded by leafy streets and multimillion-dollar homes. Farther northwest is Paramount Canada's Wonderland, a theme park, and Black Creek Pioneer Village, which re-creates a mid-19th-century community. A bit farther out, in the town of Kleinburg, is the outstanding McMichael Canadian Art Collection. Most people visit the northeastern suburban section of Toronto for the hands-on Ontario Science Centre in North York and the outstanding Toronto Zoo in Scarborough, but the sprawling Edward Gardens are also a draw. Directly east of downtown is Greektown, which is centered around Danforth Avenue (called simply The Danforth), and southeast is The Beaches, a bohemian, waterfront neighborhood perfect for a boardwalk stroll and some shopping. Huge and lovely High Park is the highlight of southwest Toronto, but West Indian, German, Polish, and Ukrainian enclaves attract those hungering for homemade ethnic treats.

GREAT ITINERARIES

Toronto in 5 Days

To see and experience all that is Toronto, you should plan a stay of at least a week. Five days is enough to see many of the highlights: the Art Gallery of Ontario, the CN Tower, the SkyDome, Harbourfront, Casa Loma, and plenty of the neighborhoods from Kensington Market and Chinatown to Little Italy and Yorkville. These itineraries don't include side trips to Niagara Falls and the festivals at Stratford and Niagara-on-the-Lake, so you'd need to adjust your plans to include them.

DAY 1: The four icons of modern Toronto are close enough together that they can all be visited on a single, albeit busy, day. Start at Queen and Bay streets at the eye-shape City Hall. (Its quaint predecessor, Old City Hall, is across the street.) Walk one block east to the Eaton Centre, at Yonge Street. The atrium-style roof is worth a peek even if you don't stay to browse the 300 or so shops. Next, head south on Bay Street through the Financial District, with its handsome skyscrapers; head west on Front Street to the spectacular CN Tower. It's not hard to find—just look up. Take the speedy elevator to the observation deck and then lunch at the 360 Revolving Restaurant.

Next, pay a visit to the tower's neighbor, the spectacular SkyDome. You should buy tickets ahead of time for a Toronto Blue Jays baseball game. Or, if the stadium is not in use, you can take a guided tour (call ahead). Leaving the SkyDome, walk or take a taxi south to Queen's Quay Terminal, part of the city's Harbourfront Centre. There's plenty to do here, from shopping and browsing the galleries to taking an impromptu pottery-making class. As the sun sets, take a stroll along the waterfront and then head to one of the great restaurants nearby. The streetcar running along the center of Queen's Quay (make sure the sign in front says Union) will take you back uptown to Union subway station.

DAY 2: Prepare for a mix of culture and shopping. Spend the morning exploring the original Chinatown—laid out west along Dundas Street behind City Hall—all the way over to the "new" Chinatown, in and around the busy Spadina Avenue–Dundas Street intersection. Cross Spadina and turn right for the colorful Kensington Market. Settle into a restaurant along Baldwin Street (there are several comprising Baldwin Village) or walk south on Spadina to Queen Street West (five short blocks) and make a left to check out the funky shopping district with restaurants and cafés. Spend the afternoon at the Art Gallery of Ontario (at Dundas and McCaul streets), with its outstanding Henry Moore collection; come back for brunch at the Atrium. In the evening, pick your favorite ethnic cuisine and head to one of the city's excellent restaurants.

DAY 3: Begin the day amid the Yorkville boutiques, at the northwest corner of Yonge and Bloor Streets. Cobblestone streets, shops in restored Victorian residences, and outdoor cafés (plenty with strong Italian espresso) may charm the credit cards out of your pocket. Before the country's most chic shops settled here, Yorkville was a hippie haven in the 1960s, attracting emerging musical artists Joni Mitchell and Gordon Lightfoot. The shops spill onto Bloor Street West, and the strip between Yonge Street and Avenue Road is sometimes referred to as Toronto's 5th Avenue. Your next stop is the nearby Royal Ontario Museum, at Bloor West and Queen's Park, with pieces from the worlds of art, archaeology, and science; even though some galleries are closed due to ongoing refurbishment, plan to spend some time here. (Across the street is the Gardiner Museum of Ceramic Art, and a short walk west on Bloor Street West is the Bata Shoe Museum at St. George Street.) In the evening, take in a play, a concert, or a comedy show at Second City.

DAY 4: If you're here in summer, take the subway south to Union Station and then walk to the docks at the foot of Bay Street and Queen's Quay to catch a ferry to the Toronto Islands; the view of the city skyline is an added plus. Make sure you know which of the many islands suits you best; in summer, particularly on weekends, kids have the run of Centre Island. In winter, take the kids to the Ontario Science Centre, with its engaging exhibits and demonstrations. The Science Center is 11 km (7 mi) northeast of downtown. Another far-flung spot worth a visit is the McMichael Canadian Art Collection, an outstanding museum with works by Canadian and First Nations artists, on 100 wooded acres. When you're back downtown in the evening, look for a place where you can dine alfresco—patio dining, as the locals say—or head to hip College Street in Little Italy.

DAY 5: Roam some special neighborhoods in Toronto. Purchase a TTC Day Pass, which allows unlimited use of transit vehicles after 9:30 AM Monday through Friday (all day Saturday and Sunday) and is available at subway stations. Some areas to the east of downtown are Rosedale, an affluent neighborhood with antiques shops, and The Danforth, with Greek restaurants. South of The Danforth is Cabbagetown, which has handsome 19th-century homes, and just below it is the center of the gay community at Church and Wellesley Streets. King Street East is Toronto's new home furnishings and design district, and streetcars running east from here will take you to the Beaches, a great place to stroll the lakefront and shop. The Esplanade area at Front Street has an increasing number of trendy eateries, but St. Lawrence Market, with stalls of prepared and fresh foods, has been here forever. West of downtown along Bloor Street is the artsy Annex community, and south along Spadina is the western border of the University of Toronto campus. The surrounding residential area has cafés and good second-hand bookstores, particularly around Harbord Street. You find intriguing eateries everywhere.

If You Have More Time

Drive to the Niagara Peninsula and Niagara Falls or the refined town of Niagara-on-the-Lake. Get tickets for a play at the Shaw or Stratford festivals (April to November). The wineries and restaurants of the Wine Region are also within easy reach.

If You Have 3 Days

If it's your first visit, select a couple of landmarks: tour the CN Tower and see a game at the SkyDome, then visit Harbourfront. On your second day, visit Chinatown and Kensington Market, spend the early afternoon at the Art Gallery of Ontario, then browse the shops of Queen Street West. Begin your third day in Yorkville and visit the Royal Ontario Museum. Spend the rest of the day in whichever neighborhood most appeals to you or at one of the farther-flung sights such as Casa Loma or the Toronto Islands.

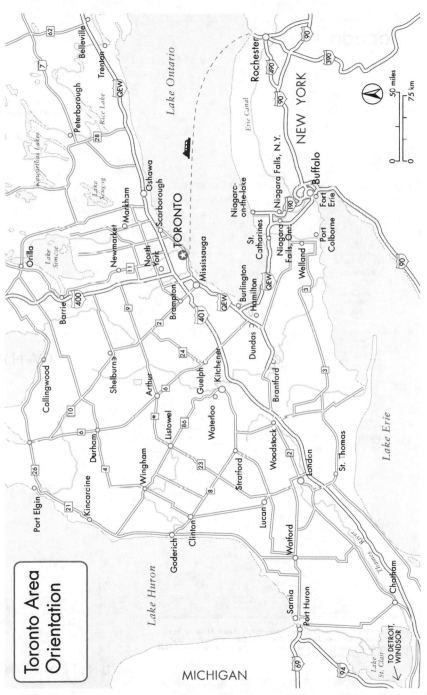

Toronto Area Orientation

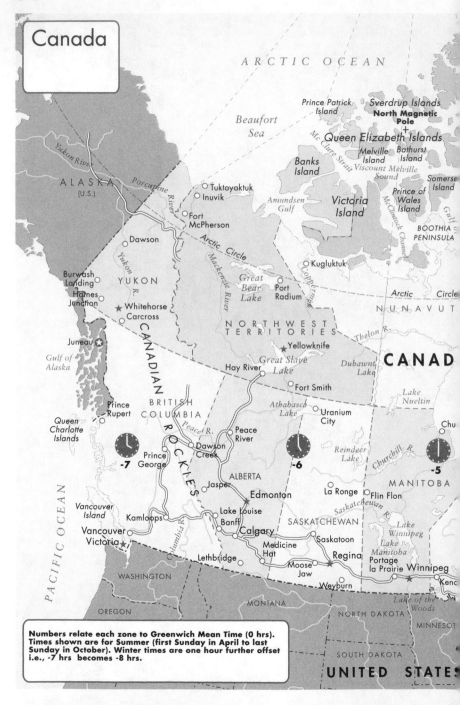

Canada

ARCTIC OCEAN

Beaufort Sea

Prince Patrick Island
Sverdrup Islands
North Magnetic Pole
+
Queen Elizabeth Islands

Banks Island

Melville Island
Viscount Melville Sound
Bathurst Island

Somerset Island

Prince of Wales Island

McClintock Channel

BOOTHIA PENINSULA

ALASKA (U.S.)

Yukon River

Porcupine River

Tuktoyaktuk
Inuvik

Fort McPherson

Amundsen Gulf

Victoria Island

Dawson

Arctic Circle

Mackenzie River

Kugluktuk

Copperme

Arctic Circle

NUNAVUT

Burwash Landing
Haines Junction

YUKON

Yukon R.

Whitehorse
Carcross

Great Bear Lake

Port Radium

Juneau

Gulf of Alaska

CANADIAN

NORTHWEST TERRITORIES

Yellowknife

Thelon R.

CANAD

Hay River
Great Slave Lake

Dubawnt Lake

Lake Nueltin

Fort Smith

Prince Rupert

BRITISH COLUMBIA

Athabasca Lake

Uranium City

Chu

Queen Charlotte Islands

ROCKIES

Peace R.

Peace River

Dawson Creek

Reindeer Lake

Churchill R.

-7
Prince George

-6

-5

Jasper

ALBERTA

La Ronge
Flin Flon

MANITOBA

Edmonton

Saskatchewan R.

PACIFIC OCEAN

Vancouver Island

Kamloops

Lake Louise
Banff

Saskatoon

Lake Winnipeg

Vancouver
Victoria

Columbia

Calgary

SASKATCHEWAN

Lake Manitoba

Medicine Hat

Lethbridge

Moose Jaw

Regina

Portage la Prairie
Winnipeg

WASHINGTON

Weyburn

Kenc

OREGON

MONTANA

NORTH DAKOTA

Lake of the Woods

MINNESOT

SOUTH DAKOTA

UNITED STATES

Numbers relate each zone to Greenwich Mean Time (0 hrs).
Times shown are for Summer (first Sunday in April to last
Sunday in October). Winter times are one hour further offset
i.e., -7 hrs becomes -8 hrs.

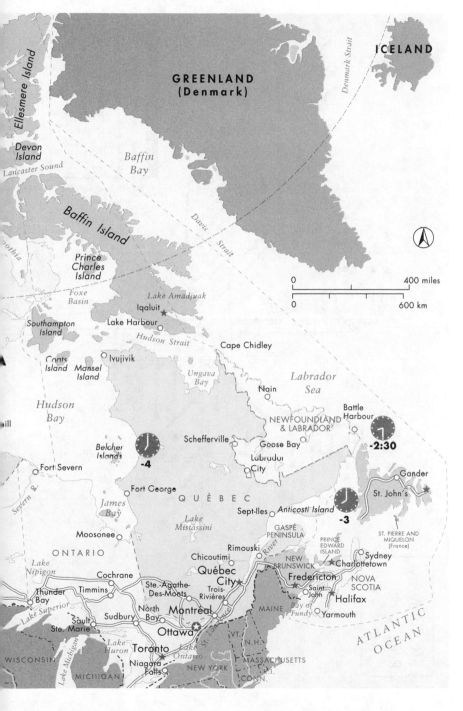

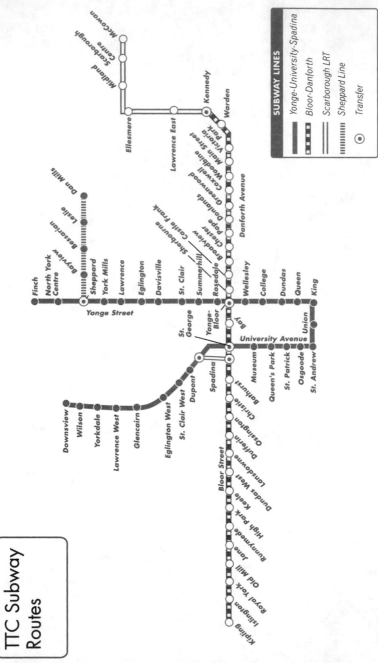

TTC Subway Routes

SUBWAY LINES

Yonge-University-Spadina
Bloor-Danforth
Scarborough LRT
Sheppard Line

◉ Transfer

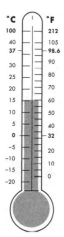

°C		°F
100		212
40		105
37		98.6
30		90
25		80
20		70
15		60
10		50
5		40
0		32
−5		20
−10		10
−15		
−20		0

The temperature can often fall below freezing from late November into March and can be brutal in January and February. That simple fact alone may discourage some tourists, but also attracts skiing and skating enthusiasts. In the often-bleak winter months, underground shopping concourses allow you to walk through much of the downtown area and avoid the cold.

Some of the best theater, ballet, opera, and concerts take place between May and September; both the Stratford and Shaw festivals, in venues each about a 90-minute drive from Toronto, are in full swing from mid-April or May through November. Toronto has year-round engagements of major theater productions.

Toronto is most pleasant to walk around and simply enjoy from late spring through early fall, when there are outdoor concerts and open-air dining—and the entire city seems to come to life. On the other hand, some hotels drop their prices up to 50% in the off-season, particularly December and January.

Climate

Toronto's climate can be harsh in December, January, and February, and sometimes in March and late November. Prolonged snowfalls rarely come to the northern shores of Lake Ontario, and many a December and January snowfall soon melts away. Spring can be brief, and a (hot) summer can last through much of June, July, August, and even September. The gorgeous autumn colors are seen best just north of the city and throughout the myriad parks; temperatures are moderate at this time.

Lake Ontario often cools the city air in summer and warms it in winter.

The following are average daily maximum and minimum temperatures for Toronto.

🔊 Forecasts **Weather Channel Connection** ☎ 900/932-8437 95¢ per minute from a Touch-Tone phone ⊕ www.weather.com.

TORONTO

Jan.	30F	−1C	May	64F	18C	Sept.	71F	22C
	18	−8		47	8		54	12
Feb.	32F	0C	June	76F	24C	Oct.	60F	16C
	19	−7		57	14		45	7
Mar.	40F	4C	July	80F	27C	Nov.	46F	8C
	27	−3		62	17		35	2
Apr.	53F	12C	Aug.	79F	26C	Dec.	34F	1C
	38	3		61	16		23	−5

ON THE CALENDAR

Top seasonal events in Toronto include the Caravan celebrations in June, Carnival Toronto (aka Caribana) in July, the Toronto International Film Festival in September, and the city's New Year's Eve Party at Nathan Phillips Square in front of City Hall.

Telephone numbers are given for a number of events; for further details about these and others, contact **Tourism Toronto** (☎ 416/203–2500 or 800/363–1990 ⊕ www.torontotourism.com). The commercial site, www.toronto.com, has information on all things Toronto.

WINTER

December

First Night Toronto, Celebration of the Arts (☎ 416/341–3143), a popular "no-booze," family-oriented celebration, takes place in many locations all over downtown from the 29th to the 31st.

Designs in Ice is a winter tradition and ice-sculpture competition held in downtown Toronto.

New Year's Eve at City Hall is celebrated in Nathan Phillips Square.

January

The **Niagara Falls Festival of Lights** (☎ 800/563–2557), which starts in late November, is an extravaganza of colored lights in the parks surrounding the falls.

The **Toronto International Boat Show** (☎ 905/951–0009) draws throngs of would-be and actual sailors to Exhibition Place to ogle state-of-the-art nautical toys.

February

The **WinterCity Festival** celebrates the season with ice-skating shows, plays, and a restaurant week.

March

Canada Blooms (☎ 416/447–8655), the country's biggest flower show, is held at the Metro Toronto Convention Centre.

SPRING

April

Shaw Festival (☎ 905/468–2172), which presents plays by the British curmudgeon George Bernard Shaw and his contemporaries, is held in Niagara-on-the-Lake and continues through November.

Stratford Festival (☎ 416/363–4471 or 800/567–1600), a theater festival featuring the best in classical and contemporary repertoire—especially the works of William Shakespeare—continues into November.

June

Gay & Lesbian Pride Week (☎ 416/927–7433) includes cultural and political programs and a parade.

Metro Toronto International Caravan (☎ 416/856–6482), held over 10 days in mid-June in various ethnic communities, finds locals eating their way around the globe while attending various performances, such as those of Indonesian puppets or North African belly dancers.

NorthbyNortheast (☎ 416/863–6963), aka N×NE, is a three-day music fest and conference in mid-June with mostly new pop and rock.

The du Maurier Downtown Jazz Festival (☎ 416/928–2033), in late June, has featured such greats as Sarah Vaughan, Miles Davis, Dizzy Gillespie, and Branford Marsalis over the years.

SUMMER

July

The Mariposa Folk Festival (☎ 705/329–2333) is the longest-running folk festival in North America; it takes place in Bracebridge, a pretty little town several hours north of Toronto.

Carnival Toronto (Caribana; ☎ 877/672–2742) is a 10-day cultural showcase with Caribbean music, dance, and arts put on by the West Indian communities. One highlight is a spectacular parade of brightly dressed revelers.

The **Molson Indy Toronto** (☎ 416/872–4639), one of the major events in the CART (Championship Racing Auto Teams) racing season, is held over a three-day period at the city's Exhibition Place. Besides races, there are themed attractions and a consumer and trade show with racing merchandise and auto-related displays.

The **Beaches International Jazz Festival** (☎ 416/698–2152), in late July, literally fills the streets with music as Canadian and international musicians perform in cafés and bistros, as well as on streets, balconies, and rooftops.

Aug.–Sept.

Canadian National Exhibition (the Ex; ☎ 416/393–6090), the biggest fair in the country, has rides, entertainment, displays, and just about anything else you can think of. It's held (as it has been since 1879) at its namesake grounds on the Lake Ontario waterfront.

FALL

September

Toronto International Film Festival (☎ 416/967–7371) brings together cinematographers and film stars from many countries for premieres and awards. Film buffs can view more than a hundred new and classic films during the event.

October

International Festival of Authors (☎ 416/973–4000) at Harbourfront Centre brings in major writers from around the world—Saul Bellow, Margaret Atwood, and A. S. Byatt have all participated. This is one of Toronto's major cultural experiences.

November

Royal Agricultural Winter Fair (☎ 416/263–3400), held annually since 1922 at Exhibition Place, is North America's most prestigious agricultural fair; among its many events is the International Royal Horse Show.

PLEASURES & PASTIMES

Ethnic Neighborhoods You can encounter markets, clothes, music, newspapers, cuisines, and customs from around the world in Toronto. If you walk around long enough, you may hear everything from Hindi to Greek. You can pick up a sari on Gerrard Street East, purchase Chinese herbal medicines on Dundas Street, and browse for French books on Queen Street West.

Museums Toronto is the place to explore often overlooked Canadian art, particularly at the Art Gallery of Ontario and the McMichael Canadian Art Collection in Kleinburg. The Royal Ontario Museum presents a brilliant and wildly diverse collection, including mummies and musical instruments. (Note that a refurbishment until 2006 means that some galleries are closed.) The city also has offbeat museums devoted to the study of hockey (Hockey Hall of Fame), design (The Design Exchange), ceramics (George R. Gardiner Museum of Ceramic Art), and even shoes (Bata Shoe Museum).

Patches of Green The city has lush ravines, parks with jogging paths, and a handful of islands for R&R and outdoor activities. Miniparks throughout downtown burst with flowers and have public sculpture, historical plaques, and, of course, benches for resting tired feet. Nathan Phillips Square has live music and a farmer's market in summer; High Park, west of downtown, has a summer Shakespeare series; Edwards Gardens in North York is the city's botanical gardens.

Playing it Up Toronto has venues for American favorites like baseball (the Toronto Blue Jays) and basketball (the Toronto Raptors). But ice hockey is a national mania; children barely able to walk learn to toddle around on skates, then move to league play when they're around 10, and generally keep going as long as their knees hold out. Maple Leaf tickets are a scarce commodity, even among locals. Never sampled Canadian football? See an Argonauts game; the play is faster and (locals say) more exciting than the American version.

Shopping The city that created Club Monaco and M.A.C. cosmetics has everything from haute couture to ethnic markets. The city's megamall, the Eaton Centre, vies with boutiques on Bloor Street West and Yorkville for shoppers' attention. Unique areas to explore include the St. Lawrence and Kensington markets; funky Queen Street West, with its street-smart shops; Chinatown, loaded with bargains; Queen Street East, with vintage and antiques stores; King Street East, for modern home furnishings; and Queen's Quay Terminal, a delightful converted warehouse on the waterfront.

Wining & Dining After each of Toronto's immigration waves, an intriguing new batch of restaurants opened, including Hungarian schnitzel after the 1956 revolution and Vietnamese in the 1970s. The city's diverse dining scene yields a bit of everything, including contemporary Canadian fare. Wine lists include excellent regional and international varietals. In summer, do as the locals and dine alfresco, a cherished Toronto pastime.

FODOR'S CHOICE

The sights, restaurants, hotels, and other travel experiences on these pages are our editors' top picks—our Fodor's Choices. They're the best of their type in the Toronto area—not to be missed and always worth your time. In the Toronto chapters that follow, you will find all the details. For Fodor's Choices outside the city, see chapter 7.

LODGING

$$$$	**The Fairmont Royal York.** When the district of Old Toronto was new, this hotel hosted the traveling elite. The landmark property still has time-tested traditional rooms and contemporary amenities and services within reach.
$$$$	**Four Seasons Toronto.** The most exclusive property in town has a great Yorkville location, fine service, and afternoon tea—what could be more civilized?
$$$$	**The Old Mill Inn.** Stroll through the formal garden and then have dinner beside the large stone hearth before tucking into your four-poster bed. You might think you've died and gone to England.
$$$$	**SoHo Metropolitan Hotel.** Ultra chic meets ultra luxury, with stunning glass sculptures, the finest Italian Frette linens, and a sinful bakery on-site.
$$$$	**Windsor Arms.** Should you use the Bentley limo to go shopping, or would you rather lounge in your regal room and be waited on by 24-hour butler service? Decisions, decisions.
$$$-$$$$	**Le Royal Meridien King Edward.** This downtown grande dame reflects the elegance of its 1903 opening date. Gentility and attention to detail are the rule.
$$$-$$$$	**Hotel Le Germain Toronto.** A design-driven hotel in Toronto is big news. This one in the Entertainment District is a beauty, and small enough to call your urban hideout.
$-$$	**Beaconsfield Bed & Breakfast.** You can relax on awning-covered balconies at this 1882 Victorian mansion, which is filled with art and individual character. Breakfasts include fruit grown organically in the backyard garden.

BUDGET LODGING

¢-$	**Helga's Place Bed & Breakfast.** An indoor pool and solarium make this North York spot unique among the city's B&Bs.
¢	**Neill-Wycik College Hotel.** This college dorm becomes Toronto's best value from early May through late August. All rooms come with phones and Continental breakfast.

RESTAURANTS	
$$$–$$$$	**Bistro 990.** No need to put on airs; first-rate French cuisine here is served pretention-free in comfortable elegance.
$$–$$$$	**Flow.** The bright and the beautiful of Yorkville flow through this neighborhood showplace of Venetian art glass and exotic woods.
$$–$$$$	**Lobby.** Traditional favorites take on a twist at the hottest, newest dining concept in town. Mac-and-cheese with foie gras, anyone?
$$–$$$	**Brasserie Aix.** A mix of classic and modern French fare comes swiftly to the always-booked leather banquettes at this Little Italy standout.
$$–$$$	**Over Easy.** The all-day-breakfast menu at this casual spot includes maple-leaf shape pancakes.
$$–$$$	**Xacutti.** The cliché-free menu takes you on a culinary journey through Asia, with avant-garde accessories. Book your ticket, er, table now.
$–$$$	**Christina's.** Yes, the waitstaff delivers the classic Greek dish you ordered, but they may also break into dance when the live music plays on the weekend.

AFTER HOURS

Canoe. This swanky bar with a panoramic view from the 54th floor of the Toronto Dominion Centre is popular with the financial crowd.

The Guvernment. Eight lounges and dance clubs, each with its own theme, are part of this chic Harbourfront complex.

Massey Hall. Near-perfect acoustics makes this spot number one for seeing fine musical acts and other performers.

The Paddock. An arts-and-media crowd fill this cozy art-deco bar, which has lots of dark wood and tasty food and drink.

The Rivoli. Cutting-edge performance art, new music, and hip poetry draw black-clad intellectuals to this club.

Second City. Many *Saturday Night Live* regulars got their start at the Toronto offshoot of the famed Chicago comedy club; Mike Myers is one alum.

Top O' The Senator. All that jazz and a smoky, old-fashioned room—what more could retro romantics want?

QUINTESSENTIAL TORONTO

Art Gallery of Ontario. Among a stellar array of art, the Henry Moore collection—the world's largest public holding of the sculptor's work—stands out.

CN Tower. The world's tallest freestanding structure, and its glass-floor observation deck, is not to be missed.

High Park. City residents come to play among the almost 400 acres of parkland west of the city.

Massey Hall. This music venue near Queen's Park is credited with having near-perfect acoustics.

St. Lawrence Market. Shop for upscale cheese and sausage varieties below where the city's first government met in this 1844 market hall.

Toronto Maple Leafs. Hockey's toughest ticket to score is Toronto's team, but it's worth the effort for a true Canadian experience.

QUINTESSENTIAL ONTARIO

The Shaw Festival, Niagara-on-the-Lake. George Bernard Shaw and his contemporaries hold forth for a half year in lovely Niagara-on-the-Lake.

The Stratford Festival, Stratford. The play's the thing in Stratford from May through November; the rest of the year is spent preparing for the onslaught of Shakespeare fans.

SHOPPING

Eaton Centre. It's big (300 stores) and it's crowded, but this downtown mall is also an architectural stunner. You'll find fashions, food, and films here—as well as a flock of fiberglass Canada geese.

Holt Renfrew. Dress up your house and yourself at this high-end shop in the Bloor-Yorkville fashion hotbed. It carries couture lines you can't find anywhere else in Toronto.

Kensington Market. Amble along rows of choice global goods, including food and clothing, at this outdoor bazaar.

Mountain Equipment Co-op. Get into a natural state of mind while rappelling down the rock-climbing wall or browsing among a myriad of backpacks, tents, sleeping bags, bike racks—and everything you never thought you needed to brave the great outdoors.

SMART TRAVEL TIPS

Finding out about your destination before you leave home means you won't squander time organizing everyday minutiae once you've arrived. You'll be more streetwise when you hit the ground and better prepared to explore the aspects of Toronto that drew you here in the first place. The organizations in this section can provide information to supplement this guide; contact them for up-to-the-minute details. Happy landings!

ADDRESSES

Most city streets are organized on a grid system: with some exceptions, street numbers start at zero from Lake Ontario and increase as you go north. On the east–west axis, Yonge (pronounced "young") Street, Toronto's main thoroughfare, is the dividing line: you can expect higher numbers the farther away you get from Yonge. For example, the 2300 block of Bloor Street West is near Jane Street; 100 Front Street East is at the corner of Jarvis Street.

AIR TRAVEL TO & FROM TORONTO

Numerous daily trips to Toronto are typical for most airlines serving the city. Allow extra time for passing through customs and immigration, which are required for all passengers, including Canadians. The 2½-hour advance boarding time recommended for international flights is applied to Canada. Fortunately, the Toronto airport has check-in kiosks for Air Canada flights, which cut back on time spent in line.

BOOKING

When you book, look for nonstop flights and remember that "direct" flights stop at least once. Try to avoid connecting flights, which require a change of plane. Two airlines may operate a connecting flight jointly, so ask whether your airline operates every segment of the trip; you may find that the carrier you prefer flies you only part of the way. To find more booking tips and to check prices and make online flight reservations, log on to www. fodors.com.

CARRIERS

When flying internationally, you must usually choose between a domestic carrier, the national flag carrier of the country you are visiting, and a foreign carrier from a third country. National flag carriers have the greatest number of nonstops. Domestic carriers may have better connections to your hometown and serve a greater number of gateway cities. Third-party carriers may have a price advantage.

Toronto is served by American, Delta, Northwest, United, US Airways, Air Canada, Air Canada's Tango, as well as more than a dozen European and Asian carriers with easy connections to many U.S. cities. An Air Canada affiliate, Air Canada Jazz, flies from the small Toronto City Centre Airport to Ottawa, Montréal, and London, Ontario. Toronto is also served within Canada by CanJet, JetsGo, West Jet, and Air Transat, a charter airline.

From the United Kingdom, Canadian charter line Air Transat offers flights to Toronto, though not in winter. (Canadian charter carriers fly among many major Canadian cities, and usually offer lower rates than Air Canada.) British Airways also has direct flights to Toronto.

🛪 **Major Airlines Air Canada** 📞 800/776-3000 ⊕ www.aircanada.com. **American** 📞 800/433-7300 ⊕ www.aa.com. **Continental** 📞 800/525-0280 ⊕ www.continental.com. **Delta** 📞 800/241-4141 ⊕ www.delta.com. **Northwest** 📞 800/225-2525 ⊕ www.nwa.com. **United** 📞 800/241-6522 ⊕ www.united.com. **US Airways** 📞 800/428-4322 ⊕ www.usairways.com.

🛪 **Smaller Airlines Air Canada Jazz** 📞 416/925-2311 or 888/247-2262 ⊕ www.flyjazz.ca. **Air Transat** 📞 877/872-6728 ⊕ www.airtransat.com. **CanJet** 📞 800/809-7777 ⊕ www.canjet.com. **JetsGo** 📞 866/448-5888 ⊕ www.jetsgo.net. **WestJet** 📞 888/937-8538 ⊕ www.westjet.com. **Tango** 📞 888/247-2262 ⊕ www.flytango.com.

🛪 **From the U.K. Air Canada** 📞 0870/524-7226 ⊕ www.aircanada.com. **British Airways** 📞 0845/722-2111 ⊕ www.britishairways.com.

CHECK-IN & BOARDING

Always **find out your carrier's check-in policy.** Plan to arrive at the airport about two hours before your scheduled departure time for domestic flights and 2½ to 3 hours before international flights. You may need to arrive earlier if you're flying from one of the busier airports or during peak air-traffic times. Note that weather conditions can affect whether or not your plane to and from Toronto will leave on time. Brace yourself for the possibilities of delays in winter. To avoid delays at airport-security checkpoints, try not to wear any metal. Jewelry, belt and other buckles, steel-toe shoes, barrettes, and underwire bras are among the items that can set off detectors.

Assuming that not everyone with a ticket will show up, airlines routinely overbook planes. When everyone does, airlines ask for volunteers to give up their seats. In return, these volunteers usually get a several-hundred-dollar flight voucher, which can be used toward the purchase of another ticket, and are rebooked on the next flight out. If there are not enough volunteers, the airline must choose who will be denied boarding. The first to get bumped are passengers who checked in late and those flying on discounted tickets, so get to the gate and check in as early as possible, especially during peak periods.

Always **bring a government-issued photo I.D.** to the airport; even when it's not required, a passport is best. U.S. Customs and Immigration maintains offices at Pearson International Airport in Toronto; U.S.-bound passengers should arrive early enough to clear customs before their flight.

Security measures at Canadian airports are similar to those in the United States. Be sure you're not carrying anything that could be construed as a weapon: a letter opener, Swiss Army knife, or a toy weapon, for example. Arriving passengers from overseas flights might find a beagle in a green coat sniffing their luggage; he's looking for forbidden agricultural products, including illegal drugs.

CUTTING COSTS

The least expensive airfares to Toronto are priced for round-trip travel and must usually be purchased in advance. Airlines generally allow you to change your return date for a fee; most low-fare tickets, however, are nonrefundable. It's smart to call a number of airlines and check the Internet; when you are quoted a good price, book it on the spot—the same fare may not be available the next day, or even the next hour. Always check different routings and look into using alternate airports. Also, price off-peak flights, which may be significantly less expensive than others. Travel agents, especially low-fare specialists (⇨ Discounts and Deals), are helpful.

Consolidators are another good source. They buy tickets for scheduled flights at reduced rates from the airlines, then sell them at prices that beat the best fare available directly from the airlines. Sometimes you can even get your money back if you need to return the ticket. Carefully read the fine print detailing penalties for changes and cancellations, purchase the ticket with a credit card, and confirm your consolidator reservation with the airline.

🖪 Consolidators AirlineConsolidator.com ☎ 888/468-5385 ⊕ www.airlineconsolidator.com; for international tickets. **Best Fares** ☎ 800/576-8255 or 800/576-1600 ⊕ www.bestfares.com; $59.90 annual membership. **Cheap Tickets** ☎ 800/377-1000 or 888/922-8849 ⊕ www.cheaptickets.com. **Expedia** ☎ 800/397-3342 or 404/728-8787 ⊕ www.expedia.com. **Hotwire** ☎ 866/468-9473 or 920/330-9418 ⊕ www.hotwire.com. **Now Voyager Travel** ✉ 45 W. 21st St., 5th fl., New York, NY 10010 ☎ 212/459-1616 🖷 212/243-2711 ⊕ www.nowvoyagertravel.com. **Onetravel.com** ⊕ www.onetravel.com. **Orbitz** ☎ 888/656-4546 ⊕ www.orbitz.com. **Priceline.com** ⊕ www.priceline.com. **Travelocity** ☎ 888/709-5983, 877/282-2925 in Canada, 0870/111-7060 in the U.K. ⊕ www.travelocity.com.

🖪 Courier Resources Air Courier Association/Cheaptrips.com ☎ 800/282-1202 ⊕ www.aircourier.org or www.cheaptrips.com; $29 annual membership. **International Association of Air Travel Couriers** ☎ 308/632-3273 ⊕ www.courier.org; $45 annual membership. **Now Voyager Travel** ✉ 45 W. 21st St., 5th fl., New York, NY 10010 ☎ 212/459-1616 🖷 212/243-2711 ⊕ www.nowvoyagertravel.com.

ENJOYING THE FLIGHT

State your seat preference when purchasing your ticket, and then repeat it when you confirm and when you check in. For more legroom, you can request one of the few emergency-aisle seats at check-in, if you are capable of lifting at least 50 pounds—a Federal Aviation Administration requirement of passengers in these seats. Seats behind a bulkhead also offer more legroom, but they don't have underseat storage. Don't sit in the row in front of the emergency aisle or in front of a bulkhead, where seats may not recline.

Ask the airline whether a snack or meal is served on the flight. If you have dietary concerns, request special meals when booking. These can be vegetarian, low-cholesterol, or kosher, for example. It's a good idea to pack some healthful snacks and a small (plastic) bottle of water in your carry-on bag. On long flights, try to maintain a normal routine, to help fight jet lag. At night, get some sleep. By day, eat light meals, drink water (not alcohol), and **move around the cabin** to stretch your legs. For additional jet-lag tips consult *Fodor's FYI: Travel Fit & Healthy* (available at bookstores everywhere).

None of the major airlines or charter lines permit smoking.

FLYING TIMES

Flying time to Toronto is 1½ hours from New York and Chicago and 4½ hours from Los Angeles.

HOW TO COMPLAIN

If your baggage goes astray or your flight goes awry, complain right away. Most carriers require that you **file a claim immediately.** The Aviation Consumer Protection Division of the Department of Transportation publishes *Fly-Rights*, which discusses airlines and consumer issues and is available online. You can also find articles and information on mytravelrights.com, the Web site of the nonprofit Consumer Travel Rights Center.

🖪 Airline Complaints Aviation Consumer Protection Division ✉ U.S. Department of Transportation, C-75, Room 4107, 400 7th St. SW, Washington, DC 20590 ☎ 202/366-2220 ⊕ airconsumer.ost.dot.gov. **Federal Aviation Administration Consumer Hotline** ✉ for inquiries: FAA, 800 Independence Ave. SW, Washington, DC 20591 ☎ 800/322-7873 ⊕ www.faa.gov.

RECONFIRMING

Check the status of your flight before you leave for the airport. You can do this on your carrier's Web site, by linking to a flight-status checker (many Web booking services offer these), or by calling your carrier or travel agent. It's not necessary to confirm international flights from Canada to the United States.

AIRPORTS & TRANSFERS

Flights into Toronto land at the three terminals of Lester B. Pearson International Airport (airport code YYZ), commonly called the Toronto Airport, 32 km (20 mi) northwest of downtown. The stunning Terminal 1 opened in early 2004, serving mostly Air Canada domestic flights. A handful of provincial flights land at tiny Toronto City Centre Airport (often called the Island Airport) in the Toronto Islands.

🚩 **Airport Information Lester B. Pearson International Airport** ☎ 416/776-3000 ⊕ www. torontoairport.ca. **Toronto City Centre Airport** ☎ 416/203-6942 ⊕ www.torontoport.com/TCCA.htm.

AIRPORT TRANSFERS

Although Pearson International Airport is not far from downtown, the drive can take well over an hour during weekday rush hours (6:30–9:30 AM and 3:30–6:30 PM). Taxis to a hotel or attraction near the lake cost C$40 or more and have fixed rates to different parts of the city. You must pay the full fare from the airport, but it's often possible to negotiate a lower fare from downtown to the airport, where airport cabs compete with regular city cabs. It's illegal for city cabs to pick up passengers at the airport, unless they are called—a time-consuming process, but sometimes worth the wait. The fare is about C$35.

Pacific Western Transportation Service offers 24-hour Airport Express coach service daily to several major downtown hotels and the Toronto Coach Terminal (commonly called the Bay Street Bus Station). It costs C$15.50 one-way, C$26.75 round-trip. Pickups are from the Arrivals levels of all three terminals at Pearson. Look for the curbside bus shelter, where tickets are sold.

GO Transit interregional buses transport passengers to the Yorkdale and York Mills

subway stations from Terminal 2 (Arrivals Level) and Terminal 1's Level 5 for C$3.65 one-way. Service can be irregular and luggage space limited.

Air Canada Jazz provides bus transportation for its customers between the Fairmont Royal York Hotel, across the street from Union Station, and the Harbourfront ferries, which serve the Toronto City Centre Airport.

Two Toronto Transit Commission (TTC) buses run from any of the airport terminals to the subway system. Bus 192 connects to the Kipling subway station; Bus 58 links to the Lawrence West station. Luggage space is limited and no assistance is given, but the price is only C$2.25 in exact change. (⇨ Bus Travel within Toronto)

If you rent a car at the airport, ask for a street map of the city. Highway 427 runs south some 6 km (4 mi) to the lakeshore. Here you pick up the Queen Elizabeth Way (QEW) east to the Gardiner Expressway, which runs east into the heart of downtown. If you take the QEW west, you'll find yourself swinging around Lake Ontario, toward Hamilton, Niagara-on-the-Lake, and Niagara Falls.

🚩 **Airport Buses Go Transit** ☎ 416/869-3200 or 888/438-6646 ⊕ www.gotransit.com. **Pacific Western Transportation Service** ☎ 905/564-6333 or 800/387-6787 ⊕ www.torontoairportexpress.com. **Toronto Transit Commission (TTC)** ☎ 416/393-4636 or 416/393-8663 for information, 416/393-4100 for lost and found ⊕ www.ttc.ca.

BIKE TRAVEL

Residents bike around the city, which has some designated paths, but short-term visitors might want to stick with the easy-to-use public transportation system, which reaches nearly every city corner.

BIKES IN FLIGHT

Most airlines accommodate bikes as luggage, provided they are dismantled and boxed; check with individual airlines about packing requirements. Some airlines sell bike boxes, which are often free at bike shops, for about $15 (bike bags can be considerably more expensive). International travelers often can substitute a bike for a piece of checked luggage at no charge; otherwise, the cost is about $100.

BOOKS

FICTION

Margaret Atwood, a prolific poet and novelist, is regarded as a stateswoman of sorts in her native Canada. Her novel *Cat's Eye* is set in northern Canada and Toronto. Alice Munro writes about small-town life in Ontario in *The Progress of Love*. Anne Michaels's poetic novel *Fugitive Pieces* and Camilla Gibb's *Mouthing the Words* involve children brought to Toronto with different yet traumatic pasts. Carol Shields (*The Stone Diaries*) and Michael Ondaatje (*The English Patient* and *Anil's Ghost*) are internationally known Canadian authors.

NONFICTION

Andrew Malcolm gives a cultural and historical overview of the country in *The Canadians*. *Why We Act Like Canadians: A Personal Exploration of Our National Character* is one of Pierre Berton's many popular nonfiction books focusing on Canada's history and culture; another is *Niagara: A History of the Falls*. *Short History of Canada,* by Desmond Morton, is a historical account of the country. *Local Colour—Writers Discovering Canada,* edited by Carol Marin, is a series of articles about Canadian places by leading travel writers. Thomas King, Cheryl Calver, and Helen Hoy collaborated on *The Native in Literature,* about the literary treatment of Native Canadians.

BUSINESS HOURS

Post offices are closed weekends. During the week most are open from 8 to 6, or from 9 to 7. The Beer Store and the LCBO (Liquor Control Board of Ontario), which sell beer and wine and liquor, respectively, close on holidays, so plan ahead.

BANKS & OFFICES

Most banks are open Monday through Thursday 10–5 and Friday 10–6. Some banks are open longer hours and also on Saturday morning. All banks are closed on national holidays. Most banks have automatic teller machines (ATMs) that are accessible around the clock.

GAS STATIONS

As in most large North American urban areas, many highway and city gas stations in and around Toronto are open 24 hours daily, although there's rarely a mechanic on duty Sunday. Smaller stations close at 7 PM.

MUSEUMS & SIGHTS

The variety of museums in Toronto also reflects opening and closing times: none are consistent, and it is best to phone ahead or check a museum's Web site. Opening hours of sites and attractions are denoted in this book by a clock icon.

PHARMACIES

The two main pharmacy chains, Shoppers Drug Mart and Pharma Plus, have several locations throughout the city that are open either until midnight or open 24 hours.

SHOPS

Most retail stores are open Monday through Saturday 10 to 6 and many now open on Sunday (generally noon to 5) as well. Downtown stores are usually open until 9 PM seven days a week. Some shops are open Thursday and/or Friday evenings, too. Shopping malls tend to be open weekdays from 9 or 10 AM to 10 PM, Saturday from 9 AM to 6 PM, and Sunday from noon to 5 PM. Convenience stores tend to be open 24 hours, seven days a week.

BUS TRAVEL TO & FROM TORONTO

Most buses arrive at the Toronto Coach Terminal, which serves a number of lines, including Greyhound (which has regular service to Toronto from all over the United States), Trentway-Wagar, Ontario Northland, Penetang-Midland Coach Lines (PMCL), and Can-AR. The trip takes 6 hours from Detroit, 2 to 3 hours from Buffalo, and 11 hours from Chicago and New York City.

FARES & SCHEDULES

Information on fares and departure times is available online or by phone.

PAYING

Tickets are purchased at the Toronto Coach Terminal before boarding the buses.

RESERVATIONS

Most bus lines do not accept reservations. You should plan on picking up your tickets at least 45 minutes before your bus's scheduled departure time.

☎ **Bus Information Can-AR** ☎ 905/564-1242 ⊕ www.can-arcoach.com. **Greyhound Lines of Canada Ltd.** ☎ 416/594-1010 or 800/661-8747 ⊕ www.greyhound.ca. **Toronto Coach Terminal** ✉ 610 Bay St., just north of Dundas St. W., Downtown ☎ 800/461-8558. **Trentway-Wagar** ☎ 800/461-7661 ⊕ www.coachcanada.com. **Ontario Northland** ☎ 705/472-4500 or 800/363-7512 ⊕ www.ontc.on.ca. **Penetang-Midland Coach Lines** ☎ 800/461-1767 ⊕ www.pmcl.on.ca.

BUS TRAVEL WITHIN TORONTO

Toronto Transit Commission (TTC) buses and streetcars link with every subway station to cover all points of the city. Service is generally excellent, with buses and streetcars covering major city thoroughfares about every 10 minutes; suburban service is less frequent. Although the subway stops running at 2 AM, the bus service operates from 1 to 5:30 AM on Bloor and Yonge streets, and as far north as Steeles. (⇨ Subway and Streetcar Travel)

FARES & SCHEDULES

All buses accept exact change, tickets, or tokens. Paper transfers are free; pick one up from the driver when you pay your fare (or show the driver the transfer from your subway station of origin). The single fare for buses (and streetcars and subways) is C$2.25; an all-day unlimited-use pass is C$7.75; five-fare tickets are available for C$9.50; 10 tickets or tokens are C$19.

Pay attention to the quirky rules of the day pass. It's good for unlimited travel for one person, weekdays after 9:30 AM or all day Saturday. On Sunday and holidays, it's good for up to six persons (maximum two adults) for unlimited travel. If you plan to stay in Toronto for a month or longer, consider the Metropass, a photo-identity card (C$98.75) that allows unlimited rides during one calendar month.

Be sure to **pick up a free Ride Guide,** available in most subways. This handy guide, published annually by the TTC, shows nearly every major place of interest in the city and how to reach it by public transit. The TTC's telephone information line provides directions in 20 languages.

☎ **Bus Information Toronto Transit Commission (TTC)** ☎ 416/393-4636 ⊕ www.ttc.ca.

PAYING

Tokens or tickets may be purchased from staffed booth or vending machines at subway stations or from many convenience stores. The fare is collected at boarding, and transfers may be used for connecting to another bus, streetcar, or subway on your trip; note that they're time-sensitive to prevent misuse.

CAMERAS & PHOTOGRAPHY

Photographers should consider a winter trip. Toronto and its surrounding country take on a whole new glamour when they're buried deep in snow.

The *Kodak Guide to Shooting Great Travel Pictures* (available at bookstores everywhere) is loaded with tips.

☎ **Photo Help Kodak Information Center** ☎ 800/242-2424 ⊕ www.kodak.com.

EQUIPMENT PRECAUTIONS

Don't pack film or equipment in checked luggage, where it is much more susceptible to damage. X-ray machines used to view checked luggage are extremely powerful and therefore are likely to ruin your film. Try to ask for hand inspection of film, which becomes clouded after repeated exposure to airport X-ray machines, and keep videotapes and computer disks away from metal detectors. Always keep film, tape, and computer disks out of the sun. Carry an extra supply of batteries, and be prepared to turn on your camera, camcorder, or laptop to prove to airport security personnel that the device is real.

CAR RENTAL

Rates in Toronto begin at C$49 a day and C$290 a week for an economy car with unlimited mileage. This does not include tax on car rentals, which is 15%. If you prefer a manual-transmission car, check whether the rental agency of your choice offers stick shifts; some companies, such as Avis, don't in Canada.

🚗 Major Agencies **Alamo** ☎ 800/522-9696 ⊕ www.alamo.com. **Avis** ☎ 800/331-1084, 800/ 879-2847 in Canada, 0870/606-0100 in the U.K., 02/ 9353-9000 in Australia, 09/526-2847 in New Zealand ⊕ www.avis.com. **Budget** ☎ 800/527-0700, 0870/156-5656 in the U.K. ⊕ www.budget. com. **Dollar** ☎ 800/800-6000, 0124/622-0111 in the U.K., where it's affiliated with Sixt, 02/9223-1444 in Australia ⊕ www.dollar.com. **Hertz** ☎ 800/654-3001, 800/263-0600 in Canada, 0870/844-8844 in the U.K., 02/9669-2444 in Australia, 09/256-8690 in New Zealand ⊕ www.hertz.com. **National Car Rental** ☎ 800/227-7368, 0870/600-6666 in the U.K. ⊕ www.nationalcar.com.

CUTTING COSTS

For a good deal, book through a travel agent who will shop around. If you're doing your own legwork, call the branch directly to compare prices quoted from the toll-free number. Also, price local car-rental companies—whose prices may be lower still, although their service and maintenance may not be as good as those of major rental agencies—and research rates on the Internet. Discount Car and Truck Rental and New Frontier typically have less expensive rates. Shuttles from the airport serve their off-site branches, which are often along nearby Dixon Road. Enterprise, a well-known agency, also operates off-site and may have less expensive rates.

Remember to ask about required deposits, cancellation penalties, and drop-off charges if you're planning to pick up the car in one city and leave it in another. If you're traveling during a holiday period, also make sure that a confirmed reservation guarantees you a car.

🚗 Local Agencies **Discount Car and Truck Rental** ☎ 416/249-5800 ⊕ www.discountcar.com. **Enterprise** ☎ 800-736-8222 or 416/798-1465 ⊕ www. enterprise.com. **New Frontier** ☎ 800/567-2837 or 416/675-2000 ⊕ www.newfrontiercar.com.

INSURANCE

When driving a rented car you are generally responsible for any damage to or loss of the vehicle. You also may be liable for any property damage or personal injury that you may cause while driving. Before you rent, see what coverage you already have under the terms of your personal auto-insurance policy and credit cards.

REQUIREMENTS & RESTRICTIONS

In Canada your own driver's license is acceptable. In Ontario, drivers must be 21. Agreements may require that the car not be taken out of Canada, including the U.S. side of Niagara Falls.

SURCHARGES

Before you pick up a car in one city and leave it in another, ask about drop-off charges or one-way service fees, which can be substantial. Note, too, that some rental agencies charge extra if you return the car before the time specified in your contract. To avoid a hefty refueling fee, fill the tank just before you turn in the car, but be aware that gas stations near the rental outlet may overcharge. The cost for additional drivers may be an additional C\$10 per day.

CAR TRAVEL

Your driver's license may not be recognized outside your home country. International driving permits (IDPs) are available from the American and Canadian automobile associations and, in the United Kingdom, from the Automobile Association and Royal Automobile Club. These international permits, valid only in conjunction with your regular driver's license, are universally recognized; having one may save you a problem with local authorities.

Given the high price of gas and the ease of Toronto's public transportation system, car travel is recommended only for those who wish to drive to sites and attractions outside the city, such as the Niagara wine region, Niagara Falls, and live theater at Stratford or Niagara-on-the-Lake. The city of Toronto and its suburbs (Oakville, Oshawa, and Mississauga, for example) have excellent transit systems that are inexpensive, clean, and safe.

EMERGENCY SERVICES

The Canadian Automobile Association (the Canadian version of AAA and AA) has

24-hour road service; membership benefits are extended to U.S. AAA members.

F Canadian Automobile Association ☎ 416/221-4300 or 800/268-3750 ✉ info@central.on.caa.ca ⊕ www.caa.ca.

FROM THE U.S.

Drivers must carry owner registration and proof of insurance coverage, which is compulsory in Canada. The Canadian Non-Resident Inter-Provincial Motor Vehicle Liability Insurance Card, available from any U.S. insurance company, is accepted as evidence of financial responsibility in Canada. The minimum liability coverage in Canada is C$200,000, except in Québec, where the minimum is C$50,000. If you are driving a car that is not registered in your name, carry a letter from the owner that authorizes your use of the vehicle.

Expect a wait at major border crossings. The wait at peak visiting times can be 60 minutes. If you can, avoid crossing on weekends and holidays at Detroit–Windsor, Buffalo–Fort Erie, and Niagara Falls, New York–Niagara Falls, Ontario, when the wait can be even longer.

Highway 401, which can stretch to 16 lanes in metropolitan Toronto, is the major link between Windsor, Ontario (and Detroit), and Montréal, Québec. There are no tolls anywhere along it, but you should be warned: between 6:30 and 9:30 each weekday morning and from 3:30 to 6:30 each afternoon, the 401 can become very crowded, even stop-and-go; plan your trip to avoid rush hours. A new toll highway, the 407, offers quicker travel; there are no tollbooths, but cameras photograph license plates and the system bills you, if it has your address. The 407 runs roughly parallel to the 401 for a 65-km (40-mi) stretch immediately north of Toronto.

If you're driving from Niagara Falls (U.S. or Canadian) or Buffalo, New York, take the Queen Elizabeth Way, which curves along the western shore of Lake Ontario and eventually turns into the Gardiner Expressway, which flows right into downtown. Yonge Street, which divides the west side of Toronto from the east, begins at the lakefront and continues north for

1,612 km (1,000 mi), though it's name changes to Highway 11 at Orillia.

F Insurance Information Insurance Bureau of Canada ☎ 416/362-9528, 800/387-2880 in Canada ⊕ www.ibc.ca.

GASOLINE

Gas prices in Canada have been on the rise. At this writing, the per-liter price was between 80¢ and 85¢. Gas stations are plentiful; many are self-service, and part of small convenience stores. Large stations are open 24 hours; smaller ones close after the dinner rush. For up-to-date prices, go to ⊕ www.torontogasprices.com.

Distances are always shown in kilometers, and gasoline is always sold in liters. (A gallon has 3.8 liters.)

PARKING

Toronto has green parking-meter boxes everywhere. Parking tickets net the city C$50 million annually, so they are frequently given out. Boxes are computerized; one hour costs C$2, payable with coins—the dollar coin (the "loonie"), the two dollar coin (the "toonie"), and nickels, dimes, and quarters are accepted—or a credit card (AE, MC, or V). Parking lots are found under office buildings, or on side streets near main thoroughfares. Costs can be exorbitant, especially if you park in a lot near a sports or entertainment venue. The best way around is by public transit or taxi.

ROAD CONDITIONS

Toronto residents rarely heed crosswalk signals, so use caution in driving along downtown streets.

RULES OF THE ROAD

By law, you are required to wear seat belts and to use infant seats in Ontario. Fines can be steep. Right turns are permitted on red signals, unless otherwise posted. You must come to a complete stop before making a right turn on red. Pedestrian crosswalks are sprinkled throughout the city, marked clearly by overhead signs and very large painted yellow Xs. Pedestrians have the right of way in these crosswalks. The speed limit in most areas of the city is 50 kph (30 mph) and usually within the

90–110 kph (50–68 mph) range outside the city.

Ontario is a no-fault province, and minimum liability insurance is C$200,000. If you're driving across the Ontario border, bring the policy or the vehicle registration forms and a free Canadian Non-Resident Insurance Card from your insurance agent. If you're driving a borrowed car, also bring a letter of permission signed by the owner.

Driving motorized vehicles while impaired by alcohol is taken seriously in Ontario and results in heavy fines, imprisonment, or both. It's illegal to refuse to take a Breathalyzer test. The possession of radar-detection devices in a car, even if they are not in operation, is illegal in Ontario. Studded tires and window coatings that do not allow a clear view of the vehicle interior are forbidden.

CHILDREN IN TORONTO

Travelers crossing the border with children should **carry identification for them** similar to that required by adults (i.e., passport or birth certificate). Children traveling with one parent or other adult should **bring a letter of permission** from the other parent, parents, or legal guardian. Divorced parents with shared custody rights should **carry legal documents establishing their status.** *Fodor's Around Toronto with Kids* (available in bookstores everywhere) can help you plan your days together.

If you are renting a car, don't forget to arrange for a car seat when you reserve. For general advice about traveling with children, consult *Fodor's FYI: Travel with Your Baby* (available in bookstores everywhere).

F Local Information City Parent ✉ Metroland Printing, 467 Speers Rd., Oakville, ON L6K 3S4 ☎ 905/815–0017.

BABYSITTING

Christopher Robin Services covers metropolitan Toronto, with a five-hour daily and four-hour nightly minimum; the cost is C$9 an hour. Also check out *City Parent*, a superior monthly newspaper for parents, which has listings of activities and local agencies. It's online at ⊕ www.cityparent.com/cityparent and free at li-

braries, bookstores, supermarkets, nursery schools, several banks, and even at many McDonald's restaurants. You can also find sitters registered at ⊕ www.canadiansitter.ca, which is a database of qualified sitters.
F Agencies Christopher Robin Services ☎ 416/483–4744.

FLYING

If your children are two or older, ask about children's airfares. As a general rule, infants under two not occupying a seat fly at greatly reduced fares or even for free. But if you want to guarantee a seat for an infant, you have to pay full fare. Consider flying during off-peak days and times; most airlines will grant an infant a seat without a ticket if there are available seats. When booking, confirm carry-on allowances if you're traveling with infants. In general, for babies charged 10% to 50% of the adult fare you are allowed one carry-on bag and a collapsible stroller; if the flight is full, the stroller may have to be checked or you may be limited to less.

Experts agree that it's a good idea to use safety seats aloft for children weighing less than 40 pounds. Airlines set their own policies: if you use a safety seat, U.S. carriers usually require that the child be ticketed, even if he or she is young enough to ride free, because the seats must be strapped into regular seats. And even if you pay the full adult fare for the seat, it may be worth it, especially on longer trips. Do **check your airline's policy about using safety seats during takeoff and landing.** Safety seats are not allowed everywhere in the plane, so get your seat assignments as early as possible.

When reserving, request children's meals or a freestanding bassinet (not available at all airlines) if you need them. But note that bulkhead seats, where you must sit to use the bassinet, may lack an overhead bin or storage space on the floor.

LODGING

Most hotels in Toronto allow children under a certain age to stay in their parents' room at no extra charge, but others charge for them as extra adults; be sure to **find out the cutoff age for children's discounts.**

The Delta Chelsea Inn maintains a supervised Children's Creative Center and allows children under 18 to stay free with their parents.

⚑ Best Choices Delta Chelsea Inn ✉ 33 Gerrard St., Toronto, ON M5G 1Z4 ☎ 416/595-1975 or 800/243-5732.

SIGHTS & ATTRACTIONS
Places that are especially appealing to children are indicated by a rubber-duckie icon (🦆) in the margin.

CONCIERGES
Concierges, found in many hotels, can help you with theater tickets and dinner reservations: a good one with connections may be able to get you seats for a hot show or prime-time dinner reservations at the restaurant of the moment. You can also turn to your hotel's concierge for help with travel arrangements, sightseeing plans, services ranging from aromatherapy to zipper repair, and emergencies. **Always tip** a concierge who has been of assistance (⇨ Tipping).

CONSULATES
All international embassies are in Ottawa, there are some consulates in Toronto. The Consulate General of the United States does not permit food, cell phones, pagers, personal organizers, tape recorders, cameras, or other electronic devices in its building. There is no storage for these items, so do not bring any of them with you.

⚑ Australia Australian Consulate General ✉ 175 Bloor St. E., Suite 1100 ☎ 416/323-1155 ⊕ www.ahc-ottawa.org ⊙ Weekdays 9-1:00 and 2-4:30.

⚑ United Kingdom British Consulate General ✉ 777 Bay St., Suite 2800 ☎ 416/593-1290 ⊕ www.britainincanada.org/Contact/toronto.htm ⊙ Weekdays 9-4:30.

⚑ United States Consulate General of the United States ✉ 360 University Ave. ☎ 416/595-1700 ⊕ www.usconsulatetoronto.ca/content/index.asp ⊙ Weekdays 8:30-1.

CONSUMER PROTECTION
Whether you're shopping for gifts or purchasing travel services, **pay with a major credit card** whenever possible, so you can cancel payment or get reimbursed if there's a problem (and you can provide documen-

tation). If you're doing business with a particular company for the first time, contact your local Better Business Bureau and the attorney general's offices in your state and (for U.S. businesses) the company's home state as well. Have any complaints been filed? Finally, if you're buying a package or tour, always consider travel insurance that includes default coverage (⇨ Insurance).

⚑ BBBs Council of Better Business Bureaus ✉ 4200 Wilson Blvd., Suite 800, Arlington, VA 22203 ☎ 703/276-0100 ᴀ 703/525-8277 ⊕ www.bbb.org.

CUSTOMS & DUTIES
When shopping abroad, keep receipts for all purchases. Upon reentering your country, **be ready to show customs officials what you've bought.** Pack purchases together in an easily accessible place. If you think a duty is incorrect, appeal the assessment. If you object to the way your clearance was handled, note the inspector's badge number. In either case, first ask to see a supervisor. If the problem isn't resolved, write to the appropriate authorities, beginning with the port director at your point of entry.

IN AUSTRALIA
Australian residents who are 18 or older may bring home A$400 worth of souvenirs and gifts (including jewelry), 250 cigarettes or 250 grams of cigars or other tobacco products, and 1,125 ml of alcohol (including wine, beer, and spirits). Residents under 18 may bring back A$200 worth of goods. Members of the same family traveling together may pool their allowances. Prohibited items include meat products. Seeds, plants, and fruits need to be declared upon arrival.

⚑ Australian Customs Service ᴀ Regional Director, Box 8, Sydney, NSW 2001 ☎ 02/9213-2000 or 1300/363-263, 02/9364-7222 or 1800/803-006 quarantine-inquiry line ᴀ 02/9213-4043 ⊕ www.customs.gov.au.

IN NEW ZEALAND
All homeward-bound residents may bring back NZ$700 worth of souvenirs and gifts; passengers may not pool their allowances, and children can claim only the

concession on goods intended for their own use. For those 17 or older, the duty-free allowance also includes 4.5 liters of wine or beer; one 1,125-ml bottle of spirits; and either 200 cigarettes, 250 grams of tobacco, 50 cigars, *or* a combination of the three up to 250 grams. Meat products, seeds, plants, and fruits must be declared upon arrival to the Agricultural Services Department.

New Zealand Customs ✉ Head office: The Customhouse, 17–21 Whitmore St., Box 2218, Wellington ☎ 09/300–5399 or 0800/428–786 ⊕ www.customs. govt.nz.

IN TORONTO

American and British visitors may bring in the following items duty-free: 200 cigarettes, 50 cigars, and 7 ounces of tobacco; 1 bottle (1.1 liters or 40 imperial ounces) of liquor or wine, or 24 355-ml (12-ounce) bottles or cans of beer for personal consumption. Any alcohol and tobacco products in excess of these amounts is subject to duty, provincial fees, and taxes. You can also bring in gifts up to a total value of C$750.

A deposit is sometimes required for trailers (refunded upon return). Cats and dogs must have a certificate issued by a licensed veterinarian that clearly identifies the animal and certifies that it has been vaccinated against rabies during the preceding 36 months. Seeing-eye dogs are allowed into Canada without restriction. Plant material must be declared and inspected. There may be restrictions on some live plants, bulbs, and seeds. With certain restrictions or prohibitions on some fruits and vegetables, visitors may bring food with them for their own use, providing the quantity is consistent with the duration of the visit.

Canada's firearms laws are significantly stricter than those in the United States. All handguns and semiautomatic and fully automatic weapons are prohibited and cannot be brought into the country. Sporting rifles and shotguns may be imported provided they are to be used for sporting, hunting, or competition while in Canada. All firearms must be declared to Canada Customs at the first point of entry. Failure to declare firearms will result in their seizure, and criminal charges may be made. Regulations require visitors to have a confirmed "Firearms Declaration" to bring any guns for sporting, hunting, or competition into Canada; a fee of C$50 applies, good for one year. For more information, contact the Canadian Firearms Centre.

Canada Customs and Revenue Agency ✉ 2265 St. Laurent Blvd. S, Ottawa, ON K1G 4K3 ☎ 800/ 267–5177 for international and non-resident inquiries ⊕ www.ccra-adrc.gc.ca. **Canadian Firearms Centre** ☎ 800/731–4000 ⊕ www.cfc-ccaf.gc.ca/en/ default.asp. **U.S. Customs Service** ✉ 1300 Pennsylvania Ave. NW, Room 6.3D, Washington, DC 20229 ⊕ www.customs.gov ☎ 202/354–1000 ✉ Complaints c/o 1300 Pennsylvania Ave. NW, Room 5.4D, Washington, DC 20229.

IN THE U.K.

From countries outside the European Union, including Canada, you may bring home, duty-free, 200 cigarettes or 50 cigars; 1 liter of spirits or 2 liters of fortified or sparkling wine or liqueurs; 2 liters of still table wine; 60 ml of perfume; 250 milliliters of toilet water; plus £145 worth of other goods, including gifts and souvenirs. Prohibited items include meat products, seeds, plants, and fruits.

HM Customs and Excise ✉ Portcullis House, 21 Cowbridge Rd. E, Cardiff CF11 9SS ☎ 0845/010– 9000 or 0208/929–0152, 0208/929–6731 or 0208/ 910–3602 complaints ⊕ www.hmce.gov.uk.

IN THE U.S.

U.S. residents who have been out of the country for at least 48 hours may bring home, for personal use, $800 worth of foreign goods duty-free, as long as they haven't used the $800 allowance or any part of it in the past 30 days. This exemption may include 1 liter of alcohol (for travelers 21 and older), 200 cigarettes, and 100 non-Cuban cigars. Family members from the same household who are traveling together may pool their $800 personal exemptions. For fewer than 48 hours, the duty-free allowance drops to $200, which may include 50 cigarettes, 10 non-Cuban cigars, and 150 ml of alcohol (or 150 ml of perfume containing alcohol). The $200 allowance cannot be combined with other individuals' exemptions, and if you exceed it, the full value of all the goods will be taxed. Antiques, which the U.S. Bureau of Customs and Border Protection defines as objects more than 100 years old, enter duty-free, as do original works of art done entirely by hand, including paintings, drawings, and sculptures. This doesn't apply to folk art or handicrafts, which are in general dutiable.

You may also send packages home duty-free, with a limit of one parcel per addressee per day (except alcohol or tobacco products or perfume worth more than $5). You can mail up to $200 worth of goods for personal use; label the package PERSONAL USE and attach a list of its contents and their retail value. If the package contains your used personal belongings, mark it AMERICAN GOODS RETURNED to avoid paying duties. You may send up to $100 worth of goods as a gift; mark the package UNSOLICITED GIFT. Mailed items do not affect your duty-free allowance on your return.

To avoid paying duty on foreign-made high-ticket items you already own and will take on your trip, register them with Customs before you leave the country. Consider filing a Certificate of Registration for laptops, cameras, watches, and other digital devices identified with serial numbers or other permanent markings; you can keep the certificate for other trips. Otherwise, bring a sales receipt or insurance form to show that you owned the item before you left the United States.

🚩 **U.S. Bureau of Customs and Border Protection** ✉ for inquiries and equipment registration, 1300 Pennsylvania Ave. NW, Washington, DC 20229 ⊕ www.customs.gov ☎ 877/287-8667, 202/354-1000 ✉ for complaints, Customer Satisfaction Unit, 1300 Pennsylvania Ave. NW, Room 5.5D, Washington, DC 20229.

DISABILITIES & ACCESSIBILITY

Travelers with disabilities do not have the same blanket legal protection in Canada that they have in the United States. Indeed, some facilities aren't easy to use in a wheelchair—the subway and bus systems in Toronto, for example. Newer sites and

attractions are well equipped for people who use wheelchairs or who have a sight or hearing impairment.

The Canadian Paraplegic Association National Office has information about touring in Canada. Community Information Toronto provides information on various facilities, as well as social and health services for people with disabilities; it's open Monday–Friday from 8 AM to 10 PM, weekends and statutory holidays from 10 to 10.

🚩 **Local Resources Canadian Paraplegic Association National Office** ✉ 1101 Prince of Wales Dr., Ottawa K2C 3W7 ☎ 613/723-1033 ⊕ www.canparaplegic.org. **City accessibility planner** ☎ 416/338-0338. **Community Information Toronto** ☎ 416/397-4636 ⊕ www.communityinformationtoronto.ca.

LODGING

Many of the major hotels in the **$$–$$$$** range have wheelchair-accessible rooms. These include The Sutton Place Hotel, InterContinental Toronto Centre, Le Royal Meridien King Edward Hotel, and Toronto Marriott Eaton Centre. Call for details.

RESERVATIONS

When discussing accessibility with an operator or reservations agent, ask hard questions. Are there any stairs, inside *or* out? Are there grab bars next to the toilet *and* in the shower/tub? How wide is the doorway to the room? To the bathroom? For the most extensive facilities meeting the latest legal specifications, opt for newer accommodations. If you reserve through a toll-free number, consider also calling the hotel's local number to confirm the information from the central reservations office. Get confirmation in writing when you can.

SIGHTS & ATTRACTIONS

Thanks to increased awareness and government-incentive programs, most major attractions—museums, churches, theaters—are equipped with ramps and lifts to handle wheelchairs. National and provincial institutions—parks, public monuments, and government buildings—are generally accessible. Tourism Toronto's

Toronto with Ease is an annual publication with accessibility information on sights, hotels, and getting around. It's available free upon request or online at ⊕ www.enablelink.org, a thorough Canadian accessibility Web site. It's always best to call for information about a particular attraction and ask for details.

TRANSPORTATION
The Toronto Transit Commission (TTC) offers a bus service called Wheel-Trans for people with disabilities who are unable to use regular public vehicles.

Transportation to and from Pearson International Airport is available for travelers with disabilities through Wheel-Trans. Three limousine companies—Aaroport, MacIntosh, and Airline Limousine—operate wheelchair-accessible vans. By pre-arrangement, people with disabilities can be picked up or dropped off at points in all three of the airport's terminals.

Greyhound/Trailways will transport a person with a disability along with one companion for the price of a single fare provided you book at least three days in advance. Amtrak requests 24-hour notice to provide Redcap service and special seats. Passengers with disabilities are entitled to a 25% discount on the normal discount coach fare; for best service, mention your disability when booking. To file a complaint about transportation obstacles at airports (including flights) or railroads, contact the Director, Accessible Transportation Directorate, at the Canadian Transportation Agency (⊕ www.cta-otc.gc.ca).

⚑ Complaints Aviation Consumer Protection Division for airline-related problems. **Departmental Office of Civil Rights** ⊠ for general inquiries, U.S. Department of Transportation, S-30, 400 7th St. SW, Room 10215, Washington, DC 20590 ☎ 202/366-4648 🖷 202/366-9371 ⊕ www.dot.gov/ost/docr/index.htm. **Disability Rights Section** ⊠ NYAV, U.S. Department of Justice, Civil Rights Division, 950 Pennsylvania Ave. NW, Washington, DC 20530 ☎ ADA information line 202/514-0301, 800/514-0301, 202/514-0383 TTY, 800/514-0383 TTY ⊕ www.ada.gov. **U.S. Department of Transportation Hotline** ☎ for disability-related air-travel problems, 800/778-4838 or 800/455-9880 TTY.

In Canada: **Accessible Transportation Directorate** ⊠ 15 Eddy St., Hull, QC K1A 0N9 ☎ 819/997-6828 or 800/883-1813. **Council of Canadians with Disabilities** ⊠ 294 Portage Ave., Suite 926, Winnipeg, MB R3C 0B9 ☎ 204/947-0303 🖷 204/942-4625. **⚑ Services Aaroport, MacIntosh** ☎ 416/225-1555 for both. **Airline Limousine** ☎ 905/676-3210. **Amtrak** ☎ 800/872-7245. **Greyhound/Trailways** ☎ 800/752-4841. **Toronto Transit Commission (TTC)** ☎ 416/393-4222, 416/393-4555 TTY for advance and same-day reservations, 416/481-2523 phone and TDD for routes and schedules, 416/393-4111 for customer service. **Wheel-Trans** ☎ 416/393-4111.

TRAVEL AGENCIES
In the United States, the Americans with Disabilities Act requires that travel firms serve the needs of all travelers. Some agencies specialize in working with people with disabilities.

⚑ Travelers with Mobility Problems Access Adventures/B. Roberts Travel ⊠ 206 Chestnut Ridge Rd., Scottsville, NY 14624 ☎ 585/889-9096 ⊕ www.brobertstravel.com ✉ dltravel@prodigy.net, run by a former physical-rehabilitation counselor. **CareVacations** ⊠ No. 5, 5110-50 Ave., Leduc, AB T9E 6V4 ☎ 780/986-6404 or 877/478-7827 🖷 780/986-8332 ⊕ www.carevacations.com, for group tours and cruise vacations. **Flying Wheels Travel** ⊠ 143 W. Bridge St., Box 382, Owatonna, MN 55060 ☎ 507/451-5005 🖷 507/451-1685 ⊕ www.flyingwheelstravel.com.

DISCOUNTS & DEALS
Be a smart shopper and compare all your options before making decisions. A plane ticket bought with a promotional coupon from travel clubs, coupon books, and direct-mail offers or purchased on the Internet may not be cheaper than the least expensive fare from a discount ticket agency. And always keep in mind that what you get is just as important as what you save.

DISCOUNT RESERVATIONS
To save money, look into discount reservations services with Web sites and toll-free numbers, which use their buying power to get a better price on hotels, airline tickets (⇨ Air Travel), even car rentals. When booking a room, always **call the hotel's local toll-free number** (if one is available) rather than the central

reservations number—you'll often get a better price. Always ask about special packages or corporate rates.

When shopping for the best deal on hotels and car rentals, look for guaranteed exchange rates, which protect you against a falling dollar. With your rate locked in, you won't pay more, even if the price goes up in the local currency.

☎ Airline Tickets **Air 4 Less** ☎ 800/AIR4LESS; low-fare specialist.

☎ Hotel Rooms **Accommodations Express** ☎ 800/444-7666 or 800/277-1064 ⊕ www. accommodationsexpress.com. **Hotels.com** ☎ 800/ 246-8357 ⊕ www.hotels.com. **RMC Travel** ☎ 800/ 245-5738 ⊕ www.rmcwebtravel.com. **Turbotrip. com** ☎ 800/473-7829 ⊕ www.turbotrip.com.

PACKAGE DEALS

Don't confuse packages and guided tours. When you buy a package, you travel on your own, just as though you had planned the trip yourself. Fly/drive packages, which combine airfare and car rental, are often a good deal. In cities, ask the local visitor's bureau about hotel packages that include tickets to major museum exhibits or other special events.

EATING & DRINKING

The restaurants we list are the cream of the crop in each price category. For more information about dining in each neighborhood, including a price chart, *see* Chapter 2.

WINE, BEER & SPIRITS

Wine, beer, and spirits are available at most Toronto eating establishments which have an LCBO license (Liquor Control Board of Ontario). Some smaller restaurants or bars may only have a wine and beer license. The "last call for alcohol" happens in bars and most restaurants at 1:50 AM; bars close at 2:30 AM. Liquor can only be served later if the establishment has applied for a special license to coincide with a major city-wide event—the annual Toronto Film Festival in September, for example—when some bars and restaurants can serve alcohol until 4 AM.

EMERGENCIES

For a complete listing of emergency services, you can always check the Yellow Pages or ask for assistance at your hotel desk. The Dental Emergency Service operates from 8 AM to midnight. Many Pharma Plus Drugmarts are open until midnight; some branches of Shoppers Drug Mart are open 24 hours.

☎ Doctors & Dentists **Dental Emergency Service** ✉ 1650 Yonge St. ☎ 416/485-7121. **Medvisit Doctors House Call Service** ☎ 416/631-3000.

☎ Emergency Services **Police and ambulance** ☎ 911.

☎ Hospitals **St. Michael's Hospital** ✉ 30 Bond St. ☎ 416/360-4000 **Toronto General Hospital** ✉ 200 Elizabeth St. ☎ 416/340-3111 or 416/340-3946 for emergencies.

☎ Hot Lines **Ambulance, fire, and police** ☎ 911.

☎ Pet Care **Veterinary Emergency Clinic** ✉ 1180 Danforth Ave. ☎ 416/465-3501.

☎ Late-Night & 24-Hour Pharmacies **Pharma Plus Drugmart** ✉ Church St. and Wellesley St. E, Church and Wellesley ☎ 416/924-7769. **Shoppers Drug Mart** ✉ 700 Bay St., Downtown ☎ 416/979-2424 ✉ 2500 Hurontario St., Mississauga ☎ 905/896-2500.

GAY & LESBIAN TRAVEL

Toronto and avidly competes for gay visitors. The heart of the city's large, visible, and active gay and lesbian community is near Church and Wellesley streets in eastern downtown.

The annual Pride Toronto Parade, held in late June, is the biggest street event of the year in Toronto, attracting well over 500,000 spectators and capping a week of cultural activities. The beach most frequented by gays and lesbians in the Toronto area is Hanlan's Point on the northwest tip of the Toronto Islands. It is now officially a clothing-optional beach, given sanction by City Council in 1999.

Consult the Pink Pages, an annual reference directory (found in various bookstores and bars) for Toronto's gay and lesbian community or pick up a free copy of *XTRA!* or *Fab*, biweekly newspapers available on the streets around the Church–Wellesley area. *XTRA!* runs a Gay Community Information Line and can

even send you a copy of the newspaper before your trip. The 519 Community Centre can provide information about events, bars, and more. Different Roads Travel, Kennedy Travel, and Now, Voyager will help you tailor your vacation, as will Skylink Travel and Tour, which caters to lesbian travelers. Tourism Toronto publishes a biannual Gay Travel Guide, a booklet written by locals-in-the-know.

For details about the American gay and lesbian scene, consult *Fodor's Gay Guide to the USA* (available in bookstores everywhere).

Gay- & Lesbian-Friendly Travel Agencies Different Roads Travel ⊠ 8383 Wilshire Blvd., Suite 520, Beverly Hills, CA 90211 ☎ 323/651-5557 or 800/429-8747 (Ext. 14 for both) 🖷 323/651-3678 ✉ lgernert@tzell.com. **Kennedy Travel** ⊠ 130 W. 42nd St., Suite 401, New York, NY 10036 ☎ 212/840-8659, 800/237-7433 🖷 212/730-2269 ⊕ www.kennedytravel.com. **Now, Voyager** ⊠ 4406 18th St., San Francisco, CA 94114 ☎ 415/626-1169 or 800/255-6951 🖷 415/626-8626 ⊕ www.nowvoyager.com. **Skylink Travel and Tour** ⊠ 1455 N. Dutton Ave., Suite A, Santa Rosa, CA 95401 ☎ 707/546-9888 or 800/225-5759 🖷 707/636-0951; serving lesbian travelers.

Local Resources Fab ⊠ 11 Church St., Ste. 200 ☎ 416/925-5221 ⊕ www.fabmagazine.com. **519 Community Centre** ⊠ 519 Church St. ☎ 416/392-6874. **Gay Community Information Line** ☎ 416/925-9872. **Pride Toronto Parade** ⊕ www.pridetoronto.com. **Tourism Toronto** ☎ 416/203-2500 or 800/363-1990 ⊕ www.torontotourism.com. **XTRA!** ⊠ 491 Church St., Suite 200, M4Y 2C6 ☎ 416/925-6665.

HOLIDAYS

Canadian national holidays for 2005 are as follows: New Year's Day, Good Friday, Easter Monday, Victoria Day (May 23), Canada Day (July 1), Simcoe Day (August 8), Labour Day (September 5), Thanksgiving (October 10), Remembrance Day (November 11), Christmas, and Boxing Day (December 26).

INSURANCE

The most useful travel-insurance plan is a comprehensive policy that includes coverage for trip cancellation and interruption, default, trip delay, and medical expenses (with a waiver for preexisting conditions).

Without insurance you'll lose all or most of your money if you cancel your trip, regardless of the reason. Default insurance covers you if your tour operator, airline, or cruise line goes out of business. Trip-delay covers expenses that arise because of bad weather or mechanical delays. Study the fine print when comparing policies.

U.K. residents can buy a travel-insurance policy valid for most vacations taken during the year in which it's purchased (but check preexisting-condition coverage). British and Australian citizens need extra medical coverage when traveling overseas. Always **buy travel policies directly from the insurance company**; if you buy them from a cruise line, airline, or tour operator that goes out of business you probably won't be covered for the agency or operator's default, a major risk. Before making any purchase, review your existing health and homeowner's policies to find what they cover away from home.

Travel Insurers In the U.S.: Access America ⊠ 6600 W. Broad St., Richmond, VA 23230 ☎ 800/284-8300 🖷 804/673-1491 or 800/346-9265 ⊕ www.accessamerica.com. **Travel Guard International** ⊠ 1145 Clark St., Stevens Point, WI 54481 ☎ 715/345-0505 or 800/826-1300 🖷 800/955-8785 ⊕ www.travelguard.com. **In the U.K.: Association of British Insurers** ⊠ 51 Gresham St., London EC2V 7HQ ☎ 020/7600-3333 🖷 020/7696-8999 ⊕ www.abi.org.uk. In Canada: **RBC Insurance** ⊠ 6880 Financial Dr., Mississauga, ON L5N 7Y5 ☎ 800/565-3129 🖷 905/813-4704 ⊕ www.rbcinsurance.com. In Australia: **Insurance Council of Australia** ⊠ Insurance Enquiries and Complaints, Level 3, 56 Pitt St., Sydney, NSW 2000 ☎ 1300/363683 or 02/9251-4456 🖷 02/9251-4453 ⊕ www.iecltd.com.au. In New Zealand: **Insurance Council of New Zealand** ⊠ Level 7, 111-115 Customhouse Quay, Box 474, Wellington ☎ 04/472-5230 🖷 04/473-3011 ⊕ www.icnz.org.nz.

LANGUAGE

Canada is a bilingual country: it has two official languages, French and English. In some provinces and cities, road signs appear in both official languages. But Toronto is the Anglophone center of Canada, and 99% of the people living here will speak to you in English.

LODGING

In Toronto you have a choice of luxury hotels, moderately priced modern properties, and smaller, older hotels with perhaps fewer conveniences but more charm.

Expect accommodations to cost more in summer than in the off-season (except for places such as ski resorts, where winter is high season). When making reservations, **ask about special deals and packages.** Big-city hotels that cater to business travelers often offer weekend packages, and many city hotels offer rooms at up to 50% off in winter. If you're planning to visit a major city or resort area in high season, **book well in advance.** Also be aware of any special events or festivals that may coincide with your visit and fill every room for miles around. The winter ski-season is high season for resorts and lodges, so plan accordingly. For approximate costs, *see* the dining price chart *in* chapter 3.

BED & BREAKFASTS

Be sure to **check out the B&B's Web site,** which may have useful information, although you should also find out how up-to-date it is. Room quality varies from house to house as well, so **ask to see a room before making a choice.**
🏠 Bed & Breakfast Metropolitan Registry of Toronto ☎ 416/964-2566. The Downtown Toronto Association of B&B Guest Houses ☎ 416/410-3938 ⊕ www.bnbinfo.com.
🏠 Reservation Services Toronto Convention & Visitors Association 🖂 416/203-2600 ✏ toronto@tourcvb.com ⊕ www.torontotourism. com.

HOME EXCHANGES

If you would like to exchange your home for someone else's, join a home-exchange organization, which will send you its updated listings of available exchanges for a year and will include your own listing in at least one of them. It's up to you to make specific arrangements.
🏠 Exchange Clubs HomeLink International 📪 Box 47747, Tampa, FL 33647 ☎ 813/975-9825 or 800/638-3841 ♨ 813/910-8144 ⊕ www.homelink. org; $110 yearly for a listing, online access, and catalog; $70 without catalog.

MAIL & SHIPPING

In Canada you can buy stamps at the post office or from vending machines in most hotel lobbies, railway stations, airports, bus terminals, many retail outlets, and some newsstands. If you're sending mail to or within Canada, **be sure to include the postal code** (six digits and letters). Note that the suite number may appear before the street number in an address, followed by a hyphen. The postal abbreviation for Ontario is ON.

Main postal outlets for products and services in the downtown area include Adelaide Street Post Office. Near the Marriott, the Delta Chelsea Hotel, and the Eaton Centre is the Atrium on Bay Post Office; and one block southeast of the major Bloor-Yonge intersection is Postal Station "F."
🏠 Post Offices Adelaide Street Post Office 🖂 31 Adelaide St. E ☎ 416/214-2353. Atrium on Bay Post Office 🖂 595 Bay St. ☎ 416/506-0911. Postal Station "F" 🖂 50 Charles St. E ☎ 416/413-4815.

POSTAL RATES

Within Canada, postcards and letters up to 30 grams cost 49¢; between 31 grams and 50 grams, the cost is 80¢; and between 51 grams and 100 grams, the cost is 98¢. Letters and postcards to the United States cost 80¢ for up to 30 grams, 98¢ for between 31 and 50 grams, and C$1.60 for up to 100 grams. Prices do not include GST (Goods and Services Tax).

International mail and postcards run C$1.40 for up to 20 grams, C$1.96 for 21 to 50 grams, and C$3.20 for 51 to 100 grams.

RECEIVING MAIL

Mail may be sent to you care of General Delivery, Toronto Adelaide Post Office, 36 Adelaide Street East, Toronto, On. M5C 1J0.

American Express allows its clients—cardholders and those who purchase traveler's checks or travel services—to pick up mail (with proper ID) from its office at 50 Bloor Street West on the concourse level (☎ 416/967-3411).

SHIPPING PARCELS

Customs forms are required with international parcels. Parcels sent regular post typically take up to two weeks. The fastest service is Federal Express, which has a 24-hour branch on Lakeshore Boulevard.

⁊ Shipping Resources FedEx ⊠ 215 Lakeshore Blvd. E., at Sherbourne St., Downtown ☎ 800/463-3339.

MEDIA

Toronto is Canada's English-language media capital. All the major TV networks (including cable) are located here, as are the two national daily newspapers and the flagship government-subsidized television/radio network, the Canadian Broadcasting Corporation (CBC). Most of the larger ISPs (Internet service providers) are also found in Ontario's capital city.

NEWSPAPERS & MAGAZINES

Canada's two national daily newspapers, the *National Post* and the *Globe and Mail,* are available at newsstands in Canada and in major foreign cities. Toronto's metropolitan daily newspaper is the *Toronto Star; The Toronto Sun* is a daily tabloid. Prices for daily papers average between 50 and 75 cents each. *Now* and *eye* are weekly, free tabloids (distributed on Thursday) that cover the entertainment scene very well. *Toronto Life* is the city's glossy magazine, with features on local culture and good coverage of the restaurant and shopping scenes. *Maclean's* is Canada's main general-interest magazine. It covers arts and culture as well as politics.

RADIO & TELEVISION

U.S. television dominates Toronto's airwaves—Fox, PBS, NBC, CBS, and ABC are readily available. Canada's two major networks, the public Canadian Broadcasting Corporation (CBC) and the private CTV, along with the Can-West Global Network, broadcast about a dozen Canadian-produced programs along with many U.S. shows during prime time. The selection of Canadian-produced current-affairs programs, however, is much larger. The CBC also has a parallel French-language network, Radio-Canada.

With more than 42 standard cable stations to choose from, international visitors at hotels can view CNN, BBC, and RAI. Local stations of note include *City-TV* (much local content), *Showcase* (all drama and excellent foreign films), *TVOntario* (a public broadcaster with excellent local and imported shows), *CFMT Multilingual TV* (a myriad of languages and content) and, of course, *CBC Newsworld,* Canada's homegrown version of CNN. The popular cultural channel *Bravo* is also based here.

The CBC operates the country's only truly national radio network. In fact, it operates four of them, two in English and two in French. Its Radio 1 network, broadcast on the AM band, has a daily schedule rich in news, discussion, and current-affairs programs. One of the most popular shows, "As It Happens," takes a quirky and highly entertaining look at national, world, and weird events every evening at 6. Radio 2, broadcast on FM, emphasizes music and often features live classical concerts by some of Canada's best orchestras, opera companies, and choral groups. The two French-language networks more or less follow the same pattern.

MONEY MATTERS

Throughout this book, unless otherwise stated, all prices, including dining and lodging, are given in Canadian dollars.

Toronto is the country's most expensive city. The following are typical prices: a soda (pop), C$1.25–C$1.75; glass of beer, C$3–C$6; a sandwich, C$6; a taxi, as soon as the meter is turned on, C$2.50, and C$1 for every kilometer (½ mi); movie admission for one, about C$11.

Prices throughout this guide are given for adults. Substantially reduced fees are almost always available for children, students, and senior citizens. (⇨ Taxes)

ATMS

ATMs are available in most bank, trust-company, and credit-union branches across the country, as well as in many convenience stores, malls, and gas stations.

CREDIT CARDS

Throughout this guide, the following abbreviations are used: **AE**, American Express; **D**, Discover; **DC**, Diners Club; **MC**, MasterCard; and **V**, Visa.

🖬 Reporting Lost Cards American Express ☏ 800/528-4800. **Diners Club** ☏ 800/234-6377. **Discover** ☏ 800/347-2683. **MasterCard** ☏ 800/307-7309. **Visa** ☏ 800/336-8472.

CURRENCY

U.S. dollars are widely accepted, although you won't get the exchange rate offered at banks. Some hotels, restaurants, and stores are skittish about accepting U.S. and even Canadian currency over $20 due to counterfeiting, so **be sure to get small bills when you exchange money or visit an ATM.** Traveler's checks (some are available in Canadian dollars), major U.S. credit cards, and debit or check cards with a credit card logo are accepted in most areas.

The units of currency in Canada are the Canadian dollar (C$) and the cent, in almost the same denominations as U.S. currency ($5, $10, $20, 1¢, 5¢, 10¢, 25¢, etc.). The $1 and $2 bill are no longer used; they have been replaced by $1 and $2 coins (known as a "loonie," because of the loon that appears on the coin, and a "toonie," respectively). At this writing the exchange rate was US$1 to C$1.37, £1 to C$2.43, AUD$1.01 to C$1, and NZD$1.16 to C$1.

CURRENCY EXCHANGE

For the most favorable rates, **change money through banks.** Although ATM transaction fees may be higher abroad than at home, ATM rates are excellent because they're based on wholesale rates offered only by major banks. You won't do as well at exchange booths in airports or rail and bus stations, in hotels, in restaurants, or in stores. To avoid lines at airport exchange booths, get a bit of local currency before you leave home.

🖬 Exchange Services International Currency Express ✉ 427 N. Camden Dr., Suite F, Beverly Hills, CA 90210 ☏ 888/278-6628 orders 🖷 310/278-6410 🌐 www.foreignmoney.com. **Thomas Cook International Money Services** ☏ 800/287-7362 orders and retail locations 🌐 www.travelex.com.

PACKING

You may want to **pack light** because airline luggage restrictions are tight. What you pack depends more on the time of year than on any dress code. For winter, you need your warmest clothes, in many layers, and waterproof boots. In summer, loose-fitting, casual clothing will see you through both day and evening events. It's a good idea to pack a sweater or shawl for cool evenings or restaurants that run their air-conditioners full blast. Men will need a jacket and tie for the better restaurants and many of the night spots. Jeans are as popular in Toronto as they are elsewhere and are perfectly acceptable for sightseeing and informal dining. Be sure to **bring comfortable walking shoes.** Consider packing a bathing suit for your hotel pool.

In your carry-on luggage, pack an extra pair of eyeglasses or contact lenses and enough of any medication you take to last a few days longer than the entire trip. You may also ask your doctor to write a spare prescription using the drug's generic name, as brand names may vary from country to country. In luggage to be checked, **never pack prescription drugs, valuables, or undeveloped film.** And don't forget to carry with you the addresses of offices that handle refunds of lost traveler's checks. Check *Fodor's How to Pack* (available at online retailers and bookstores everywhere) for more tips.

To avoid customs and security delays, carry medications in their original packaging. Don't pack any sharp objects in your carry-on luggage, including knives of any size or material, scissors, and corkscrews, or anything else that might arouse suspicion.

To avoid having your checked luggage chosen for hand inspection, don't cram bags full. The U.S. Transportation Security Administration suggests packing shoes on top and placing personal items you don't want touched in clear plastic bags.

CHECKING LUGGAGE

You're allowed to carry aboard one bag and one personal article, such as a purse or a laptop computer. Make sure what you carry on fits under your seat or in the overhead bin. Get to the gate early, so you can board as soon as possible, before the overhead bins fill up.

Baggage allowances vary by carrier, destination, and ticket class. On international flights, you're usually allowed to check two bags weighing up to 70 pounds (32 kilograms) each, although a few airlines allow checked bags of up to 88 pounds (40 kilograms) in first class. Some international carriers don't allow more than 66 pounds (30 kilograms) per bag in business class and 44 pounds (20 kilograms) in economy. On domestic flights, the limit is usually 50 to 70 pounds (23 to 32 kilograms) per bag. In general, carry-on bags shouldn't exceed 40 pounds (18 kilograms). Most airlines won't accept bags that weigh more than 100 pounds (45 kilograms) on domestic or international flights. Check baggage restrictions with your carrier before you pack.

Airline liability for baggage is limited to $2,500 per person on flights within the United States. On international flights it amounts to $9.07 per pound or $20 per kilogram for checked baggage (roughly $640 per 70-pound bag), with a maximum of $634.90 per piece, and $400 per passenger for unchecked baggage. You can buy additional coverage at check-in for about $10 per $1,000 of coverage, but it often excludes a rather extensive list of items, shown on your airline ticket.

Before departure, itemize your bags' contents and their worth, and label the bags with your name, address, and phone number. (If you use your home address, cover it so potential thieves can't see it readily.) Include a label inside each bag and **pack a copy of your itinerary.** At check-in, make sure each bag is correctly tagged with the destination airport's three-letter code. Because some checked bags will be opened for hand inspection, the U.S. Transportation Security Administration recommends that you leave luggage unlocked or use the plastic locks offered at check-in. TSA screeners place an inspection notice inside searched bags, which are re-sealed with a special lock.

If your bag has been searched and contents are missing or damaged, file a claim with the TSA Consumer Response Center as soon as possible. If your bags arrive damaged or fail to arrive at all, file a written report with the airline before leaving the airport.

⑦ Complaints U.S. Transportation Security Administration Consumer Response Center ☎ 866/ 289-9673 ⊕ www.tsa.gov.

PASSPORTS & VISAS

When traveling internationally, carry your passport even if you don't need one (it's always the best form of I.D.) and **make two photocopies of the data page** (one for someone at home and another for you, carried separately from your passport). If you lose your passport, promptly call the nearest embassy or consulate and the local police.

U.S. passport applications for children under age 14 require consent from both parents or legal guardians; both parents must appear together to sign the application. If only one parent appears, he or she must submit a written statement from the other parent authorizing passport issuance for the child. A parent with sole authority must present evidence of it when applying; acceptable documentation includes the child's certified birth certificate listing only the applying parent, a court order specifically permitting this parent's travel with the child, or a death certificate for the nonapplying parent. Application forms and instructions are available on the Web site of the U.S. State Department's Bureau of Consular Affairs (⊕ www.travel.state.gov).

ENTERING CANADA

Citizens and legal residents of the United States do not need a passport or a visa to enter Canada, but proof of citizenship (a birth certificate or valid passport) and some form of photo identification will be requested. Naturalized U.S. residents should carry their naturalization certificate. Permanent residents who are not citizens should carry their "green card." U.S. residents entering Canada from a third country must have a valid passport, naturalization certificate, or "green card."

Citizens of the United Kingdom need only a valid passport to enter Canada for stays of up to six months.

PASSPORT OFFICES

The best time to apply for a passport or to renew is in fall and winter. Before any trip, check your passport's expiration date, and, if necessary, renew it as soon as possible.

⊞ Australian Citizens Passports Australia ☎ 131-232 ⊕ www.passports.gov.au.
⊞ New Zealand Citizens New Zealand Passports Office ☎ 0800/22-5050 or 04/474-8100 ⊕ www.passports.govt.nz.
⊞ U.K. Citizens U.K. Passport Service ☎ 0870/521-0410 ⊕ www.passport.gov.uk.

REST ROOMS

Toronto is often noted for its cleanliness, which fortunately extends to its public rest rooms. In the downtown shopping areas, large chain bookstores and department stores are good places to stop. If you dart into a coffee shop, you may be expected to make a purchase. Gas stations downtown do not typically have rest rooms. Only a few subway stations have public rest rooms; their locations are noted on the subway map posted above the doors in each car on the train.

SENIOR-CITIZEN TRAVEL

To qualify for age-related discounts, mention your senior-citizen status up front when booking hotel reservations (not when checking out) and before you're seated in restaurants (not when paying the bill). Be sure to have identification on hand. When renting a car, ask about promotional car-rental discounts, which can be cheaper than senior-citizen rates.

⊞ Educational Programs Elderhostel ✉ 11 Ave. de Lafayette, Boston, MA 02111-1746 ☎ 877/426-8056, 978/323-4141 international callers, 877/426-2167 TTY 🖷 877/426-2166 ⊕ www.elderhostel.org.

SHOPPING

Toronto has some of the most stylish shops in the country, but it's the city's markets that make it a mecca for shoppers, especially Kensington and the flea markets on the harbor front.

SMART SOUVENIRS

Skip the maple products and Canadian flag mugs and take home a Roots T-shirt (C$25) or sweatshirt (C$50)—or a gorgeous leather jacket or bag—from the quality Canadian clothing shop. A Hudson Bay Company blanket (C$200–C$400) is a timeless purchase, and the selection of winter apparel and outdoor activity goods may be better than at home. Or **pick up a Canadian novel or CD** that hasn't yet migrated to your hometown.

WATCH OUT

Americans should note that it is illegal for them to buy Cuban cigars and to take them home.

SIGHTSEEING TOURS

BOAT TOURS

If you want to get a glimpse of the skyline, try a boat tour. Toronto Tours runs one-hour tours of the harbor from mid-April through late October, which cost about C$24. There are many boat tour companies operating all along the boardwalk of the Harbourfront; it's up to you to decide which one best suits your interest and pocketbook.

To further your appreciation for manmade beauty, Great Lakes Schooner Company lets you see Toronto's skyline from the open deck of the tall ship *Challenge*. Tours are available early May to the end of September and cost about C$36, depending on length.

⊞ Tour Companies Great Lakes Schooner Company ☎ 800/267-3866 ⊕ www.greatlakesschooner.com. **Toronto Tours** ☎ 416/869-1372 ⊕ www.torontotours.com.

BUS TOURS

For a look at the city proper, take one of the many available bus tours. Toronto City Tours (part of Toronto Tours) offers 1½-, 2-, and 3-hour guided tours in 24-passenger buses, from C$29 to C$49.

If you want the freedom to get on and off the bus when the whim strikes, take a hop-on, hop-off tour. Olde Town Toronto Tours has London-style double-decker buses and turn-of-the-century trolleys. Both take you around the city on a two-hour loop. A ticket good for 24 hours costs C$31. Tours leave every 20 minutes in summer, every two hours in winter. The company also has tours to Niagara Falls.

From April through November, Gray Line
Sightseeing Bus Tours has tours starting at
the bus terminal daily from 10 to 2, on the
hour; the cost is C$31.

⑦ Tour Companies Toronto Tours ☎ 416/869-1372
⊕ www.torontotours.com. **Gray Line Sightseeing
Bus Tours** ✉ 610 Bay St., north of Dundas St.
☎ 800/353-3484 ⊕ www.grayline.ca. **Olde Town
Toronto Tours** ☎ 800/350-0398.

SPECIAL-INTEREST TOURS

If roaming around the city makes you
yearn for nature, Call of the Wild leads
guided trips of different lengths—dogsledding and cross-country skiing in winter,
canoeing and hiking in summer—in Algonquin Provincial Park and other areas in
southern Ontario. Prices include transportation from Toronto. Toronto Field
Naturalists schedules about 150 guided
tours during the year, each focusing on
some aspect of nature (geology, wildflowers) and with starting points accessible by
public transit. The Bruce Trail Association
arranges day and overnight hikes around
Toronto and its environs.

Tourism Toronto can provide further information about special-interest tours.

⑦ Tour Operators Bruce Trail Association ⊕ Box
857, Hamilton ON L8N 3N9 ☎ 800/665-4453
⊕ www.brucetrail.org. **Call of the Wild** ☎ 905/
471-9453 ⊕ www.call-wild.com. **Toronto Field Naturalists** ☎ 416/593-2656 ⊕ www.sources.com/tfn.
Tourism Toronto ☎ 416/203-2500 or 800/363-1990
⊕ www.torontotourism.com.

WALKING TOURS

To get a feel for Toronto's outstanding cultural diversity, Heritage Toronto has free
guided walking tours on weekends and occasional holiday-Mondays from mid-April
to early October. They last 1½ to 2 hours
and cover one neighborhood or topic, such
as the historic theater block.

The Royal Ontario Museum runs 1½- to
2-hour Rom Walk tours on such topics as
the Toronto Underground PATH System,
Historic Toronto, and Cabbagetown. A
few free walks are given weekly.

A Taste of the World runs food-, literary-,
and ghost-theme tours of various lengths
in several neighborhoods. A Saturday-
morning Kensington Foodies Roots Walk

through historic Kensington Market is a
multisensory experience where you can
you sample the local delicacies. Reservations are essential.

⑦ Tour Operators Heritage Toronto ☎ 416/338-
0684 ⊕ www.heritagetoronto.org. **Royal Ontario
Museum** ☎ 416/586-8097 ⊕ www.rom.on.ca. **A
Taste of the World** ☎ 416/923-6813 ⊕ www.
torontowalksbikes.com.

STUDENTS IN TORONTO

Persons under 18 years of age who are not
accompanied by their parents should **bring
a letter from a parent or guardian** giving
them permission to travel to Canada.

⑦ I.D.s Services STA Travel ✉ 10 Downing St.,
New York, NY 10014 ☎ 212/627-3111, 800/777-0112
24-hr service center ⊟ 212/627-3387 ⊕ www.sta.
com. **Travel Cuts** ✉ 187 College St., Toronto, On.
M5T 1P7 ☎ 800/592-2887 in the U.S., 416/979-2406
or 866/246-9762 in Canada ⊟ 416/979-8167
⊕ www.travelcuts.com.

SUBWAY & STREETCAR TRAVEL

The Toronto Transit Commission (TTC),
which operates the buses, streetcars, and
subways, is safe, clean, and reliable. There
are two subway lines, with 60 stations
along the way: the Bloor/Danforth line,
which crosses Toronto about 5 km (3 mi)
north of the lakefront, from east to west,
and the Yonge/University line, which loops
north and south, like a giant "U," with the
bottom of the "U" at Union Station. A
light rapid transit (LRT) line extends service to Harbourfront along Queen's Quay.

From Union Station you can walk underground (or via the Skywalk) to the Metro
Toronto Convention Centre and to many
hotels, including the InterContinental
Toronto Centre, the Fairmont Royal York,
Toronto Hilton, and Sheraton Centre—a
real boon in inclement weather.

FARES & SCHEDULES

One fare plus a transfer wherever you
enter the system permits continuous travel
on several vehicles to make a single trip.
The fare is C$2.25 in exact change or one
ticket/token. Tokens and tickets are sold in
each subway station and many convenience stores. All vehicles accept tickets,
tokens, or exact change, but you must **buy
tickets and tokens before you board.** For

information on discount passes and routes, *see* Bus Travel within Toronto, *above.*

Subway trains stop running at 2 AM, but bus service runs from 1 to 5:30 AM along Bloor and Yonge streets, and as far north on Yonge as Steeles Avenue.

Streetcars that run 24 hours include those on King Street, Queen Street, and College Street. Other streetcar lines run along Queen's Quay and Harbourfront, Spadina Avenue, and Dundas Street. All of them, especially the King line, are interesting rides with frequent service. **Riding the city's streetcars is a great way to capture the flavor of the city,** since you pass through many neighborhoods.

🚋 Subway & Streetcar Information **Toronto Transit Commission (TTC)** (☎ 416/393-4636 or 416/393-8663 for information, 416/393-4100 for lost and found ⊕ www.ttc.ca).

TAXES

A Goods and Services Tax (GST) of 7% applies on virtually every transaction in Canada except for the purchase of basic groceries.

In addition to imposing the GST, Ontario levies a sales tax of 8% on most items purchased in shops and on restaurant meals. (Be aware that with taxes and tip, **you will pay at least 30% more than your food and beverage total when dining out.**) Toronto has a 5% hotel tax, but the provincial sales tax does not apply to lodging.

REFUNDS

You can **get a GST refund** on purchases taken out of the country and on short-term accommodations of less than one month, but not on food, drink, tobacco, car or motor-home rentals, or transportation; rebate forms, which must be submitted within 60 days of leaving Canada, may be obtained from certain retailers, duty-free shops, customs officials, and from the Canada Customs and Revenue Agency. Instant cash rebates up to a maximum of C$500 are provided by some duty-free shops when you leave Canada. Always **save your original receipts** from stores and hotels (not just credit-card receipts), and **be sure the name and address of the**

establishment is shown on the receipt. Original receipts are not returned. To be eligible for a refund, receipts must total at least C$200, and each receipt must show a minimum purchase of C$50.

For information about provincial tax refunds, call Tourism Toronto's toll-free visitor information line. Ontario does not tax goods shipped directly by the vendor to the visitor's home address.

🛈 **Revenue Canada** ✉ 2265 St. Laurent Blvd. S, Ottawa, ON K1G 4K3 ☎ 506/636-5064, 800/461-9999 in Canada ⊕ www.ccra-adrc.gc.ca. **Tourism Toronto** ☎ 416/203-2500, 800/363-1990 in North America ⊕ www.torontotourism.com.

TAXIS

Taxi fares cost C$2.75 for the first ⅕ km (roughly ⅒ mi), C$1.37 for each km thereafter, and 25¢ for each 33 seconds not in motion. A 25¢ surcharge is added for each passenger in excess of four. The average fare to take a cab across downtown is C$8–C$9. The largest companies are Beck, Co-op, Diamond, Metro, and Royal. For more information, call the Metro Licensing Commission.

🚕 Taxi Companies **Beck** ☎ 416/751-5555. **Co-op** ☎ 416/504-2667. **Diamond** ☎ 416/366-6868. **Metro** ☎ 416/504-8294. **Royal** ☎ 416/785-3322. **Metro Licensing Commission** ☎ 416/392-3000.

TIME

Toronto is on Eastern Standard Time (EST), the same as New York. The city is three hours ahead of Pacific Standard Time (PST), which includes Vancouver and Los Angeles, and is one hour behind Atlantic Standard Time, which is found in the Maritime Provinces. The Province of Newfoundland and Labrador is one and a half hours ahead of Toronto.

TIPPING

Tips and service charges are not usually added to a bill in Toronto. In general, tip 15% of the total bill. This goes for food servers, barbers and hairdressers, and taxi drivers. Porters and doormen should get about C$2 a bag. For maid service, leave at least C$2 per person a day (C$3 in luxury hotels).

American money is welcome at a majority of establishments (a U.S. $1 tip is worth about C$1.37), so don't worry if you run out of Canadian money.

TOURS & PACKAGES

Because everything is prearranged on a prepackaged tour or independent vacation, you spend less time planning—and often get it all at a good price. You also may want to consider purchasing the CityPass; in early 2004, Toronto became the first Canadian city to join these US-based value-added ticket books. For C$46, you can gain admission to the Art Gallery of Ontario, the CN Tower, Casa Loma, the Ontario Science Centre, the Royal Ontario Museum, and the Toronto Zoo. You save about $45 and avoid the sometimes long ticket lines. For more information, go to ⊕ www.citypass.com. The companies listed below offer multiday tours in and around Toronto.

BOOKING WITH AN AGENT

Travel agents are excellent resources. But it's a good idea to collect brochures from several agencies, as some agents' suggestions may be influenced by relationships with tour and package firms that reward them for volume sales. If you have a special interest, find an agent with expertise in that area; the American Society of Travel Agents (ASTA; ⇨ Travel Agencies) has a database of specialists worldwide. You can log on to the group's Web site to find an ASTA travel agent in your neighborhood.

Make sure your travel agent knows the accommodations and other services of the place being recommended. Ask about the hotel's location, room size, beds, and whether it has a pool, room service, or programs for children, if you care about these. Has your agent been there in person or sent others whom you can contact?

Do some homework on your own, too: local tourism boards can provide information about lesser-known and small-niche operators, some of which may sell only direct.

BUYER BEWARE

Each year consumers are stranded or lose their money when tour operators—even large ones with excellent reputations—go out of business. So check out the operator. Ask several travel agents about its reputation, and try to **book with a company that has a consumer-protection program.** (Look for information in the company's brochure.) In the United States, members of the National Tour Association and the United States Tour Operators Association are required to set aside funds to cover payments and travel arrangements in the event that the company defaults. It's also a good idea to choose a company that participates in the American Society of Travel Agents' Tour Operator Program; ASTA will act as mediator in any disputes between you and your tour operator.

Remember that the more your package or tour includes, the better you can predict the ultimate cost of your vacation. Make sure you know exactly what is covered, and beware of hidden costs. Are taxes, tips, and transfers included? Entertainment and excursions? These can add up. ⚑ Tour-Operator Recommendations **American Society of Travel Agents** (ASTA) ⊠ 1101 King St., Suite 200, Alexandria, VA 22314 ☎ 703/739-2782 or 800/965-2782 24-hr hot line 🖷 703/739-3268 ⊕ www.astanet.com. **National Tour Association** (NTA) ⊠ 546 E. Main St., Lexington, KY 40508 ☎ 859/226-4444 or 800/682-8886 🖷 859/226-4404 ⊕ www.ntaonline.com. **United States Tour Operators Association** (USTOA) ⊠ 275 Madison Ave., Suite 2014, New York, NY 10016 ☎ 212/599-6599 🖷 212/599-6744 ⊕ www.ustoa.com.

TRAIN TRAVEL TO & FROM TORONTO

Amtrak has service from New York and Chicago to Toronto (both 12 hours), providing connections between Amtrak's U.S.-wide network and VIA Rail's Canadian routes. VIA Rail runs trains to most major Canadian cities; travel along the Windsor–Québec City corridor is particularly well served. Amtrak and Via Rail operate from Union Station on Front Street between Bay and York streets. You can walk underground to a number of hotels from the station. There is a cab stand outside the main entrance of the station.

CLASSES

Trains to Toronto may have two tiers of service, business class and reserved coach class (C$105 one-way from New York). Business class is usually limited to one car, and benefits include more legroom, meals, and complimentary alcoholic beverages.

CUTTING COSTS

Substantial discounts are available on VIA Rail if you book at least five days in advance (call VIA Rail Canada for fares and schedules). If you're planning to travel a lot by train, **look into the Canrail pass.** It allows 12 days of coach-class travel within a 30-day period; sleeping cars are available, but they sell out very early and must be reserved at least a month in advance during high season (June through mid-October), when the pass is C$741 (discounts for youths and seniors). Low-season rate (October 16 through May) is C$461. The pass is not valid during the Christmas period (December 15 through January 5). For more information and reservations, contact a travel agent in the U.S. In the United Kingdom, Long-Haul Leisurail represents both VIA Rail and Rocky Mountaineer Railtours.

Train travelers can **check out the 30-day North American RailPass** offered by Amtrak and VIA Rail. It allows unlimited coach–economy travel in the U.S. and Canada. You must reserve seats for your whole itinerary when purchasing the pass. The cost is C$1,004 from June to October 15 and C$711 at other times.

FARES & SCHEDULES

🚆 **Train Information Amtrak** ☎ 800/872-7245 ⊕ www.amtrak.com. **Long-Haul Leisurail** ⌂ Box 113, Peterborough, PE3 8HY U.K. ☎ 01733/335-599. **Rocky Mountaineer Railtours** ☎ 800/665-7245. **Union Station** ✉ 65-75 Front St., between Bay and York Sts. ☎ 416/366-8411. **VIA Rail Canada** ✉ Front St. W. at Bay St. ☎ 888/842-7245 or TTY 888/268-9503 ⊕ www.viarail.ca.

PAYING

Major credit cards, debit cards, and cash are accepted. Traveler's checks are accepted in Canadian and U.S. currencies; for others, go to the Currency Exchange kiosk on the main level of the station.

RESERVATIONS

Reservations are strongly urged for intercity and inter-provincial travel and for journeys to and from the United States. If your ticket is lost, it is like losing cash, so guard your ticket closely. If you lose your reservation number, your seat can still be accessed by using your name or the train you have been booked on.

TRANSPORTATION AROUND TORONTO

Toronto Transit Commission (TTC) buses, streetcars, and subways are safe, clean, and easy to use. There's no reason to have a car, unless you need one to visit farther-flung sights.

TRAVEL AGENCIES

A good travel agent puts your needs first. Look for an agency that has been in business at least five years, emphasizes customer service, and has someone on staff who specializes in your destination. In addition, **make sure the agency belongs to a professional trade organization.** The American Society of Travel Agents (ASTA)—the largest and most influential in the field with more than 20,000 members in some 140 countries—maintains and enforces a strict code of ethics and will step in to help mediate any agent-client disputes involving ASTA members if necessary. ASTA (whose motto is "Without a travel agent, you're on your own") also maintains a Web site that includes a directory of agents. (If a travel agency is also acting as your tour operator, *see* Buyer Beware *in* Tours and Packages.)

🚆 **Local Agent Referrals American Society of Travel Agents (ASTA)** ✉ 1101 King St., Suite 200, Alexandria, VA 22314 ☎ 703/739-2782 or 800/965-2782 24-hr hot line 🖷 703/739-3268 ⊕ www.astanet.com. **Association of British Travel Agents** ✉ 68-71 Newman St., London W1T 3AH ☎ 020/7637-2444 🖷 020/7637-0713 ⊕ www.abta.com. **Association of Canadian Travel Agencies** ✉ 130 Albert St., Suite 1705, Ottawa, Ontario K1P 5G4 ☎ 613/237-3657 🖷 613/237-7052 ⊕ www.acta.ca. **Australian Federation of Travel Agents** ✉ Level 3, 309 Pitt St., Sydney, NSW 2000 ☎ 02/9264-3299 🖷 02/9264-1085 ⊕ www.afta.com.au. **Travel Agents' Association of New Zealand** ✉ Level 5, Tourism and Travel House, 79 Boulcott St., Box 1888, Wellington

6001 ☎ 04/499-0104 🖷 04/499-0786 ⊕ www.taanz.org.nz.

VISITOR INFORMATION

Learn more about foreign destinations by checking government-issued travel advisories and country information. For a broader picture, consider information from more than one country. 🔊 **Canadian Tourism Commission** ☎ 613/946-1000 ⊕ www.canadatourism.com. **Ontario Tourism Marketing Partnership** ✉ 10th Floor, Hearst Block, 900 Bay St., Toronto, ON M7A 2E1 ☎ 800/668-2746 ⊕ www.ontariotravel.net. **Tourism Toronto** ✉ 207 Queen's Quay W, Suite 509, Box 106, M5J 1A7 ☎ 416/203-2600 or 800/363-1990 ⊕ www.torontotourism.com. **Traveller's Aid Society** ✉ Union Station, arrivals level and basement level, Room B23 ☎ 416/366-7788 ✉ Pearson Airport, Terminal I, arrivals level, past Customs, near Area B ☎ 905/676-2868 ✉ Pearson Airport, Terminal 2, between international and domestic arrivals ☎ 905/676-2869 ✉ Pearson Airport, Terminal 3, arrivals level, near international side ☎ 905/612-5890. 🔊 **In the U.K.** Visit **Canada Center** ✉ 62-65 Trafalgar Sq., London WC2 5DY ☎ 0891/715-000, 50p per minute peak rate and 45p per minute cheap rate. 🔊 **Government Advisories U.K. Foreign and Commonwealth Office** ✉ Travel Advice Unit, Consular Division, Old Admiralty Building, London SW1A 2PA ☎ 020/7008-0232 or 020/7008-0233 ⊕ www.fco.gov.uk/travel. **Australian Department of Foreign Affairs and Trade** ☎ 02/6261-1299 Consular Travel Advice Faxback Service ⊕ www.dfat.gov.au. **New Zealand Ministry of Foreign Affairs and Trade** ☎ 04/439-8000 ⊕ www.mft.govt.nz.

WEB SITES

Do check out the World Wide Web when planning your trip. You'll find everything from weather forecasts to virtual tours of famous cities. Be sure to visit Fodors.com (⊕ www.fodors.com), a complete travel-planning site. You can research prices and book plane tickets, hotel rooms, rental cars, vacation packages, and more. In addition, you can post your pressing questions in the Travel Talk section. Other planning tools include a currency converter and weather reports, and there are loads of links to travel resources.

The site of the City of Toronto, www.city.toronto.on.ca, has helpful material about everything from local politics to public transit. The monthly magazine *Toronto Life* (⊕ www.torontolife.com) and the weekly alternative papers *Now* (www.nowtoronto.com) and *Eye* (www.eye.net) list the latest art and nightlife events and carry information about dining, shopping, and more. Another site, www.toronto.com, has links to the *Toronto Star* and information about topics including sports and dining out.

EXPLORING TORONTO

BEST PLACE TO WALK ON AIR
Glass Floor Level at the CN Tower ⇨*p.15*

CITY HALL REDUX
St. Lawrence Market ⇨*p.9*

LEAFIEST SPOT FOR A STROLL
Cabbagetown ⇨*p.35*

BEST WAY TO GET BENEATH THE SURFACE
The Underground City ⇨*p.13*

FOR ART'S SAKE
Art Gallery of Ontario ⇨*p.21*

Updated by
Bruce Bishop

"TORONTO IS LIKE NEW YORK, AS RUN BY THE SWISS", actor Peter Ustinov is rumored to have said. Indeed, this is a big, beautiful, and efficient city, one that has emerged from relative obscurity over the past half century to become the center of culture, commerce, and communications in Canada. That Toronto's star is ascendant is no surprise. With its colorful ethnic mix, rich history, and breathtaking architecture, Toronto is nonstop adventure for the willing tourist. Twice-daily high-speed ferry service between Rochester, New York, and Toronto, begun in 2004, now makes it even easier to get to the city. To get a sense of how big, various, and magical Toronto is, the best place to start is the CN Tower, the tallest freestanding structure in the world. From this vantage point, you can get a bird's-eye view of the city's striking skyline and unique geography.

The city officially became Toronto on March 6, 1834, but its roots are much more ancient than that. A Frenchman named Etienne Brûlé was sent into the not-yet-Canadian wilderness in the early 1600s by the famous explorer Samuel de Champlain to see what he could discover. And he discovered plenty: the river and portage routes from the St. Lawrence to Lake Huron, possibly Lakes Superior and Michigan, and, eventually, Lake Ontario. Of course the Huron peoples had known about these places for centuries; they had long called the area between the Humber and Don rivers "Toronto," which is believed to mean "place of meetings." Later it developed into a busy village named Teiaiagon, and then it was the site of a French trading post. After the British won the Seven Years' War in the late 1700s, the trading post became a British town named York (1793). Finally, the city we know today was born, once again going back to the name Toronto.

The city followed the usual history of colonial towns of the 19th century: it was invaded by the Americans in 1812; there were several devastating fires; there was a rebellion in 1837; and there was a slow but steady increase in its population of white Anglo-Saxon Protestants, from about 9,000 in the 1830s to well over 500,000 before the outbreak of World War II, at which time they outnumbered the non-WASPs by five to two. In the past six decades, Toronto has metamorphosed into a diverse city, where colorful ethnic enclaves mix with imposing banks and government buildings—making this a wonderful town to explore.

In 1998 the six communities that made up the Municipality of Metropolitan Toronto (which itself was created in 1953 to help alleviate growing pains faced by the community with the rapid increase in immigration following the end of World War II) became a megacity under the name City of Toronto. Nevertheless, reminders of those five cities and one borough from the pre-megacity era (Toronto, Etobicoke, North York, Scarborough, York, and East York, respectively) still show up on shop signs, as part of postal addresses, and in the names of subway stations and newly established civic-service centers.

The city's population numbers more than 4.5 million, and its residents—including Canada's largest gay and lesbian community—come from countries around the world and from all manner of ethnic backgrounds. A hundred different languages can be heard on the streets, from

Hindi to Greek to French. Street signs in Toronto are mostly in English—
and in the predominant language of the neighborhood. Weekly and daily
newspapers are published in myriad languages.

Toronto is a city of activity. After New York, it's the second largest destination for live theater on the continent. Every September the city hosts
an international film festival. (Toronto is a top location for the film industry, too). In mid-2003 the ground was broken for the city's first home
to both the Canadian Opera Company and the National Ballet of
Canada. Benefactors include native son Isadore Sharp, founder of Four
Seasons Hotels and Resorts. When the 2,000-seat, C$100-million opera
house opens in 2006, it will be called the Four Seasons Centre for the
Performing Arts. Additionally, Toronto has numerous sports teams, including the popular Toronto Blue Jays, who play at the SkyDome.

Toronto's less-traveled parts include its original Chinatown, laid out west
along Dundas Street and running all the way to "new" Chinatown, near
the Spadina Avenue/Dundas Street intersection. From here it's just a short
walk to the outdoor, European-style Kensington Market, which abounds
in fresh vegetables, poultry, and meats. Toronto is also a city filled with
boutiques, restaurants, and cafés, and of course there are plenty of
shops—above ground and in the Underground City, an 11-km-long (7-
mi-long) subterranean walkway lined with eateries, shops, banks, medical offices, and theaters.

Often-overlooked gems of Toronto are the beach-fringed Toronto Islands.
These eight tree-lined islands—and more than a dozen smaller islets that
sit in Lake Ontario just off the city's downtown—offer a welcome touch
of greenery. They've been attracting visitors since 1833, especially during summer, when the more than 550 acres of parkland on the islands
are most irresistible. From any of the islands you have spectacular views
of Toronto's skyline, especially as the setting sun turns the city's skyscrapers to gold, silver, and bronze.

Getting Your Bearings

The boundaries of what Torontonians consider downtown, where most
of the city sights are located, are subject to debate, but everyone agrees
on the southern cutoff—Lake Ontario and the Toronto Islands. The other
coordinates of the rectangle that comprise the city core are Bathurst Street
to the west, Parliament Street to the east, and Eglinton Avenue to the
north. Beyond these borders are numerous Greater Toronto sights that
make excellent morning, afternoon, or full-day excursions. An ideal way
to get a sense of the city's layout is from one of the observation decks
at the CN Tower on a clear day; the view is especially lovely at sunset.

Most city streets are organized on a grid system: with some exceptions,
street numbers start at zero at the lake and increase as you go north.
On the east–west axis, Yonge (pronounced "young") Street, Toronto's
main thoroughfare, is the dividing line: you can expect higher numbers
the farther away you get from Yonge.

Traffic is dense and parking expensive within the city core. If you have
a car with you, leave it at your hotel when exploring the city and use it
for excursions to outlying attractions or to towns like Stratford. In the

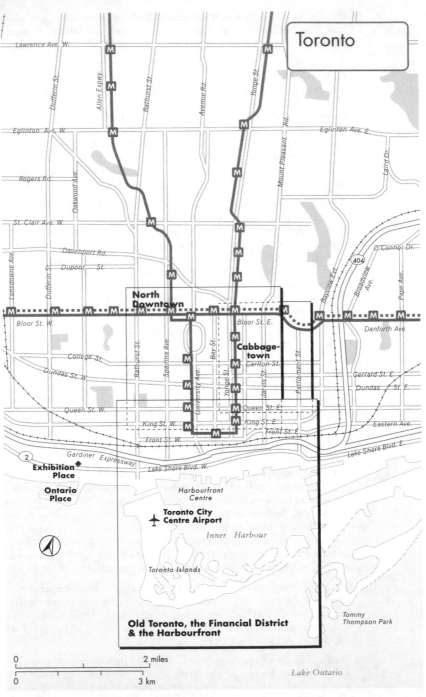

Toronto

Lawrence Ave. W.

Dufferin St.

Allen Expwy.

Bathurst St.

Avenue Rd.

Yonge St.

Eglinton Ave. W.

Eglinton Ave. E.

Mount Pleasant Rd.

Laird Dr.

Rogers Rd.

Oakwood Ave.

St. Clair Ave. W.

Lansdowne Ave.

Davenport Rd.

O'Connor Dr.

Dupont St.

Dufferin St.

Bayview Ext.

Broadview Ave.

Pape Ave.

404

North Downtown

Bloor St. W.

Bloor St. E.

Danforth Ave.

College St.

Bathurst St.

Spadina Ave.

Cabbage-town

Carlton St.

Dundas St. W.

University Ave.

Bay St.

Yonge St.

Jarvis St.

Parliament St.

Gerrard St. E.

Dundas St. E.

Queen St. W.

Queen St. E.

King St. W.

King St. E.

Eastern Ave.

Front St. W.

Front St. E.

Gardiner Expressway

Lake Shore Blvd. W.

Lake Shore Blvd. E.

2

Exhibition Place

Ontario Place

Harbourfront Centre

✈ **Toronto City Centre Airport**

Inner Harbour

Toronto Islands

Tommy Thompson Park

Old Toronto, the Financial District & the Harbourfront

Lake Ontario

| 0 | | | 2 miles |
| 0 | | | 3 km |

city, use the excellent Toronto Transit System (TTC)—it costs C$2.25 a ride, or C$7.75 for an all-day pass—or take taxis.

Old Toronto

In this district, which runs from Yonge Street east to Parliament Street and from King Street south to the lake, Toronto got its municipal start as the village of York in 1793. In 1834, the year the little community was erected into a city, the area, described as a ward, was renamed in honor of Canada's patron saint, St. Lawrence. A pleasing natural disorder now prevails in this neighborhood, which blends old and new buildings, residential and commercial space. Within the space of a few blocks you can walk past the huge canopy of the 1960s-era Hummingbird Centre, where crowds throng for a ballet, to converted late-19th- and early-20th-century warehouses hosting an array of modern stores, to a hall that has operated as a market since the early 1800s.

Numbers in the text and in the margin correspond to points of interest on the Old Toronto, the Financial District & the Harbourfront map.

a good walk

Start your tour at the northwest corner of Yonge and Front streets, where the **Hockey Hall of Fame and Museum ❶ ☛** is housed in a decommissioned branch of the Bank of Montréal. After having your fill of hockey's golden moments, turn left and walk a short block north on Yonge to Wellington and turn left again. Walk less than half the block, then enter BCE Place, a striking skyscraper built in the 1980s. The reassembled stones of the former 15 Wellington Street West—the oldest building on this walk—are in the BCE Place concourse. The elegant Greek Revival bank was one of the earliest (1845) projects of William Thomas, the architect who also designed the St. Lawrence Hall. Return to, and cross, Yonge Street; head another short block north to Colborne, where on the right you see the **Trader's Bank ❷**, the city's first skyscraper. From here, go one block north to King, turn right, and walk one short block to Victoria Street. Across Victoria is the beautiful Le Royal Meridien King Edward Hotel, a 1903 structure by E. J. Lennox, who also designed Old City Hall, Massey Hall, and Casa Loma.

A little farther east, on the corner of King and Church, is the impressive Anglican **St. James Cathedral ❸**. Directly south of the church is the Toronto Sculpture Garden, a small landscaped park with waterfalls. Head north one block on Church to Adelaide; two blocks to the east (look for the flags and postal drop box) is **Toronto's First Post Office ❹**, where you can transact your 21st-century postal business using 19th-century implements. Return 1½ blocks west to Jarvis; a block south at King is the elegant **St. Lawrence Hall ❺**. Continue south one block on Jarvis to **St. Lawrence Market ❻**; you're now on Front Street again, and from here it's two blocks west to the **Flatiron Building ❼**. As you continue west from here on Front to your starting point, Yonge Street, you pass the St. Lawrence Centre and the Hummingbird Centre, two large performing-arts venues. The Hummingbird opened as the O'Keefe Centre in 1960 with the world premiere of the musical *Camelot*.

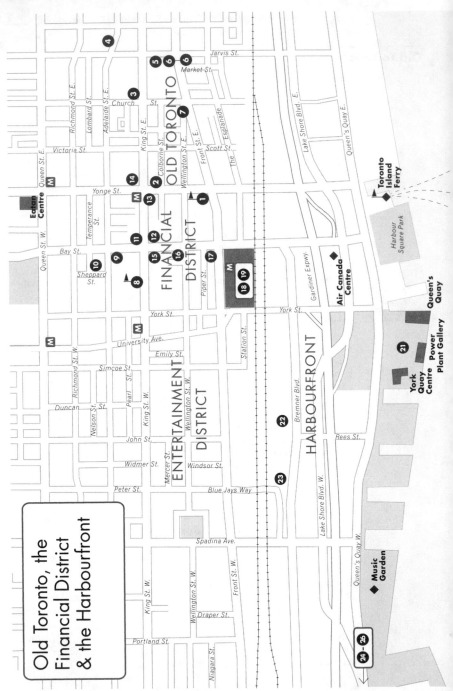

Old Toronto, the
Financial District
& the Harbourfront

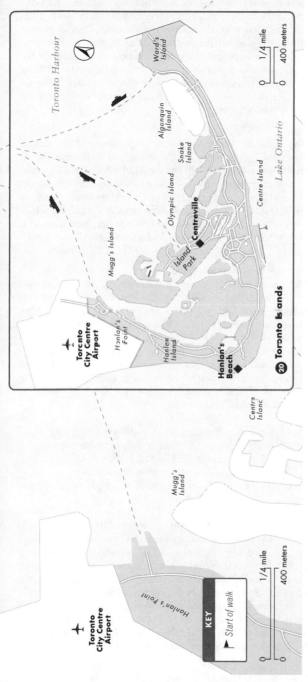

⑳ Toronto Islands

TIMING This walk takes from 45 minutes for the buildings alone to a half day to include time at the hockey museum, market, post office, and cathedral. If you add the adjacent Cabbagetown or Financial District to your tour, you could easily spend an interesting full day in the area. For those out to photograph scenic cityscapes, one of the best views is that of the Flatiron Building in early morning or late afternoon, with the building framed by the sunlit skyscrapers behind it. If you want to catch the farmers setting out their wares at the St. Lawrence Market, you should arrive as early as 5 AM on Saturday.

What to See

❼ Flatiron Building. Similarly shaped relatives live in wedge-shape lots all over North America. This building, on the triangle of Wellington, Scott, and Front streets, was erected in 1892 as the head office of the Gooderham and Worts distilling company and still hosts important offices. On the back of the building, a witty trompe-l'oeil mural by Derek Besant is drawn around the windows. The mural depicts even larger windows, which look like the windows on the south side of Front Street. The illusion? It appears that the whole thing has been tacked up on the wall and is peeling off. ⊠ *Front St. between Church and Scott Sts., Old Toronto.*

★ ▶ ❶ **Hockey Hall of Fame and Museum.** Even if you're not a hockey fan, it's worth a trip here to see this shrine to Canada's favorite sport. Exhibits include the original 1893 Stanley Cup, as well as displays of goalie masks, skate and stick collections, great players' jerseys, video displays of big games, and a replica of the Montréal Canadiens' locker room. The details of the beautifully ornate 1885 building, a former Bank of Montréal branch designed by architects Darling & Curry, have been well preserved: note the richly carved Ohio stone and the Hermès figure supporting the chimney near the back of the building. ⊠ *30 Yonge St., Old Toronto* ☏ *416/360–7765* ⊕ *www.hhof.com* ⊠ *C$12* ☉ *Weekdays 10–5, Sat. 9:30–6, Sun. 10:30–5.*

┌─────────┐
│ **need a** │
│ **break?** │
└─────────┘
BCE Place (⊠ 42 Yonge St., between Front and Wellington, Old Toronto), a modern office and retail complex cleverly designed to incorporate the Bank of Montréal building and other older structures under a glass roof, is not only one of the most impressive architectural spaces in Toronto—the atrium is also a pleasant place to sit and enjoy a cup of coffee.

❸ **St. James Cathedral.** Even if bank towers dwarf it now, this Anglican church with noble Gothic spires has the tallest steeple in Canada. Its illuminated spire clock once guided ships into the harbor, which used to be much closer to the church (everything built south of Front Street is landfill). This is the fourth St. James Cathedral on this site; the third burned down in the Great Fire of 1849. As part of the church's bicentennial in 1997, a new peal of bells was installed. Stand near the church most Sundays 30 minutes before the 11 AM service and you can be rewarded with a glorious concert of ringing bells. ⊠ *65 Church St., at King St., Old Toronto* ☏ *416/364–7865* ⊕ *www.stjamescathedral.on.ca.*

5 **St. Lawrence Hall.** Standing on the site of the area's first town hall, the St. Lawrence Hall, built in 1850–51, demonstrates Renaissance Revival architecture at its finest. Erected for musical performances and balls, it is here that Jenny Lind sang, where antislavery demonstrations were held, and where P. T. Barnum first presented the midget Tom Thumb. Take time to admire the exterior of this architectural gem, now used for everything from concerts to wedding receptions and graduation parties. ⊠ *157 King St. E, Old Toronto* ☎ *416/392–7130.*

6 **St. Lawrence Market.** Built in 1844 as the first true Toronto city hall, the building now has an exhibition hall upstairs—the Market Gallery—where the council chambers once stood. The building continues to serve the citizens of the city as a food market, which began growing up around the city hall in the early 1900s. The market is renowned for its local and imported foods such as fresh shellfish, sausage varieties, and cheeses. The plain brick building across Front Street, on the north side, is open only on Saturday morning as a farmers' market; it's a cornucopia of fine produce and homemade jams, relishes, and sauces from farms just north of Toronto. ⊠ *Front and Jarvis Sts., Old Toronto* ☎ *416/392–7219* ⊕ *www.stlawrencemarket.com* ☉ *Tues.–Sat. 8–6; farmers' market Sat. 5 AM–2 PM.*

Fodor'sChoice
★

4 **Toronto's First Post Office.** Dating from 1833, this working post office continues to use quill pens, ink pots, and sealing wax. Exhibits include reproductions of letters from the 1820s and 1830s. Distinctive cancellation stamps are used on all outgoing cards and letters. ⊠ *260 Adelaide St. E, Old Toronto* ☎ *416/865–1833* ⊕ *www.townofyork.com* ☒ *Free* ☉ *Weekdays 9–4, weekends 10–4.*

2 **Trader's Bank.** It's fun to see the early-20th-century equivalent of the CN Tower. At 15 stories, this was the first "skyscraper" of the city when it went up in 1906, complete with an observation deck. Trader's Bank building is still owned by Canadian Pacific Railway, the largest private employer in Canada (planes, trains, hotels, and more). ⊠ *67 Yonge St., Old Toronto.*

The Financial District

Those striking, often magnificent high-rises that form the greatest part of Toronto's skyline are banks, banks, and banks. Every one of Canada's major banks has its headquarters in downtown Toronto, between University Avenue and Yonge Street. The fact that many of the older properties have now been included on the city's Inventory of Buildings of Architectural and Historical Importance proves Toronto is making a concerted effort to preserve its history. Only two cheers though—there was massive destruction of great 19th-century buildings in the early 20th century.

The most interesting aspect of a Financial District walk is the architectural variety of the skyscrapers—temples to steel construction that reflect the prosperity of the steel industry in Canada. Many banks have more than one building named for them. Most of the towers have bank branches, restaurants, and retail outlets on their ground floors and are connected to the Underground City of shops and tunnels, so you have many easy choices for a snack or to change money along the way.

Numbers in the text and in the margin correspond to points of interest on the Old Toronto, the Financial District & the Harbourfront map.

a good walk

Start the tour at the St. Andrew TTC station on the northwest corner of University and King. Walk one short block west on King past York Street, where you see the huge **First Canadian Place** ⑧ ☛ complex, which includes the Toronto Stock Exchange. Leave First Canadian Place by the Adelaide Street exit and proceed a half block east on Adelaide to the corner of Bay Street, to the **Canada Permanent Trust Building** ⑨ and the **Bay-Adelaide Park** ⑩, tucked in from the street. From here, head a block south on Bay Street to King, where the **Bank of Nova Scotia** ⑪ inhabits the northeast corner, with the Scotia Tower just to the east. Cross King to the **Canadian Imperial Bank of Commerce** ⑫ buildings, with their distinct architectural styles, and then go a half block east to Yonge Street, where on the southwest corner of Yonge and King you come to the **Dominion Bank** ⑬. At the northeast corner of the same intersection is the original **Royal Bank** ⑭ building.

Now walk back west along King Street to Bay, and the **Toronto-Dominion Centre (TD Centre)** ⑮. A block south on Bay Street is the **Design Exchange** ⑯, the wonderful art-deco building that housed the old Toronto Stock Exchange. Continue south on Bay Street for less than a block to reach the modern **Royal Bank Building and Plaza** ⑰; **Union Station** ⑱, where the trains of the national, intercity, and Toronto transit system meet, is just across Front Street from here. You can descend from Union Station into Toronto's vast **Underground City** ⑲, a warren worthy of its own tour.

TIMING   The walk outlined encompasses a little more than 1½ km (1 mi). Stock Market Place at the Toronto Stock Exchange and the Design Exchange exhibits take about 45 minutes each, and if you come between noon and 2 during summer, you might catch a concert. Taking into account stops for the TSE and Design Exchange and a snack and/or concert, the tour should run two to three hours. This area is adjacent to Old Toronto, and the two tours together would fill a pleasant day.

What to See

⑪ **Bank of Nova Scotia.** Built between 1949 and 1951 and partially replaced by the ScotiaBank Tower just to the east, this bank has sculptural panels inspired by Greek mythology above its large windows. In the lobby, bas-reliefs symbolize four regions of Canada; look up to see a brightly colored gilt plaster ceiling. Other interesting details include the original stainless-steel-and-glass stairway with marine motifs and the marble counters and floors. The north wall relief depicts some of the industries and enterprises financed by the bank. ⊠ *44 King St. W, Financial District* ☎ *416/866–6161.*

⑩ **Bay-Adelaide Park.** Designed to be a plaza for a building that fell victim to the recession of the early 1990s, the park was nevertheless completed in 1993 as an homage to those who worked on it. The multistory indoor-outdoor space includes a water sculpture, a monument dedicated to construction workers, and a tropical plant collection. ⊠ *Yonge St. between Richmond and Adelaide Sts., Financial District.*

9 **Canada Permanent Trust Building.** Built in the roaring '20s, this skyscraper was designed in New York wedding-cake style. Look up at the ornate stone carvings that grace both the lower and top stories, where stylized faces peer down to the street below. You can walk through the imposing vaulted entrance with its polished brass doors; even the elevator doors in the foyer are embossed. The spacious banking hall has a vaulted ceiling, marble walls and pillars, and a marble floor with mosaic borders. ⊠ *320 Bay St., Financial District* ☎ *416/361–8600.*

12 **Canadian Imperial Bank of Commerce.** The first of the "twin" Bank of Commerce buildings went up in the two years following the stock-market crash of 1929, but hard times didn't mean stinting on details: the stunning interior has marble floors, limestone walls, and bronze vestibule doors decorated with an array of animals and birds. Murals in the alcoves on either side of the entrance trace the history of transportation. The bronze elevator doors are richly decorated, the vaulted banking hall is lit by chandeliers, and each desk has its own lamp. South of the old tower, set slightly back around a plaza at 243 Bay Street, is the bank's 57-story stainless-steel counterpart, designed by I. M. Pei in the early 1970s. ⊠ *25 King St. W, Financial District* ☎ *416/980–2211.*

★ **16** **Design Exchange.** A delightful example of streamlined moderne design, a later and more austere version of art deco, this building is clad in polished pink granite and smooth buff limestone, with stainless-steel doors. Between 1937 and 1983 the DX (as it's now known) was the home of the Toronto Stock Exchange. Don't miss the witty stone frieze carved above the doors—a banker in top hat marching behind a laborer and sneaking his hand into the worker's pocket. (Only in Canada, where socialism has always been a strong force, would you find such a political statement on the side of a stock exchange.) In the early 1990s, the building reopened as a nonprofit center devoted to promoting Canadian design. The permanent collection contains examples of contemporary and older decorative arts, furniture, graphic design, housewares, lighting, and tableware. The old trading floor is now used for rotating exhibits—check their Web site or the local papers for information. On the ground floor a café, Kubo, is good for dim sum and drinks. ⊠ *234 Bay St., Financial District* ☎ *416/ 363–6121* ⊕ *www.dx.org* ▦ *C$8* ☉ *Weekdays 10–6, weekends noon–5.*

13 **Dominion Bank.** Frank Darling, the designing architect here, was also responsible for the voluptuous Bank of Montréal branch at Yonge and Front streets. The 1913–14 Dominion Bank is a classic Chicago-style skyscraper that retains its original facade. The upper 46 stories have been turned into 550 luxury condos and commercial space. ⊠ *1–5 King St. W, at Yonge St., Financial District.*

▶ **8** **First Canadian Place.** The 72 stories of this 1970s building are faced with white marble to contrast with the black of the Toronto-Dominion Centre to the south and with the nearby silver of I. M. Pei's Bank of Commerce tower. First Canadian Place is also known as the Bank of Montréal tower, but it's best known for being the home of the ⇨ **Toronto Stock**

Exchange. It's also interesting as an early and successful real estate project of the Reichman brothers, who later came to fiscal grief when their Canary Docks project in London, England, failed to capture the imagination—and rental contracts—of that city's financial community. ⊠ *100–130 King St. W, Financial District* ☎ *416/363–4669.*

⑭ Royal Bank. The 1913 building that predated the structure of the same name on Bay and Front streets can't quite match the newer building for glitter, but it's no slouch in the decorative department. Note the distinctive cornice, the overhanging roof, the sculpted ox skulls above the ground-floor windows, and the classically detailed leaves at the top of the Corinthian columns. Today the once wide-awake banking floor has been taken over by a company that sells mattresses. ⊠ *2 King St. E, Financial District* ☎ *416/364–6200.*

⑰ Royal Bank Building and Plaza. In this case, all that glitters *is* gold: the exterior is coated with 2,500 ounces of the precious ore to keep the heat in and the cold out (or vice versa, depending on the season). Designed by the gifted Torontonian Boris Zerafa, who was also involved in the creation of the Richmond-Adelaide Centre and the ScotiaBank Tower, this 1976 building is a classic. It's "a palette of color and texture as well as mass," in Zerafa's own words. The surface creates gorgeous reflections of sky, clouds, and other buildings; this is the jewel in the crown of the Toronto skyline. The building, dramatic in almost any light, is especially stunning in a full-force sunset. ⊠ *200 Bay St., Financial District* ☎ *416/974–3940.*

★ ⑮ Toronto-Dominion Centre (TD Centre). Mies van der Rohe, a virtuoso of modern architecture, designed this five-building masterwork, though he died in 1969 before the last building was finished in 1985. As with his acclaimed Seagram Building in New York, Mies stripped these buildings to their skin and bones of bronze-color glass and black-metal I-beams. The TD Centre's tallest building, the Toronto Dominion Bank Tower, is 56 stories high. The only decoration consists of geometric repetition, and the only extravagance is the use of rich materials, such as marble counters and leather-covered furniture. The setting is far from austere, however. In summer, the plazas and grass are full of office workers eating lunch and listening to one of many free outdoor concerts. Inside the low-rise square banking pavilion at King and Bay streets is a virtually intact Mies interior.

Inside the TD Centre's Aetna Tower is the **Gallery of Inuit Art,** (⊠ 79 Wellington St. W ☎ 416/982–8473 ⊠ Free ☉ Weekdays 8–6, weekends 10–4). It's one of just a few such galleries in North America. The collection, equal to that of the Smithsonian, focuses on Canada's huge and unexplored northern frontier. ⊠ *55 King St. W, Financial District.*

need a break? If you like to sit on a bench and watch the world go by, you won't find a better spot than nearby **King Street West.** Grab a hot dog (or a veggie dog), take a seat, and watch theatergoers and maybe even actors walk by. Don't like hot dogs? Don't worry: Italian, Greek, French, and Canadian restaurants and bars can all be found next to the theaters for pre- and post-show action.

⑧ Toronto Stock Exchange (TSE). Here beats the pulse of the Canadian economy, and to help the public better understand how it all works, the TSE runs Stock Market Place, a dynamic state-of-the-art visitor and education center. The history and mystery of stocks and bonds, money markets, and diversified funds are explained through entertaining and interactive displays. It's only open to the public on Fridays. ⊠ *First Canadian Place, 100–130 King St. W, between Bay and York Sts., Financial District* ☎ *416/947–4670* ⊕ *www.tse.com* ⊠ *Free* ☼ *Fri. 10–5.*

⑲ Underground City. This subterranean universe, which lays claim to being the world's largest pedestrian walkway, emerged in the mid-1960s partly to replace the retail services in small buildings that were demolished to make way for the latest round of skyscrapers, and partly to protect office workers from the harsh winter weather. As each major building went up, its developers agreed to build and to connect their underground shopping areas with others and with the subway system. You can walk from beneath Union Station to the Fairmont Royal York hotel, the Toronto-Dominion Centre, First Canadian Place, the Sheraton Centre, The Bay, Eaton Centre, and City Hall without ever seeing the light of day. You encounter everything from art exhibitions to buskers (the best are the winners of citywide auditions, who are licensed to perform throughout the subway system) and walkways, fountains, and trees. There are underground passageways in other parts of the city—one beneath Bloor Street and another under College Street (both run from Yonge to Bay streets)—but this is the city's most extended subterranean network. Maps to guide you through this labyrinth are available in many downtown news and convenience stores.

⑱ Union Station. Popular historian Pierre Berton wrote that the planning of Union Station recalled "the love lavished on medieval churches." Indeed, this train depot that anchors the financial district both visually and symbolically can be regarded as a cathedral built to serve the god of steam. Designed in 1907, and opened officially in 1927 by the Prince of Wales, it has a 40-foot-high ceiling of Italian tile and 22 pillars weighing 70 tons apiece. The vast main hall, with its lengthy concourse and light flooding in from arched windows at each end, was designed to evoke the majesty of the country that spread out by rail and imagination from this spot. To this end, too, the names of the towns and cities across Canada that were served by the country's two railway lines, Grand Trunk (which was to become part of today's Canadian National) and Canadian Pacific, are inscribed on a frieze that runs along the inside of the hall. Train travel declined and the building came very near to being demolished in the 1970s, but public opposition eventually proved strong enough to save it, and Union Station is now a vital commuter hub. Commuter, subway, and long-distance trains arrive and depart from here. ⊠ *65–75 Front St. W, between Bay and York Sts., Old Toronto.*

Harbourfront

The new century has brought a renewed interest in Toronto's Harbourfront. Cranes dot the skyline, as condominium buildings seemingly appear overnight. Pedestrian traffic increases as temperatures rise in spring and summer. Everyone wants to be overlooking, facing, or playing in or on Lake Ontario. The lakefront is appealing for strolls, and myriad recreational and amusement options make it ideal for those traveling with children. Some of the city's most expensive residential real estate is here, along with shops and parks. A light rapid transit (LRT) line joins Union Station with the Harbourfront, and another LT line, the 510 Spadina, stops at numerous locations along Harbourfront and busy Spadina Avenue. In 2004 the federal government pledged C$25 million to create Canada Square, a gathering place of green space, a floating boardwalk, and a lakeside promenade.

Before the drastic decline of trucking reduced the Great Lakes trade, due to the 1970s oil crisis, Toronto's waterfront was an important center for shipping and warehousing. It fell into commercial disuse and the area was sadly neglected for a long time after. The Gardiner Expressway, Lake Shore Boulevard, and a network of rusty rail yards stood as hideous barriers to the natural beauty of Lake Ontario; the area overflowed with grain silos, warehouses, and malodorous towers of malt, used by local breweries. In the 1980s, the city began work to develop the waterfront for people-friendly purposes, and the trend continues today.

Numbers in the text and in the margin correspond to points of interest on the Old Toronto, the Financial District & the Harbourfront map.

a good tour

The waterfront area explored here is roughly 4 km (2½ mi) long; after visits to Harbourfront Centre, the SkyDome, or the CN Tower, you might want to proceed by car or taxi because the distances between sights increase and the walking gets a bit more awkward. Start your tour at the Harbourfront stretch between Yonge and Bay streets, south of the Westin Harbour Castle Hotel ▶. The docks here are the embarkation point for ferries to the **Toronto Islands** ⑳, and the surrounding plaza has a festive air, with its balloon sellers and vendors of hot dogs, cotton candy, and ice cream. When you return from the islands, walk west on Queen's Quay West about ½ km (¼ mi) to **Harbourfront Centre** ㉑; along the way you see Toronto's amateur sailors taking their boats out on the lake. From here, head north on York Street, then west on Bremner Boulevard about 1¼ km (¾ mi) to the **CN Tower** ㉒ (you walk under highway bridges, but persevere). Next to the CN Tower is the **SkyDome** ㉓. No game today? Tours of the SkyDome are available.

Walk south on Rees Street back to Queen's Quay West, then proceed west 1½ km (1 mi) to Bathurst Street. Walk north on Bathurst about ½ km (¼ mi); under the expressway you see the entrance to **Fort York** ㉔ on your left. From Fort York, go south on Bathurst, then west 1 km (½ mi) on Lake Shore Boulevard to **Exhibition Place** ㉕, home to the Canadian National Exhibition (CNE; mid-August to Labor Day) and the National Trade Centre. Also on the Exhibition Place grounds is Canada's Sports Hall of Fame. When you're finished exploring, use the pedestrian bridge to cross Lake Shore Boulevard to **Ontario Place** ㉖, a lakeside amusement park built by the provincial government.

TIMING   All the attractions on this tour are open year-round, but the milder weather from May through October makes exploring them easier and more pleasant; it's also the best time to find the sights in full operation. The walk alone takes about one hour, at a strolling rate. If you're going to the Toronto Islands, add 45 minutes just to cross the bay and return on the same ferry. Depending on your interest in the various sights in the area, you can spend anywhere from a half day to three days here.

What to See

🕐 ㉒ **CN Tower.** The tallest freestanding tower in the world is 1,815 feet and
Fodor'sChoice 5 inches high—and yes, it's listed in the *Guinness Book of World*
★ *Records.* The CN Tower is tall for a reason: prior to the opening of this telecommunications tower in 1976, so many tall buildings had been built over the previous decades that lower radio and TV transmission towers were having trouble broadcasting. The C$63-million building weighs 130,000 tons and contains enough concrete to build a curb along Highway 401 from Toronto to Kingston, some 262 km (162 mi) to the east. It's worth a visit if the weather is clear, despite the steep fee. Six glass-front elevators zoom up the outside of the tower. The elevators travel at 20 feet per second and the ride takes less than a minute—a rate of ascent similar to that of a jet-plane takeoff. Each elevator has one floor-to-ceiling glass wall—three opaque walls make the trip easier on anyone prone to vertigo. Also, an elevator attendant chatters away during each ride, putting almost everyone at ease.

There are four observation decks to choose from. The **Glass Floor Level** is about 1,122 feet above the ground, and is just as the name describes. It's like walking on a cloud. This could well be the most photographed indoor location in the city—lie on the transparent floor and have your picture taken from above like countless before you. Don't worry, the glass floor has the strength to support 85,000 pounds. Above is the **Look Out Level,** at 1,136 feet; one floor more, at 1,150 feet, is the excellent **360 Revolving Restaurant.** (If you're here to dine at the restaurant, your elevator fee is waived.) At an elevation of 1,465 feet, the **Sky Pod** is the world's highest public observation gallery. All the levels provide spectacular panoramic views of Toronto, Lake Ontario, and the Toronto Islands. On really clear days you can often see Lake Simcoe to the north and the mist rising from Niagara Falls to the south.

On the ground level, the **Marketplace at the Tower** has 12,500 square feet of shopping space with quality Canadian sports and travel items and souvenirs, along with a shop selling Inuit art. There's also the **Fresh Market Cafe,** with seating for 300; the **Maple Leaf Cinema,** which screens the 15-minute documentary *To the Top,* about the building of the Tower; and the **Themed Arcade,** with the latest in virtual-game experiences, including extreme sports like Alpine Racer and TopSkater. One of the most popular attractions at the Tower is **Thrill Zone,** on the ground level. For an added fee, digital animation allows you to experience the thrill—without the risk—of bungee jumping, hang gliding, or tightrope walking from the top of the CN Tower to nearby office buildings.

Peak visiting hours are 11 to 4, particularly on weekends; you may wish to work around them. Hours for rides and attractions vary. ✉ *301 Front St. W, Harbourfront* ☎ *416/868–6937, 416/362–5411 restaurant* ⊕ *www.cntower.ca* ⛶ *First three observation levels C$19, Sky Pod*

C$26.50, combined packages C$32 ⊙ *Sun.–Thurs. 10–10, Fri. and Sat. 10–10:30 PM.*

㉕ Exhibition Place. The Canadian National Exhibition (CNE or "the Ex") takes place the last two weeks of August and Labor Day weekend, attracting more than 3 million people each year. It began in 1879 as primarily an agricultural show, and there are still livestock exhibits. The Ex is a noisy, crowded, often entertaining collection of carnival workers pushing C$5 balloons, plus tummy-turning midway rides, bands, horticultural and technological exhibits, parades, dog swims, horse shows, and (sometimes) top-notch performances. The latter have included stadium appearances by Elton John and Shania Twain. **Canada's Sports Hall of Fame** in the center of the CNE grounds includes touch-screen computers with autobiographies, highlights of famous careers, and sports quizzes. Avoid taking a car to the Ex; parking is insufficient and always terribly overpriced. Instead, take one of the numerous buses and streetcars labeled "Exhibition." ⊠ *Lake Shore Blvd. between Strachan Ave. and Dufferin St., Harbourfront* ☎ *416/263–3600, 416/260–6789 for Hall of Fame* ⊕ *www.explace.on.ca* ⊠ *Free* ⊙ *Hall of Fame weekdays 9–5.*

★ ㉔ Fort York. The most historic site in Toronto is a must for anyone interested in the origins of the city. The founding of Toronto occurred in 1793 when the British built Fort York to protect the entrance to the harbor during Anglo-American strife. Twenty years later the fort was the scene of the bloody Battle of York, in which explorer and general Zebulon Pike led U.S. forces against the fort's outnumbered British, Canadian, and First Nations defenders. The Americans won this battle—their first major victory in the War of 1812—and burned down the provincial buildings during a six-day occupation. A year later British forces retaliated when they captured Washington and torched its public buildings, including the Executive Mansion. A tale people love to tell in Toronto is that a subsequent application of whitewash to cover the charred wood gave rise to the sobriquet "White House," a term first used on presidential letterhead by Teddy Roosevelt years later. Today Fort York's defensive walls surround Canada's largest collection of original War of 1812 buildings. Exhibits include restored barracks, kitchens, and gunpowder magazines, plus changing museum displays. ⊠ *100 Garrison Rd., between Bathurst St. and Strachan Ave., Harbourfront* ☎ *416/392–6907* ⊕ *www.city.toronto.on.ca/culture/fort_york.htm* ⊠ *C$5* ⊙ *Jan.–late May, weekdays 10–4, weekends 10–5; late May–early Sept., daily 10–5.*

★ ℭ ㉑ Harbourfront Centre. Stretching from just west of York Street to Spadina Avenue, this culture-and-recreation center is a match for San Francisco's Pier 39 and Baltimore's Inner Harbor and is one of the highlights of a visit to Toronto. The original Harbourfront opened in 1974, rejuvenating more than a mile of city waterfront that had deteriorated badly. Today Harbourfront Centre, a streamlined version of the original concept, draws more than 3 million visitors to the 10-acre site each year.

Queen's Quay Terminal (⊠ 204 Queen's Quay W ☎ 416/203–0510 ⊕ www.queens-quay-terminal.com) at Harbourfront Centre is a former Terminal Warehouse building, where goods shipped to Toronto were stored before being delivered to shops all over the city. In 1983 it was transformed into a magnificent, eight-story building with 30 delightful specialty shops, eateries, the handsome, 450-seat Premiere Dance Theatre—and harbor views.

Exhibits of contemporary painting, sculpture, architecture, video, photography, and design are mounted at the **Power Plant** (✉ 231 Queen's Quay W ☎ 416/973–4949 ⊕ www.thepowerplant.org ⛛ C$4 ⊘ Tues. and Thurs.–Sun. noon–6, Wed. noon–8; tours Sat. and Sun. at 2 and 4, Wed. at 6:30). It can be spotted by its tall red smokestack. It was built in 1927 as a power station for the Terminal Warehouse's ice-making plant. Wednesday from 5 PM to 8 PM, admission is free.

York Quay Centre (✉ 235 Queen's Quay W ☎ 416/973–4000, 416/973–4866 rink info, 416/973–4963 craft studio) hosts concerts, theater, readings, and even skilled artisans. The Craft Studio, for example, has professional craftspeople working in ceramics, glass, metal, and textiles from February to December, in full view of the public. A shallow pond outside is used for canoe lessons in warmer months and as the largest artificial ice-skating rink in North America in more wintry times. At the nearby Nautical Centre, many private firms rent boats and give lessons in sailing and canoeing.

Among the seasonal events in Harbourfront Centre are the Ice Canoe Race in late January, Winterfest in February, a jazz festival in June, Canada Day celebrations and the Parade of Lights in July, the Authors' Festival and Harvest Festival in October, and the Swedish Christmas Fair in November. ✉ *Administrative offices, 110 Queen's Quay W, Harbourfront* ☎ *416/973–4000 event hotline, 416/973–4600 offices* ⊕ *www.harbourfrontcentre.com.*

> **need a break?**
>
> There are plenty of places inside **Queen's Quay** for a quick sandwich, freshly squeezed juice, or ice-cream concoctions. You can also check out one of the food trucks outside, selling peel-on French fries, with salt and vinegar, if you like.

Music Garden. Developed by renowned cellist Yo-Yo Ma and garden designer Julie Moir Messervy, this park was planned for Boston, but when that venue fell through, Toronto was the pair's next choice. The park's concept is based on J. S. Bach's *Cello Suite No. 1* (which consists of six movements—Prelude, Allemande, Courante, Sarabande, Minuet, and Gigue), as interpreted by Yo-Yo Ma. Each movement is reflected in the park's elaborate design, using undulating riverscape, a forest grove of wandering trails, a swirling path through a wildflower meadow, a conifer grove, a formal flower parterre, and giant grass steps. ✉ *South side of Queen's Quay W, west of Spadina Ave., Harbourfront* ☎ *416/338–0338.*

★ ⓒ ㉖ **Ontario Place.** The waterfront entertainment complex stretches along three man-made islands and includes Soak City, downtown Toronto's only water park; pedal boats at Bob's Boat Yard; Wilderness Adventure Ride; and Mars Simulator Ride. The **Cinesphere,** an enclosed dome with a six-story movie screen, uses the world's first IMAX projection system, a Canadian invention. The 16,000-seat outdoor **Molson Amphitheatre** stages nightly performances by singers and rock groups throughout summer, and the **Atlantis Pavilions** is a 32,000-square-foot entertainment and dining facility. Live children's entertainment on two stages is included in the admission price to the park. The Big Comfy Couch, Clifford the Big Red Dog, and other children's favorites are featured. For the best value, the Play All Day Pass allows unlimited use of most rides and attractions including daytime Cinesphere IMAX and large-format films. Weekends in September bring several annual events to this venue: the Great White North Dragon Boat Challenge, the Toronto In-Water Boat Show, and the Fall Fishing Festival and Kids' Fishing Derby. ⊠ *955 Lakeshore Blvd. W, across from Exhibition Place, Harbourfront* ☎ *866/ 663–4386 recording* ⊕ *www.ontarioplace.com* ⊠ *Gate admission C$13, pass C$29* ⊙ *Late May–early Sept., daily 10–9.*

★ ⊙ ㉓   **SkyDome.** One of Toronto's most famous landmarks, the SkyDome is home to baseball's Blue Jays, and was the world's first stadium with a fully retractable roof. One way to see the huge 52,000-seat stadium is to buy tickets for a Blue Jays game or one of the many other events that take place here. You might watch a cricket match, Wrestlemania, a monster-truck race, a family ice show, or a rock concert—even the large-scale opera *Aida* has been performed here. You can also take a one-hour guided walking tour. Depending on several factors, you may find yourself in the middle of the field, in a press box, in the dressing rooms, or, if a roof tour is available, 36 stories above home plate on a catwalk. There's also a 15-minute film. Tour times vary based on when daytime events are scheduled. ⊠ *1 Blue Jays Way, tour entrance at Front and John Sts., between Gates 1 and 2, Old Toronto* ☎ *416/341–2770 for tours, 416/341–3663 for events and shows, and 416/341–1234 or 888/654–6529 for Blue Jays information* ⊕ *www.skydome.com* ⊠ *Tour C$12.50* ⊙ *Tours daily.*

★ ⊙ ⑳   **Toronto Islands.** Though sometimes referred to in the singular, there are actually eight narrow, tree-lined islands plus more than a dozen smaller islets in Lake Ontario just off the city's downtown, providing a welcome touch of greenery. They've been attracting visitors since 1833, and why not? The more than 550 acres of parkland are irresistible, and it's usually a few degrees cooler than it is in the city. You have spectacular views of Toronto's skyline, especially as the setting sun turns the Royal Bank Tower and other skyscrapers to gold, silver, and bronze.

Sandy beaches fringe the islands, the best ones being those on the southeast tip of Ward's Island, the southernmost edge of Centre Island, and the west side of Hanlan's Island. In 1999 a portion of Hanlan's Beach that had long been used by nude bathers was officially declared "clothing-optional" by Toronto's City Council. The declaration regarding Ontario's only legal nude beach passed without protest or incident—perhaps a testament to the truly international flavor of the city. The section frequented by gays and lesbians is at the easterly end; the "straight" section is more westerly. Overlapping occurs, however, and there is a nice, tolerant attitude here in general. There are free changing rooms near each beach.

Lake Ontario's water has at times been declared unfit for swimming, so check reports before you go. Swimming in the lagoons and channels is prohibited. In summer, Centre Island has rowboat and canoe rentals. Pack a cooler with picnic fixings or something you can grill on one of the park's barbecue pits. Note that the consumption of alcohol in a public park is illegal in Toronto. The winter can be bitter cold on the islands, but snow-shoeing and cross-country skiing with downtown Toronto over your shoulder is appealing to many. There are supervised wading pools, baseball diamonds, volleyball nets, and tennis courts—even a Frisbee course.

All transportation on these interconnected islands comes to you compliments of your feet: no cars (except for emergency and work vehicles) are permitted. The boardwalk from Centre Island to Ward's Island is 2½ km (1½ mi) long. Centre Island gets so crowded that no bicycles are allowed on its ferry from the mainland during summer weekends. Consider renting a bike for an hour or so once you get there and working your way across the islands. (Bike rentals can be found south of the Centre Island ferry docks on the Avenue of the Islands.)

There are more than a dozen rides, including a restored 1890s merry-go-round with at least four dozen hand-carved animals, at the children's amusement park **Centreville** (✉ Centre Island ☎ 416/203–0405 ⊕ www. centreisland.ca ✉ Day pass C$23 ⊙ Late May–early Sept., weekdays 10:30–6, weekends 10:30–8; early-Sept.–Oct., weekends 10:30–6). It's modeled after a late-19th-century village, with shops, a town hall, and a small railroad station. The Far Enough Farm (free) has all kinds of animals to pet and feed, including piglets, geese, and cows. There's no entrance fee to the modest 14-acre park, although there's a charge for rides. Instead of buying tickets, consider a day pass.

You may want to take one of the equally frequent ferries to Ward's or Hanlan's Islands. Both islands have tennis courts and picnic and sunbathing spots. Late May through early September, the ferries run between the docks at the bottom of Bay Street and the Ward's Island dock between 6:30 AM and 12:45 AM; for Centre and Hanlan's islands, they begin at 8 AM. They run roughly at half-hour intervals most of the working day and at quarter-hour intervals during peak times such as summer evenings and weekends. On Canada Day (July 1) the lines are very slow-moving. In winter, the ferries run only to Ward's Island on a limited schedule. ✉ *Ferries at foot of Bay St. and Queen's Quay, Harbourfront* ☎ *416/392–8186 for island information, 416/392–8193 for ferry information* ✉ *Ferry C$6 one way.*

Along Dundas & Queen Streets

Every city has its heart, and the areas along Dundas and Queen Streets typify Toronto's ethnic makeup and youthful appeal. To locals, Dundas West can only mean Chinatown and Kensington Market, and Queen West has always been bohemian—albeit now slightly more chic—and was the home of '90s comedy troupe Kids in the Hall and pop-rockers Barenaked Ladies. The sprawling town square, two city halls, two-block-long Eaton Centre, and a major art museum are here, too; it's an area full of variety in architecture, purpose, and tone.

Numbers in the text and in the margin correspond to points of interest on the North Downtown Toronto map.

a good walk

Start at the corner of **Spadina Avenue** ㉗ ⌐ and Nassau Street. Walk two blocks west on Nassau to Bellevue Avenue, turn left, and go south to Denison Square and the Kiever Synagogue, a lovely leftover from the early- and mid-20th-century immigration of Russian and Polish Jews to this area. Just to the southeast, at the corner of Denison Square and Augusta Avenue, **Bellevue Square** ㉘ is a pretty little park with shade trees. Take Augusta Avenue one short block north to Baldwin Street, walk two short blocks east to Kensington Avenue and the overflowing stalls of **Kensington Market** ㉙. Continue south one block on Kensington to Dundas and turn left (east) back to Spadina. On the east side you'll see the Chinese Home for the Aged, which signals the approach to Toronto's original **Chinatown** ㉚ (there are four in the Greater Toronto Area), one block south on Spadina at Dundas.

After exploring this lively area, head east on Dundas for about four blocks to the **Art Gallery of Ontario** ㉛, a large beige building; you can visit its annex, the Grange, Toronto's oldest brick building and an earlier home to the gallery's collection. If you want to see more art, across the street is the **Ontario College of Art and Design Gallery** ㉜ and the Rosalie Sharpe Pavillion, which has contemporary multimedia exhibitions. Head three blocks south from the Grange on McCaul Street to Queen Street, then go three short blocks east to busy University Avenue. At the northwest corner sits **Campbell House** ㉝, a restored chief justice's residence.

Cross University, go north one block to Armoury Street, turn right and almost immediately take a left onto Centre Avenue to visit the **Museum for Textiles** ㉞. Now head south on Centre and east on Armory Street, where you approach the City Hall complex from behind. Continue along the concrete path, passing on your left a small park with a waterfall, until you reach Bay Street. Walk south on Bay: at the northwest corner of Bay and Queen you see the expanse of Nathan Phillips Square, the public plaza in front of **City Hall** ㉟. After visiting the modern building and **Old City Hall** ㊱ diagonally across the square, turn left, walk a short block to Yonge Street, and approach **Eaton Centre** ㊲, a gigantic shopping, office, and hotel complex. Exiting the huge mall at Yonge and Dundas, take Dundas three blocks east to Bond Street and then go south a short distance on Bond to the **Mackenzie House** ㊳.

TIMING

Although it's always nicest to stroll around in warm weather, wintertime brings skating, Christmas caroling, and other festive activities to Nathan Phillips Square. Chinatown is at its busiest (and most fun) on Sunday, but be prepared for very crowded sidewalks and much jostling. Kensington is great any time, although it can feel a bit sketchy at night. The walk itself is just under 3 km (2 mi) long and should take about an hour. The Campbell and Mackenzie houses merit at least half an hour each, the Art Gallery and the Grange an hour or more. And, of course, Chinatown can gobble up an entire afternoon.

What to See

③ Art Gallery of Ontario. From extremely modest beginnings in 1900, the
Fodor'sChoice AGO (as it's known) is now in the big leagues in terms of exhibitions
★ and support. In early 2004, "Transformation AGO" was launched—a
major expansion designed by world-renowned architect (and Toronto
native son) Frank Gehry. With a 20% increase in overall building size,
allowing for 97,000 square feet of additional gallery space, completion
is expected in early 2008, at a cost of C$194.8 million. Torontonians
will not recognize the new AGO, as Gehry plans a monumental glass
and titanium facade to be built over the main building.

Current exhibits will remain open during construction. The **Henry Moore
Sculpture Centre** has the largest public collection of Moore's sculpture
in the world. People of all ages can enjoy climbing in and around Henry
Moore's large *Two Forms* sculpture, which is just outside the AGO, on
McCaul Street. The **Canadian Wing** includes major works by such north-
ern lights as Emily Carr, Cornelius Krieghoff, David Milne, and Homer
Watson. The AGO also has a growing collection of works by such world-
famous artists as Rembrandt, Hals, Van Dyck, Hogarth, Reynolds,
Chardin, Renoir, de Kooning, Rothko, Oldenburg, Picasso, Rodin, Degas,
Matisse, and many others. Visitors of any age can drop by the **Anne Tan-
nenbaum Gallery School** on Sunday and explore painting, printmaking,
and sculpting in Toronto's most spectacular studio space. Admission to
AGO also gains you entrance to **The Grange,** an adjoining Georgian-style
house museum built in 1817–18 and donated to the city in 1911. The
columned front and delicately balanced wings only hint at the delightful details of the interior. Wednesday evenings are free after 6 PM. ⊠ *317
Dundas St. W, Chinatown* ☎ *416/979–6648* ⊕ *www.ago.net* ⊡ *C$12*
⊙ *Tues., Thurs., and Fri. 11–6, Wed. 11–8:30, Sat. and Sun. 10–5:30.*

need a break? You can have a light, healthy snack in the shadow of two Rodin
sculptures at the Art Gallery of Ontario's **Agora Grill** (⊠ 317
Dundas St. W, Downtown ☎ 416/979–6612). Weekend brunches,
from 11 to 3, are particularly popular here. The restaurant is open
for lunch (from noon to 2:30) and brunch only.

㉘ Bellevue Square. This little park with shady trees, benches, and a wading pool and playground is a good place to rest after a visit to Kensington Market. ⊠ *Denison Sq. and Augusta Ave., Downtown.*

㉝ Campbell House. The stately Georgian mansion of Sir William Campbell,
the sixth chief justice of Upper Canada, is now one of Toronto's most
charming house museums. Built in 1822 in another part of town, the Campbell House was moved to this site in 1972. It has been tastefully restored
with elegant early-19th-century furniture. Costumed guides detail the social life of the upper class. Note the model of the town of York as it was
in the 1820s, and the original kitchen. ⊠ *160 Queen St. W, Queen West*
☎ *416/597–0227* ⊡ *C$4.50* ⊙ *Oct.–mid-May, weekdays 9:30–4:30; mid-
May–Oct., weekdays 9:30–4:30, weekends noon–4:30.*

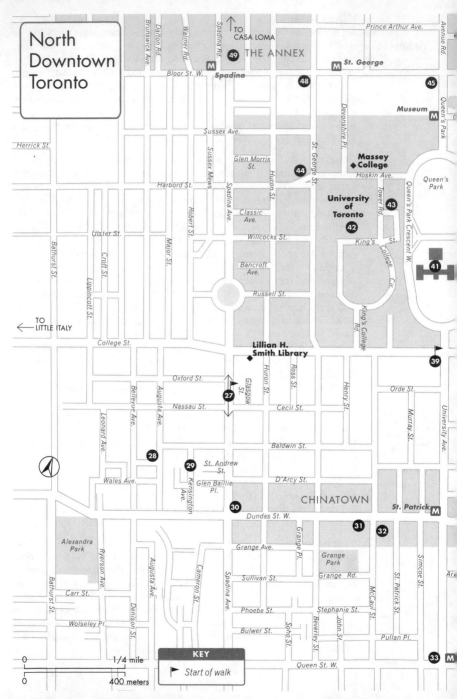

North Downtown Toronto

TO CASA LOMA

THE ANNEX

Prince Arthur Ave.

Avenue Rd.

49

M St. George

48

45

Bloor St. W.

M Spadina

Museum

M

Queen's Park

Herrick St.

Sussex Ave.

Glen Morris St.

44

Massey ♦ College

Hoskin Ave.

Queen's Park

Harbord St.

Classic Ave.

University of Toronto

42

43

Ulster St.

Willcocks St.

King's St.

41

Bancroft Ave.

Russell St.

TO LITTLE ITALY

College St.

Lillian H. Smith Library ♦

39

Oxford St.

27

Glasgow St.

Orde St.

Nassau St.

Cecil St.

28

Baldwin St.

St. Andrew St.

29

Glen Baillie Pl.

D'Arcy St.

Wales Ave.

CHINATOWN

St. Patrick

30

Dundas St. W.

M

Grange Ave.

31

32

Alexandra Park

Grange Park

Grange Rd.

St. Patrick St.

Sullivan St.

Carr St.

Phoebe St.

Stephanie St.

Wolseley Pl.

Bulwer St.

Pullan Pl.

33 M

0 — 1/4 mile

0 — 400 meters

Queen St. W.

Queen Street West is lined with cafés and restaurants. Consider the **Queen Mother Café** (✉ 208 Queen St. W, Queen West ☎ 416/598–4719), a neighborhood institution popular with art students and broadcast-media types. Serving Lao-Thai cuisine, the "Queen Mum" is open until 1 AM for wholesome meals and fabulous desserts at reasonable prices.

★ ㉚ **Chinatown.** You pass shops selling silk kimonos (for less than half the price elsewhere), lovely sake sets, Chinese herbs, and fresh-caught fish in Toronto's Chinatown, one of the largest in North America. On Sunday, up and down Spadina Avenue and along Dundas Street, Chinese music blasts from storefronts, cash registers ring, and bakeries, markets, herbalists, and restaurants, such as **Spadina Garden** (114 Dundas St. W), do their best business of the week.

Spadina and Dundas streets were for years the anchor of Toronto's Chinatown. When a new city hall was built in the 1960s, many of the residents were uprooted from the area behind the old building, and Chinatown began to spread west. Today, Chinatown—which now has to be described as the main or original Chinatown, as three other areas with large Chinese populations have sprung up elsewhere in metropolitan Toronto—covers much of the area of Spadina Avenue from Queen Street to College Street, running along Dundas Street nearly as far east as Bay Street. The population is more than 100,000, which is especially impressive when you consider that just over a century ago there was only a single Chinese resident, Sam Ching, who ran a hand laundry on Adelaide Street. A huge wave of immigration that began some three decades ago continues today. You can start a walk through this lively, interesting area on Elizabeth Street, just north of City Hall, and walk north to Dundas Street, then either east toward Bay Street or west to Spadina Avenue. ✉ *Along Dundas St. from Spadina Ave. to Nathan Phillips Sq.*

㉟ **City Hall.** Toronto's modern city hall was the outgrowth of a 1958 international competition to which some 520 architects from 42 countries submitted designs. The winning presentation by Finnish architect Viljo Revell was controversial—two curved towers of differing height. But there is a logic to it all—an aerial view of the City Hall shows a circular council chamber sitting like an eye between the two tower "eyelids" containing offices of 44 municipal wards, with 44 city councillors. A remarkable mural within the main entrance, *Metropolis,* was constructed by sculptor David Partridge from 100,000 common nails. Revell died before his masterwork was opened in 1965, but within months the City Hall became a symbol of a thriving city, with a silhouette as recognizable in its own way as the Eiffel Tower. The positive influence that the development of this building has had on Toronto's civic life is detailed in Robert Fulford's book *Accidental City.*

Annual events at City Hall include the Spring Flower Show in late March; the Toronto Outdoor Art Exhibition in early July; and the yearly Cavalcade of Lights from late November through Christmas, when more than 100,000 sparkling lights are illuminated across both new and old city halls.

In front of City Hall, 9-acre **Nathan Phillips Square** (named after the mayor who initiated the City Hall project) has become a gathering place, whether for royal visits, protest rallies, picnic lunches, or concerts. The reflecting pool is a delight in summer, and even more so in winter, when office workers skate at lunchtime. The park also holds a Peace Garden for quiet meditation and Henry Moore's striking bronze sculpture *The Archer*. On New Year's Eve, crowds gather here for Toronto's answer to New York City's Times Square countdown madness. ⊠ *100 Queen St. W, Downtown* ☎ *416/338–0338, 416/338–0889 TDD* ⊕ *www.city.toronto.on.ca* ☉ *Weekdays 8:30–4:30.*

❸ **Eaton Centre.** The 3-million-square-foot Eaton Centre shopping mall has been both praised and vilified since it was built in the 1970s, but it remains incredibly popular. From the graceful glass roof, arching 127 feet above the lowest of the mall levels, to Michael Snow's exquisite flock of fiberglass Canada geese floating poetically in open space, to the glass-enclosed elevators, porthole windows, and nearly two dozen long and graceful escalators, there is plenty to appreciate.

Such a wide selection of shops and eateries can be confusing, so here's a simple guide: Galleria Level 1 contains two food courts; popularly priced fashions; photo, electronics, and music stores; and much "convenience" merchandise. Level 2 is directed to the middle-income shopper; Level 3, suitably, has the highest elevation, fashion, and prices. In the late 1990s a branch of eatons (formerly Eaton's) opened here, even after most of the chain's stores across Canada had closed and the family's merchant dynasty had come to an end. The Centre now retains the famous family's name, but the biggest tenants are Sears and the Canadian flagship store of Swedish retail giant H & M (which was scheduled to open in late 2004). The southern end of Level 3 has a skywalk that connects the Centre to the seven floors of The Bay (formerly Simpsons) department store, across Queen Street.

Safe, well-lit parking garages with spaces for some 1,800 cars are sprinkled around Eaton Centre. The building extends along the west side of Yonge Street all the way from Queen Street up to Dundas Street (with subway stops at each end). ⊠ *220 Yonge St., Downtown* ☎ *416/598–8560* ⊕ *www.torontoeatoncentre.com* ☉ *Weekdays 10–9, Sat. 9:30–7, Sun. noon–6.*

The Café at the Church of the Holy Trinity (⊠ 10 Trinity Sq., facing Bay St., Downtown ☎ 416/598–4521 ⊕ www.holytrinitytoronto. org) is a charming eatery serving sandwiches, soups, pastries, and tea. It's open weekdays 9 to 5. The church itself is fully operational and available for quiet contemplation in the midst of one of downtown Toronto's busiest sections.

❷ **Kensington Market.** The steamy, smelly, raucous, European-style marketplace titillates all the senses. On any given day you can find Russian rye breads, barrels of dill pickles, fresh fish on ice, mountains of cheese, and bushels of ripe fruit. Crates of chickens and rabbits can both amuse and horrify. Kensington's collection of vintage-clothing stores is the best in the city.

Kensington Market sprang up in the early 1900s, when Russian, Polish, and Jewish inhabitants set up stalls in front of their houses. Since then, the market—named after the area's major street—has become a United Nations of stores. Unlike the members of the UN, however, these vendors get along well with one another. Jewish and Eastern European shops sit side by side with Portuguese, Caribbean, and East Indian ones, as well as with a sprinkling of Vietnamese, Japanese, and Chinese establishments. Al Waxman, the deceased local star of Canadian television's long-running sitcom *King of Kensington* (and American TV's *Cagney & Lacey*), is now immortalized in a bronze statue here. Saturday is the best day to visit, preferably by public transit; parking is difficult. Note that many stores are closed on Sunday. ✉ *Bordered by College St. on the north, Spadina Ave. on the east, Dundas St. on the south, and Augusta Ave. on the west, Kensington Market* ☉ *Daily dawn–dusk.*

need a break?

Hole-in-the-wall eateries flourish around Kensington Market. **Cafe La Gaffe** (✉ 24 Baldwin St., Kensington Market ☎ 416/596–2397) is filled with customers chatting about theater, art, and politics over coffee and large portions of chicken brochettes, grilled fish, and fresh veggies. The tiny front patio, overlooking what locals call Baldwin Village, is great for people-watching in summer, and the ambience is definitely Parisian, though the establishment is owned by a Bermudian-Canadian.

③ **Mackenzie House.** Once home to journalist William Lyon Mackenzie, who was born in Scotland at the end of the 18th century and emigrated to Canada in 1820, the National Historic Site is now a museum and library. Mackenzie started a newspaper that so enraged the powers that be (a clique known as "the Family Compact") that they dumped all his type into Lake Ontario. An undeterred Mackenzie stayed on to be elected the first mayor of Toronto in 1834 and is said even to have designed the coat of arms of his new city; his grandson, William Lyon Mackenzie King, became the longest-serving prime minister in Canadian history.

Mackenzie served only one year as mayor. Upset with the government big shots in 1837, he gathered about 700 supporters and marched down Yonge Street to try to overthrow the government. His minions were roundly defeated, and Mackenzie fled to the United States with a price on his head. When the Canadian government granted him amnesty many years later, he was promptly elected to the legislative assembly and began to publish another newspaper. By this time, though, Mackenzie was so down on his luck that some friends bought his family this house. Mackenzie enjoyed the place for but a few depressing years, and died in 1861. Among the period furnishings and equipment preserved here is the fiery Scot's printing press. ✉ *82 Bond St., Downtown* ☎ *416/392–6915* 💰 *C$3.50, holidays C$5* ☉ *Tues.–Fri. noon–4, weekends noon–5.*

off the beaten path

THE BEACHES – Queen Street West represents the city's cutting edge, but The Beaches (or The Beach) neighborhood, 15 minutes east via streetcar on Queen Street, is old-school bohemian. This area of pricey real estate, bordered by Woodbine Avenue on the west and Neville Park Road to the east, has a funky flair *and* a small-town feel. It's easy to spend an afternoon strolling the delightful yet crowded (in summer) boardwalk along the shore of Lake Ontario. Musicians often perform at the several public parks fronting the boardwalk, where you're also likely to see artists selling their wares. You could also do some leisurely window-shopping on Queen Street East, which is lined with quaint antiques stores and specialty boutiques and shops. An annual international jazz festival in July attracts over 400 musicians and thousands of listeners to this laid-back community.

One of the more unusual neighborhood stores is the **Three Dog Bakery** (✉ 2014 Queen St. E, The Beaches ☎ 416/693–3364), a bakery for dogs. For something to drink in The Beaches, you can stop at one of several Irish pubs, such as **Murphy's Law** (✉ 1702 Queen St. E, The Beaches ☎ 416/690–5516). **Licks** (✉ 1962 Queen St. E, The Beaches ☎ 416/362–5425) is a neighborhood restaurant institution for great burgers and ice cream.

㉞ Museum for Textiles. Ten galleries showcase cultural displays—men's costumes from northern Nigeria, for example—as well as the latest in contemporary design. Rugs, cloth, and tapestries from around the world are exhibited. Wednesday evenings (5 to 8) admission is pay-what-you-can. ✉ *55 Centre Ave., Downtown* ☎ *416/599–5321* ⊕ *www. museumfortextiles.on.ca* 🔲 *C$8* ⊙ *Tues., Thurs., and Fri. 11–5, Wed. 11–8, weekends noon–5.*

㊱ Old City Hall. Opened in 1899, and used until 1965 when "new" City Hall was built across the street, the old municipal building is still going strong as the home of the provincial courts, county offices, and the marriage bureau. This imposing building was designed by E. J. Lennox, who was also the architect for Casa Loma and the King Edward Hotel. Note the huge stained-glass window as you enter. The fabulous gargoyles above the front steps were apparently the architect's witty way of mocking certain turn-of-the-20th-century politicians; he also carved his name under the eaves on all four faces of the building. The building has been filmed, inside and out, for countless domestic and international TV shows and feature films. It's been made even more famous by the hundreds of gay and lesbian marriages which have been performed here since the summer of 2003. ✉ *60 Queen St. W, Downtown* ☎ *416/327–5675* ⊙ *Weekdays 8:30–5.*

㉜ Ontario College of Art and Design Gallery. The college's gallery, across the street from the Art Gallery of Ontario, shows works by students, faculty, and alumni. OCAD is probably Canada's foremost art and design institution, with a prestigious history—several of Canada's Group of Seven landscape painters taught here—and a vibrant future. The gallery is an important exhibition space for emerging Canadian artists and designers. Be sure to walk a few steps south on McCaul Street to see the 2004 addition to the College, Sharp Centre for Design: a space-age platform hovering over the main building which houses classrooms and studio space. ☒ *Rosalie Sharp Pavilion, 285 Dundas St. W, Chinatown* ☎ *416/ 977–6000 Ext. 262* ⊕ *www.ocad.on.ca* ☜ *Free* ☉ *Wed.–Sat. noon–6.*

► ㉗ **Spadina Avenue.** Spadina, running from the lakeshore north to College Street, has never been fashionable. For decades it has housed a collection of inexpensive stores, factories that sell wholesale if you have connections, ethnic-food and fruit stores, and eateries, including some first-class, if modest-looking, Chinese restaurants. Each new wave of immigrants—Jewish, Chinese, Portuguese, East and West Indian, South American—has added its own flavor to the mix, but Spadina-Kensington's basic bill of fare is still bargains galore. Here you can find gourmet cheeses, fresh (not fresh-frozen) ocean fish, fine European kitchenware at half the prices of Yorkville stores, yards of remnants piled high in bins, designer clothes minus the labels, and the occasional rock-and-roll nightspot and interesting greasy spoon. A streetcar line runs down the wide avenue to Front Street.

Toronto's widest street has been pronounced "Spa-*dye*-nah" for a century and a half, but it really should be called "Spa-*dee*-na," as it is derived from an Ojibway word, meaning hill, with that pronunciation. The history behind Spadina Avenue's width—it is 132 feet wide, double the width of almost every other old street in town—goes back to 1802, when a 27-year-old Irish physician named William Warren Baldwin came to muddy York. He soon married a rich young woman, built a pleasant home where Casa Loma and Spadina House now sit, and decided to cut a giant swath through the forest from Bloor Street down to Queen Street so they could look down, literally and socially, on Lake Ontario. Alas, their view disappeared in 1874, when a thankless granddaughter sold the land at the crescent just above College Street for the site of Knox College. The college vacated the building several decades later and moved to the University of Toronto campus. Now covered with vines, the Victorian building still sits in the crescent, a number of the chestnut trees planted by Dr. Baldwin remaining on the west side. Little else remains of Dr. Baldwin's Spadina, except for a handful of Victorian mansions.

Around Queen's Park

Bounded by College Street to the south, Church Street to the east, Bloor Street to the north, and Spadina Avenue to the west, this midtown area is a political, cultural, and intellectual feast. Its heart is the large, oval Queen's Park, south of which is the seat of the Ontario Provincial Legislature, and to the east and west the University of Toronto's main campus, which straddles the park and occupies about 160 acres. The park area abuts the Yorkville shopping district, the high-end shopping on Bloor Street between Yonge and Avenue Road. The gay- and lesbian-friendly neighborhood of Church and Wellesley and the Rosedale residential area are nearby.

Numbers in the text and in the margin correspond to points of interest on the North Downtown Toronto map.

a good walk

Start at the northeast corner of University Avenue and College Street (Queen's Park TTC station), where you face the green expanse of **Queen's Park** 39 ⚑. If you're traveling with kids, you might want to detour two blocks to the right (east) on College Street until you come to Bay Street and the fascinating **Toronto Police Museum and Discovery Centre** 40. Return to University Avenue and go north. University Avenue splits into Queen's Park Circle. Follow Queen's Park Crescent East; when you reach Wellesley Street West you find a traffic light and a safe way to cross the stream of four-lane traffic toward the pink **Ontario Legislative Building** 41, on the site originally granted to King's College, the University of Toronto's precursor.

After visiting the parliament buildings, return to Wellesley Street West and go left (west) under an overpass onto the **University of Toronto** 42 (U of T) campus. The large green area before you is King's College Circle. The circle includes some of the oldest college buildings, such as the domed Convocation Hall, and some of the newest, such as the poured-concrete Medical Sciences building. Take Tower Road north from King's College Circle; almost immediately to your left is the large Romanesque Revival University College, which was originally the city's first nonsectarian college. Now a part of the U of T campus, the building houses the Public Affairs and Alumni Development Department, which provides visitor information, maps, and guided tours. It's a short block north on Tower Road to neo-Gothic **Hart House** 43, a student center.

Turn right from Hart House and walk less than a block north along another green area until you reach Hoskin Avenue. Cross north at the traffic light and take a left. When, after a long block, you get to Devonshire Place, you see Massey College, whose handsome buildings and enclosed courtyard were designed by Canadian architect Ron Thom. Past students have included the late Robertson Davies, one of Canada's finest novelists. Continue west on Hoskin for another block until you reach the corner of St. George Street, where you can glimpse a linked trio of poured-concrete buildings. The one closest is the library school; the monstrous one in the middle is Robarts Library; and the southernmost building houses the **Thomas Fisher Rare Book Library** 44.

If you don't want to visit the rare-books library, turn right (east) at the traffic light where Tower Road meets Hoskin Avenue; in about a block, Hoskin curves and becomes Queen's Park Crescent. Walk north on the crescent; where the street straightens out again, the TTC's Museum subway stop is on your left. Beyond it is the large, stone **Royal Ontario Museum** 45, or ROM, one of Canada's finest museums. Across the street from ROM's main entrance is the **George R. Gardiner Museum of Ceramic Art** 46. At this point you are on the edge of **Yorkville** 47, an elegant shopping district, but don't be distracted (unless you can't resist, of course). On the north end of ROM is Bloor Street; take it west one long block to St. George Street to visit the **Bata Shoe Museum** 48. Catercorner from the museum is the York Club, one of the landmarks of **The Annex** 49, a neighborhood that attracts the intellectual set.

TIMING The Queen's Park walk is good any time of year because many of the attractions bring you indoors. Excluding a stroll around The Annex, the walk alone should take about a half hour at a strolling pace. The walk and a visit to the legislature and one or two of the museums or libraries would make a nice half-day (or more) program; allot at least one hour each for the Royal Ontario and Gardiner museums.

What to See

49 The Annex. Born in 1887, when the burgeoning town of Toronto engulfed the area between Bathurst Street and Avenue Road north from Bloor Street to the Canadian Pacific Railway tracks at what is now Dupont Street, the countrified Annex soon became an enclave for the well-to-do; today it attracts an intellectual set. Timothy Eaton of department-store fame built a handsome structure at 182 Lowther Avenue (since demolished). The prominent Gooderham family, owners of a distillery, erected a lovely red castle at the corner of St. George Street and Bloor Street, now the home of the exclusive York Club.

As Queen Victoria gave way to King Edward, the old rich gave way to the new rich and ethnic groups came and went, until the arrival of the ultimate neighborhood wrecker—the developer. Many Edwardian mansions were demolished to make room for very ugly 1960s-era apartment buildings.

Still, The Annex, with its hundreds of attractive old homes, can be cited as a prime example of Toronto's success in preserving lovely, safe streets within the downtown area. Examples of late-19th-century architecture can be spotted on Admiral Road, Lowther Avenue, and Bloor Street, west of University Avenue. Round turrets, pyramid-shape roofs, and conical (some even comical) spires are among the pleasures shared by some 20,000 Torontonians who live in this vibrant community, including professors, students, writers, lawyers, and other professional and artsy types. Bloor Street between Spadina and Palmerston keeps them fed and entertained with its bohemian collection of used-record stores, crafts shops run by eccentrics, and restaurants, from elegant Italian to hearty Polish and aromatic Indian. Keep your eyes open, too; you may run into one of Canada's better-known authors, such as Michael Ondaatje, Jane Jacobs, or Daniel Richler (Mordecai's son). ⊠ *Bordered by Bathurst St. to the west, St. George St. to the east, Bloor St. W to the south, and Dupont St. to the north.*

48 Bata Shoe Museum. Created by Sonja Bata, wife of the founder of the Bata Shoe Company, this collection contains 10,000 varieties of foot coverings and, through the changing fashions, highlights the craft and sociology of making shoes. Some items date back more than 4,000 years. Pressurized sky-diving boots, iron-spiked shoes used for crushing chestnuts, and smugglers' clogs are among the items on display. Elton John's boots have proved wildly popular, but Napoléon's socks give them a run for the money. Admission is free the first Tuesday of every month. ⊠ *327 Bloor St. W, The Annex* 🕾 *416/979-7799* ⊕ *www. batashoemuseum.ca* 🖙 *C$6* ☉ *Tues., Wed., Fri., and Sat. 10–5, Thurs. 10–8, Sun. noon–5.*

☾ **Casa Loma.** A European-style castle, Casa Loma was commissioned by Sir Henry Pellatt, a soldier and financier, who picked up architectural ideas from some of Europe's finest mansions. This great folly has 98 rooms, two towers, creepy passageways, and lots of secret panels. The home's architect, E. J. Lennox, also designed Toronto's Old City Hall and the King Edward Hotel. Pellatt spent over C$3 million to construct his dream (that's in 1913 dollars), only to lose it to the taxman just over a decade later. Some impressive details are the giant pipe organ, the reproduction of Windsor Castle's Peacock Alley, the majestic, 60-foot-high ceiling of the Great Hall, and the mahogany-and-marble stable, reached by a long, underground passage. The rooms are copies of those in English, Spanish, Scottish, and Austrian castles. This has been the location for many a horror movie and period drama—and for an episode of the BBC's *Antiques Roadshow.* Self-guided audio tours are available in eight languages. A tour is a good 1½-km (1-mi) walk, so wear sensible shoes. ⊠ *1 Austin Terr., Forest Hill* ☎ *416/923–1171* ⊕ *www. casaloma.org* ⊑ *C$12* ⊗ *Daily 9:30–4.*

㊻ **George R. Gardiner Museum of Ceramic Art.** This collection of rare ceramics includes 17th-century English delftware and 18th-century yellow European porcelain; its pre-Colombian collection dates to Olmec and Maya times. An extensive refurbishment (adding a third floor) has closed the museum to the public until October 2005. ⊠ *111 Queen's Park Crescent, The Annex* ☎ *416/586–8080* ⊕ *www.gardinermuseum. on.ca* ⊑ *C$10* ⊗ *Mon. and Wed.–Fri. 10–6, Tues. 10–8, weekends 10–5.*

㊸ **Hart House.** A neo-Gothic student center built in 1911–1919, Hart House represents the single largest gift to the University of Toronto. Vincent Massey, a student here at the turn of the 20th century, regretted the absence of a meeting place and gym for students and convinced his father to build one. It was named for Vincent's grandfather, Hart, the founder of Massey-Ferguson, once the world's leading supplier of farm equipment. Originally restricted to male students, Hart House has been open to women since 1972.

Soldier's Tower, attached to the Hart House, with its 51-bell carillon, was erected in 1923 as a memorial to university community members who fell in World War I. Names of alumni killed in later wars have since been added.

The stained-glass windows and vaulted ceiling in the Great Hall of Hart House are impressive, but so is Chef Suzanne Baby's cuisine at the resident **Gallery Grill** (☎ 416/978–2445 ⊗ Sept.–May, weekdays and Sun. noon–3). Try roasted monkfish or house-made duck sausage and a caramel nut tart with passion-fruit sauce, for example. ⊠ *U of T, 7 Hart House Circle, Queen's Park* ☎ *416/978–2452* ⊕ *www.utoronto.ca/harthouse.*

☉ **Lillian H. Smith Branch of the Toronto Public Library.** Honoring the memory of the city's first children's librarian, this branch maintains nearly 60,000 items in three children's collections, ranging from the 14th century to the present. In addition, the Merril Collection of Science Fiction, Speculation and Fantasy includes about 50,000 items, on everything from parapsychology to UFOs. The Electronic Resource Centre has public terminals for online access. ⊠ *239 College St., between Spadina Ave. and St. George St., Downtown* ☎ *416/393–7746* ⊕ *www.tpl.toronto.on.*

ca 🖘 *Free* ☉ *Library Mon.–Thurs. 10–8:30, Fri. 10–6, Sat. 9–5; children's and Merril collections Sun.–Fri. 10–6, Sat. 9–5.*

> **off the beaten path**

LITTLE ITALY – Once a quiet strip of College Street with just a few unfrequented clothing shops and the odd obstinate pizzeria, Little Italy (College Street, west of Bathurst Street between Euclid Avenue and Shaw Street) has since become the hippest place in Toronto. New, ethnic restaurants open weekly, bars and coffeehouses are packed into the night, and every corner holds fashionable cafés and diners to match. This is the southern edge of the city's Italian community, and though not much remains of this heritage—most Italians have moved to North York—the flavor lingers on some menus and at a few food markets.

㊶ Ontario Legislative Building. Like City Hall, the home to the provincial parliament was the product of an international contest among architects, in this case won by a young Briton residing in Buffalo, New York. The 1893 Romanesque Revival building, made of pink Ontario sandstone, has a wealth of exterior detail; inside, the huge, lovely halls echo half a millennium of English architecture. The long hallways are hung with hundreds of oils by Canadian artists, most of which capture scenes of the province's natural beauty. Take one of the frequent (on the hour from mid-May to early September, less often the rest of the year) tours to see the chamber where the 130 MPPs (Members of Provincial Parliament) meet. The two heritage rooms—one each for the parliamentary histories of Britain and Ontario—are filled with old newspapers, periodicals, and pictures. The many statues that dot the lawn in front of the building, facing College Street, include one of Queen Victoria and one of Canada's first prime minister, Sir John A. Macdonald. The lawn is also the site of Canada Day celebrations and the occasional political protest. These buildings are often referred to simply as Queen's Park, after the park surrounding them, or as the parliament buildings. ⊠ *1 Queen's Park, Queen's Park* ☎ *416/325–7500* 🖘 *Free* ☉ *Guided tour mid-May–early-Sept., daily 10–4, weekends 9–4; early-Sept.–mid-May, weekdays 10–4.*

▶ **㊴ Queen's Park.** Many visitors consider this to be the heart of Toronto. Surrounding the large oval-shape patch of land are medical facilities to the south, the University of Toronto to the west and east, and the Royal Ontario Museum to the north. To most locals, Queen's Park is chiefly synonymous with politics, as the Ontario Legislative Building sits in the middle of this charming urban oasis. ⊠ *Queen's Park Circle between College St. and Bloor St. W, Queen's Park.*

> **off the beaten path**

ROSEDALE – The posh residential neighborhood northeast of Queen's Park has the charm of curving roads (it's one of the few neighborhoods to have escaped the city's grid pattern), many small parks and large trees, and a jumble of oversize late-19th-century and early-20th-century houses in Edwardian, Victorian, Georgian, and Tudor styles. In the 1920s, Sheriff William Jarvis and his wife, Mary, settled here on a 200-acre estate in what was then the country. She named her home Rosedale for the wildflowers that bloomed in profusion. Most of the roses are gone now, as are the magnificent trees for which Elm Avenue was named. Though some of the fine old houses have been carved up into small apartments, the neighborhood is still the home of old and new wealth and many who wield power. ⊠ *Bounded by Yonge St., the Don Valley Pkwy., St. Clair Ave., and the Rosedale Ravine.*

★ ☾ ㊺ **Royal Ontario Museum.** Since its inception in 1912, the ROM, Canada's largest museum, has amassed more than 6 million items. What makes the ROM unique is that science, art, and archaeology exhibits are all appealingly presented under one roof. A C$200-million refurbishment project (called Renaissance ROM) is currently underway and is expected to continue until late 2006. The museum's 230,000 square feet of public space will gain 40,000 square feet. Architect Daniel Libeskind (the designer of the Jewish Museum in Berlin) has designed a new building for several new galleries on and around the existing buildings—an ultramodern edifice termed "The Crystal," with slanting walls and metal cladding. A highlight of Renaissance ROM will be the Learning Centre—a state-of-the-art educational facility for the 220,000 schoolchildren expected annually. Permanent exhibits will be closed depending on the area of construction; the museum's Web site lists current closings.

Two of the ROM's most popular exhibits are the **Evolution Gallery,** with its ongoing audiovisual program on Darwin's theories of evolution, and the **Dinosaur Collection.** The **Herman Herzog Levy Gallery** exhibits a stunning range of large and colorful textiles, paintings, and prints from the museum's acclaimed Asian collection; the **Asian Sculpture Gallery** displays 25 stone Buddhist sculptures dating from the 2nd through 16th centuries; and the **Gallery of Korean Art** is North America's largest permanent gallery devoted to Korean art and culture. Admission is free on Friday. ⊠ *100 Queen's Park, Queen's Park* ☏ *416/586–5549* ⊕ *www.rom. on.ca* ⊡ *C$15* ⊙ *Mon.–Thurs., Sat., and Sun. 10–6, Fri. 10–9:30.*

㊹ **Thomas Fisher Rare Book Library.** Early writing artifacts such as a Babylonian cuneiform tablet, a 2,000-year-old Egyptian papyrus, and books dating to the beginning of European printing in the 15th century are shown here in rotating exhibits, which change three times annually. Subjects of these shows might include Shakespeare, Galileo, Italian opera, or contemporary typesetting. ⊠ *U of T, 120 St. George St., Queen's Park* ☏ *416/978–5285* 🖨 *416/978–1667* ⊕ *www.library.utoronto.ca/fisher* ⊡ *Free* ⊙ *Weekdays 9–4:45.*

☾ ㊵ **Toronto Police Museum and Discovery Centre.** Highlights are a replica of a 19th-century police station, an array of firearms, and exhibits about infamous crimes. Interactive displays include law-and-order quizzes and the opportunity to study your own fingerprints. Kids can have fun with the 1914 paddy wagon, car-crash videos, and, especially, a Harley Davidson they can jump on. They can also enjoy climbing in and out of a car sliced in half and hearing a dispatcher squawk at them. Tours are self-guided only. ⊠ *40 College St., Queen's Park* ☏ *416/808–7020* ⊕ *www. torontopolice.on.ca/museum* ⊡ *Donations accepted* ⊙ *Weekdays 10–4:30.*

Toronto Reference Library. Designed by one of Canada's most admired architects, Raymond Moriyama, who also created the Ontario Science Centre, this library is arranged around a large atrium, affording a wonderful sense of open space. Among the highlights is a fabric sculpture, Lyra, designed by artist Aiko Suzuki; it hangs over the pool and waterfall in the foyer. Glass-enclosed elevators glide swiftly and silently up and down one side of the atrium, allowing you to admire the banners that hang from the ceiling, announcing the collections on each floor. One-third of the more than 4 million items—spread across 45 km (28 mi) of shelves—are open to the public. Audio carrels are available for listening to your choice among the nearly 30,000 music and spoken-word recordings. Open Saturday 2–4 and by appointment, the **Arthur Conan Doyle Room** is of special interest to Baker Street regulars. It houses the world's finest public collection of Holmesiana, including records, films, photos, books, manuscripts, letters, and even cartoon books starring Sherlock Hemlock of *Sesame Street.* ⊠ *789 Yonge St., Yorkville* ☎ *416/395–5577* ⊕ *www. tpl.toronto.on.ca* ☉ *Mon.–Thurs. 10–8, Fri. and Sat. 10–5, Sun. 1:30–5.*

㊷ **University of Toronto.** Almost a city unto itself, U of T has a staff and student population of more than 50,000. The institution dates to 1827, when King George IV signed a charter for a "King's College in the Town of York, Capital of Upper Canada." The Church of England had control then, but by 1850 the college was proclaimed nondenominational, renamed the University of Toronto, and put under the control of the province. Then, in a spirit of Christian competition, the Anglicans started Trinity College, the Methodists began Victoria, and the Roman Catholics begat St. Michael's; by the time the Presbyterians founded Knox College, the whole thing was almost out of hand. Now the 10 schools and faculties are united and they welcome anyone who can meet the admission standards and afford the tuition, which, thanks to government funding, is reasonable. The architecture is interesting, if uneven, as one might expect at a campus that's been built in bits and pieces over 150 years. Walking tours leave from the Nona Macdonald Visitors Centre. June through August there are historical campus walks in addition to general, daily tours. ⊠ *Visitor center, 25 King's College Circle, Queen's Park* ☎ *416/978–5000* ⊕ *www.utoronto.ca* ☒ *Tours free* ☉ *Tours weekdays at 11 and 2, weekends at 11.*

㊼ **Yorkville.** Toronto's Rodeo Drive or Madison Avenue is packed with restaurants, galleries, specialty shops, and high-price stores specializing in designer clothes, furs, and jewels. It's also the neighborhood where much of the excitement takes place in September during the annual Toronto International Film Festival. This is said by many to be the world's most people-friendly film festival, where the public actually gets to see premieres and hidden gems and attend industry seminars. Klieg lights shine over skyscrapers, bistros serve alcohol until 4 AM, cafés teem with the well-heeled, and everyone practices their air kisses. ⊠ *Bordered by Avenue Rd., Yonge and Bloor Sts., and Yorkville Ave., Yorkville.*

need a break? In the heart of the city's gay and lesbian neighborhood, **Zelda's** (⊠ 542 Church St., Church and Wellesley ☎ 416/922–2526) is a popular bar and restaurant frequented by twentysomethings and baby boomers of every sexual orientation. The outdoor patio provides must-see people-watching from late spring to late fall.

Cabbagetown

The area that the late Cabbagetown-born-and-bred novelist and short-story writer Hugh Garner described in his 1950 novel *Cabbagetown* as "the world's largest Anglo-Saxon slum" has turned into one of downtown's most popular neighborhoods. Mockingly named by outsiders for the cabbages that grew on tiny lawns and were cooked in nearly every house, the moniker is used with a combination of inverse pride and almost wistful irony today. Beginning in the 1970s, rehabbers turned houses that sold in the C$25,000 range into ones that now fetch C$500,000 and more—part of the insistent gentrification of Toronto's downtown. Although there are few tourist attractions per se here, it's fun to stroll around and enjoy the architectural diversity of this funky residential area. The enclave extends roughly from Parliament Street on the west—about 1½ km (1 mi) due east of Yonge Street—to the Don River on the east, and from Bloor Street on the north to Queen Street East on the south.

Numbers in the text and in the margin correspond to points of interest on the Cabbagetown map.

a good walk

Start at the beginning of **Spruce Street** 🟢 ⚑ and walk east to **Spruce Court** 🟢, one of the city's earliest low-income housing projects and now a residential cooperative. Around the corner to the right, on **Sumach Street** 🟢, is the building that once housed the Ontario Women's Medical College. Now turn around and walk north past the attractive terrace full of homes built as workers' cottages. Turn left on **Carlton Street** 🟢, where you can see some of the area's largest homes. Continue west to **Metcalfe Street** 🟢, which, thanks to all its trees, fences, and unbroken rows of terraces, is one of the most beautiful streets in Toronto. Look down on the sidewalk on the east side nearest Carlton Street to see a utility-hole cover from the Victorian era, bearing the date 1889, before proceeding north.

Turn left now and head west along **Winchester Street** 🟢 and the Hotel Winchester, erected in 1881. To the south on **Parliament Street** 🟢 is an imposing row of large Victorian houses; most of the buildings on the west side date from the 1890s, though the storefronts of the commercial area are from the 20th century. Walk north on Parliament to the beautiful St. James Cemetery. From the cemetery, turn left (east) along **Wellesley Street East** 🟢, which comes to an end at Wellesley Park. Framing the park are parts of the Don Valley, the Necropolis Cemetery, and a row of houses to the south. Proceed south through Wellesley Park, and turn right along Amelia Street to Sumach Street. Head south again, past Winchester Street, and make a left (east) into Riverdale Park, which once hosted the city's main zoo and is now home to **Riverdale Farm** 🟢, a living-history farm museum.

TIMING The Cabbagetown walk covers 3 km–5 km (2 mi–3 mi) and should take an hour or two at a leisurely pace. Because the main reason to explore the neighborhood is its architecture, a clear day in any season is the best time to visit.

What to See

53 **Carlton Street.** Some of Cabbagetown's largest homes, dating from the late 19th century, are on this street. **No. 288** is a Second Empire house built in 1882 of solid brick with white stone trim. **No. 286,** next door, was built in 1883 and has the familiar steep gable and bargeboard trim. Check out the wrought-iron cresting over the round bow window. **No. 295,** an earlier house of Victorian-Gothic design, was originally the home of an executive of Toronto's first telephone company—this wondrous machine was envisioned by Alexander Graham Bell in Brantford, Ontario, just an hour west of Toronto—and had one of the first telephones in the city.

54 **Metcalfe Street.** The rows of trees, fences, and terraces along this street make it one of Toronto's most beautiful. Superimposed on the side of the simple but picturesque Victorian **No. 37** are 1891 and 1912 additions in beaux-arts classical forms. The Romanesque **St. Enoch's Presbyterian Church,** at the northeast corner of Metcalfe and Winchester streets, was erected in 1891.

56 **Parliament Street.** This busy commercial and residential Cabbagetown street is particularly noteworthy for its late-19th-century houses. **Nos. 502–508,** erected in 1879, are among the largest and most elaborately decorated Second Empire structures still standing in Toronto. The apartment towers of **St. James Town,** built in the 1960s, have been reviled ever since because they wiped out many attractive older homes.

Laid out in the 1840s, **St. James Cemetery,** at the northeast corner of Parliament and Wellesley Streets, contains the graves of many of Toronto's prominent citizens from the days when the place was still called York, as well as some of the more interesting burial monuments in Toronto. While you are at the St. James Cemetery, observe the small yellow-brick Gothic **Chapel of St. James-the-Less,** built in 1858 and considered one of the most beautiful church buildings in the country.

⑧ 58 Riverdale Farm. Not only is this museum one of Toronto's most delightful attractions and a special treat for children, but it's also free. The most interesting structure is the original Pennsylvania German–style barn, built in 1858 and moved to the farm in 1975 from suburban Markham, 23 mi north of the city. Inside are various implements, such as a light sleigh from the early 20th century and an exact replica of the type of Conestoga wagon used by German-speaking immigrants early in the 19th century. Demonstrations of crafts such as quilting and spinning are offered daily. Riverdale Farm's permanent residents include Clydesdale horses, cows, sheep, goats, pigs, donkeys, ducks, geese, chickens, and a small assortment of domestic animals. The farm also has a 59-herb garden and a garden of corn and grains. Bring along bathing suits for very young children—the lovely park adjacent to the farm has a wading pool. ✉ *Riverdale Park, 201 Winchester St., Cabbagetown* ☎ *416/ 392–6794* ⊕ *www.riverdaletoronto.com/riverdale_farm/* ✆ *Free* ⊙ *May–Oct., daily 9–6; Nov.–Apr., daily 9–4.*

51 Spruce Court. Now a residential cooperative, at Spruce and Sumach streets, it was originally constructed between 1913 and 1926 for the Toronto Housing Company as one of the city's earliest and most attractive low-income housing projects. The individual units not only provided modern conveniences and street access but also opened onto a grassy courtyard.

50 Spruce Street. This street in the heart of Cabbagetown is of architectural note. The little brick cottage set far back from the road at **No. 35** was built in 1860–61 and was once home to the dean of Trinity College Medical School. The fence also dates from the 19th century. **No. 41** was built in 1871 and served until 1903 as a medical school; it has now been recycled as part of a residential development. Its history is outlined on the Toronto Historical Board plaque on its front lawn. **Nos. 119–133** on Spruce Street are characteristic of Toronto's residential architecture between 1875 and 1890. These workers' cottages were erected in 1887 in Second Empire style, typified by high mansard roofs punctuated by dormers with marvelous details such as carved wooden brackets and metal decorative devices.

52 Sumach Street. Of particular historical importance on this Cabbagetown street is **No. 289.** Now a private residence, this building was once the Ontario Women's Medical College, built in 1889 and a forerunner of Women's College Hospital. Canada's less-than-enlightened attitudes toward women barred them from medical schools and city hospitals. The attractiveness of this brick-and-stone structure demonstrates the suc-

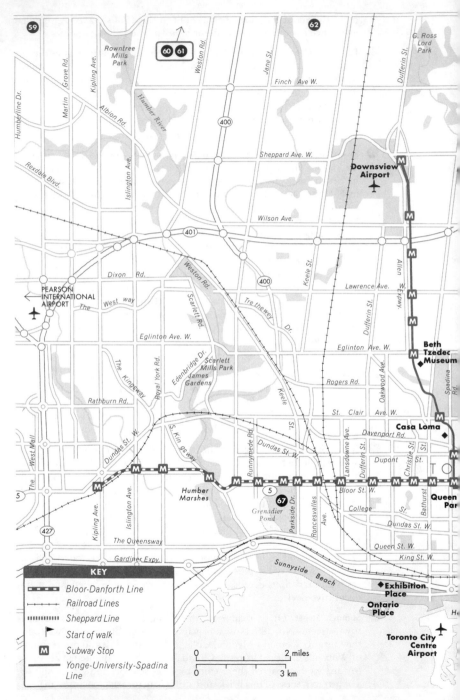

59

60 61

62

G. Ross
Lord
Park

Rowntree
Mills
Park

Weston Rd.

Jane St.

Finch Ave W.

Dufferin St.

Humberline Dr.

Martin Grove Rd.

Kipling Ave.

Albion Rd.

Humber River

400

Sheppard Ave. W.

Downsview
Airport ✈

M

Rexdale Blvd.

Wilson Ave.

401

M

M

Dixon Rd.

Weston Rd.

400

Keele St.

Lawrence Ave.

Allen Expwy.

M

PEARSON
INTERNATIONAL
AIRPORT ✈

The West way

Scarlett Rd.

Trethewey Dr.

Dufferin St.

M

Eglinton Ave. W.

Eglinton Ave. W.

M

Beth
Tzedec
Museum ◆

The Kingsway

Royal York Rd.

Edenbridge Dr.

Scarlett
Mills Park
James
Gardens

Keele

Rogers Rd.

Oakwood Ave.

Spadina Rd.

Rathburn Rd.

S. Kingsway

St. Clair Ave. W.

M

Casa Loma ◆

West Mall

Dundas St. W.

Davenport Rd.

Lansdowne Ave.

Dufferin St.

Dupont

Christie St.

St.

T

M M

M

Humber
Marshes

Dundas St. W.

5

67

M M M Runnymede Rd. M M M M M M M M M M M M

Bloor St. W.

Bathurst

Queen
Par

5

Islington Ave.

Grenadier
Pond

Parkside Dr.

Roncesvalles Ave.

College

St.

427

The Queensway

Dundas St. W.

Kipling Ave.

Gardiner Expy.

Queen St. W.

King St. W.

Sunnyside Beach

◆ Exhibition
Place

Ontario
Place

H

Toronto City
Centre ✈
Airport

KEY

▪▪▪▪ Bloor-Danforth Line

+‒+‒+ Railroad Lines

▪▪▪▪▪▪ Sheppard Line

⌐ Start of walk

Ⓜ Subway Stop

Yonge-University-Spadina
Line

0 _____ 2 miles

0 _____ 3 km

cess with which Victorian architects and builders managed to integrate institutions into mostly residential streetscapes.

57 **Wellesley Street East.** A variety of architectural styles decorate the Cabbagetown section of this street. **No. 314,** built in 1889–90, has stonework around the windows and carved stone faces above the door and in the keystones.

From 1848 to 1888 **Wellesley Park,** at the far east end of Wellesley Street East, was the site of the area's major industry—the P. R. Lamb Glue and Blacking Factory. Today it's a small, pleasant neighborhood park and playground, surrounded by the Don Valley, the Necropolis Cemetery, and a row of houses to the south.

55 **Winchester Street.** As you stroll along this Cabbagetown street, keep an eye out for the repeated sunburst patterns of carved wood in many of the gables and the large amount of stained glass, much of it original and some of it reinstalled by lovers of Victoriana. The **Hotel Winchester,** a venerable but sadly decaying building at the southeast corner of Winchester and Parliament, is one of the neighborhood's most prominent structures. It opened in 1888 as the Lake View Hotel, so named because from its roof one could see all the way south to the blue waters of Lake Ontario.

Necropolis Cemetery is the resting place of many of Toronto's pioneers. Among the most famous (and notorious) are Toronto's first mayor, William Lyon Mackenzie, who led a revolt against the city in 1837; Samuel Lount and Peter Matthews, two of Mackenzie's followers, who were hanged for their part in that rebellion; and George Brown, founder of the *Globe* newspaper and one of the fathers of Canada's Confederation. The beautiful chapel, gate, and gatehouse of the nonsectarian burial ground, erected in 1872, constitute one of the most picturesque groupings of small Victorian buildings in Toronto. The Necropolis is also known for its great variety of trees, flowering shrubs, and rare and exotic plants. ⊠ *200 Winchester St., at Sumach St., Cabbagetown* ☎ *416/923–7911* ☉ *Mid-May–mid-Sept., daily 8–8; mid-Sept.–mid-May, daily 8–5:30.*

Greater Toronto

Explore beyond the downtown areas to find the ethnic enclaves, parks, museums, and attractions that make Toronto interesting. High Park is the city's main green space and has Shakespeare productions in summer. Edwards Gardens, in North York, is the city's botanical gardens. The McMichael Canadian Art Collection, north of the city, is an exceptional gallery not to be missed for its Group of Seven pieces. Black Creek Pioneer Village, a living-history museum, and Paramount Canada's Wonderland, an enormous theme park, are extremely kid-friendly. A short drive may provide a needed urban escape for you, as it does for many Torontonians.

Numbers in the margin correspond to points of interest on the Greater Toronto map.

TIMING Plan to explore each Greater Toronto sight independently or to combine a couple of sights in one trip. You can reach High Park via public transportation, but a car is necessary for visiting the Kortright Centre and Black Creek Pioneer Village, and is helpful for getting to other sights. A special GO Transit bus serves Paramount Canada's Wonderland in summer.

What to See

⟳ 🆂 **Black Creek Pioneer Village.** Less than a half-hour drive from downtown is a rural, mid-19th-century living-history-museum village that makes you feel as though you've gone through a time warp. Black Creek Pioneer Village is a collection of more than three dozen 19th- and early-20th-century buildings that have been moved to their current site—a town hall, a weaver's shop, a printing shop, a blacksmith's shop, and a school complete with dunce cap. The mill dates from the 1840s and has a 4-ton wooden waterwheel that grinds up to a hundred barrels of flour a day (bags are available for purchase).

As men and women in period costumes go about the daily routine of mid-19th-century Ontario life, they explain what they're doing and how they do it, and answer questions. Free wagon rides, farm animals, and a decent restaurant contribute to a satisfying outing. In winter, you can also skate, toboggan, or hop on a sleigh ride. ✉ *1000 Murray Ross Pkwy., corner of Jane St. and Steeles Ave., North York* ☎ *416/736–1733* ⊕ *www.blackcreek.ca* ⊠ *C$11, parking C$6* ⊙ *May–June, weekdays 9:30–4, weekends 11–5; July–Aug., weekdays 10–5, weekends 11–5; Oct.–Apr., weekdays 9:30–4, weekends 11–4:30.*

🆖 **The Danforth.** This area along Danforth Avenue has a dynamic ethnic mix, although it's primarily a Greek community. Once English-settled (although it was named after Asa Danforth, an American contractor who cut a road into the area in 1799), the neighborhood is now Italian, Greek, East Indian, Latin American, and, increasingly, Chinese. But a large percentage of the 120,000 Greek Canadians in metropolitan Toronto live here, and the area is still referred to as "Greektown." Late-night taverns, all-night fruit markets, and some of the best ethnic restaurants in Toronto abound. ✉ *Bounded by the Don Valley Pkwy. to the west and Warden Ave. to the east The Danforth.*

★ ⟳ 🆄 **Edwards Gardens.** The beautiful 35-acre gardens (once owned by industrialist Rupert Edwards) flow into one of the city's most visited ravines. Paths wind along colorful floral displays and exquisite rock gardens. Refreshments and picnic facilities are available, but no pets are allowed. There's also a signposted "teaching garden." For a great ravine walk, start at the gardens' entrance and head south through Wilket Creek Park and the winding Don River Valley. Pass beneath the Don Valley Parkway and continue along Massey Creek. After hours of walking (or biking, or jogging) through almost uninterrupted park, you reach the southern tip of Taylor Creek Park on Victoria Park Avenue, just north of The Danforth. From here you can catch a subway back to your hotel. ✉ *Entrance at southwest corner of Leslie St. and Lawrence Ave. E, North York* ⊙ *Daily dawn–dusk.*

★ ⏾ **⑰** **High Park.** One of North America's loveliest parks, High Park (at one time the privately owned countryside "farm" of John George Howard, Toronto's first city architect) is especially worth visiting in summer, when the many special events include professionally staged Shakespeare productions. Hundreds of Torontonians and guests arrive at dinnertime and picnic on blankets before the show. Admission is by donation.

The small **Grenadier Pond** in the southwest corner of High Park is named after the British soldiers who, it is said, crashed through the soft ice while rushing to defend the town against invading American forces in 1813. The pond is home to thousands of migrating birds. You can fish in its well-stocked waters, either from the shore or from a rented rowboat. There are Sunday-afternoon concerts in summer and supervised skating in winter.

At the South end of High Park, near Colborne Lodge, is the **High Park Zoo** (☎ 416/392–8186 ⊙ Daily dawn–dusk). It's more modest than the Toronto Zoo, but it's a lot closer to downtown and it's free. Even young children won't tire walking among the deer, Barbary sheep, peacocks, rabbits, and buffalo.

Colborne Lodge (☎ 416/392–6916 ▣ C$3.50 ⊙ Jan.–Mar., weekends noon–4; Apr.–Dec., weekdays 9:30–4, weekends noon–5) was built more than 150 years ago by John George Howard on a hill overlooking Lake Ontario. This Regency-style "cottage" contains its original fireplace, bake oven, and kitchen, as well as many of Howard's own drawings and paintings. From High Park subway station, enter the park and follow signs for the lodge.

Other highlights of the 398-acre park are a large swimming pool, tennis courts, fitness trails, and hillside gardens with roses and sculpted hedges. To get here, take the TTC to the High Park station and walk south; you can also take the College Street streetcar to the eastern end of the park and walk west. There's limited parking along Bloor Street north of the park, and along the side streets on the eastern side. ⊠ *Bordered by Bloor St. W, the Gardiner Expressway, Parkside Dr., and Ellis Park Rd. Main entrance off Bloor St. W at High Park Ave., Southwest Toronto* ☎ *416/392–1111, 416/392–1748 walking tours.*

Kortright Centre for Conservation. Only 15 minutes north of the city, this delightful conservation center has three aquariums and more than 16 km (10 mi) of hiking trails through forest, meadow, river, and marshland. In winter, some of the trails are reserved for cross-country skiing (bring your own skis or snowshoes and dress warmly). In the magnificent woods, there have been sightings of foxes, coyotes, rabbits, deer, wild turkeys, pheasants, chickadees, finches, and blue jays. Seasonal events include a winter carnival, a spring maple-syrup festival, and a Christmas crafts fair. To get here, drive 3 km (2 mi) north along Highway 400, exit west at Major Mackenzie Drive, and continue south 1 km (½ mi) on Pine Valley Drive to the gate. ⊠ *9550 Pine Valley Dr., Woodbridge* ☎ *905/832–2289* ⊕ *www.kortright.org* ▣ *C$5* ⊙ *Daily 10–4.*

★ **⑥** **McMichael Canadian Art Collection.** On 100 acres of lovely woodland in Kleinburg, 30 km (19 mi) northwest of downtown, the McMichael is the only major gallery in the country with the mandate to collect Canadian art exclusively. The museum holds impressive works by Tom Thomson, Emily Carr, and the Group of Seven landscape painters, as well as their early-20th-century contemporaries. These artists were inspired by the wilderness and sought to capture it in bold, original styles. First Nations art and prints, drawings, and sculpture by Inuit artists are well represented. Strategically placed windows help you appreciate the scenery as you view art that took its inspiration from the vast outdoors. Inside, wood walls and a fireplace set a country mood. ⊠ *10365 Islington Ave., west of Hwy. 400 and north of Major Mackenzie Dr., Kleinburg* ☎ *888/ 213–1121* ⊕ *www.mcmichael.on.ca* ☜ *C$15, parking C$5* ⊙ *May–Oct., daily 10–5; Nov.–Apr., daily 10–4.*

★ ☾ ❻ **Ontario Science Centre.** It has been called a museum of the 21st century, but it's much more than that. Where else can you stand at the edge of a black hole, work hand-in-clamp with a robot, or land on the moon? Even the building itself is extraordinary: three linked pavilions float gracefully down the side of a ravine and overflow with exhibits that make space, technology, and communications fascinating. A dozen theaters show films that bring the natural world to life. Demonstrations of glassblowing, papermaking, lasers, electricity, and more take place regularly throughout the day; check the schedule when you arrive. The museum has a cafeteria, a restaurant, and a gift store with a cornucopia of books and scientific doodads. Take Yonge Street subway from downtown to Eglinton station, and No. 34 Eglinton East bus to Don Mills Road stop, then walk ½ block south. ⊠ *770 Don Mills Rd., at Eglinton Ave., North York* ☎ *416/696–1000* ⊕ *www.osc.on.ca* ☜ *C$14, parking C$8* ⊙ *Early Sept.–late May, daily 10–5; late May–early Sept., 10–6.*

☾ ❻ **Paramount Canada's Wonderland.** Yogi Bear, Fred Flintstone, and Scooby Doo are part of Canada's first theme park, filled with more than 200 games, rides, restaurants, and shops. Favorite attractions include Kidzville, home of the Rugrats, and the Top Gun looping inverted jet coaster. In Nickelodeon Central, three rides star Nickelodeon characters Jimmy Neutron, Dora the Explorer, and Arnold from *Hey Arnold!* The Whitewater Bay wave pool, the Black Hole water slide, and a children's interactive water play area are all a part of Splash Works, the 20-acre on-site water park. Look for the strolling Star Trek characters, the Paramount Studio Store, miniature golf, and batting cages as well.

Entertainment includes concerts, musicals, sea-lion shows, and cliff divers. The high-quality **Kingswood Music Theatre** stages excellent pop and rock acts and has many ethnic music festivals and concerts throughout the summer. There are 7,000 reserved seats under a covered pavilion and 8,800 additional seats on the sloping lawn.

Check newspapers, chain stores, and hotels for discount tickets and coupons. The park is close to Toronto—it's barely 30 minutes north of downtown by car or via the "Wonderland Express" GO Bus from the Yorkdale and York Mills subway stations. ⊠ *9580 Jane St., Vaughan* ☎ *905/832–7000, 905/832–8131 Kinswood Theatre tickets* ⊕ *www. canadas-wonderland.com* ☜ *Rides passport C$50, grounds C$30* ⊙ *June–early Sept., daily 10–10; early Sept.–mid-Oct., weekends 10–dusk.*

★ ☾ ⑥③ **Toronto Zoo.** With its varied terrain, from river valley to dense forest, the Rouge Valley was an inspired choice of site for this 710-acre zoo in which mammals, birds, reptiles, and fish are grouped according to their natural habitats. Enclosed, climate-controlled pavilions have botanical exhibits, such as the Africa pavilion's giant baobab tree. A daily program of activities might include chats with animal keepers, and animal and bird demonstrations. Look over an Events Guide, distributed at the main entrance, to help plan your day. An "Around the World Tour" takes approximately three hours and includes the Africa, Americas, Australasia, and Indo-Malayan pavilions. From June through early September, the Zoomobile can take you through the outdoor exhibit area.

The African Savanna is the country's finest walking safari, a dynamic reproduction that brings rare and beautiful animals and distinctive geological landscapes to the city's doorstep. You can also dine in the Savanna's Safari Lodge and camp overnight in the Bush Camp (reservations required). Coming with kids? You may want to visit the Children's Web (open June through August) for its backyard bug, butterfly, and pond displays; playground; and pony rides. In the Marco Polo area, you can take a camel ride (May through September, daily; October through May, weekends only). Rides cost extra. Parking is free from November through April. It's a 30-minute drive east from downtown, or take Bus 86A from Kennedy subway station. ✉ *Meadowvale Rd. (Exit 396 off Hwy. 401), Scarborough* ☎ *416/392–5900, 416/392–9106 or 416/392–5947 for camping reservations* ⊕ *www.torontozoo.com* ✉ *C$18, parking C$8* ☾ *Mid-Mar.–late May and early Sept.–mid-Oct., daily 9–6; late May–early Sept., daily 9–7:30; Oct.–mid-Mar., daily 9–4:30.*

☾ ⑤⑨ **Wild Water Kingdom.** The largest park of its kind in Canada, Wild Water Kingdom has huge water slides, river rapids, giant outdoor hot tubs, a fantastic wave pool, and a delightful area for younger children to splash around in. The most popular slides are the Midnight Express and the Night Rider, which send riders into darkness and out again. The Caribbean Cove swimming pool is enjoyed by adults who love being able to purchase tropical cocktails at the bar. ✉ *7855 Finch Ave. W., off Hwy. 427, Brampton* ☎ *905/794–0565 or 866/794–9453* ⊕ *www.wildwaterkingdom. com* ✉ *C$25.50, parking C$6* ☾ *Early June–late June, daily 10–6; late June–late Aug., daily 10–8; late Aug.–early Sept., daily 10–6.*

WHERE TO EAT

By Sara
Waxman

IMMIGRATION FLOURISHES IN TORONTO, and no matter if you've come from a far-flung corner of the world, you can often find home cooking here. Multi-ethnic Little Italy (which has as many French and Chinese restaurants as Italian), a half dozen Chinatowns (urban and suburban), the Greek area of The Danforth, and Little India are just some of the neighborhoods full of restaurants. Southeast Asian cooking—Korean, Vietnamese, Laotian, Thai, and Malaysian—is taking local taste buds by storm with flavors like chili, ginger, lemongrass, coconut, lime, and tamarind. The abundant fresh produce of the province, once exclusively filtered through French, British, and Italian cooking techniques, now benefits from the sweet and pungent flavors of the Middle East and the soulful dishes of Latin America as well. In one short block of Baldwin Street at Kensington Market, there are 23 eateries—you might call it the United Nations of gastronomy.

The Toronto restaurant scene is in a state of perpetual motion. New restaurants open at a vigorous rate to meet the demands of a savvy dining public. Even formal haute cuisine establishments, which had all but faded into Toronto's gastronomic history, are experiencing a renaissance, joining the ever-swelling ranks of bistros, trattorias, tapas bars, noodle bars, wine bars, and smart cafés. Red meat has made a comeback, but along with steak houses have come more vegetarian-friendly restaurants. The dining-out scene is the most exciting in decades. In fact, a popular TV show, *Opening Soon*, visits new restaurants in the days and weeks before opening, finishing with their premieres.

Brilliant young chefs such as Susur Lee (Susur, Lee's) and Claudio Aprile (Senses) stay ahead of the public's evolving taste by drawing from a number of Asian cuisines and spiffing up classical French and Continental preparations. Rather than following tradition, today's young chefs are creating their own trends and their own signature dishes. And the public speaks out about the results, loudly: everyone who sits in a restaurant is a critic, and word of mouth has closed unsuccessful eateries faster than you can say "overcooked food and patronizing service." Successful chefs cook with the premise that every ingredient is in season—somewhere in the world—just hours away from landing in their sauté pans. Though utterly fresh fish and seafood were once difficult to come by, you can now feast on fish which were swimming in the Azores, Caribbean, or Arctic waters not long before.

Recommending restaurants in an up-and-coming foodie destination is a difficult task. There's not enough space to mention many worthy kitchens in the suburbs and outlying areas. Whatever restaurant you choose, it's hard to go wrong in a town where globalization has created a clientele with a sophisticated palate and a demand for high-quality international cuisines.

Old Toronto & The Financial District

American–Casual

$$$–$$$$ ✕ **Reds Bistro & Bar.** Pine beams, etched glass, hanging pots and pans, and cheery prints make this 300-seat bistro a breath of country air in a

KNOW-HOW

Dress Dress in Toronto restaurants is casual but neat. In the fashionable spots downtown, especially Yorkville, Queen Street, and Little Italy, diners always look pulled together in trendy and classic attire. In the more elegant and expensive restaurants, men are likely to feel more comfortable wearing a jacket. We mention dress only when men are required to wear a jacket or a jacket and tie.

Mealtimes Lunch typically starts at 11:30 or noon and dinner service begins around 5:30 or 6. Many restaurants close between lunch and dinner (roughly the hours of 2:30 to 5:30). On weekdays, kitchens usually close around 10:30 PM. Chinatown, Yorkville, Danforth, and the area around Queen's Park have a few late-night spots. There are few all-night restaurants in the city. Unless otherwise noted, the restaurants listed in this guide are open daily for lunch and dinner.

Reservations Reservations are always a good idea; we mention them only when they're essential or not accepted. Book as far ahead as you can. (Large parties should always call to check the reservations policy.)

Smoking Toronto restaurants prohibit smoking. Some let diners get away with smoking in outdoor dining areas.

WHAT IT COSTS In Canadian dollars				
	$$$$	**$$$**	**$$**	**$**	**¢**
AT DINNER	over C$30	C$20–C$30	C$12–C$20	C$8–C$12	under C$8

Prices are per person for a main course at dinner time.

neighborhood of office towers. And the reasonably priced but fancy-sounding dishes won't max out your credit card. Each day of the week brings a special, such as roast duck breast with black currant fig, or simply a 12-ounce sirloin. Desserts are big enough for sharing. The wine list, heavy on reds (hence the name of the place), is a great read. ⊠ 77 *Adelaide St. W, Financial District* ☎ 416/862–7337 ☰ AE, DC, MC, V ⊗ *Closed Sun. No lunch Sat.*

$–$$ ✕**Beer Bistro.** A renowned beer writer–taster and a creative chef have teamed up in a happy/hoppy partnership where beer is king. Each menu item uses beer as an ingredient: the chef pan-fries catfish and pairs it with black-eyed peas and orzo cooked with Pilsner; a chunky beef stew is slowly braised in La Maudite to melting tenderness. Start with a flight of beer in 3-ounce tasting glasses, to be drunk from mild to bold. The casual, comfortable, modern interior includes a huge angled mirror on the wall above the kitchen, which allows a peek into the heart of the restaurant. ⊠ 18 *King St. E, Financial District* ☎ 416/861–9872 ☰ AE, DC, MC, V ⊗ *Closed Sun.*

Where to Eat in Downtown Toronto

★ $–$$ ✕ **Marché.** Herbs grow in pots, fresh fruits and vegetables are piled high, an enormous snowbank holds bright-eyed fish and fresh seafood, and fresh pasta spews from pasta makers, ready to be cooked to order. This old-world market square in a downtown office tower is really a self-service restaurant. A rotisserie roasts lacquer-crisp game birds and European sausages. Bread and croissants are baked before your eyes, and pizza is prepared to order. This high-concept, low-price dining adventure is open daily 7:30 AM–2 AM. Smaller versions, called Marchelinos, are all over town. ✉ *BCE Place, 42 Yonge St., Financial District* ☎ *416/366–8986* ▭ *AE, DC, MC, V.*

Canadian

★ $$$–$$$$ ✕ **Canoe.** Look through huge windows on the 54th floor of the Toronto Dominion Bank Tower and enjoy the breathtaking view of the Toronto Islands and the lake while you dine. Classics include foie gras and truffles. Boutique game dishes are lighter treatments of local products. A seven-course tasting menu takes you from coast to coast. Desserts, such as fireweed honey-butter tart with roasted plum sauce and cream, are quite serious. ✉ *Toronto-Dominion Center, 66 Wellington St. W, 54th fl., Financial District* ☎ *416/364–0054* ⚓ *Reservations essential* ▭ *AE, DC, MC, V* ⊙ *Closed weekends.*

Contemporary

$$$$ ✕ **Bymark.** Wood, glass, and water create drama in a space anchored by a 5,000-bottle wine "cellar" inside a two-story glass column. The menu offers delectability and perfection: poached sea scallops with seared foie gras, crème fraîche, and sake beurre blanc; an 8-ounce grilled U.S. Prime grade beef burger with molten Brie de Meaux and grilled porcini. And there's service to match. The bar one floor up oozes extreme comfort and has a good view. In summer, sit on the patio overlooking architect Mies van der Rohe's TDC Plaza. ✉ *66 Wellington St. W, concourse level, Financial District* ☎ *416/777–1144* ⚓ *Reservations essential* ▭ *AE, DC, MC, V* ⊙ *Closed Sun.*

$$$–$$$$ ✕ **Rosewater Supper Club.** Thronelike blue velvet banquettes for two or four sit atop hardwood and marble floors in a historic building with 22-foot-high ceilings. Here beautifully prepared food is served to beautiful people. You might try prosciutto ham of Parma with sweet melon, or buffalo mozzarella and heirloom tomato terrine. You can trust the freshness of halibut, ginger-steamed with white-wine sauce. The menu changes with the market. Prime beefsteaks, served with vegetables and potatoes, come from Canada's cattle country. Not ready to commit to dinner? The bar is an after-five hot spot. ✉ *19 Toronto St., Old Toronto* ☎ *416/214–5888* ▭ *AE, DC, MC, V* ⊙ *Closed Sun. No lunch Sat.*

Delicatessen

$–$$ ✕ **Shopsy's.** In 1945, when the three Shopsowitz brothers came into the business started by their parents in 1921, you'd pay 8¢ for a corned-beef sandwich. Today Shopsy's belongs to a food conglomerate, and such a sandwich costs C$5.75. The corned beef, always freshly cooked and firm, is piled on fresh rye bread slathered with mustard; there's nothing like it. Soups are satisfying, salads are huge, and hot dogs are legendary. The deli often has a wait at peak hours. ✉ *33 Yonge St., Downtown*

☏ 416/365–3333 ✉ 1535 Yonge St., Midtown ☏ 416/967–5252 ⊟ AE, DC, MC, V.

Irish

$$ ✕ **PJ O'Brien.** A meal of Irish Kilkenny Ale-battered fish-and-chips, Irish stew, or corned beef and cabbage ends with bread pudding steeped in whiskey and custard, just like Gran made. Close your eyes and think of Dublin. The dining room has polished-wood floors, furniture, and moldings, a collection of antique musical instruments, a brigade of lively servers, and an engaging kitchen. Upstairs there's an even cozier bar than the one on the main floor. ✉ 39 Colborne St., Old Toronto ☏ 416/815–7562 ⊟ AE, DC, MC, V ☾ Closed Sun.

Italian

$$–$$$$ ✕ **Romagna Mia Osteria Pizzeria.** Traditional Emilia-Romagna regional cooking and congenial and casual service fly under the flag of the familiar and promising red-checkered tablecloth. Sautéed duck breast, atop crispy polenta with vegetables in a luscious San Giovese wine reduction, is special indeed—and so are the homemade pastas. For theatrics, order risotto; rice imported from Vercelli is finished table-side in a hollowed wheel of Parmigiano-Reggiano. It's authentic and wonderful. ✉ 106 Front St. E, Downtown ☏ 416/363–8370 ⊟ AE, DC, MC, V ☾ Closed Sun.

$–$$ ✕ **Masquerade Caffè Bar.** An eclectic array of primary-color furnishings, stoves, and Murano-glass mosaics fills this Fellini-esque environment. The daily-changing Italian menu lists a variety of risottos, divine ravioli, and a choice of *panini*—Italian sandwiches on homemade breads with scrumptious meat, cheese, and veggie fillings. Zabaglione, whipped to a thick, frothy cream and poured over fresh fruit, is a knockout dessert. ✉ BCE Place, Front and Yonge Sts., Financial District ☏ 416/363–8971 ⊟ AE, DC, MC, V.

Japanese

★ $$–$$$ ✕ **Nami.** In this large, attractive restaurant, you can eat at tables, the sushi bar, in a tatami room with nontraditional wells under the tables, or at the *robatta* (a cooking grill surrounded by an eating counter). You're likely to see a chef toss all manner of edibles on the grill: soft-shell crab, skewers of scallops and shrimp, and asparagus, which is raised to its highest potential when prepared this way. Dinner combos at a table or booth include soup, salad, tempura, chicken yakitori, or a beef or salmon teriyaki dish, rice, and dessert. ✉ 55 Adelaide St. E, Old Toronto ☏ 416/362–7373 ⊟ AE, DC, MC, V ☾ Closed Sun. No lunch Sat.

Seafood

★ $$$ ✕ **Starfish.** Patrick McMurray won the 48th World Oyster Opening Championship in Galway, Ireland, by cleanly shucking 30 oysters in 3 minutes, 47 seconds. In his smart, naturally comfortable restaurant, he is a walking encyclopedia of oyster lore. McMurray gives you a still-quivering pink scallop, an Emerald Cove, a Belon, or a Malpeque and informs you of the qualities of each. His oven-roasted black cod, East Coast lobsters, crisp salads, and homemade desserts will make you fall for Starfish hook, line, and sinker. ✉ 200 Adelaide St. E, Downtown ☏ 416/366–7827 ⌕ Reservations essential ⊟ AE, DC, MC, V ☾ Closed Sun. No lunch Sat.

Harbourfront

Steak

$$$-$$$$ ✕ **Harbour Sixty Steakhouse.** Walk up stone steps to the Corinthian columns and the grand neoclassical entrance of the restored Harbour Commission building. A baroque-inspired foyer leads to a gold-tone granite bar. Luxury indeed—when you are eating the finest basic foodstuffs, an opulent dining room is the only way to go. Beyond the bar is an open kitchen, with a cooler stocked with ruby-red tuna steaks, lobsters on ice, oysters, bright Atlantic salmon, and steaks. Slowly roasted prime rib is delicious. Fresh salmon and tuna are grilled to your taste. Sit in comfortable oversize armchairs or spacious curved and upholstered booths. ⊠ *60 Harbour St., Harbourfront* ☎ *416/777–2111* ⊟ *AE, DC, MC, V* ☾ *No lunch weekends.*

Along Dundas, Queen & King Streets

Chinese

★ **$$$-$$$$** ✕ **Lai Wah Heen.** The mahogany-color Peking duck is wheeled in on a trolley and presented with panache. Excellent choices from the 100-dish inventory include wok-fried shredded beef and vegetables in a crisp potato nest. At lunch, the dim sum is divine: translucent dumplings and pastries burst with juicy fillings of shark's fin sprinkled with bright red lobster roe, and shrimp dumplings with green tops look like baby bok choy. The service is formal, in an elegant room with a sculpted ceiling, etched-glass turntables, and silver serving dishes. ⊠ *Metropolitan Hotel, 118 Chestnut St., 2nd fl., Chinatown* ☎ *416/977–9899* ⌕ *Reservations essential* ⊟ *AE, DC, MC, V.*

$-$$$ ✕ **Wah Sing.** Just one of a jumble of Asian restaurants clustered on a tiny Kensington Market street, this meticulously clean and spacious restaurant has two-for-the-price-of-one lobsters (in season, which is almost always). They're scrumptious and tender, with black-bean sauce or ginger and green onion. You can also choose giant shrimps Szechuan-style or one of the lively queen crabs from the tank. Chicken and vegetarian dishes for landlubbers are good, too. ⊠ *47 Baldwin St., Kensington Market* ☎ *416/599–8822* ⊟ *MC, V.*

$-$$ ✕ **Spadina Garden.** The Chen family has owned Spadina Garden for more than a decade, and the restaurant's dishes are Toronto classics. This is largely the cuisine of inland northwest China, so there is no tank of finny creatures to peruse. Start with barbecued honey-garlic spareribs or spring rolls before moving on to serious entrées. Orange beef is a dark and deliciously saucy dish seasoned with dried orange peel and hot red peppers; sliced beef is served with black mushrooms and oyster sauce. The room itself is calm, with standard black lacquer, high-back chairs, and red-paper lanterns. ⊠ *114 Dundas St. W, Chinatown* ☎ *416/977–3413 or 416/977–3414* ⊟ *AE, MC, V.*

$-$$ ✕ **Tiger Lily's Noodle House.** Many come to the bright, hand-painted café for real egg rolls and shrimp-and-spinach pot stickers in a light lemony glaze. But the real attraction is the noodles, cooked in many ways and combinations; Hawaiian duck long-rice soup, redolent with coconut lemongrass, plump with chicken and seafood, is one option. Soups include noodles, wontons, meat or vegetable broth, and garnishes of barbecued pork, Shanghai chicken, or veggies. Black-bean beef is special. If you want your Chinese food steeped in tradition, not grease, you'll find double happiness here. ⊠ *257 Queen St. W, Queen West* ☎ *416/ 977–5499* ▤ *AE, MC, V.*

Contemporary

★ **\$\$\$\$** ✕ **Senses Bakery & Restaurant.** Chef Claudio Aprile's flavor matchings are flawless: foie gras is seared on a fine mesh grill and served with quince *tarte tatin* (upside-down tart), assorted berries, and caramelized orange peel. A simple item like roast lamb salad is partnered with cashews, smoked paprika oil, kumquat preserves, and baked green-tea noodles. Braised black beef ribs, slow cooked to melting, with black truffle gnocchi is the upscale rendition of meat and potatoes. Subdued shades of gray and beige velvets decorate the 36-seat dining room. Senses Café serves breakfast and light meals daily between noon and 8 PM (C\$8–C\$12). *SoHo Metropolitan Hotel* ⊠ *328 Wellington St. W, Entertainment District* ☎*416/935–0400* ▤*AE, DC, MC, V* ⊘ *Closed Mon. and Tues. No lunch.*

\$\$\$\$ ✕ **Susur.** The country's most renowned chef, Susur Lee, has a unique, eclectic Asian style. His reverse set menu begins with the principal course, with subsequent dishes diminishing in size and weight. Appetizers may include braised oxtail and tapioca ravioli; main-course choices might be venison with Italian lentils and currants or fresh fish with black-olive sauce and grapes. Subtle recessed lighting in the square, white room changes from shades of pink to blues and greens. Choose a white leather booth or dining table and prepare for a wait between courses—keeping in mind that the food is worth it. ⊠ *601 King St. W, Downtown* ☎ *416/603–2205* ⌂ *Reservations essential* ▤ *AE, MC, V* ⊘ *Closed Sun. No lunch.*

\$\$\$–\$\$\$\$ ✕ **Torch Restaurant.** Stained-glass windows, sumptuous booths, and private Victorian-style dinettes are reminiscent of an old San Francisco steak house. The rousing selection of appetizers and salads includes a caramelized onion-and-goat-cheese tart and renowned crab cakes. Main-course portions are generous. Fresh pickerel, what some call fisherman's steak, comes with sweet-corn succotash and tomato cucumber relish. Steak frites with spicy mayonnaise are among the city's best, though there are many fans of this kitchen's braised red cabbage, mashed potatoes with liver, and caramelized onions side dishes. Do leave room for extraordinary sticky-toffee pudding with vanilla ice cream. ⊠*253 Victoria St., Downtown* ☎ *416/364–7517* ▤ *AE, DC, MC, V* ⊘ *Closed Mon. No lunch.*

\$\$\$–\$\$\$\$ ✕ **Ultra Supper Club.** Walk through an unassuming entrance to an interior courtyard with a handsome garden. Past glass doors to the right is the dining room, left is the lounge, divided by shimmering fabrics hung from the ceiling. Start with a fricassee of wild mushrooms with fresh herbs and garlic in rich veal au jus, and go on to lobster and sweetbread ravioli, or grouper with sweet-tart carrot-and-coriander reduction. Servers attend to you caringly. At around 11, tables are removed and a sea of dancers who know the right moves fills the polished wood floor. ⊠ *314 Queen St. W, Queen West* ☎ *416/263–0330* ▤ *AE, DC, MC, V.*

\$\$\$–\$\$\$\$ ✕ **YYZ.** Beautiful people with disposable income vie with the decor for attention at this sleek, energy-charged spot. In summer, the patio is the place to be seen. On the seasonal menu, look for spicy hot and cold shrimp avocado with mango and cucumber salad, pan-seared Pacific halibut, and roasted veal tenderloin wrapped in prosciutto with sage gnocchi. Bar snacks excel; these include crunchy spiced pecans and black sesame crackers. You can order off the late menu until 12:30, making this a great post-theater stop. ⊠ *345 Adelaide St. W, Entertainment District* ☎ *416/ 599–3399* ⌾ *Reservations essential* 🖃 *AE, DC, MC* ⊘ *No lunch.*

$$$ ✗ **Crush Wine Bar.** They've sandblasted the natural-brick walls and polished the original wood floor in this old building, with great results, and an open kitchen lets you see the corps of chefs at work. The four-course prix fixe menu is a dreamscape of the chef's expertise and might include wild sockeye salmon, black bass with orange crust, oven-roasted squab, and passion fruit mousse in chocolate puff pastry. A sommelier does wine pairings by the glass with panache and recommends just the right tipple for duck ravioli with roasted garlic or bison rib eye with red-wine reduction. ⊠ *455 King St. W, Downtown* ☎ *416/977–1234* ⌾ *Reservations essential* 🖃 *AE, DC, MC, V* ⊘ *Closed Sun.*

$$ ✗ **Lee's.** When what you really want is a garlic Cornish game hen sandwich or a "festive dish"—made from 19 vegan, seafood, or meat ingredients—come to Lee's. Meals are created with a mix of Southeast Asian and Western styles and sensibilities, served on dishes handmade in mainland China and Hong Kong. No need to commit to a Susur-style dining event; this spot is perfect for a pre- or post-theater meal or an intriguing lunch, as well as a full-scale dinner. ⊠ *603 King St. W, Downtown* ☎ *416/603–2205* ⌾ *Reservations essential* 🖃 *AE, MC, V* ⊘ *Closed Sun.*

French

★ $$$$ ✗ **The Fifth.** Enter through The Easy, a main-floor dance club, and take a freight elevator to The Fifth, a semiprivate dining club and loft space with the right balance of formality and flirtation. The mood is industrial-strength romantic. In winter, sit on a sofa in front of a huge fireplace; in summer, dine on a gazebo terrace. The ever-changing seasonal menu is haute French. A thimble of caviar, a slice of foie gras, a fillet of sole, and a cut of beef are all given a classic French interpretation. ⊠ *225 Richmond St. W, Downtown* ☎ *416/979–3005* ⌾ *Reservations essential* 🖃 *AE, DC, MC, V* ⊘ *Closed Sun.–Wed. No lunch.*

Italian

$$–$$$$ ✗ **KitKat Bar & Grill.** Owner Al Carbone welcomes everyone like longlost family. You can dine at window tables in the front, perch at the long bar, enjoy the privacy of an old-fashioned wooden booth, or sit at a picnic table in the rear. Portions are enormous. An antipasto platter for two is a meal, and pastas, seafood, roast chicken, and grilled steak are all delectable. This eclectic and eccentric southern Italian eatery is built around a massive tree. A theater-district locale means pre- and post-theater hours are really busy. ⊠ *297 King St. W, Entertainment District* ☎ *416/977– 4461* 🖃 *AE, DC, MC, V* ⊘ *No lunch weekends.*

★ $–$$ ✗ **Il Fornello.** Pizza aficionados especially love Il Fornello's 10-inch thincrust pie, baked in a wood-burning oven. Orchestrate your own medley from 50 to 60 traditional and exotic toppings. A new chef has brought the kitchen upmarket, while keeping prices low. Try pasta with braised leg of lamb, or risotto cooked with veal shank and topped with pine nuts and lemon zest. The *zuppa de pesce* is a larger-than-expected bowl of tomato-basil broth brimming with poached fish and shellfish. You might not want to share the molten chocolate cake or lemon tart. Food sensitivities and allergies are taken seriously. ⊠ *214 King St. W, Downtown* ☎ *416/977–2855* ⊠ *207 Queen's Quay W, Harbourfront* ☎ *416/861–1028* ⊠ *1560 Yonge St., Midtown* ☎ *416/920–8291* ⊠ *35 Elm St., Downtown* ☎ *416/598–1766* ☰ *AE, MC, V.*

Malaysian

$$ ✕ **Matahari Grill.** It's hard to pass up any of the dishes here, so you might order the Matahari platter, which includes a sampling of satays, *keropok* (spicy rice crackers), and *achar-archar* (marinated cabbage, green beans, pickled cucumber, carrot, and pineapple salad topped with peanuts and sesame seeds). Or you could enjoy the *assam matahari* (scallops, prawns, calamari, tomatoes, and mushrooms, poached in spicy tamarind broth). The seafood curry grill has scallops, prawns, calamari, tomatoes, and okra served in a tantalizing coconut-curry broth. In summer there is a tiny outdoor patio, but most people prefer the pretty, sophisticated decor inside. ⊠ *39 Baldwin St., Kensington Market* ☎ *416/596–2832* ⚑ *Reservations essential* ☰ *AE, DC, MC, V* ☻ *Closed Mon. No lunch weekends.*

Pan-Asian

$$–$$$$ ✕ **Monsoon.** A fragrant, eclectic consort of Pan-Asian cuisine is served in a dining-and-lounge environment. The black-brown color scheme makes for a serene yet dynamic space with laid-back sophistication. Begin your culinary affair with grilled tiger prawns in a cup of guacamole made with Asian spices, or with the chef's daily dim sum creation for two. Travel on to organic beef tenderloin with miso mashed potatoes or yellowfin tuna on wasabi *rosti* (potato pancake). A must on the side are sweet yam fries with soy chile *sambal* (spicy peanut sauce). ⊠ *100 Simcoe St., Downtown* ☎ *416/979–7172* ☰ *AE, DC, MC, V* ☻ *No lunch weekends.*

Seafood

★ $$–$$$ ✕ **Rodney's Oyster House.** This playful, basement raw bar is a hotbed of bivalve variety frequented by dine-alones and showbiz types. Among the options are soft-shell steamers, quahogs, and "Oyster Slapjack Chowder," plus salty Aspy Bays from Cape Breton or perfect Malpeques from owner Rodney Clark's own oyster beds in Prince Edward Island. A zap of Rodney's own line of condiments or a splash of vodka and freshly grated horseradish are certain eye-openers. Shared meals and half orders are okay. Be sure to ask about the daily white-plate specials. ⊠ *469 King St. W, Downtown* ☎ *416/363–8105* ☰ *AE, DC, MC, V* ☻ *Closed Sun.*

Vegetarian

$$ ✕ **Fressen.** A feast of herbivorous cuisine jumps off the page of a menu totally free of meat and dairy, although dishes are designed with eggs. Vegetable soups are silken and perfumed with coconut milk and ginger; pasta dishes are plump with mushrooms and vegetables. Desserts like the chocolate terrine amaze. Sip a groove juice (made from cucumber, celery, kale, and other greens) while you wait for your main course. It's all served in a room decorated by natural materials: ceiling pipes are covered by woven twigs, and piles of rocks and herb-filled jars enhance the environment. ⊠ *478 Queen St. W, Queen West* ☎ *416/504–5127* ☰ *MC, V* ☻ *No lunch weekdays.*

The Annex & Little Italy

Cafés

¢ ✕ **Future Bakery & Café.** A European-style bread and dessert bakery also serves Old European recipes like beef borscht, buckwheat cabbage rolls, and potato-cheese pierogies slathered with thick sour cream. This place is beloved by the pastry-and-coffee crowd, health-conscious foodies looking for fruit salad with homemade yogurt and honey, students wanting generous portions, and people-watchers from 7 AM to 2 AM. A St. Lawrence Market branch just sells bread and pastries. ⊠ *483 Bloor St. W, The Annex* ☎ *416/922–5875* ⌂ *Reservations not accepted* ⊠ *St. Lawrence Market, 95 Front St. E, Downtown* ☎ *416/366–7259* ⊟ *MC, V.*

Cajun/Creole

$$–$$$ ✕ **Southern Accent.** This funky Cajun and Creole restaurant sits on a street made for browsing the antiques shops, bookstores, and galleries that line it. You can perch at the bar, order a martini and hush puppies, and chat with the resident psychic. Whimsical knickknacks adorn every inch of the place. Dining rooms on two floors offer a changing, market-fresh menu. Fortunately, there are some constants—bayou chicken (southern fried, with dark and spicy sauce); cracker catfish (a fillet coated with spiced crackers) served with lime tartar sauce; and shrimp étouffée with caramelized vegetables. ⊠ *595 Markham St., The Annex* ☎ *416/536–3211* ⊟ *AE, DC, MC, V* ⊙ *Closed Mon. No lunch.*

Eclectic

★ $$$–$$$$ ✕ **Splendido.** Even the most hard to please will thrill to the four- or six-course chef's tasting menus, which might include poached green and white asparagus with lobster foam, and Alberta lamb rib eye with wild leeks and morel mushrooms. The menu crisscrosses the country, with wood-burning oven-roast whole fish, short ribs of beef, or prime beef strip steak. The kitchen is peerless and the front of the house functions like a fine Swiss watch. A huge, black, iron chandelier serves as the focal point in one of the city's most beautifully balanced rooms, which are painted in shades of caramel, cream, and taupe. ⊠ *88 Harbord St., The Annex* ☎ *416/929–7788* ⌂ *Reservations essential* ⊟ *AE, DC, MC, V* ⊙ *Closed Mon. No lunch Tues.–Sun.*

$$–$$$ ✕ **Messis.** The chef-owner keeps an eye on the fresh market produce and a skillful hand in the kitchen, resulting in some of the freshest, prettiest dishes around. Herb-marinated veal loin and a rack of New Zealand lamb with Southern Comfort rosemary glaze show the chef's talent for inspired comfort food. Enjoy grilled free-range cornish hen with Pommery mustard glaze and a sauté of red potatoes, mushrooms, sundried tomatoes, celery root, fennel, and spinach with red wine. Messis is a favorite for small celebrations because of lovely desserts like a phyllo package of wild blueberries and white chocolate. The summer patio twinkles with lights at night. ⊠ *97 Harbord St., The Annex* ☎ *416/920–2186* ⊟ *AE, DC, MC, V* ⊙ *No lunch Sat.–Mon.*

$–$$ ✕ **350 Fahrenheit.** Almost any food plan can be accommodated at this modern, sleek café: Atkins, Zone, Blood Type, Suzanne Somers, South Beach, and more. It's Nirvana for vegetarians, the heart healthy, and the food conscious. Each menu item lists calorie count, protein, carb, fat, and fiber amount. They do the research, calculate, and cook, you eat—silken puree of lentils, Mexican smoked chicken and hominy stew, marinated salmon pinwheels. Fresh green peas, pungent with turmeric and thyme, fill flaky pastry triangles; grilled chicken breast with lime glaze sits atop chopped avocado and tomato salad. Here there's no need to cheat. ⊠ *467 Bloor St. W, The Annex* ☎ *416/929–2080* ☰ *AE, DC, MC, V* ⊘ *No lunch Sun.*

French

$$–$$$ ✕ **Brasserie Aix.** Glide through the handsome front bar past the tables and
Fodor's Choice into a dining room of lovely proportions lined with red leather banquettes
★ and illuminated by discreet lighting. Choose from a mix of traditional and modern French dishes—a bowl of wine-poached mussels or a *brandade de morue*—a savory whip of potato, salt cod, garlic, and olive oil. Cornish hen is roasted with green olives and citrus peel. Grilled calves' liver is flattered by Pommery mustard and crisp, thin frites. ⊠ *584 College St., Little Italy* ☎ *416/588–7377* ⌖ *Reservations essential* ☰ *AE, MC, V.*

$$ ✕ **Le Paradis.** University types, writers, and actors from the surrounding neighborhood come to this authentic French bistro-on-a-budget for the ambience and gently priced wine list. Steak and frites, crisp herb-roasted chicken, and exotic *tajine de volaille* (a Moroccan stew of chicken, prunes, olives, and a shopping list of seasonings) get the creative juices flowing. It's the kind of place you search for in France. ⊠ *166 Bedford Rd., The Annex* ☎ *416/921–0995* ☰ *AE, DC, MC, V.*

Pan-Asian

$$–$$$ ✕ **Xacutti.** The cliché-free menu is pure joy; the avant-garde decor and
Fodor's Choice table settings are a study in chic minimalism. The culinary journey be-
★ gins the moment you're handed a menu, which divides dishes into small, large, and sides. It's worth stopping for a few of each. Small dishes include barbecue cinnamon-guava pork ribs with grilled star fruit or Mumbai noodles with tiger prawns, vegetables, and toasted cashews in Silk Road Curry. Large dishes include a dramatic tandoori salmon in rice paper with curry leaves and tangerine miso. Sunday brunch draws the city's trendsetters. ⊠ *503 College St., Little Italy* ☎ *416/323–3957* ⌖ *Reservations essential* ☰ *AE, DC, MC, V* ⊘ *No lunch weekdays.*

$$–$$$ ✕ **Tempo.** The beat here is buoyant—with music, with the crowd at the bar, and with servers flying about. All the while, three chefs calmly make sushi hand rolls and Asian fusion dishes, such as roasted salted cod with sundried figs, chickpeas, and tempura fiddlehead ferns. Small plates of smoky tuna carpaccio or tempura soft-shell crab take a detour through the peppery hills of Thailand. Even lemongrass soup and tiger shrimp are high on the hot-and-spicy scale. To experience the freshest, sometimes most unusual offerings (such as barramundi ceviche), ask for the *omakase*, which means chef's choice. ⊠ *596 College St., Little Italy* ☎ *416/531–2822* ⌖ *Reservations essential* ☰ *AE, MC, V* ⊘ *Closed Sun. No lunch Mon.–Sat.*

Portuguese

★ **$$$–$$$$** ✕ **Chiado.** The exquisite fish, which form the menu's basis, are flown in from the Azores and Madeira. You might have bluefin tuna or *peixe espada* (scabbard fish). Traditional Portuguese dishes include *açorda*, in which seafood is folded into a thick, custard-like soup made with bread and eggs. There's much for meat eaters, too—for example, a roasted rack of lamb sparkles with Douro wine sauce. Choose from a fine selection of appetizers at Senhor Antonio's tapas bar. French doors lead to a dining room with polished wood floors, tables set with starched white napery, and plum velvet armchairs—all relaxed elegance. ⊠ *864 College St. W, Little Italy* ☎ *416/538–1910* ⌦ *Reservations essential* ⊟ *AE, DC, MC, V* ⊗ *No lunch weekends.*

Around Queen's Park, Church-Wellesley & Yorkville

American–Casual

$$–$$$ ✕ **Over Easy.** The real draw here is the best French toast around, pre-
Fodor'sChoice pared with caramelized bananas and pure maple syrup. The all-day break-
★ fast menu includes the Eggstro (eggs baked and smothered in a three-cheese sauce) and an unimaginable Big Breakfast (three sunny-side-ups, a maple-leaf shape pancake, a ladle full of molasses-tinged baked beans, chopped garlic and bacon, a grilled tomato, a bowl of home fries with onions, and two big strips of crisp double-smoked bacon). ⊠ *208 Bloor St. W, Queen's Park* ☎ *416/922–2345* ⌦ *Reservations not accepted* ⊟ *AE, DC, MC, V* ⊗ *No dinner.*

$–$$ ✕ **7 West Cafe.** It's surprising how many people hunger for pasta primavera or a bagel melt at 3 AM. Luckily, such cravings can be indulged at this 24-hour haven for the hip and hungry. Everything comes with a green salad, and every item is homemade. Soups like Moroccan lentil and vegetarian chili are delicious. The dinner-size sandwiches (grilled honey-and-herb chicken breast, for example) are huge. All three floors here are chic and trendy. ⊠ *7 Charles St. W, Queen's Park* ☎ *416/928–9041* ⊟ *AE, MC, V.*

Canadian

$$$–$$$$ ✕ **Pangaea.** In this tranquil room with an aura of restrained sophistication, unprocessed seasonal ingredients and the freshest produce are always used. Soups—such as wild-rabbit soup with chicken broth, wood-ear mushrooms, cattail hearts, and fresh ginger—are unique; salads are creative constructions of organic greens. Soy-honey-glazed quail comes with tempura onion rings; veal, Australian lamb, and caribou are served with truffle-whipped potatoes. Vegetarians can find bliss in this caring kitchen, too. ⊠ *1221 Bay St., Yorkville* ☎ *416/920–2323* ⊟ *AE, DC, MC, V.*

Contemporary

$$–$$$$ ✕ **Flow.** Gorgeous wood, artisanal glass, natural polished stone, and dra-
Fodor'sChoice matic lighting on two levels help make this a not-to-be-missed show-
★ place. At lunch, there are salads like roasted shrimp with Japanese eggplant. Dinner appetizers include rare-beef salad and seared foie gras toasts. Of the entrées, the seafood and fish platter for two is a knockout; the veal porterhouse and the barbecued Canadian rib eye are favorites. Vegans have options, too, and there's a kids menu. The glamorous bar, hosting live music on weekends, serves steak sandwiches, grilled short ribs, tempura shrimp rolls, and more. Afternoon tea is splendid. ⊠ *133 Yorkville Ave., Yorkville* ☎ *416/925–2143* ⊟ *AE, DC, MC, V.*

$$–$$$$ ✕ **Lobby.** Passersby ogle the white, overstuffed sofas and white coffee
Fodor'sChoice tables in windows open to the street in summer. No, it is not a furni-
★ ture store; it's the front lounge of the hottest, newest dining concept in

town. Sit at bar tables or behind white, sheer curtains in the dining room. Munch on an ahi tuna BLT or a hefty 8-ounce grilled Kobe beef burger with garlic truffle mayo. Take a leap of faith and have the mac-and-cheese capped with seared foie gras, or savor tuna tartare or hearts of romaine with smoked salmon. Spectacular desserts delight as well. ⊠ *192 Bloor St. W, Yorkville* ☎ *416/929–7169* ▤ *AE, MC, V* ☉ *Closed Mon.*

$$–$$$ ✕ **Carens Wine & Cheese.** Two levels of casual dining and a cozy protected patio provide an intimate respite for a small meal, pre- or posttheater, or whenever. Pick out a selection of carefully chosen imported cheeses, paired with a glass of wine, or try a fabulous Stilton cheese–stuffed burger topped with mushrooms sauteéd in cognac. Lovely seasonal soups, a few pasta selections, and a piece of good chocolate cake for dessert: who could ask for anything more? ⊠ *158 Cumberland Ave., Yorkville* ☎ *416/962–5158* ▤ *AE, DC, MC, V.*

Eclectic

$$$–$$$$ ✕ **Boba.** Owners Bob Bermann and Barbara Gordon (Boba) are a sophisticated culinary couple who cook in a charming brick house personalized with robust and gorgeous color. The dishes they've dreamed up are original and delicious—rice-paper-wrapped chicken breast on Thai black rice and big-eye tuna grilled rare with coconut noodles, mango and avocado salsa, and black bean sauce are customer favorites. For a heartier dish, try the traditional grilled Black Angus strip loin with Yukon Gold frites. Vegetarian dinners are spontaneously invented. Boba has one of the city's prettiest patios for summer dining. ⊠ *90 Avenue Rd., Yorkville* ☎ *416/961–2622* ▤ *AE, DC, MC, V* ☉ *No lunch.*

★ $$ $$$$ ✕ **Studio Café.** At this well lit, comfortable café—a combination hotel coffee shop, restaurant, and contemporary glass-and-art gallery—you can have a full Japanese or Canadian breakfast. Trendsetting dishes include a complex Asian stir-fry; chicken curry with all the chutneys, pickles, and sauces; and risotto with sautéed leeks and tomatoes. Still, sandwiches such as smoked turkey clubhouse with cranberry sauce, and one of the city's best beef burgers—with roasted onions, mushrooms, and aged cheddar—are what draw the foodies. ⊠ *Four Seasons Toronto hotel, 21 Avenue Rd., north of Bloor St., Yorkville* ☎ *416/964–0411* ▤ *AE, DC, MC, V.*

French

★ $$$$ ✕ **Truffles.** This restaurant serves contemporary French cuisine rooted in authentic French flavors. Appetizers include thyme-roasted sweetbreads with lentil ragout and the signature spaghettini with truffle foam. Entrées such as pepper-seared loin of venison or truffled honey squab breast are pleasures for the palate. An early dinner (at 6) offers a three-course, fixed-price menu for a mere C$31—quite a bargain, considering this kitchen has won countless international dining awards. An extraordinary multicourse tasting menu is also available. ⊠ *Four Seasons Toronto hotel, 21 Avenue Rd., Yorkville* ☎ *416/928–7331* ⚠ *Reservations essential* ▤ *AE, DC, D, MC, V* ☉ *Closed Sun. No lunch.*

$$$–$$$$ ✕ **Bistro 990.** A superior kitchen pairs seamlessly here with bistro in-
Fodor'sChoice formality. Start your experience with traditional pâté de maison, part-
★ nered with quince marmalade, wine preserves, and plenty of homemade croutons. Oven-roasted halibut with salsa and feta cheese is a treat, and a roasted half chicken with herb garlic au jus crackles with crispness

and Provençal flavor. Ask about the wild game dish of the day. Faux stone walls stenciled with Cocteau-esque designs, sturdily upholstered chairs, and a tiled floor make it sophisticated but comfortable. ⊠ *990 Bay St., Church–Wellesley* ☎ *416/921–9990* ♿ *Reservations essential* ☰ *AE, DC, MC, V* ☉ *Closed Sun. No lunch Sat.*

★ **$$$$$**   ✕ **Michelle's Bistro.** A decidedly romantic slice of Paris in Toronto: candles shimmer at each table, cushions on banquettes create personal comfort zones, and live music on weekends adds panache. In spring a thousand tulips grace the front patio, in summer the flower garden and twinkling lights invite you to linger, and in winter snow drapes quietly over the evergreens. The typical French kitchen uses seasonal ingredients. The omelet of the day, a salad niçoise, and pert servers keep everyone happy. ⊠ *162 Cumberland St., Yorkville* ☎ *416/944–1504* ☰ *AE, DC, MC, V.*

Indian

★ **$–$$**   ✕ **The Host.** Dine in the garden room among flowering plants or in the handsome main room. Waiters rush around carrying baskets of hot *naan* (a gorgeous, puffy flat bread) from the oven. An excellent dish is tandoori *machi*, whole fish baked in a tandoor oven and served on a sizzling plate with onion and coriander. Sliced tender lamb is enfolded in a curry of cashew nuts and whole cardamom. End your meal with such exotic Indian desserts as little round cakes soaking in rosewater-scent honey. ⊠ *14 Prince Arthur St., Yorkville* ☎ *416/962–4678* ♿ *Reservations essential* ☰ *AE, MC, V.*

Italian

★ **$$–$$$$**   ✕ **Sotto Sotto.** A coal cellar in a turn-of-the-20th-century home was dug out, its stone walls and floor polished, and a restaurant created in what has become a dining oasis for locals and international jet-setters alike. The menu of more than 20 pasta dishes gives a tantalizing tug at the taste buds. *Orecchiette* ("ear-shape" disks of pasta), with a toss of prosciutto, mushrooms, black olives, and fresh tomatoes, is a symphony of textures. Gnocchi is made daily. Cornish hen is marinated, pressed, and grilled to a juicy brown, and the swordfish and fresh fish of the day are beautifully done on the grill. ⊠ *116-A Avenue Rd., Yorkville* ☎ *416/962–0011* ☰ *AE, DC, MC, V* ☉ *No lunch.*

$$–$$$ ✕ **Bellini.** Never wavering from its focus on elegance, good taste, classic food, and professional service, Bellini has stood the test of time. How can one choose from among dishes such as butter-braised lobster and sea scallops with green and white asparagus in lobster basil broth, or the siren call of Provimi veal osso buco with vegetable ragu and lemon-thyme au jus, or risotto of lobster, honey mushrooms, mascarpone cheese, and chervil? It's easier to sample with the prix fixe menu, C$37 per person including a half bottle of red wine. ⊠ *101 Yorkville Ave. W, Yorkville* ☎ *416/929–9111* ☰ *AE, DC, MC, V* ☉ *No lunch.*

Pan-Asian

$–$$ ✕ **Indochine.** A century of French colonization influenced Vietnamese cuisine, and China also left an indelible stamp. Indochine reflects these influences with stunning appetizers. Six crab preparations or the beef curry, rich in flavor, make good entrées. Purple-basil beef is a popular Chinese-style dish. Vegetarians go for the noodle soups, fragrant with tamarind and lemongrass. Try Vietnamese coffee—a filtered mix of milk, sugar, and strong coffee. ✉ *4 Collier St., Yorkville* ☎ *416/922–5840* 🖃 *AE, DC, MC, V* ☉ *No lunch Sun.*

¢–$$ ✗ **Spring Rolls.** Torontonians embrace Pan-Asian spring rolls as if they'd cut their teeth on these appetizers. You too can choose from the enormous hot or cold selection. A Thai red curry comes with jasmine rice, chilies, and herb-touched coconut milk, and leaves you breathless. ✉ *687 Yonge St., Queen's Park* ☎ *416/972–7655* 🖚 *Reservations essential* ✉ *693 Yonge St., Queens Park* ☎ *416/972–7655* ✉ *85 Front St., Midtown* ☎ *416/365–7655* ✉ *40 Dundas St. W, Chinatown* ☎ *416/585–2929* 🖃 *AE, MC, V.*

Steak

$$$–$$$$ ✗ **Morton's.** Just when you thought this top-notch international chain couldn't possibly get better, they have added glorious new steak variations to their repertoire, including steak au poivre, with yummy peppercorn-cognac sauce; filet Oskar, topped with crab, asparagus, and béarnaise; and filet Diane, with sautéed mushrooms in a rich mustard sauce. Of course you can still dine on a New York strip or a 48-ounce porterhouse. All beef is shipped chilled, not frozen, from one Chicago supplier. The interior has a handsome, wood-panel clubbiness. ✉ *4 Avenue Rd., Yorkville* ☎ *416/925–0648* 🖃 *AE, D, MC, V.*

Cabbagetown

French

★ $$–$$$$ ✗ **Provence Delices.** This pretty French-style villa is a 25-year-old Cabbagetown landmark with faux-painted walls, a potbellied stove, and a pretty summer patio. The eight-item sampling menu satisfies the curious with a tartare of scallops, a bread *tartine* (open-face sandwich) with cured salmon, goat cheese, and garlic mayo, a chicken roulade with orange sauce, and other small dishes. If classic Provençal fish soup appeals, this is the place to try it. Duck confit with olive sauce is crisp and juicy all at the same time. Authentic patisserie, including tarte tatin, with caramelized apples and a buttery crust, makes a fine ending. ✉ *12 Amelia St., Cabbagetown* ☎ *416/924–9901* 🖃 *AE, MC, V.*

Greater Toronto

Chinese

$$–$$$ ✗ **Mandarin.** Diners may be weak in the knees at the sight of the smorgasbord of Chinese food. First, heap your plate with salad-bar selections and large shrimp in the shell, and then attack the hot-and-sour soup, the wonton soup, or both. The food has no MSG and no preservatives. Servers explain each dish and invite you to come back for more honey-garlic ribs, deep-fried shrimp and chicken wings, breaded chicken, spring rolls, sweet-and-sour dishes, chicken curry, mixed vegetables, seafood stir-fries, and more—even sliced beef with gravy and roast potatoes. Desserts include tarts, cookies, and ice cream. Seniors get a 10% discount. ✉ *2200 Yonge St., at Eglinton Ave., Midtown* ☎ *416/486–2222* 🖃 *AE, MC, V* ✉ *2206 Eglinton Ave. E, at Birchmont St., Scarborough* ☎ *416/288–1177* 🖃 *AE, MC, V.*

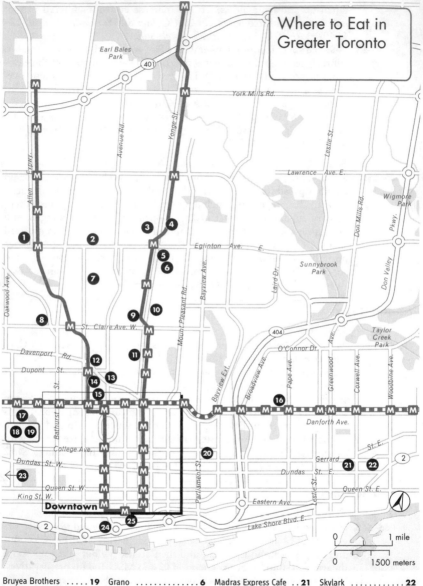

Where to Eat in Greater Toronto

Contemporary

★ **$$$$** ✕ **North 44.** A lighting engineer has created a refined, sophisticated environment where appetizers such as Parma ham with mascarpone-stuffed figs, frisée salad, and a lobster taco with crisp beet wrapper, jicama salad, and scallion awaken your taste buds. Just try to choose from chef-owner Marc McEwen's creative and exciting main courses, including whole roasted Dover sole in brown butter and a crisp shoestring basket, and braised lamb shank with fried-onion-potato mousse. There are more than 50 wines sold by the glass, enough to complement any dish. ✉ *2537 Yonge St., 4½ blocks north of Eglinton Ave., Midtown* ☎ *416/ 487–4897* ☰ *AE, MC, V* ☾ *Closed Sun. No lunch.*

★ **$$–$$$** ✕ **Centro.** Restaurateur Tony Longo continues to set standards of excellence. Fine regional ingredients filter through a Mediterranean style in specialties such as snowy white, baked halibut partnered with market-fresh veggies. Gnocchi and egg *tagliolini* (paper-thin noodles) are so like the fine pasta in Italy you may want to sing. Capon holds a trove of foie gras mousse at its heart and gets unexpected zip from sundried cherries in orange-and-balsamic-vinegar sauce. The wine list has an uncommon depth and breadth, and service is urbane and attentive. Natural colors and unique lighting create a subdued sophistication. ✉ *2472 Yonge St., at Eglinton Ave., Midtown* ☎ *416/483–2211* ⌦ *Reservations essential* ☰ *AE, DC, MC, V* ☾ *Closed Sun. No lunch.*

French

★ **$$–$$$** ✕ **Pastis Express.** Menu items are etched into the frosted-glass windows and plastered walls are the color of the morning sun in Provence. Expect pure bistro fare here, like homemade ravioli with snails and garlic herb butter, and fish-and-chips. Thick saffron-flavor fish soup, plump with fish and crustaceans, comes with three tidy add-ons: rouille, croutons, and grated cheese. A tasting plate of three French minidesserts satisfies. The food is good, but this place could run on the Gallic charm of owner George Gurnon alone. ✉ *1158 Yonge St., at Summerhill, Midtown* ☎ *416/928–2212* ☰ *AE, DC, MC, V* ☾ *Closed Sun. and Mon. No lunch.*

Greek

$–$$$ ✕ **Christina's.** Who doesn't have a foodie love affair with Greek dips? Here

FodorsChoice they're served individually or as a large platter combination, *pikilia*

★ *mezedakia,* that comes with warm pitas. A bottle of Greek wine and specials like *saganaki,* an iron plate of Kefalograviera cheese flamed in brandy, and you may shout "Opa" with the waiters. Order a fish or meat mixed grill and the tray of food almost covers the table. This cheery place, with the colors of the Aegean Sea and sun on the walls, has live music and uninhibited Greek dancing—by patrons and staff alike—on weekends. ✉ *492 Danforth Ave., The Danforth* ☎ *416/463–4418* ☰ *A, DC, MC, V.*

Indian

$ ✕ **Skylark.** A few miles east of downtown, owner Gurnam Multani extends a jovial welcome and leads you to a blue-clothed table where you must make a decision: buffet or menu. Most people help themselves to a dozen or so buffet items, including salads, vegetables cooked in sweet cream, and chickpeas and mung beans in a rich onion sauce. Vegans can eat well. Other dishes on the menu (and sometimes on the buffet) in-

BEST AL FRESCO DINING

AT THE FIRST SIGN OF WARM WEATHER, and until the evenings turn cool in September, Torontonians hit the deck, the patio, the courtyard, and the rooftop terrace. White plastic tables and chairs sprout around every restaurant that has a patch of frontage to call its own.

In summer, wildflowers and groves of trees in Yorkville burst into bloom. **Sassafraz** (✉ 100 Cumberland St., Yorkville ☎ 416/964–2222) is encircled by a patio that's filled from noon until 2 AM. A light-wrapped tree glimmers in the garden at **Michelle's Bistro** (✉ 162 Cumberland St., Yorkville ☎ 416/944–1504).

Hemingways (✉ 142 Cumberland St., Yorkville ☎ 416/968–2828) brings in the locals and fans from the burbs who climb the stairs to a flower-filled roof garden. The who's who gather at the city's glamour spot, **Flow** (✉ 133 Yorkville Ave., Yorkville ☎ 416/925–2143). The patio at **Amber** (✉ 119 Yorkville Ave., Yorkville ☎ 416/926–9037) is for cool, late-night kind of people. The patio at **Prego della Piazza** (✉ 150 Bloor St. W, Yorkville ☎ 416/920–9900), flanked by the Church of the Redeemer, is a summer favorite.

Kensington Market is home to melting-pot cuisine. **Last Temptation** (✉ 12 Kensington Ave., Kensington Market ☎ 416/599–2551) has a funky patio that's a great spot for spicy roti. Relish great guacamole and fajitas in the open air at **Margaritas** (✉ 14 Baldwin St., Kensington Market ☎ 416/977–5525).

East of downtown, the passage to Indian cuisine is filled with exciting sights and sounds. Sit at an outdoor table at **Madras Express Cafe** (✉ 1438-A Gerrard St., Little India ☎ 416/461–7470) and eat a masala dosa, a folded, foot-long, crunchy rice-flour pancake filled with potato and mustard seed.

When they're rolling up the sidewalks elsewhere, the Greek area of The Danforth is just getting lively. Bouzouki music fills the air, and dozens of Greek restaurants are filled with night owls nibbling from traditional appetizer platters. The sidewalk patio at **Christina's** (✉ 513 Danforth Ave., Danforth ☎ 416/465–1751) is a good place to check out the Greek scene. A popular place to sit at crowded outdoor tables and sip ouzo is **Myth** (✉ 417 Danforth Ave., Danforth ☎ 416/461–8383).

The Italians practically invented the art of sipping espresso outdoors and watching the world go by. Little Italy is packed with multi-ethnic restaurants, pizza parlors, wine bars, and pool halls. The 70-seat patio at **Bruyea Brothers** (✉ 640 College St., Little Italy ☎ 416/532–3841) is a haven for urban food and cool drinks. Window walls open to the street so that the patio combines with the front of the restaurant at **Giovanna** (✉ 637 College Ave., Little Italy ☎ 416/538–2098). **Trattoria Giancarlo** (✉ 41 Clinton St., Little Italy ☎ 416/533–9619) has tasty grilled meats you can savor at outdoor picnic tables.

The Entertainment District teems with suited after-work crowds. If you see an empty table, take it. Queen Street, between University Avenue and Bathurst Street, is filled with Gen-X dining adventure. **The Rivoli** (✉ 322 Queen St. W, Queen West ☎ 416/596–1908) is a hot oudoor spot. The rear garden at the **Queen Mother Café** (✉ 208 Queen St. W, Queen West ☎ 416/598–4719) is a cool place for East–West dishes. Way west, **The Drake Hotel** (✉ 1150 Queen St. W, Queen West ☎ 416/531–5042) has an interesting rooftop patio made even more intriguing by the pretty clientele.

clude lamb curry and chicken *Muglai*, a spicy, northern-Indian dish with cream sauce and cashews. The bargain gets even better when Mr. Multani strolls by offering just-baked naan. ⊠ *1433 Gerrard St. E, Little India* ☎ *416/469–1500* ▭ *AE, MC, V.*

Italian

★ **$$–$$$$** ✕ **Il Mulino.** A ceiling arched like the ancient wine cellars of Italy, a cool gray-and-white color scheme, sculpted leather chairs, and subdued lighting make for comfort, while the food makes for joy. Begin with elegant octopus carpaccio or wild mushroom *agnolotti* (crescent-shape stuffed pasta) with veal juice and walnut sauce, then graduate to a whole baby black bass, cleanly filleted in the kitchen. Carnivores love the handsome breaded veal chop. End the evening with the chocolate volcano—warm chocolate cake with decadent molten interior. ⊠ *1060 Eglinton Ave. W, Midtown* ☎ *416/780–1173* ▭ *AE, DC, MC, V* ☺ *No lunch Sat.–Mon.*

★ **$$–$$$$** ✕ **Mistura.** The buzz of this place often settles on Mistura's combination of comfort and casual luxury and its innovative menu. Choose from one of more than a dozen delectable starters, like savory Maryland crab cakes with lemon aioli on chopped salad, or grilled calamari. Duck two ways—crispy confit or roasted breast with port-infused dried cherries—is a specialty. Balsamic glazed lamb ribs are always a hit. Veal ravioli is just one of the homemade pastas. Daily whole fish is a carefully thought-out triumph. Vegetarians are given their due with dishes like red-beet risotto. ⊠ *265 Davenport Rd., ½ block west of Avenue Rd., Midtown* ☎ *416/515–0009* ▭ *AE, DC, MC, V* ☺ *No lunch.*

★ **$–$$$** ✕ **Grano.** What started as a bakery and take-out antipasto bar has grown into a cheerful collage of the Martella family's Italy. Come for animated talk, good food, and great bread in lively rooms with faux-ancient plaster walls, wooden tables, and bright chairs. Choose, if you can, from 40 delectable vegetarian dishes and numerous meat and fish antipasti. Lucia's homemade gnocchi and ravioli are divine, as is the white-chocolate-and-raspberry pie. ⊠*2035 Yonge St., between Eglinton and Davisville Aves., Midtown* ☎ *416/440–1986* ▭ *AE, DC, MC, V* ☺ *Closed Sun.*

★ **$$** ✕ **Filippo's Gourmet Pizza.** LIFE IS LIKE A PIZZA—THE MORE YOU PUT IN, THE RICHER IT GETS is written on a slate map of Italy that hangs on the wall of this charming spot. A big wooden display table inside beckons with antipasti—polenta and olives, potato and fried onion, crisp green beans, and grilled peppers and eggplant. Bruschetta is piled high with chopped tomato and fresh basil. The enthusiasm of owner Filippo DiNatale is transferred to all his dishes—rigatoni with fennel, capers, anchovies; rich and creamy risottos; and wonderful pizzas handmade to order. ⊠ *744 St. Clair Ave. W, Midtown* ☎ *416/658–0568* ▭ *AE, MC, V.*

Japanese

$–$$$ ✕ **Edo.** Aficionados of Japanese food may have to stop themselves from ordering everything on the menu. Even the uninitiated are mesmerized by the intriguing dishes servers carry, including plates of *yaki kinoko* (grilled mushrooms or thickly sliced eggplant baked to a silken texture with both sweet and sour flavors). If soft-shell crab is on the menu, it's a worthy choice. The chef is an artist with sushi and sashimi, but if you can't decide, the set menus give you a balanced and exciting Japanese meal. ⊠*484*

Eglinton Ave. W, Midtown ☎ *416/481–1370* ⊙ *No lunch* ⌨ *Reservations essential* 🖃 *AE, DC, MC, V* ✉ *431 Spadina Rd., Midtown* ☎ *416/482–8973* ⌨ *Reservations essential* 🖃 *AE, DC, MC, V.*

Seafood

★ **$$$–$$$$**   ✕ **Joso's.** This two-story restaurant displays intriguing wall hangings, sensuous paintings of nudes and the sea, and signed celebrity photos. The kitchen prepares dishes from the Dalmatian side of the Adriatic Sea, and members of the international artistic community who frequent the place adore the unusual and healthful array of seafood and fish. The black risotto with squid is a must. Grilled prawns, their charred tails pointing skyward, is a dish often carried aloft by speed-walking servers. ✉ *202 Davenport Rd., Midtown* ☎ *416/925–1903* ⌨ *Reservations essential* 🖃 *AE, DC, MC, V* ⊙ *Closed Sun. No lunch Sat.*

WHERE TO STAY

Updated by
Jack Kohane

GIVEN THAT MORE THAN 100 LANGUAGES and dialects are spoken in the greater Toronto area, it's not surprising that much of the downtown hotel market is international-business-traveler savvy. High-speed wireless Internet connections are standard at most high-end properties, and generous work spaces and business services abound. But these same core hotels are close to tourist attractions—the Harbourfront and the Toronto Islands, the cavernous SkyDome, the Air Canada Centre, and the Royal Ontario Museums. Not wanting to miss out on potential customers, hotels like the Four Seasons, the Delta Chelsea, and the Sheraton Centre Toronto have instituted perks for the younger set, like complimentary milk and cookies, kid-size bathrobes, and children's day camp. Another key trend in Toronto's downtown lodgings is the emergence of small, upscale, boutique hotels, such as the Hotel Le Germain, the Pantages Hotel, and the opulent SoHo Metropolitan. There are a growing number of bed-and-breakfasts and hostels in different urban neighborhoods as well.

City-center accommodations are usually within a 10- to 15-minute walk of Yonge Street and the glittering lights of the exciting Entertainment District, the soaring office towers of the Financial District, the shops of Eaton Centre (Canada's most famous shopping magnet), and the cool patio bars and art galleries of the Queen West. In the city's quiet east end, there's a mix of high-density high-rises and large tracts of park. Although not close to downtown attractions, hotels such as Inn on the Park and the Hilton Suites Conference Centre & Spa in Markham are within a 15-minute drive of the Ontario Science Centre and the Toronto Zoo. Within a 15-minute drive west of downtown is the forested High Park and the meandering Humber River, an area where there are few major hotels but an ample array of quaint B&Bs and the lovely Old Mill Inn to choose among. Lester B. Pearson International Airport is 29 km (18 mi) northwest of downtown; airport hotels are airport hotels, but staying in this area also means quick connections to cities beyond, such as Niagara.

Even though the breadth of lodging choices and price ranges are on par with other cities of its size, the attractive exchange rate of the Canadian dollar against most other international currencies really sets this metropolis apart as a lodgings bargain. When booking, remember to first ask about discounts and packages. Even the most expensive properties regularly reduce their rates during low-season lulls and on weekends. Discounts from 20% to 50% are not uncommon. If you're a member of a group (examples: seniors, students, auto club, or the military), you may also get a deal. Downtown hotels regularly have specials that include theater tickets, meals, or museum passes. It never hurts to ask for these kinds of perks up front.

Downtown

$$$$
Fodor'sChoice
★

Four Seasons Toronto. Some of Toronto's most luxurious guest rooms are here, in fashionable Yorkville. Appointments include antique-style writing desks, comfortable robes, oversize towels, and fresh flowers. Many of the corner rooms have furnished balconies, and some rooms have bay windows that open. Ask for upper rooms to get views facing downtown and the lake. The Studio Café serves Italian and Mediterranean dishes,

3

The lodgings we list are the cream of the crop in each price category. Properties are assigned price categories based on the range from their least expensive standard double room at high season (excluding holidays) to the most expensive. We always list the facilities that are available—but we don't specify whether they cost extra: when pricing accommodations, always ask what's included and what costs extra.

Services Unless otherwise noted in individual descriptions, all the hotels listed have private baths, central heating, air-conditioning, and private phones. Almost all hotels have data ports or high-speed Internet access and phones with voice mail. Most large hotels have video or high-speed checkout capability, and many can arrange babysitting. Diversions such as Web TV, in-room video games, VCRs, and CD players are also provided in many hotels.

Bringing a car to Toronto can be a headache unless your hotel provides free parking. Garages cost around $20 per day, and street-side parking is not available in most neighborhoods.

Reservations Hotel reservations are a necessity—hotels fill up quickly, so book your room as far in advance as possible. Summer is the busiest time, and if you plan on visiting during the Caribana Festival (late July) or during the Toronto International Film Festival (September), note that hordes of visitors will be joining you in a search for a room.

Be aware that the city is a popular destination for leisure travelers, and it also draws many conventions. These conventions book huge blocks of hotel rooms, particularly in April through November. (This can mean annoying lobby bustle, but it also tends to ensure that properties in this competitive town have plenty of amenities and high levels of service.) If conventioneers bother you, ask the hotel in which you're interested whether any large gatherings will coincide with your stay.

What it Costs In addition to the dollar advantage you get if you're paying with U.S. currency, there are other ways to save money during a visit. Many hotels that cater to business travelers cut rates for weekends—these rates sometimes start on Thursday—and these hotels typically have special packages for couples and families, too. Toronto hotels typically slash rates a full 50% in January and February, a boon for skiers. Smaller hotels and apartment-style accommodation downtown are also moderately priced (and therefore popular in summer).

WHAT IT COSTS In Canadian dollars				
	$$$$	$$$	$$	$	¢
FOR 2 PEOPLE	over $250	$175–$250	$125–$175	$75–$125	under $75

Prices are for two people in a standard double room in high season (excluding 7% GST, 5% room tax, and optional service charge)

THE ANNEX

Bloor St. W.

Lennox St.

Herrick St.

TO AIRPORT STRIP

Sussex Ave.

Harbord St.

Ulster St.

Willcocks St.

Russell St.

College St.

Hoskin Ave.

Queen's Park

QUEEN'S PARK

St. Jo

Wellesley

LITTLE ITALY

College St.

Oxford St.

Nassau St.

Cecil St.

Baldwin St.

D'Arcy St.

College St.

Orde St.

Elm St.

CHINATOWN

Dundas St. W.

Alexandra Park

Sullivan St.

Grange Park

Grange Rd.

Armoury St.

Robinson St.

Wolseley St.

Butwer St.

Renfrew Pl.

Pullan Pl.

QUEEN STREET WEST

Queen St. W.

Richmond St. W.

Camden St.

Adelaide St. W.

ENTERTAINMENT DISTRICT

Nelson St.

Pearl St.

King St. W.

Mercer St.

Wellington St. W.

FIN D

Heenan Pl.

Where to Stay in Toronto

Front St. W.

Station St.

0   1/4 mile

0   400 meters

ROSEDALE

YORKVILLE

CHURCH-WELLESLEY

OLD TORONTO

and is one of the best business lunches in town. The more formal Truffles restaurant has contemporary French cuisine and an acclaimed wine list. ☒ *21 Avenue Rd., Yorkville M5R 2G1* ☎ *416/964–0411 or 800/ 819–8053* 🖶 *416/964–2301* ⊕ *www.fourseasons.com* 🛏 *230 rooms, 150 suites* ♿ *2 restaurants, in-room data ports, cable TV, indoor-outdoor pool, health club, bicycles, bar, lobby lounge, babysitting, business services, parking (fee), no-smoking floors* ▭ *AE, D, DC, MC, V.*

$$$$ 🛏 **Pantages Hotel.** The contemporary design hints at the Far East, with clean lines, gleaming hardwood flooring, and brushed steel accents. Down duvets and pillows, 27-inch LCD flat-screen televisions, and wi-fi Internet come standard in all rooms. Many rooms have sofa beds, closeted washer/dryer units, and nifty work/breakfast tables that fit neatly over beds. The hotel owes its name to the legendary Pantages Theatre (now Canon Theatre), next door. Room views are unspectacular—you might look onto the neighboring building's fire escape or have a ho-hum vista of downtown skyscrapers. The spa is a selling point, with its water therapies, massage, and yoga. At this writing, elements of the hotel and spa are under construction but should be ready early 2005. ☒ *200 Victoria St., at Schuter St., Downtown M5B 1V8* ☎ *416/362–1777 or 866/ 852–1777* 🖶 *416/214–5618* ⊕ *www.pantageshotel.com* 🛏 *85 rooms, 26 suites* ♿ *Restaurant, room service, some kitchens, minibars, lounge, cable TV with movies, gym, spa, bar, laundry facilities, concierge, Internet, business services, meeting rooms, parking (fee), no-smoking floors* ▭ *AE, D, DC, MC, V* ▯⃝ *CP.*

$$$$ 🛏 **Park Hyatt Toronto.** The experience here is *très* New York Park Avenue. Elegant guestrooms are a generous 300 to 400 square feet, with wide windows overlooking Queen's Park and Lake Ontario. Two-level loft suites have designer kitchenettes, and the 2,500-square-foot Algonquin Suite affords three different skyline views. Set aside time for the signature Mandarin Honey Body Glow treatment at the hotel's Stillwater Spa or a drink at the rooftop bar. For beef lovers, there's Morton's steak house. ☒ *4 Avenue Rd., at Bloor St. W, Yorkville M5R 2E8* ☎ *416/ 925–1234 or 800/778–7477* 🖶 *416/924–4933* ⊕ *www.parktoronto.hyatt. com* 🛏 *346 rooms* ♿ *2 restaurants, in-room data ports, cable TV, health club, spa, bar, Internet, business services, parking (fee), no-smoking floors* ▭ *AE, D, DC, MC, V.*

$$$$ 🛏 **Sheraton Centre.** Views from this hotel in the city center are marvelous— to the south are the CN Tower and the SkyDome; to the north, both city halls. Guest rooms and suites have pillow-top mattresses, crisp bed linens, and cozy duvets. Club Level rooms have bathrobes and provide access to the complimentary Continental breakfast and cocktail hour at the 43rd-floor Club Level Lounge. Children's programs are available in summer. ☒ *123 Queen St. W, Entertainment District M5H 2M9* ☎ *416/ 361–1000 or 800/325–3535* 🖶 *416/947–4873* ⊕ *www.sheraton.com* 🛏 *1,302 rooms, 75 suites* ♿ *3 restaurants, coffee shop, in-room data ports, cable TV, indoor-outdoor pool, gym, hot tub, sauna, spa, lobby lounge, parking (fee), no-smoking floors* ▭ *AE, DC, MC, V.*

$$$$
Fodor'sChoice
★
🛏 **SoHo Metropolitan Hotel.** Ultra-luxury is the only standard at the SoHo Met: Italian Frette linens, European down duvets, walk-in closets, solid marble bathrooms with heated floors, and upmarket bath prod-

LODGING ALTERNATIVES & RESOURCES

Apartment Rentals

If you want a home base that's roomy enough for a family and comes with cooking facilities, consider a furnished rental. Home-exchange directories sometimes list rentals as well as exchanges.

International Agents: Hideaways International (✉ 767 Islington St., Portsmouth, NH 03801 ☎ 603/430–4433 or 800/843–4433 🖷 603/430–4444 ⊕ www.hideaways.com); annual membership $145.

Local Agents: Apartments International Inc. (✉ 255 Duncan Mill Rd., Suite 604, Downtown M3B 3H9 ☎ 416/410–2400 or 888/410–2400 🖷 416/410–2410 ⊕ www.apts-intl.com).

Bridge Street Accommodations (✉ 1000 Yonge St., Suite 301, Downtown M4W 2K2 ☎ 416/923–1000, 800/667–8483 in North America 🖷 416/924–2446 ⊕ www.bridgestreet.com).

Glen Grove Suites (✉ 2837 Yonge St., Midtown M4N 2J6 ☎ 416/489–8441 or 800/565–3024 🖷 416/440–3065 ⊕ www.glengrove.com).

TorontoRent.com (✉ 1235 Bay St., Suite 400, Downtown ☎ 416/789–2812 ⊕ http://torontorent.com).

Bed-and-Breakfasts

More than a dozen private homes, all in and around downtown, are affiliated with **Toronto Bed & Breakfast** (✉ 253 College St., Box 269, Downtown M5T 1R5 ☎ 705/738–9449, 705/738–6886, or 877/922–6522 🖷 705/738–0155 ⊕ www.torontobandb.com). This free registry has charming lakeside retreats to downtown Victorian gems. Most of these B&Bs tend to fall into the less-expensive price categories. **The Downtown Toronto Association of Bed & Breakfast Guest Houses** (✉ Box 190,

Station B, M5T 2W1 ☎ 416/410–3938 🖷 416/483–8822 ⊕ www.bnbinfo.com) represents privately owned B&Bs scattered throughout downtown.

Hostels

In some 4,500 locations in more than 70 countries around the world, Hostelling International (HI), the umbrella group for a number of national youth-hostel associations, has single-sex, dorm-style beds and, at many hostels, rooms for couples and family accommodations. Toronto's hostel has private rooms for couples and families, as well as dormitory-style rooms more suitable for college-age travelers. Membership in any HI national hostel association, open to travelers of all ages, allows you to stay in HI-affiliated hostels at member rates; one-year membership is about $28 for adults (C$35 for a two-year minimum membership in Canada, £13.50 in the U.K., A$52 in Australia, and NZ$40 in New Zealand); hostels charge about $10–$30 per night.

Organizations: Hostelling International—USA (✉ 8401 Colesville Rd., Suite 600, Silver Spring, MD 20910 ☎ 301/495–1240 🖷 301/495–6697 ⊕ www.hiayh.org). **Hostelling International—Canada** (✉ 205 Catherine St., Suite 400, Ottawa, ON K2P 1C3 ☎ 613/237–7884 or 800/663–5777 🖷 613/237–7868 ⊕ www.hihostels.ca). **YHA England and Wales** (✉ Trevelyan House, Dimple Rd., Matlock, Derbyshire DE4 3YH, U.K. ☎ 0870/870–8808, 0870/770–8868, or 0162/959–2700 🖷 0870/770–6127 ⊕ www.yha.org.uk). **YHA Australia** (✉ 422 Kent St., Sydney, NSW 2001 ☎ 02/9261–1111 🖷 02/9261–1969 ⊕ www.yha.com.au). **YHA New Zealand** (✉ Level 4, Torrens House, 195 Hereford St., Box 436, Christchurch ☎ 03/379–9970 or 0800/278–299 🖷 03/365–4476 ⊕ www.yha.org.nz).

ucts. Glamour begins in the cosmopolitan open-concept lobby, where a stunning glass sculpture by noted artist Dale Chihuly (the only one of his works in Toronto visible from the street) sits in front of floor-to-ceiling glass windows, dazzling guests and passersby alike. Senses Bakery & Restaurant stakes its reputation on its braised black beef ribs with truffle gnocchi. Service here is superlative. The pastry chefs make decadent cakes, including black forest, and fabulous cookies. ⊠ *328 Wellington St. W, Entertainment District M5V 3T4* ☎ *416/599–8800 or 800/ 668–6600* 🖷 *416/599–8801* ⊕ *www.soho.metropolitan.com* ⇨ *69 rooms, 19 suites* ⚓ *Restaurant, in-room data ports, cable TV, indoor pool, health club, hot tub, spa, bar, concierge, Internet, business services, parking (fee), no-smoking floors* ⊟ *AE, DC, MC, V.*

$$$$
Fodor's Choice
★

🖵 **Windsor Arms.** Service is the motto here, with a staff-to-guest ratio of 1:6 (the highest in Canada), 24-hour butler service, and a Bentley limo available for use. Lavish suites include handmade furnishings, luxurious bedcover fabrics, state-of-the-art DVD and CD sound systems, and bathrooms with whirlpool tubs. Once you leave your room, you might sip one of the many international and exotic loose-leaf teas at the Tea Room, boogie down at Club 22, or relax at the on-site spa. The building's graceful neo-Gothic facade has been painstakingly restored, which contributes to the hotel's genteel refinement. ⊠ *18 St. Thomas St., Yorkville M5S 3E7* ☎ *416/971–9666 or 877/999–2767* 🖷 *416/921– 9121* ⊕ *www.windsorarmshotel.com* ⇨ *2 rooms, 26 suites* ⚓ *Restaurant, tea shop, in-room data ports, cable TV, in-room VCRs, indoor pool, gym, spa, bar, dance club, Internet, business services, meeting rooms, no-smoking rooms* ⊟ *AE, DC, MC, V.*

$$$–$$$$

🖵 **Delta Chelsea Hotel.** Canada's largest hotel has long been popular with families and tour groups, so be prepared for a flurry of activity here. The Family Fun Zone has a children's creative center, an arcade, a family pool, and the four-story "Corkscrew"—downtown Toronto's only heated indoor waterslide. Camp Chelsea entertains kids with supervised activities while parents step out (daily from late June to early September, Friday night and Saturday the rest of the year). The Delta Chelsea has standard kitchenettes and deluxe guestrooms, as well as one- and two-bedroom suites. ⊠ *33 Gerrard St., Downtown M5G 1Z4* ☎ *416/ 595–1975 or 800/243–5732* 🖷 *416/585–4375* ⊕ *www.deltachelsea.com* ⇨ *1,590 rooms, 18 suites* ⚓ *3 restaurants, room service, cable TV, 2 pools, health club, hot tub, sauna, billiards, 3 lounges, video game room, babysitting, children's programs (ages 3–12), dry cleaning, laundry facilities, concierge floor, business services, convention center, parking (fee), no-smoking floors* ⊟ *AE, D, DC, MC, V.*

$$$–$$$$
Fodor's Choice
★

🖵 **The Fairmont Royal York.** Built by Canadian Pacific Railway in 1929 for the convenience of passengers using nearby Union Station, the enormous lobby has classic design from the year it was constructed, including travertine walls and columns. Guest rooms are formal without being stuffy. Comfy beds have ruffled pillows, thick comforters, and classic arched wood headboards. A skylight illuminates a lap pool from above, next to a hand-painted trompe l'oeil wall mural. The signature restaurant, Epic, has the city's best Canadian whole lobster (either butter-poached, steamed, grilled, or roasted), and the snug Library Bar just might have Toronto's best martinis. ✉ *100 Front St. W, Financial District M5J 1E3* ☎ *416/368–2511 or 800/441–1414* 🖷 *416/368–9040* 🌐 *www.fairmont.com* *1,304 rooms, 61 suites* *5 restaurants, in-room data ports, minibars, cable TV, pool, health club, 4 bars, shops, Internet, business services, travel services, parking (fee), no-smoking floors* 💳 *AE, D, DC, MC, V.*

$$$–$$$$ Fodor's Choice ★ **Hotel Le Germain Toronto.** The Germain Group is known for beautiful, chic, upscale boutique hotels, and the Toronto version is no exception. A retro, redbrick exterior—accented by a soaring glass-and-stainless-steel frontage—works well with the historic architecture of the surrounding theater district. The dazzling lobby contains a library, a cappuccino bar, and a double-side, open-hearth fireplace. Sleek furnishings fill ultramodern rooms, which have plasma-screen televisions. Suites have separate bedrooms and living rooms, wet bars, fireplaces, and private terraces that afford superb views of the skyline. The restaurant, Luce (which means "light" in Italian), serves first-class cuisine. ✉ *30 Mercer St., Entertainment District M5V 1H3* ☎ *416/345–9500 or 866/345–9501* 🖷 *416/345–9501* 🌐 *www.hotelboutique.com* *122 rooms, 4 suites* *Restaurant, café, cable TV, health club, massage, business services, parking (fee), no-smoking floors* 💳 *AE, DC, MC, V* 🍽 *CP.*

$$$–$$$$ **InterContinental Toronto.** This handsome and intimate member of a respected international hotel chain is just a two-minute walk from the main Yorkville shopping area. Service is top-notch. Art-deco touches enhance the public areas and the spacious guest rooms. Signatures Restaurant is elegant, comfortably classic, and has breezy alfresco dining in season. Relax in the clublike opulence of the Harmony Lounge: perfect for noshes, tea, or cocktails after a hard afternoon of shopping. ✉ *220 Bloor St. W, Yorkville M5S 1T8* ☎ *416/960–5200 or 800/267–0010* 🖷 *416/960–8269* 🌐 *www.toronto.intercontinental.com* *210 rooms, 11 suites* *Restaurant, in-room data ports, cable TV, pool, gym, massage, sauna, lounge, parking (fee), no-smoking floors* 💳 *AE, DC, MC, V.*

★ **$$$–$$$$** **Le Royal Meridien King Edward.** Toronto's first luxury hotel, a Heritage-designated property, has attracted a well-heeled clientele since 1903. Guests have included Rudyard Kipling and the Beatles. The "King Eddy" is still opulent, with its vaulted ceiling, marble pillars, and palm trees. Guest rooms aren't large by today's standards but are furnished in a charming English Edwardian way. Elegance oozes from the crown moldings and mahogany beds. The hotel's Café Victoria and the Consort Bar (serving a light lunch menu) are favorites among the city's elite. ✉ *37 King St. E, Old Toronto M5C 1E9* ☎ *416/863–9700 or 800/543–4300* 🖷 *416/367–5515* 🌐 *www.toronto.lemeridien.com* *292 rooms, 29 suites* *Restaurant, cable TV, gym, hair salon, spa, Internet, business services, meeting rooms, parking (fee), no-smoking floors* 💳 *AE, DC, MC, V.*

★ **$$$–$$$$** **Metropolitan Hotel.** A striking, modern look carries through from the 26-story facade to the neutral color schemes and square-edged furnishings in guestrooms. Down duvets and pillows, and triple sheeting of Italian linens adorn the beds. Bathrobes are from Frette Italian linens. Suite bathrooms have marble surfaces and whirlpool tubs. Romance packages come with chocolates and a red rose placed bedside at turndown service. Dining options include Hemispheres Restaurant & Bistro, and Lai Wah Heen (which means "luxurious meeting place"), a Cantonese restaurant serving great dim sum. ⊠ *108 Chestnut St., Downtown M5G 1R3* ☎ *416/977–5000 or 800/668–6600* 🖷 *416/977–9513* ⊕ *www.metropolitan.com* ⌕ *422 rooms, 58 suites ♧ 2 restaurants, in-room data ports, cable TV, indoor pool, health club, hot tub, sauna, 2 bars, playground, Internet, business services, parking (fee), no-smoking floors* ▭ *AE, D, DC, MC, V.*

$$$–$$$$ 🏨 **Renaissance Toronto Hotel at SkyDome.** Where else can you roll out of bed and watch a baseball game, pop-star concert, or monster truck rally from the comfort of your room? This is the world's only hotel completely integrated into a world-class sports and entertainment dome. All the guest rooms are large, but the most popular are the 70 rooms overlooking the stadium, along with nine bi-level field-view suites. The price of these rooms may vary with the event. ⊠ *1 Blue Jays Way, Entertainment District M5V 1J4* ☎ *416/341–7100 or 800/237–1512* 🖷 *416/341–5091* ⊕ *www.renaissancehotels.com* ⌕ *348 rooms ♧ Restaurant, cable TV, indoor pool, hot tub, sauna, health club, lobby lounge, Internet, business services, parking (fee), no-smoking floors* ▭ *AE, DC, MC, V.*

$$–$$$$ 🏨 **Comfort Suites City Centre.** A concrete exterior is all that remains from the time before this building was converted from government to hotel use. Cream and plum colors add to the lightness in the lofty, bright guest rooms, which have elbow room to spare. A cascading waterfall and a fireplace welcome guests to the lobby. For honeymooners (or those with a sense of irony), special suites come with heart-shape whirlpool spas, fireplaces, and chilled champagne. ⊠ *200 Dundas St. E, Downtown M5A 4R6* ☎ *416/362–7700 or 877/316–9951* 🖷 *416/362–7706* ⊕ *www.toronto.com/comfortsuites* ⌕ *151 suites ♧ In-room data ports, cable TV, indoor pool, gym, hot tub, lobby lounge, Internet, business services, parking (fee), no-smoking rooms* ▭ *AE, DC, MC, V.*

★ $$–$$$$ 🏨 **Grand Hotel and Suites.** A gorgeous 30-foot tall granite facade leads into a spectacular lobby of gleaming marble, coffee-color granite pillars, and floors crowned in plush furnishings. Two-room suites with dens have a spacious living room–work space separated from the bedroom area by French doors. Oversized ambassador suites are one- or two-story, with two marble washrooms and a full granite kitchen. Grand Jacuzzi suites have king-size beds and 6-foot-long whirlpool tubs. Or you can take a dip in a heated whirlpool up on the rooftop terrace while looking out at the city and Lake Ontario. Fine dining is available at the Citrus Room. ⊠ *225 Jarvis St., Downtown M5B 2C1* ☎ *416/863–9000 or 877/324–7263* 🖷 *416/863–1100* ⊕ *www.grandhoteltoronto.com* ⌕ *117 rooms, 60 suites ♧ Restaurant, kitchenettes, refrigerators, cable TV, in-room VCRs, gym, outdoor hot tub, sauna, business services, parking (fee), no-smoking floors* ▭ *AE, DC, MC, V* †◯† *BP.*

★ $$–$$$$ 🏨 **Sutton Place Hotel.** Visiting film and stage stars stay here because of Sutton Place's commitment to service and privacy, and its luxury. Tapestries, swaths of floral arrangements, antiques, and plush chairs fill the public areas. Guest rooms have French-provincial-style furnishings, cut-crystal bedside lamps, and some antiques. On alternating floors vibrant blues and vivid roses or calming greens decorate the rooms. Luxury suites come with full kitchens and whirlpool baths. You might appreciate the proximity to the Royal Ontario Museum, trendy Yorkville shops, the Toronto Eaton Centre, and an array of excellent ethnic restaurants. ✉ *955 Bay St., Downtown M5S 2A2* 🏨 *416/324–5621 or 800/268–3790* 🖨 *416/924–1778* ⊕ *www.suttonplace.com* ⇨ *230 rooms, 64 suites* ⚫ *Restaurant, in-room data ports, minibars, cable TV, indoor pool, health club, hair salon, laundry service, concierge, business services, parking (fee), no-smoking floors* ▤ *AE, DC, MC, V.*

$$–$$$$ 🖼 **Toronto Downtown Marriott Eaton Centre.** Do you shop in your sleep? Guest rooms here are connected to Eaton Centre through an above-ground walkway. They're also larger than most in town and have high-speed Internet access. An indoor rooftop swimming pool provides a fabulous view of the city. At the airy Parkside Café on the main floor, you can sip your coffee while basking in the light pouring in from the enormous windows. Character's sports bar (renovated in 2004) has giant wide-screen TVs, arcade games, and pool tables, and serves pub fare. Or you might choose the top-notch JW's Steakhouse. ✉ *525 Bay St., Downtown M5G 2L2* 🏨 *416/597–9200 or 800/905–0667* 🖨 *416/597–9211* ⊕ *www. marriotteatoncentre.com* ⇨ *435 rooms, 24 suites* ⚫ *2 restaurants, cable TV, indoor pool, health club, billiards, lobby lounge, sports bar, Internet, business services, parking (fee), no-smoking floors* ▤ *AE, DC, MC, V.*

★ $–$$$$ 🖼 **Cawthra Square B&B Inn.** Once the residence of a sergeant in the York Militia, Cawthra Square is now a restored 4,400-square-foot gay-friendly inn. Antiques, including a queen-size mahogany canopy bed, furnish Victoria's Room. Mary's Room has a mahogany four-poster bed and private terrace. Ric's luxury suite occupies an entire floor, with two bedrooms, whirlpool bath, and terrace. The large country kitchen has tin ceilings and access to an adorable garden with a gurgling pond, flowering plants, and shrubs. Continental breakfast, served from 7:30 to 1, includes a cornucopia of fresh baked goods, as does afternoon tea. ✉ *10 Cawthra Sq., Church–Wellesley M4Y 1K8* 🏨 *416/966–3074 or 800/259–5474* 🖨 *416/966–4494* ⊕ *www.cawthrasquare.com* ⇨ *6 rooms, 4 with bath* ⚫ *Cable TV, laundry service, Internet, parking (fee); no smoking* ▤ *AE, D, MC, V* ⦿ *CP.*

$$–$$$ 🖼 **Hilton Toronto.** Golds and creamy browns grace the lobby; upstairs, guest rooms have wood floors, subtle earth tones, and modern furniture. The indoor-outdoor pool is modest, but the view of the city from the glass enclosed elevators is a thrill. Proximity to the entertainment and financial districts makes the Hilton Toronto a convenient base. There's also direct access to the PATH, an almost 27-km-long (17-mi-long) underground shopping mall that's filled with shops and restaurants. ✉ *145 Richmond St. W, Downtown M5H 2L2* 🏨 *416/869–3456 or 800/267–2281* 🖨 *416/ 869–3187* ⊕ *www.hilton.com* ⇨ *601 rooms, 47 suites* ⚫ *5 restaurants, cable TV, indoor-outdoor pool, health club, hot tub, sauna, hot tub, 2 bars, Internet, parking (fee), no-smoking floors* ▤ *AE, DC, MC, V.*

$$–$$$ 🖼 **Holiday Inn On King.** Request views of Lake Ontario, the downtown skyline, or the SkyDome at this hotel smack in the middle of the pulsating Entertainment District. Guest rooms are large by downtown standards, with modern, subdued furnishings intended for comfort, not trendsetting style. Executive suites have whirlpool baths. The outdoor swimming pool and the fitness center are on the 17th floor. There are in-room spa services available. At the Canadian Bar & Grill, works of famous Canadian artists drape the walls, and the menu items are inspired by the country itself—Alberta beef and Casa Loma salmon, for example. ✉ *370 King St. W, Entertainment District M5V 1J9* ☎ *416/599–4000 or 800/263–6364* 🖷 *416/599–7394* ⊕ *www.hiok.com* ⋐ *425 rooms* ᓚ *2 restaurants, refrigerators, cable TV, pool, gym, massage, sauna, Internet, business services, meeting rooms, parking (fee), no-smoking floors* 🖃 *AE, D, DC, MC, V.*

★ **$$–$$$** 🖷 **Radisson Plaza Hotel Admiral Toronto–Harbourfront.** You can't get much closer to Toronto's waterfront, and unobstructed Lake Ontario and verdant Toronto Islands vistas come standard with the superb lakeside location. This small hotel has an appropriately maritime design, with deep blue accents, plush seating trimmed in rich, full-grain woods, and the requisite brass embellishments in public and private rooms. The full bank of windows at Commodore's Restaurant provides a spectacular panorama of the lake. The seafood specialties are some of the finest in the city: lobster and sweet-corn bisque, grilled Atlantic salmon, and pasta with scallops lazing in dill cream sauce are delicious. ✉ *249 Queen's Quay W, Harbourfront M5J 2N5* ☎ *416/203–3333 or 800/333–3333* 🖷 *416/203–3100* ⊕ *www.radisson.com* ⋐ *157 rooms* ᓚ *2 restaurants, cable TV, pool, hot tub, squash, bar, parking (fee), no-smoking floors* 🖃 *AE, D, DC, MC, V.*

$–$$$ 🖷 **Howard Johnson Toronto Yorkville.** The look of the rooms is standard fare—traditional chain-hotel, with some exposed brick walls—and the amenities are frugal, but the location is a big asset here. The stylish boutiques, antiques shops, and funky eateries of trendy Yorkville are just around the corner, and steps from the lobby door are key public-transit intersection points. Kids under 12 stay free in their parents' rooms. Ask about discounts for seniors or auto club members. ✉ *89 Avenue Rd., Yorkville M5R 2G3* ☎ *416/964–1220 or 800/446–4656* 🖷 *416/964–8692* ⊕ *www.hojo.com* ⋐ *69 rooms* ᓚ *Dining room, in-room data ports, cable TV, lounge, business services, meeting room, parking (fee)* 🖃 *AE, DC, MC, V* ⦿ *CP.*

$–$$$ 🖷 **Novotel Toronto Centre.** A good-value, few-frills, modern hotel, the Novotel is in the heart of the ultrachic Esplanade area, near the St. Lawrence Market, the Air Canada Centre, Union Station, and the Entertainment District. A brilliant idea: some suites have bowed shower-curtain rods for more in-tub space. The fitness facilities are especially extensive for the price range. Local calls are free and all rooms have coffeemakers. The restaurant, Cafe Nicole, serves up a heaping plate of scrumptious steak frites. ✉ *45 The Esplanade, Old Toronto M5E 1W2* ☎ *416/367–8900 or 800/668–6835* 🖷 *416/360–8285* ⊕ *www.novotel.com* ⋐ *262 rooms* ᓚ *Restaurant, cable TV, indoor pool, health club, hot tub, sauna, meeting rooms, parking (fee), no-smoking floors* 🖃 *AE, DC, MC, V.*

$–$$$ 🖷 **Palmerston Inn Bed & Breakfast.** Host Judy Carr has created a classic elegance in her 1906, Greek-pillar, Georgian mansion, with single and double rooms. Period antiques grace each guest room. Bathrobes and slippers are available. Two rooms have wood-mantled fireplaces. A covered outdoor deck serves as a breakfast room in summer. In winter, breakfast is served in a dining room with original stained-glass windows. There's all-day tea and coffee and afternoon sherry. From here, it's a pleasant stroll down historic, tree-lined Palmerston Boulevard to bustling Bloor Street or to trendy College Street bars and restaurants. ✉ *322*

6 MAJOR ATTRACTIONS
ONE LOW PRICE
AVOID MOST TICKET LINES

Purchase a

and enjoy:

Casa Loma

Ontario Science Centre

Toronto Zoo

Art Gallery of Ontario

CN Tower

Royal Ontario Museum

Ask for it at the first one you visit!
Good for 9 days from first use!
For more information visit
www.citypass.com or call
(707) 256-0490.
Prices change 4/1/06.
Taxes may be added as required.

Only **$49.50** CAD
A **$99.00 Value!** (Youth 4-12 **$31.75**)
CityPass is on sale at all of the above attractions.

**CityPass is also available for: New York City · Chicago · San Francisco
Philadelphia · Seattle · Southern California · Boston**

Palmerston Blvd., The Annex M5G 2N6 ☎ *416/920–7842 or 877/ 920–7842* 🖷 *416/960–9529* ⊕ *www.palmerstoninn.com* ➷ *6 rooms* ☾ *Lounge, free parking; no a/c in some rooms, no room TVs, no smoking* ▭ *MC, V* ⑩⑪ *BP.*

$–$$ 🏨 **Casa Loma Inn.** The builder of this 1894 mansion was a wealthy downtown jeweler who obviously wanted his home to sparkle like his diamonds. Host Danuta Ruczynki has labored for years to return the redbrick structure to its former brilliance. Etched-glass transom windows have been fully restored, and carved gargoyles peer out from lintels and corner turrets. Original guest rooms have fresh bathroom tiles and tubs; though snug, windows open for a refreshing breeze. Rooms in an addition to the house are larger, some with fireplaces and whirlpool baths. Most rooms have some view of the front or rear gardens. ⊠ *21 Walmer Rd., The Annex M5R 2W7* ☎ *416/924–4540* 🖷 *416/975–5485* ⊕ *www. toronto.com/casalomainn* ➷ *27 rooms* ☾ *Some in-room hot tubs, microwaves, refrigerators, laundry facilities, parking (fee); no a/c in some rooms, no smoking* ▭ *No credit cards.*

$–$$ 🏨 **Days Hotel & Conference Centre–Toronto Downtown.** Unlike many downtown properties, the Days Hotel has resisted the temptation to increase room rates exorbitantly, attracting international travelers and conference goers. The location has the advantage of being within walking distance of the major neighborhoods, without the expense of being right in the thick of them. Functional blond-wood furnishings and sunshine-color walls lend a modern Scandinavian aesthetic to the rooms. The Beer Cellar, a new bar, and a quiet little coffee shop are on-site. ⊠ *30 Carlton St., Downtown M5B 2E9* ☎ *416/977–6655 or 800/367–9601* 🖷 *416/977–0502* ⊕ *www.dayshoteltoronto.ca* ➷ *538 rooms* ☾ *Restaurant, coffee shop, in-room data ports, refrigerators, cable TV, indoor pool, bar, babysitting, meeting rooms, parking (fee), no-smoking floors* ▭ *AE, DC, MC, V.*

$–$$ 🏨 **Hotel Victoria.** A local landmark built in 1909, the Vic is Toronto's second-oldest hotel, with a longstanding reputation for service excellence. Architectural traces of the early 20th century are evident in the columned and marbled lobby, stately crown moldings, and floor-to-ceiling windows. Rooms are rather diminutive in size, but not in cleanliness or comfort. Wingback chairs and quilted bedcovers are nice touches. ⊠ *56 Yonge St., Old Toronto M5E 1G5* ☎ *416/363–1666 or 800/363–8228* 🖷 *416/ 363–7327* ⊕ *www.hotelvictoriatoronto.com* ➷ *56 rooms* ☾ *Restaurant, cable TV, parking (fee), no-smoking floors* ▭ *AE, DC, MC, V.*

¢–$$ 🏨 **Rosedale Bed & Breakfast.** History buffs might enjoy this designated Heritage home; on display in the parlor is a large collection of rare and unusual books gathered from around the world. The 1887 redbrick town house reflects Toronto's aristocratic past, but remains intimate and homey. The French Room, with antiques, French doors, and original fireplace, is a favorite with guests. The Green Room has a cozy sleigh bed and a wet bar. ⊠ *572 Sherbourne St., Rosedale M4X 1L3* ☎ *416/927–0543* 🖷 *416/ 966–0962* ⊕ *www.rosedalebandb.ca* ➷ *6 rooms, 4 with bath* ☾ *Dining room, parking (fee); no room phones, no smoking* ▭ *V* ⑩⑪ *CP.*

$ 🏨 **Mulberry Tree Bed & Breakfast.** In addition to being a gifted chef (try his signature breakfast of paper-thin Parisian crepes), host Paul Buer is also a celebrated photographer, and images from his family's global treks fill the rooms—even the dining room doubles as a kind of gallery. Bedrooms, where antiques and plants abound, are neat as a pin. Robes are provided. A small balcony off the guest lounge overlooks an attractive garden. This grand, century-old, Heritage home sits on a serene, tree-canopied street. ⊠ *122 Isabella St., Downtown M4Y 1P1* ☏ *416/960–5249* 🖷 *416/960–3853* ⊕ *www.bbtoronto.com/mulberrytree* ➹ *4 rooms* ⌂ *Dining room, in-room data ports, cable TV, parking (fee); no room phones, no smoking* ⊟ *No credit cards* ⍩ *BP.*

¢–$ ▦ **International Living Learning Centre Residence and Pitman Hall Residence.** On the Ryerson University campus are two adjacent buildings amalgamated into one large student and summer residence with a central reservation number. From early May to late August, they open their single-occupancy, dormitory-style guest rooms to non-students. (Guests under 18 must be accompanied by an adult.) Each room has a single bed and phone. At Pittman, bathroom and kitchen facilities are shared and Continental breakfast is included. The International Centre rooms have en suite bath and cable television, but no breakfast. The central location and inexpensive prices make these residences a hard deal to beat. ⊠ *Pittman Hall, 160 Mutual St.; International Living Learning Centre, 133 Mutual St. Downtown M5B 2M2* ☏ *416/979–5296* 🖷 *416/979–5241* ⊕ *www.ryerson.ca/conference* ➹ *Pittman Hall, 550 rooms without bath; International Living Learning Centre, 252 rooms* ⌂ *Cable TV in some rooms, laundry facilities, no-smoking floors; no TVs in some rooms* ⊟ *AE, MC, V* ⊗ *Closed Sept.–Apr.*

¢–$ ▦ **Massey College Student Residence.** You can crash at the modern student residence at the University of Toronto between early May and late August. Rates vary with length of stay (daily, weekly, and monthly), by the month (May through July are higher than August), and by type of room. Single and double junior suites have shared bathrooms, and single and double senior suites have private bathrooms. Rooms are spartan, but linens, towels, and housekeeping services are provided. There's only one pay phone for the entire residence. Breakfast is included; cafeteria-style lunch costs C$6.75, dinner C$12. Massey is a stone's throw from Queen's Park and other major attractions. ⊠ *4 Devonshire Pl., Queen's Park M5S 2E1* ☏ *416/946–7843* 🖷 *416/978–1759* ⊕ *www.utoronto.ca/massey/summer.html* ➹ *40 rooms, 5 with bath* ⌂ *Cafeteria, recreation room, laundry facilities, parking (fee); no a/c, no room phones, no room TVs, no smoking* ⊟ *MC, V* ⊗ *Closed Sept.–Apr.*

★ ¢ ▦ **Neill-Wycik College Hotel.** Fifteen of the 22 floors in this college residence, near Dundas and Yonge streets, become a non-student lodging value from early May through late August. There are four apartment-style units on each floor; within each unit—equipped with linens, towels, and pillows—there are either four or five bedrooms and two bathrooms. Each unit has a common area, a television lounge, and a kitchen (bring your own dishes and utensils). The 23rd-floor roof deck has grills for guest use and a great view of the city. The 5th floor has a terrace. Continental breakfast is included, but you can upgrade to a hot meal for only C$1. ⊠ *96 Gerrard St. E, Downtown M5B 1G7* ☏ *416/977–2320 or 800/268–4358* 🖷 *416/977–2809* ⊕ *www.neill-wycik.*

com ⤴ *300 rooms without bath* ♿ *Cafeteria, kitchenettes, sauna, laundry facilities, parking (fee); no a/c in some rooms, no room TVs* ▤ *MC, V* ¶ *CP* ✆ *Closed Sept.–Apr.*

¢ ▥ **Philomena and Dave Bed & Breakfast.** Relax, lemonade in hand, on the 3rd-floor balcony overlooking a small woods after a hard day power-shopping at nearby Honest Ed's, the city's most famous discount department store, or in fashionable Yorkville. Whatever you do, this cheerful, three-story, 1910 B&B is a welcoming spot to return to. Many original fixtures remain, including quarter-cut oak doors and trim and large stained-glass bay windows. Two of the rooms have broadloom carpets and the third has original hardwood; furnishings are eclectic—traditional, solid-wood dresses and sleek, modern, Scandinavian-style closets. The family cats roam the premises freely. English, German, and Italian are spoken here. ✉ *31 Dalton Rd., The Annex M5R 2Y8* ☎ *416/ 962–2786* ☎ *416/964–8837* ⊕ *www.bbcanada.com/2072.html* ⤴ *3 rooms without bath* ♿ *Dining room, cable TV, free parking; no a/c in some rooms, no room phones, no smoking* ▤ *No credit cards* ¶ *BP.*

North & Northeast

★ $$–$$$ ▥ **Hilton Suites Conference Centre & Spa.** The building's sleek architecture of glass and marble reflect what the area is known for—high-tech industry; this is often referred to as the "Silicon Valley of the North." Standard two-room suites have a separate bedroom and a pull-out sofa in the carpeted living room, wingback chairs, and art deco-style wood furniture. Follow the gilded staircase to the Holtz Spa, which has 14 feng shui-configured treatment rooms. At the upscale Essence of Unionville restaurant, the chef's specialty is maple-infused Atlantic salmon served on a Yukon-potato pancake with apple fennel sauce. ✉ *8500 Warden Ave., Markham L6G 1A5* ☎ *905/470–8500 or 800/ 668–8800* ☎ *905/477–8611* ⊕ *www.hilton.com* ⤴ *500 suites* ♿ *3 restaurants, cable TV, indoor pool, gym, spa, squash, lounge, Internet, business services, free parking, no-smoking rooms* ▤ *AE, DC, MC, V.*

$$–$$$ ▥ **Inn on the Park.** Six hundred acres of wooded parkland, with extensive jogging trails in summer and cross-country skiing in the winter, surround the Inn on the Park. Rooms are spacious, clean, and neatly furnished with conventional beds, wood side tables, and upholstered armchairs. From July 1 through Labor Day, families fill the poolside rooms and children participate in supervised swimming and other activities. The hotel is off the Don Valley Parkway, about 20 minutes' drive from downtown and a 10-minute walk from the Ontario Science Centre. ✉ *1100 Eglinton Ave. E, North York M3C 1H8* ☎ *416/444–2561 or 877/644–4687* ☎ *416/446–3308* ⊕ *www.innontheparktoronto.com* ⤴ *269 rooms* ♿ *2 restaurants, cable TV, 2 pools (1 indoors), health club, lounge, children's programs (ages 5–12), business services, free parking, no-smoking floors* ▤ *AE, DC, MC, V.*

★ $$–$$$ ▥ **Robin's Nest Bed & Breakfast.** A reflection of dignified Edwardian Canadian life, Robin's Nest is a restored 1892 Heritage home. The luxurious master suite overlooks an English garden and has a private terrace and an adjoining library with fireplace, as well as a whirlpool tub. The tall bay windows of the Jenny Wren Suite have a view of the front garden. The Tree Tops Suite's mansard ceilings frame a nice alcove that comes complete with a lion's claw soaking tub. Welcoming touches in every room include bathrobes and complimentary sherry. ⊠ *13 Binscarth Rd., Rosedale M4W 1Y2* ☎ *416/926–9464 or 877/441–4443* 🖷 *416/926–3730* ⊕ *www.robinsnestbandbtoronto.com* 🏷 *3 suites* ♿ *Dining room, cable TV, Internet, free parking; no smoking* ⊟ *MC, V* ⦿ *BP.*

$ 🖭 **Vanderkooy Bed & Breakfast.** Built in 1910, this immaculate and cozy home has retained many of its original decorative touches, including excellent examples of Edwardian stained-glass windows, antiques, and a collection of original watercolors. Two pet cats wander the premises. A full breakfast—Canadian pea-meal bacon, eggs, preserves, and heavenly French toast from a family recipe—is served on an antique oak table surrounded by fragrant plants and overlooking a colorful garden and miniature waterfall. Start your morning with a jog through one of the city's quietest neighborhoods, or take a nature hike through Balfour Park, an almost untouched tract of ravine forest, both close at hand. ⊠ *53 Walker Ave., Downtown M4V 1G3* ☎ *416/925–8765* 🖷 *416/925–8557* ⊕ *www.bbcanada.com/1107.html* 🏷 *4 rooms, 3 with bath* ♿ *Free parking; no room phones, no room TVs, no smoking* ⊟ *No credit cards* ⦿ *BP.*

¢–$ 🖭 **Helga's Place Bed & Breakfast.** An indoor pool and solarium sur-
Fodor'sChoice   rounded by greenery make Helga's feel like a spa retreat. The 2nd floor
★   has a common room with skylights and pine ceilings, and a library. One room has a king-size bed, a fireplace, and a whirlpool tub; the other two have queen-size beds and private balconies. Breakfast is a three-course affair that might include eggs or omelets, apple pancakes, waffles, croissants, sausages or ham, and vegetarian dishes on request, including frittata and quiche. Do try Helga's own hearty poppy-seed bread. Nearby subway and bus lines can get you downtown quickly. ⊠ *180 Codsell Ave., at Sheppard Ave. W, North York M3H 3W7* ☎ *416/633–5951* 🖷 *416/636–2335* ⊕ *www.bbcanada.com/3288.html* 🏷 *3 rooms* ♿ *Cable TV, in-room VCRs, free parking; no a/c, no room phones, no smoking* ⊟ *No credit cards* ⦿ *BP.*

West and Southwest

★ $$$$ 🖭 **The Old Mill Inn.** Tucked into the Humber River valley, Old Mill is the only country inn within the city limits of Toronto. Meticulous, manicured English gardens and an enchanting three-arched stone bridge flank the Tudor-style building, constructed in 1914. Burnished mahogany and cherrywood tables, chairs, and beds (some four-poster) grace each guestroom. Gas fireplaces, large whirlpool tubs, and down duvets invite romance. Exposed stone walls and a 50-foot-high solid fir cathedral ceiling define the Old World–style manor-house restaurant. There's dinner and dancing six nights a week, luncheon buffets, and afternoon tea. It's all just 15 minutes from downtown and the airport. ⊠ *21 Old Mill Rd., at Bloor St. W, West Toronto M8X 1G5* ☎ *416/236–2641 or 866/653–6455* 🖷 *416/236–2749* ⊕ *www.oldmilltoronto.com* 🏷 *46 rooms, 13 suites* ♿ *Restaurant, in-room data ports, minibars, cable TV, gym, spa, business services, free parking; no smoking* ⊟ *AE, DC, MC, V.*

★ $$–$$$ 🖭 **The Drake Hotel.** Once a notorious flophouse, this 19th-century building is now an off-the-wall boutique hotel. Hanging near the lobby's 110-

year-old terrazzo staircase is a Rorschach ink blot mural that spans the lounge and dining room. Vintage 1950s leather couches, slightly tattered ottomans, art curios, digital art projections, and flat-screen TVs decorate guestrooms. DJs rock and roll in the lounge, the underground bar, and on the rooftop patio nightly. The on-site Yoga Den has drop-in classes. ⊠ *1150 Queen St. W, Queen West M6J 1J3* ☎ *416/531–5042* 🖷 *416/ 531–9493* ⊕ *www.thedrakehotel.ca* ↪ *19 rooms, 1 suite* ⌂ *Restaurant, café, minibar, cable TV, in-room VCRs, fitness classes, massage, 3 bars, laundry service, Internet; no smoking* ☱ *AE, MC, V.*

★ **$–$$$** 🏨 **Bonnevue Manor Bed & Breakfast Place.** True craftsmen created this 5,000-square-foot house and it shows in every enchanting nook and cranny, in the high plastered ceilings, and in the richly aged hardwood floors. Rooms at the gay-friendly inn are airy and open, with bathrooms delightfully accented by sleek pedestal sinks. A kind of nostalgic funkiness blends 19th-century antiques and a wood-burning fireplace with modern pieces. Breakfasts brim with home-baked goods, hot cereals, and omelets. It's within walking distance of High Park, Toronto's largest green space, and the white sands of Sunnyside Beach; a 10-minute drive takes you downtown. ⊠ *33 Beaty Ave., West Toronto M6K 3B3* ☎ *416/536– 1455 or 800/603–3837* 🖷 *416/533–2644* ⊕ *www.toronto.com/ bonnevuemanor* ↪ *4 rooms* ⌂ *Dining room, free parking; no a/c, no room phones, no room TVs, no smoking* ☱ *AE, MC, V* ‖○‖ *BP.*

$–$$ 🏨 **Beaconsfield Bed & Breakfast.** An artist-and-actress couple owns this
Fodor'sChoice architecturally distinct 1882 Victoria B&B in the hip Queen West area.
★ Latin American artifacts and paintings, acquired during the hosts' travels, decorate the colorful, one-bedroom Mexican Suite. Hand-painted scenic murals cover the walls and ceilings of the panoramic, two-bedroom Ontario Suite. Both have direct access to an outdoor deck overlooking the backyard garden. The third room is smaller and a bit spartan. Homegrown breakfasts might include raspberries from the hosts' yard. Eclectic stores, art galleries, and ethnic restaurants are within a few minutes' walk, and there's 24-hour streetcar service nearby. ⊠ *38 Beaconsfield Ave., Queen West M6J 3H9* ☎ *416/535–3338* 🖷 *416/535–3338* ⊕ *www. bbcanada.com/beaconsfield* ↪ *3 rooms, 2 with bath* ⌂ *Free parking; no room phones, no room TVs, no smoking* ☱ *No credit cards* ‖○‖ *CP.*

¢–$ 🏨 **Islington Bed & Breakfast House.** Host Joey Lopes takes guests on a leisurely walking tour of the surrounding Humber River valley, describing its history and abundance of flora and bird life. The gently undulating hills Islington sits among are just 20 minutes from downtown. Most guest-room furnishings are mix-and-match, with solid wood pieces; one room showcases art-deco furniture. Hanging paintings and tapestries depict scenic countryside, reflecting the local landscape. ⊠ *1407 Islington Ave., Islington Village M9A 3K5* ☎ *416/236–2707* 🖷 *416/233–3192* ⊕ *www.bbcanada.com/5812.html* ↪ *3 rooms without bath* ⌂ *Cable TV, free parking; no a/c in some rooms, no room phones, no smoking* ☱ *No credit cards* ‖○‖ *BP.*

¢ 🏨 **Marigold International Traveler's Hostel.** This charming private hostel is off the beaten path but well connected to downtown by the Dundas and the College Street streetcars. It's popular with international backpackers. There are four to six beds per room, arranged in bunks. One room with double bunk beds is used as a private room to accommodate couples or a family of four; the others are usually rented as single-sex dormitories. You can lounge (and smoke) on three sundecks and one balcony in the front and back of the building. There are coin lockers and a TV room. Free coffee, tea, and doughnuts are set out in the morning, and checkout is by 2 PM. ☒ *2011 Dundas St. W, High Park M6R 1W7* ☎ *416/536–8824* 🖷 *416/588–2678* ⮑ *11 rooms* ⚴ *Cable TV, laundry facilities, free parking; no room phones, no smoking* ☐ *No credit cards.*

The Beaches

¢–$ 🏨 **B&B My Guest Bed and Breakfast.** Bordering Greektown and Little India, there's an irresistible Victorian home situated a 30-minute walk from the neighborhood waterfront. Friendly host Teri McIver, who hails from Ireland, relishes opening her century-old home to travelers from around the world. The Blue Room has a balcony, fireplace, and two double beds with iron headboards. The Gold Room is traditionally furnished with a queen-size bed, wooden headboard, and matching side tables. A hearty hot breakfast accompanied by fruits, breads, cereals, and yogurt is served in the dining room. ☒ *17 Gledhill Ave., The Beaches M4C 5K7* ☎ *416/422–3663 or 416/826–8021* 🖷 *416/422–0465* ⊕ *www.bbmyguest.com* ⮑ *3 rooms, 1 with bath* ⚴ *Dining room, fans, cable TV, free parking; no a/c in some rooms, no smoking* ☐ *AE, MC, V* ❍❘ *CP.*

The Airport Strip

$$–$$$$ 🏨 **Holiday Inn Select.** Pleasant rooms at affordable rates are the mainstays of this chain hotel. Like most hotels along the Dixon Road airport strip, it caters mostly to the business traveler and hosts a large number of conferences. Steaks sizzle at the Metro Bar & Grill. ☒ *970 Dixon Rd., Airport M9W 1J9* ☎ *416/675–7611 or 800/465–4329* 🖷 *416/675–9162* ⊕ *www.hiselect.com* ⮑ *445 rooms, 8 suites* ⚴ *Restaurant, cable TV, indoor-outdoor pool, gym, sauna, lobby lounge, Internet, business services, meeting rooms, airport shuttle, parking (fee), no-smoking floors* ☐ *AE, DC, MC, V.*

$$–$$$$ 🏨 **Toronto Airport Marriott.** To attract the leisure traveler, the Airport Marriott gives substantial weekend discounts of up to 50%. An enormous skylight over the indoor pool, adjacent to the lobby and breakfast restaurant, ensures that a generous helping of sunshine suffuses the space. Italian marble floors and rich mahogany trims enhance the public areas. Guest rooms are standard, bright, and comfortable. ☒ *901 Dixon Rd., Airport M9W 1J5* ☎ *416/674–9400 or 800/905–2811* 🖷 *416/674–8292* ⊕ *www.marriott.com* ⮑ *424 rooms, 12 suites* ⚴ *2 restaurants, cable TV, indoor pool, health club, hot tub, sauna, lobby lounge, bar, airport shuttle, parking (fee), no-smoking rooms* ☐ *AE, DC, MC, V.*

$$$ 🏨 **Wyndham Bristol Place–Toronto Airport.** After you've collected your luggage, pick up a phone at the arrival level, call the Wyndham Bristol Place, and an airport bus can have you here in about two minutes. This has long been considered one of the ritziest of the airport strip hotels. Bedrooms have mahogany armoires, tables, and desks. A small waterfall

cascades in the lobby. For an airport property, it's fairly quiet—rooms that face east are the quietest of all. ⊠ *950 Dixon Rd., Airport West M9W 5N4* ☎ *416/675–9444 or 877/999–3223* 🖷 *416/675–4426* ⊕ *www.wyndham.com* ⤴ *287 rooms, 5 suites* ⚹ *2 restaurants, in-room data ports, minibars, cable TV, indoor pool, health club, sauna, lobby lounge, playground, Internet, convention center, airport shuttle, parking (fee), no smoking rooms* ⊟ *AE, DC, MC, V.*

$–$$$ 🏨 **Courtyard by Marriott Toronto Airport.** Room design caters to business travelers with large, well-lit desks and ergonomic chairs for added comfort during those long conference calls. The Courtyard Café serves a standard hot breakfast buffet, with cook-to-order options. A large-screen TV dominates the lounge, where there are plenty of overstuffed sofas on which to unwind. The big plus here is convenience; you're around the corner from the airport, near the major crossroads of Highways 401 and 427, and a 20-minute drive from downtown. ⊠ *231 Carlingview Dr., Airport M9W 5E8* ☎ *416/675–0411 or 866/675–0411* 🖷 *416/675–0433* ⊕ *www.marriott.com* ⤴ *168 rooms, 1 suite* ⚹ *Restaurant, cable TV, in-room data ports, indoor pool, health club, hot tub, lounge, Internet, meeting rooms, airport shuttle, parking (fee), no-smoking floors* ⊟ *AE, DC, MC, V* ⍨⍥ *CP.*

$–$$$ 🏨 **Radisson Suites Toronto Airport.** Every suite at this hotel has a separate bedroom and a living room, a full-size pull-out couch, an oversize desk, a cordless phone, two TVs, and a coffeemaker. Fox Bistro, with its large central fireplace as the focal point, is comfortable, and serves a large variety of foods. Plenty of inexpensive restaurants are nearby. Bathrobes are available. Continental breakfast comes with the business-class club rooms. The airport shuttle is C$6 one way. ⊠ *640 Dixon Rd., Airport M9W 1J1* ☎ *416/242–7400 or 800/333–3333* 🖷 *416/242–9888* ⊕ *www.radisson.com* ⤴ *216 suites* ⚹ *Restaurant, minibars, cable TV, gym, parking (fee), no-smoking floors, airport shuttle* ⊟ *AE, DC, MC, V.*

$–$$ 🏨 **Travelodge Hotel Toronto Airport Dixon Road.** Pinewood furniture, exposed brick, and a large brass fireplace in the lobby encourage you to leave Toronto's urban sprawl at the door and slip into this rustic oasis. Each room is decorated in a similar country spirit. The airport shuttle is C$6 one way. ⊠ *925 Dixon Rd., Airport M9W 1J8* ☎ *416/674–2222 or 888/483–6887* 🖷 *416/674–5757* ⊕ *www.travelodge.com* ⤴ *283 rooms* ⚹ *Restaurant, cable TV, indoor pool, gym, sauna, lobby lounge, meeting rooms, parking (fee), no-smoking floors, airport shuttle* ⊟ *AE, D, DC, MC, V.*

$ 🏨 **Carlingview Airport Inn.** There are only three floors to this modest place, but what it lacks in size, it makes up for in friendly service. Standard rooms, in beiges and creams, are brightened by silk potted plants and bouquets of colorful silk flowers to cheer up otherwise unadorned coffee tables and dressers. ⊠ *221 Carlingview Dr., off Dixon Road, Airport M9W 5E8* ☎ *416/675–1176, 416/675–3303, 877/675–3303, or 800/263–6100* 🖷 *416/675–6524* ⊕ *www.carlingview.ca* ⤴ *112 rooms* ⚹ *Restaurant, airport shuttle, free parking, no-smoking floors* ⊟ *AE, DC, MC, V* ⍨⍥ *CP.*

Camping

For a list of licensed private campgrounds and trailer parks, contact the **Ministry of Tourism and Recreation** (✉ 900 Bay St., 9th fl., Downtown ☎ 416/314–7570 or 800/668–2746 ⊕ www.ontariotravel.net).

⚘ **Glen Rouge Campground.** A forest of pine, hemlock, maple, and meadows—12,000 acres worth—makes up the park that surrounds this campground. Well-marked hiking trails provide ample exposure to the park's resident plant and animal life, including fox, rabbit, deer, wild turkey, and many other species of birds. Fishing for trout and salmon are possible here, too. Eighty-seven serviced campsites have electricity and water; there are 27 unserviced campsites and 11 pack-in tent sites. Some are riverside. The park is in the city's northeast end, near the Toronto Zoo. ✉ *Hwy. 2, 1 km (½ mi) east of Port Union Rd., Scarborough* ⌂ *Toronto Parks and Wildlife, 100 Queen St. W, M5H 2N2* ☎ *416/ 338–2267* ⊕ *www.city.toronto.on.ca/parks* ⌤ *125 sites* ▣ *C$22–C$30* ⚲ *Flush toilets, partial hook-ups (electric and water), dump station, drinking water, showers, grills, picnic tables, public telephone, play area* ▤ *MC, V* ⊗ *Closed early Sept.–mid-May.*

⚘ **Albion Hills Campground.** There's good swimming from a sandy beach at the manmade Albion Lake, and 26 km (16 mi) of mountain bike trails at the Albion Hills Conservation Authority Park. You could also rent a boat and go fishing here. There are serviced and unserviced campsites as well as pull-through sites for RVs, with 15-amp and 30-amp service and a dumping station. Washrooms and hot showers are readily available throughout the campground. It's 8 km (5 mi) north of Bolton in Caledon, near the great hiking on the Bruce Trail. ✉ *16500 Hwy. 50, 40 km (25 mi) northwest of Toronto, Caledon L0N 1P0* ☎ *800/838– 9921* ⊕ *www.trca.on.ca/parks_and_attractions* ⌤ *234 sites* ▣ *C$22–C$25* ⚲ *Flush toilets, partial hook-ups (electric and water), dump station, drinking water, showers, grills, picnic tables, electricity, public telephone, general store, swimming* ▤ *AE, DC, MC, V* ⊗ *Closed mid-Oct.–mid-May.*

⚘ **Indian Line Campground.** For campers who prefer to rough it with ease, Indian Line is the ideal choice, close to the malls and markets of Brampton. You can swim, fish, canoe, or go for a hike in the day, and at night take in a movie. It's also close to Paramount Canada's Wonderland and Wild Water Kingdom, 30 minutes from downtown Toronto. There's plenty of shade for the 240 serviced and unserviced campsites, as well as pull-through sites for RVs, with 15-amp and 30-amp service. There's a snack bar on-site. ✉ *7625 Finch Ave. W, at Hwy. 427, north of Hwy. 401, Brampton L6T 4G3* ☎ *800-304-9728* ⊕ *www.trca.on.ca/parks_and_at- tractions* ⌤ *240 sites* ▣ *C$23–C$30* ⚲ *Flush toilets, partial hook-ups (electric and water), dump station, drinking water, showers, picnic ta- bles, electricity, public telephone, general store, play area, swimming* ▤ *AE, DC, MC, V* ⊗ *Closed Nov.–Apr.*

NIGHTLIFE &
THE ARTS

4

Updated by
Hannah James

TORONTO'S STATUS AS ONE OF THE MOST MULTICULTURAL CITIES IN THE WORLD has made its arts and nightlife scene a diverse and exciting one. As the city continues to grow, new venues emerge and some existing venues are magnificently refurbished. Ambitious programs from many of the city's new performance ensembles present a rich variety of entertainment for all tastes and budgets. The city's glamorous nightlife is maintained thanks in part to the string of celebs and other film and television industry types who paint the town red while on location here. Toronto's "every-city" quality attracts the location scouts, but it's the Torontonians' reputation for being courteous and leaving the stars alone that brings them back again and again. This means it's not uncommon to brush elbows with celebrities while enjoying a night out on the town.

The best places for information on all the city's cultural events are the free weekly newspapers *NOW* and *eye Weekly* and the "What's On" section of the *Toronto Star,* which all appear on Thursday; the Saturday (weekend) *Globe and Mail* and *National Post*; and the monthly magazine *Toronto Life.* On the Web, comprehensive and up-to-the-minute listings are available from *Toronto Life* (⊕ www.torontolife.com), *eye Weekly* (⊕ www.eye.net), *NOW* (⊕ www.nowtoronto.com), and the *Toronto Star* (⊕ www.thestar.com). Other sources include ⊕ www.toronto.com and ⊕ www.canoe.ca.

On any night in Toronto, visitors can find a place or entertainment to suit their tastes. From indie rock mash-up nights where arty semiotics majors showcase obscure rock operas and art, to pumping clubs where shiny people squeeze themselves into the tightest clothes, to divey, dark clubs where you can hear fancy-finger-picking bluegrass musicians, there's something for everyone. The newest strip for the cooler-than-thou crowd is along Dundas West, where small cocktail bars bearing names such as Cocktail Molotov and the Communist Daughter are the places to see and be seen. For night-owls there are always places to hang out in Toronto, from 24-hour restaurants in Chinatown and on the Danforth to all-night clubs along Queen West and College where you can dance until dawn on weekends.

THE ARTS

Toronto is the capital of the performing arts in English-speaking Canada, but it wasn't always so. Before 1950, Toronto had no opera company, no ballet, and very little theater worthy of the title "professional." Then came the Massey Report on the Arts, one of those government-sponsored studies that usually helps put sensitive subjects on the back burner for several more years. In this case, however, all heaven broke loose—money began to come from a variety of government grants; two prominent Canadian millionaires passed away and their death taxes were put toward the creation of the Canada Council, which doled out more money; the Canadian Opera Company, CBC television, and the National Ballet of Canada were born; and a number of little theaters began to pop up, culminating in an artistic explosion throughout the 1970s in every aspect of the arts.

More than money fueled this arts explosion, though. Other factors were a massive immigration from culturally nourished countries of Eastern and Central Europe, as well as from England; a growing sense of independence from the mother country; a recognition that if Canada did not develop its own arts, then the damned Yankees would do it for them; and, in general, a growing civic and cultural maturity.

Today Toronto is, after New York and London, the largest center for English-speaking theater in the world. The city's smaller theaters have long been filled with interesting productions of the finest in classic and contemporary Canadian, English, American, and French drama. Since the 1960s the Hummingbird (formerly the O'Keefe Centre) and Royal Alexandra theaters have provided a mix of local and Broadway productions. Restored historic theaters like the Elgin/Winter Garden complex and the Canon Theatre (formerly the Pantages), plus more modern venues, like the Toronto Centre for the Arts (formerly the Ford Centre) and the Princess of Wales, explain why it can truly be called "Broadway North"—for better or for worse.

Because of the many movies that are shot here, Toronto has also garnered the nickname "Hollywood North." The availability of excellent crews, the variety of locations (Toronto has posed for everything from Paris to Vietnam), and the savings from the exchange rate between U.S. and Canadian dollars are all contributing factors. Toronto has become an excellent venue for "star gazers" over the past number of years. Sit in the right restaurant or stroll along the tony shopping avenues and you may be lucky enough to run into any number of big-name actors passing through. Richard Gere and Catherine Zeta-Jones filmed *Chicago* here and Chow Yun Fat was in town for *Bulletproof Monk*. During 2002 or 2003, you may have run into Harvey Keitel shooting *Crime Spree,* Dennis Quaid and Sharon Stone near the set of *Cold Creek Manor,* Christopher Plummer in town for *Blizzard,* or Robert De Niro fresh off the set of *Godsend.* Locals generally let the stars have their privacy, even when spotted in public, which is another reason industry types like working here. For information about productions in town during your visit, phone the **Toronto Film and Television Office** (☎ 416/392–7570 ⊕ www. city.toronto.on.ca/tfto).

Tickets

Full-price theater tickets run from as low as C$20 to as high as C$95. Tickets for pop concerts are usually C$40 to C$100, although at smaller venues the cost may drop to as low as C$20. On certain slow nights and Sunday, many theaters have Pay What You Can (PWYC) entry. Simply phone the venue and ask. Tickets for almost any event in the city can be obtained through **Ticketmaster** (☎ 416/870–8000 ⊕ www. ticketmaster.ca).

To get half-price tickets on the day of a performance, visit the **T. O. Tix booth** (✉ Yonge St. at Dundas St. ☎ 800/541–0499 or 416/536–6468 ⊕ www.theatreintoronto.com), open in good weather Tuesday through Saturday noon–6, and operated by the Toronto Theatre Alliance. Tickets for Sunday performances are sold on Saturday. In summer, the wait can be 45 minutes or more. If you arrive at around 11:15 you stand the best chance of getting the show you want. As of September 24 you can buy tickets online. All sales are final, credit cards are accepted (Visa and MasterCard), and a small service charge is added to the price of each ticket. The Web site posts a list of what's available each day or call the number above. The booth also gives out superb brochures and pamphlets on the city.

Classical Music & Opera

Major Venues

The MacMillan Theatre. University of Toronto Symphony and Opera School productions take place here. The free U of T student newspaper, *The Varsity*, found all around the campus, lists events. ⊠ *University of Toronto Faculty of Music, Edward Johnson Bldg., 80 Queen's Park Crescent, Queen's Park* ☎ *416/978–3744* ⊕ *www.music.utoronto.ca.*

The Music Gallery. The self-titled "Centre for New and Unusual Music" presents an eclectic selection of new music, world music, atonal, classical, and avant-garde jazz in a relaxed atmosphere. The main venue is **St. George the Martyr Church** (⊠ 197 John St., Entertainment District), but there are several other venues, so call or visit the Web site for times and concert info. ☎ *416/204–1080* ⊕ *www.musicgallery.org.*

Walter Hall. This is the place to see avant-garde artists and the stars of the future. The intimate venue is suited to jazz groups, baroque ensembles, and student recitals. Because it's run by the music faculty of the University of Toronto, serious and experimental jazz bands and baroque chamber orchestras are often presented during the academic year at little or no cost. The acoustics at this small theater are good, as are all sight lines. For concert listings, you can pick up the free U of T student newspaper, *The Varsity*, on campus. ⊠ *University of Toronto Faculty of Music, Edward Johnson Bldg., 80 Queen's Park Crescent, Queen's Park* ☎ *416/978–3744* ⊕ *www.music.utoronto.ca.*

Classical Music

Glenn Gould Studio. A variety of classical music companies perform here. The box office is open Tuesday through Thursday only. ⊠ *250 Front St. W, Entertainment District* ☎ *416/205–5555* ⊕ *glenngouldstudio.cbc.ca.*

Tafelmusik. Internationally renowned as one of the world's finest period ensembles, Tafelmusik presents baroque music on original instruments. ⊠ *Trinity–St. Paul's United Church, 427 Bloor St. W, The Annex* ☎ *416/964–6337* ⊕ *www.tafelmusik.org.*

The Toronto Mendelssohn Choir. This group of 180 vocalists that often performs with the Toronto Symphony was begun in 1894 by Elmer Isler and has since been applauded worldwide. It performs the *Messiah* at Christmastime. Some of the beautiful and heartbreaking music heard in the Academy Award–winning film *Schindler's List* was sung by this choir. ⊠ *Roy Thomson Hall, 60 Simcoe St., Entertainment District* ☎ *416/598–0422 or 416/872–4255* ⊕ *www.tmchoir.org.*

Toronto Symphony Orchestra. Since 1922 this orchestra has achieved world acclaim with conductors such as Seiji Ozawa, Sir Thomas Beecham, and Andrew Davis. When Canadian-born Peter Oundjian took over as artistic director in 2003 it ended several years of instability for the ensemble, and signaled further rejuvenation of an already world-class orchestra. The TSO presents about three concerts weekly at Roy Thomson Hall from September through May when they are not on tour. ⊠ *Roy Thomson Hall, 60 Simcoe St., Entertainment District* ☎ *416/593–4828 or 416/872–4255* ⊕ *www.tso.on.ca.*

Opera

Canadian Opera Company. Founded in 1950, the COC has grown to be the largest producer of opera in Canada and the fifth-largest company on the continent. From the most popular operas, such as *Carmen* and *Madame Butterfly,* to more modern or rare works, such as *The Cunning Little Vixen* and *Hansel and Gretel,* the COC has proven trustworthy and often daring. Recent versions of Verdi's *La Traviata* and Wagner's *The Flying Dutchman* were considered radical by many. The COC often hosts world-class performers and it pioneered the use of scrolling subtitles that appear above the performers, which allow the audience to follow the libretto in English in a capsulized translation. Regular performances are at the Hummingbird Centre for the Performing Arts. A number of free performances are held outdoors at the **Harbourfront Centre** (⊠ 207 Queen's Quay W), usually during the last week of August. Seating is first-come, first-served. ⊠ *Hummingbird Centre, 1 Front St. E, Old Toronto* ☎ *416/363–6671* ⊕ *www.coc.ca.*

Concert Halls

It's not uncommon for a venue to present modern dance one week, a rock or classical music concert another week, and a theatrical performance the next.

★ **Elgin and Winter Garden Theatre Centre.** This jewel in the crown of the Toronto arts scene is comprised of two former vaudeville halls, built in 1913, one on top of the other, that together form one of the last operating double-decker theater complexes in the world. From 1913 to 1928, the theaters hosted vaudeville legends like George Burns, Gracie Allen, and Charlie McCarthy. In 1928 the Winter Garden closed and the Elgin became a cinema. The Elgin's gold-leaf-and-cherub–adorned interior and the Winter Garden's nature-themed decor, complete with hand-painted walls and ceiling hung with beech braches, fell into disrepair. In the 1980s, the Ontario Heritage Foundation completed an admirable C$30-million restoration—showcasing the building's Edwardian charm and original details, such as the Elgin's nickelodeon, damask wall coverings, and gilt cherubs, and the Winter Garden's beech-branch ceiling canopy—and reopened the theaters in 1989. These stages have since hosted Broadway-caliber musicals such as *Joseph and the Amazing Technicolor Dreamcoat* (starring Donny Osmond) and *STOMP,* comedy performances, jazz concerts, a Mozart opera festival, portions of the Toronto International Film Festival, the Renaissance Theatre Company's production of *A Midsummer Night's Dream* (directed by Kenneth Branagh and starring Emma Thompson), and much more. The Elgin, downstairs, has about 1,500 seats, and is more suited to musicals; Winter Garden, upstairs, is somewhat more intimate, with about 1,000 seats. Both theaters are wheelchair accessible, and both have excellent sight lines. The best Winter Garden seats are mezzanine row A, seats 208–209, or orchestra rows E and F, seats 31–33. At the Elgin, try for orchestra row N, seats 13–14 or 41–42; row J, seats 27–29; or mezzanine row A, seats 207–209. Guided tours (C$7) are given Thursday at 5 PM and Saturday at 11 AM. ⊠ *189 Yonge St., Midtown* ☎ *416/872–5555 tickets, 416/314–2901 tours* ⊕ *www.heritagefdn.on.ca.*

Hummingbird Centre for the Performing Arts. When this theater opened in 1960 as the O'Keefe Centre it showcased the world premiere of *Camelot,* starring Julie Andrews, Richard Burton, and Robert Goulet. Renamed in 1996 after major renovations, the theater has long been the home of the Canadian Opera Company and the National Ballet of Canada. The Hummingbird also plays host to visiting comedians, rock stars, pre-Broadway shows, and post-Broadway tours. Almost anything but the most lavish opera or musical can be accommodated in the cavernous 3,223-seat hall. The acoustics, however, can be sub-par at certain seats. Try for seats close to A47–48 and avoid very front rows, such as AA and BB. ⊠ *1 Front St. E, Old Toronto* ☎ *416/872–2262* ⊕ *www. hummingbirdcentre.com.*

Fodor'sChoice
★ **Massey Hall.** It has always been cramped, but Massey Hall's near-perfect acoustics and its handsome, U-shape tiers sloping down to the stage have made it a great place to enjoy music since 1894, when it opened with a performance of Handel's *Messiah.* The nearly 2,800 seats are not terribly comfortable, and a small number are blocked by pillars that hold up the ancient structure, but Massey Hall remains a venerable place to catch the greats and near-greats of the music world, such as (in 2004) Sarah Harmer, Cyndi Lauper, and Jason Mraz. Comedians and dance troupes are also standard fare. The best seats are in rows G–M, center, and in rows 32–50 in the balcony. ⊠ *178 Victoria St., Queen's Park* ☎ *416/872–4255* ⊕ *www.masseyhall.com.*

★ **Roy Thomson Hall.** The most important concert hall in Toronto opened in 1982. It was named for the billionaire newspaper magnate known as Lord Thomson of Fleet, after his family donated C$4.5 million in his memory. In 2002 a major facelift improved the hall's acoustics as well as its aesthetics, with new blond-wood flooring and pale decorative accents. It is the home of the Toronto Symphony Orchestra and the Toronto Mendelssohn Choir, and also hosts visiting orchestras and popular entertainers. The best seats are rows H and J in the orchestra and row L upstairs. Tours (C$4) highlight the acoustic and architectural features of the striking round structure. ⊠ *60 Simcoe St., Entertainment District* ☎ *416/872–4255 tickets, 416/593–4822 Ext. 363 tours* ⊕ *www. roythomson.com.*

St. Lawrence Centre for the Arts. This center has been presenting theater, music, dance, opera, film, and forums on public issues since 1970. The two main halls are the luxuriously appointed Bluma Appel Theatre and the Jane Mallett Theatre, both venues for recitals and performances by companies like the Toronto Operetta and the Hannaford Street Silver Band. At the Bluma Appel, try for rows E–N, seats 12–20; the Jane Mallett is small enough for all seats to have good sight lines. ⊠ *27 Front St. E, Old Toronto* ☎ *416/366–7723* ⊕ *www.stlc.com.*

Toronto Centre for the Arts. Classical music concerts and other musical performances—that have included classical Indian-music ensembles and a Vietnamese pop group—are often hosted at this center, opened in 1993. The architecturally impressive complex is less than a half-hour drive north of the waterfront and is close to the North York subway stop. It has a 1,850-seat main stage, a 1,030-seat recital hall, a 200-seat studio theater, and a two-story, 5,000-square-foot art gallery. The acoustically superb **George Weston Recital Hall** is internationally renowned as one of the finest halls in North America. It features international artists and a wide array of musical styles, from classical to klezmer to jazz. The best seats off the main stage are center orchestra, especially row H, seats 128–130, and mezzanine row A, seats 230–231. ⊠ *5040 Yonge St., North York* ☎ *416/870–8000 or 416/733–9388* ⊕ *www.tocentre.com.*

Dance

Toronto's rich dance scene includes pretty, *Swan Lake* interpretations and edgy, emotionally charged modern dance performances. Dance schools range from traditional ethnic-dance studios to the National Ballet School and the Toronto Dance Theatre.

National Ballet of Canada. Canada's homegrown and internationally recognized classical ballet company was founded in 1951 by Celia Franca, an English dancer from the Sadler's Wells tradition, and is supported by infusions of dancers trained at its own school. The season runs from November through May. A series of outstanding productions, such as Kenneth MacMillan's *Manon,* John Cranko's *Taming of the Shrew* and *Romeo and Juliet,* Glen Tetley's *Alice,* and James Kudelka's *The Actress* and *The Nutcracker,* have been performed by the company, and many have moved into the permanent repertory. Mr. Kudelka, a Canadian choreographer and the company's artistic director, has directed the National Ballet to a more contemporary repertoire and is breaking the company's star system by advancing dancers from the corps and soloist ranks. Tickets run C$26–C$114. Same-day half-price tickets for students and seniors are available at the box office on the day of performance. ⊠ *Hummingbird Centre, 1 Front St. E, Old Toronto* ☎ *416/345–9595 information, 866/345–9595 tickets* ⊕ *www.national.ballet.ca.*

Premiere Dance Theatre. This is a venue for dance performances by local contemporary companies as well as visiting troupes like the internationally renowned La La La Human Steps. ⊠ *Harbourfront Centre, 207 Queen's Quay W, Harbourfront* ☎ *416/973–4000* ⊕ *www. harbourfrontcentre.com.*

Toronto Dance Theatre. With roots in the Martha Graham tradition, Toronto Dance Theatre is the oldest contemporary dance company in the city. Since its beginnings in the 1960s it has created close to 100 works, more than a third using original scores commissioned from Canadian composers. It tours Canada and has played major festivals in England, Europe, and the United States. ⊠ *Premiere Dance Theatre, Harbourfront Centre, 207 Queen's Quay W, Harbourfront* ☎ *416/973–4000* ⊕ *www. harbourfrontcentre.com.*

Film

Toronto has a devoted film audience. The result is a feast of riches—commercial first- and second-run showings, festivals, and lecture series for every taste. A loosely associated group of independent movie theaters, including the Fox, the Music Hall Royal, Revue, Kingsway, and Paradise, offers low-priced screenings of independent productions, old classics, cult films, and new commercial releases. For movie times, contact the theaters directly, or check *Now Magazine* online at www. nowtoronto.com.

First-Run & Mainstream Movies

The Cinesphere. This theater offers 70mm films—those especially made for the IMAX screen system, and popular films that benefit from the large format and 24-track sound. ⊠ *Ontario Place, 955 Lakeshore Blvd. W, Harbourfront* ☎ *416/314–9900.*

The Docks Drive-in Theatre. For an old-fashioned treat, head to the al fresco Docks Drive-in, open from spring to mid-October, weather-permitting. First-run flicks are shown on Friday, Saturday, Sunday, and Tuesday evenings, starting at approximately 9 pm. Tickets can be purchased in person at the Docks box office. ⊠ *11 Polson St., near the harbor, Harbourfront* ☎ *416/461–3625* ⊕ *www.thedocks.com/nav/drivein.htm.*

Paramount. In the heart of the Entertainment District, this megaplex shows all the latest blockbusters. For advanced tickets go to the Web site. ⊠ *John St. and Richmond St., Downtown* ☎ *416/368–5600* ⊕ *www. famousplayers.com.*

Varsity. The many screens here show new releases. Smaller VIP screening rooms have seat-side waitstaff ready to take your concession-stand orders. ⊠ *55 Bloor St. W, at Bay St., Yorkville* ☎ *416/961–6303* ⊕ *www.cineplex.com.*

Independent, Foreign & Revival Films

Carlton Cinemas. Head to this theater for rarely screened films from around the world. Foreign-language films are shown in the original language with subtitles. ⊠ *20 Carlton St., Midtown* ☎ *416/598–2309.*

Cinematheque Ontario. International film programs are presented at the Art Gallery of Ontario year-round. Series of years past have featured specific genres and exceptional directors. ⊠ *317 Dundas St. W, Midtown* ☎ *416/968–3456.*

Cumberland 4. An excellent selection of international and nonmainstream new films are shown here. Prior to the movie, slideshows displaying visual art replace the typical rapid-fire advertisements at other theaters. ⊠ *159 Cumberland St., Yorkville* ☎ *416/646–0444.*

Film Reference Library. This is the largest collection of English-language Canadian film material in the world. For a small fee, the public may view everything from posters and books to actual screenings of films in the reference selection. The library is open weekdays noon to 5. ⊠ *2 Carlton St., Midtown* ☎ *416/967–1517.*

Harbourfront Centre. Interesting retrospectives, such as one featuring early-20th-century classic Japanese film, are presented here. ⊠ *235 Queen's Quay W, Harbourfront* ☎ *416/973–4000* ⊕ *www. harbourfrontcentre.com.*

Film Festivals & Events

☺ **Sprockets: The Toronto International Film Festival for Children.** Held at the end of April each year, this festival features new works and classic films aimed at children ages 4 to 14. Call for times and venues. ☎ 416/968–3456.

Talk Cinema. This interactive cinema experience takes place Sunday mornings from November to April. Each Sunday, audiences view a film, and then listen to a guest speaker—often a director, producer, or actor—who comments on the feature and answers questions. Tickets are available for individual films or for the entire series. ☎ 416/968–3456 ⊕ www.bell.ca/filmfest.

Toronto International Film Festival. Downtown is dominated by this festival each September. The 10-day event, the third-largest of its kind in the world, attracts Hollywood's brightest stars to view the latest works of both great international directors and lesser-known independent film directors from Canada and around the world. You can get tickets in advance through a balloting process that starts in July; information can be found on the festival's Web site. Single tickets to available films can be purchased online as well. Most films are sold out early on at this hugely popular festival except for a few rush tickets, which require enduring long lines. ☎ 416/967–7371 or 416/968–3456 ⊕ www.bell.ca/filmfest.

Theater

Some of the most entertaining theater in Toronto is free, though donations are always welcome. Every summer the CanStage theater company presents **Dream in High Park** (⊠ High Park, main entrance off Bloor St. W at High Park Ave., West Toronto ☎ 416/367–8243 information, 416/368–3110 box office ⊕ www.canstage.com), quality productions of Shakespeare and contemporary works in glorious High Park's outdoor amphitheater. The productions are usually knockouts and run from July to late August. In fall, the natural amphitheater transforms into a picnic ground and family entertainment venue. The plays are under the stars, so call ahead if it is drizzling. Call for directions to the amphitheater.

Commercial Theaters

Canon Theatre. This 1920 vaudeville theater, formerly known as the Pantages Theatre, is one of the most architecturally and acoustically exciting live theaters in Toronto. In 1988–89& then-owner Cineplex Odeon refurbished the magnificent theater in preparation for the Canadian debut of *The Phantom of the Opera*. The theater itself is one of the most beautiful in the world. Designed by world-renowned theater architect Thomas Lamb, it has Doric, Ionic, and Corinthian columns, a grand staircase, gold-leaf detailing, crystal chandeliers, and working gas lamps. Most sight lines are better than might be expected at a theater with 2,250 seats—the best are, typically, in the middle of the orchestra and the front of the mezzanine. ⊠ 263 Yonge St., Downtown ☎ 416/872–1212 ⊕ www.onstagenow.com.

Princess of Wales. State-of-the-art sound and technical facilities and wonderful wall and ceiling murals by American artist Frank Stella grace this theater. The local producers of *Miss Saigon,* father-and-son team Ed and David Mirvish, built this exquisite 2,000-seat theater in 1991–93 to accommodate the technically demanding musical when no other suitable venue was available. All levels are wheelchair-accessible. If you can, book Row A, seats 29–30 in the dress circle (mezzanine), or Row B, seats 35–36 in the stalls (orchestra). ⊠ *300 King St. W, Entertainment District* ☎ *416/872–1212 or 800/461–3333* ⊕ *www.onstagenow.com.*

Royal Alexandra. Since 1907, this has been the place to be seen in Toronto. The 1,500 plush red seats, gold brocade, and baroque swirls and flourishes make theatergoing a refined experience. This was Ed Mirvish's first foray into drama and theater production, followed in the 1980s by his purchase of London's Old Vic and in the 1990s by his building of the Princess of Wales theater. Recent programs have been a mix of blockbuster musicals and a variety of dramatic productions, some touring before or after Broadway appearances. The theater is wheelchair-accessible on the 1st floor only. Avoid rows A and B; try for rows C–L center. For musicals, aim for the front rows of the first balcony. ⊠ *260 King St. W, Entertainment District* ☎ *416/872–3333 or 800/461–3333* ⊕ *www.onstagenow.com.*

Small Theaters & Companies

Buddies In Bad Times. Local thespians and playwrights present edgy, alternative performances in the country's largest gay-centered multi-theater complex. Actor Daniel MacIvor has performed here. ⊠ *12 Alexander St., Yonge and College* ☎ *416/975–8555* ⊕ *buddiesinbadtimestheatre.com.*

Factory Theatre. This is Canada's largest producer of homegrown theater. Many of the company's alternative Canadian plays have gone on to tour the country and have won prestigious awards. ⊠ *125 Bathurst St., Entertainment District* ☎ *416/504–9971* ⊕ *www.factorytheatre.ca.*

Hart House Theatre. Amateur, student, and occasional professional productions have been presented here, at the main theater space of the U of T, since 1919. ⊠ *7 Hart House Circle, Queen's Park* ☎ *416/978–8668* ⊕ *www.harthousetheatre.ca.*

Le Théâtre Français de Toronto. French-language drama of high quality is performed at this theater, whose repertoire ranges from classical to contemporary, both from France and French Canada. ⊠ *26 Berkeley St., 2nd fl., Cabbagetown* ☎ *416/534–6604* ⊕ *www.theatrefrancais.com.*

Fodor'sChoice ★ **Rivoli.** Along the Queen Street strip, the Rivoli has long been a major showcase for the more daring arts in Toronto. A back room functions as a performance space, with theater happenings, "new music" (progressive rock and jazz), improvisational comedy troupes, and more. Some nights have a cover charge, usually C$5 to C$10. Asian-influenced cuisine and good steak are served in the dining room. Dinner for two, without drinks, runs about C$35. The walls are lined with work (all for sale) by up-and-coming local artists. There's also a bar, and a pool hall upstairs. ⊠ *332 Queen St. W, Queen West* ☎ *416/596–1908 or 416/597–0794* ⊕ *www.rivoli.ca.*

★ **Tarragon Theatre.** The natural habitat for indigenous Canadian theater is in this old warehouse and railroad district. Maverick companies often rent the smaller of the Tarragon's theaters for interesting experimental works. ⊠ *30 Bridgman Ave., The Annex* ☎ *416/531–1827* ⊕ *www.tarragontheatre.com.*

Théâtre Passe Muraille. In the hip, up-and-coming area around Bathurst and Queen streets, this venue has long been the home of fine Canadian collaborative theater. ✉ *16 Ryerson Ave., Entertainment District* ☎ *416/ 504–7529* ⊕ *www.passemuraille.on.ca.*

🜏 **Lorraine Kimsa Theatre For Young People.** Productions are devoted solely to children, but unlike many purveyors of traditional children's fare, this place does not condescend, or compromise its dramatic integrity. ✉ *165 Front St. E, Old Toronto* ☎ *416/862–2222* ⊕ *www.lktyp.ca.*

NIGHTLIFE

Toronto has all kinds of music clubs, as well as lots of places to hang out or dance. Many have the life span of a butterfly, so call before you set out to make sure they're still open and offering the kind of evening you're searching for. Downtown, Adelaide Street West from University Avenue to Peter Street has spawned numerous clubs of the loud, techno variety. Many places there don't charge a cover, and those that do rarely ask more than C$10.

The stretch of College Street between Bathurst and Ossington streets, known as Little Italy, is crammed with candlelit martini bars. Beautiful people come here to sip beautiful cocktails. The nightlife in The Beaches, home of The Beaches Jazz Festival, is concentrated along Queen Street from Woodbine Avenue east to Victoria Park Avenue. Bars and clubs catering to the casual, sporty types who stroll up after playing beach volleyball, and the locals—many of whom work in the performing arts and film trades—dot the streetscape.

The intersection of Yonge Street and Eglinton Avenue—known as "Young and Eligible" by locals—is popular with young professionals. Dance clubs, pool halls, and a variety of bars and pubs are in this area.

Bars & Pubs

Have a good time in Toronto, but be aware of the strict drinking and driving laws. Police regularly stop cars to check drivers' sobriety with a breath analysis test. If you have a blood-alcohol level higher than .08%, it's the judge or jail, no matter where you're from. Under the city's liquor laws, last call in bars is 2 AM; closing time is 3 AM. The minimum drinking age is 19.

On June 1, 2004, Toronto implemented a bylaw that forbids smoking in bars, pool halls, and casinos. Some patios and separate smoking rooms—which are often oppressively smoky—are approved for smokers by the city government, but to avoid hefty fines, check with the venue prior to lighting up.

★ **Frisco's.** A landmark in the club district, this retrofitted factory attracts the high-tech and financial crowd to its restaurant and upstairs bar on Thursdays and Fridays. Shoulder to shoulder, 25- to 40-year-old singles dance and mingle. The line for the sidewalk patio starts forming at 3:30 PM, and at 9 PM for the upstairs bar. ✉ *133 John St., Entertainment District* ☎ *416/595–8201.*

Allen's. This quintessential Irish pub—an anomaly on the mostly Greek avenue—with Emerald-Isle brews on tap, is a great place to go for a quick drink or for an entire evening, since the food is better than most pub fare. ⊠ *143 Danforth Ave., East Toronto* ☎ *416/463–3086.*

Brunswick House. Students from the nearby University of Toronto make up the bulk of the crowd here. The saloon atmosphere is loud, raucous, and fun. ⊠ *481 Bloor St. W, The Annex* ☎ *416/964–2242.*

Fiddlers Green. This Victorian-style Irish pub attracts a large group of regulars. Multiple taps of ales and lagers, along with a full menu, keep the staff hopping. Drop in for a pint and discover why it claims to have the friendliest atmosphere in town. ⊠ *27 Wellesley St. E, Church and Wellesley* ☎ *416/967–9442.*

Gypsy Co-Op. The two floors of this bar accommodate a funky, stylish crowd looking for some bohemian downtown flavor. Although the decor has moved from "general store" to upscale, the Co-Op remains an important venue for an eclectic mix of who's who in the performing and visual-arts communities. ⊠ *817 Queen St. W, Queen West* ☎ *416/ 703–5069* ⊕ *www.bandofgypsies.com.*

Hemingway's. One of the most crowded singles bars in Toronto, Hemingway's is homier and less serious than other Yorkville watering holes. The bar has comfortable high-back chairs, mirrors, artsy posters, and books lining one wall. Thursday, Friday, and Saturday evenings the music is live rock and Top 40. About three-quarters of the middle- to upper-class professionals who frequent this place are regulars. ⊠ *142 Cumberland St., Yorkville* ☎ *416/968–2828.*

★ **Madison Avenue Pub.** On the edge of the U of T campus, and often filled to the gills with college students from fall to spring, "Maddy" has six levels of good food and drink. It typifies an English pub, with lots of brass, exposed brick, and dartboards. Sixteen brands of beer are on tap, and there's a large selection of bottled imports. A piano bar, billiards rooms, and plasma-screen TVs are also part of the scene. The patios are lively in summer. ⊠ *14–18 Madison Ave., The Annex* ☎ *416/927–1722.*

Myth. Great Mediterranean and Middle Eastern food are served here, in the middle of the city's Greek area, but the real action starts *après* dinner on weekends and centers around the bar. The big-screen TVs mounted in the vaulted corners play mostly movie classics, but the young, trendy customers are watching each other, not the films. ⊠ *417 Danforth Ave., East Toronto* ☎ *416/461–8383.*

★ **Smokeless Joe's.** More than 250 beers from around the world, many of which can't be found anywhere else in Ontario, are served here. Friendly staff, comfort food, and a smoke-free patio keep the bar very crowded on weekends. ⊠ *125 John St., Entertainment District* ☎ *416/591–2221.*

Wayne Gretzky's. The pre-game Blue Jays and Maple Leafs fans and the post-theater crowd from Second City comedy club across the street flock to this sports bar and family-style restaurant. When he's in town, the hockey icon and part-owner can often be seen in the crowd. The rooftop patio, open from May through September, is built around a waterfall and is considered one of the best in town. ⊠ *99 Blue Jays Way, Entertainment District* ☎ *416/979–7825.*

The Whistling Oyster. Famed for its seafood, the Oyster really rocks during happy hour (daily 4–7), when the martinis flow and dim sum and other delicacies are offered at invitingly low prices. The place is almost always packed with regulars who crowd around the bar and flirt with the waitstaff. The crowd is mainly professionals, and a good deal of pick-up business takes place every night. In fact, rumor has it the owner met his wife here. ⊠ *11 Duncan St., below street level, Entertainment District* ☏ *416/598-7707.*

Gay & Lesbian

Pegasus on Church. Locals come here to meet, shoot pool, and above all, play the interactive Internet game NTN Trivia. Pegasus is famous in Toronto for consistently being one of the top scorers on the "wired" trivia game. The music is mixed by the bartender of the day, and each one has a loyal following. ⊠ *489B Church St., Church and Wellesley* ☏ *416/927-8832* ⊕ *www.pegasusonchurch.com.*

Slack Alice. One of the oldest gay and lesbian bars in town, the Alice has a great kitchen serving steaks, pizzas, and fajitas, and provides a friendly atmosphere with nightly events, themes, and contests. ⊠ *562 Church St., Church and Wellesley* ☏ *416/969-8742* ⊕ *www.slackalice.ca.*

Woody's. A predominantly upscale male crowd, with lots of professional types, frequents Woody's. Check out the Bad Boys Night Out on Tuesday, the Best Chest Contest (men competing only) on Thursday, and the ever-changing entertainment each Sunday. ⊠ *467 Church St., Church and Wellesley* ☏ *416/972-0887* ⊕ *www.woodystoronto.com.*

Comedy Clubs

The Laugh Resort. Catch stand-up solo acts Wednesday through Saturday nights. The cover is C$7 to C$15 (no drinks included). Ensure a great seat by going early and enjoying a light preshow dinner. ⊠ *370 King St. W, Entertainment District* ☏ *416/364-5233* ⊕ *www.laughresort.com.*

Fodor'sChoice ★ Second City. Since it opened in 1973, Second City has been providing some of the best comedy in Toronto. Many alumni of this troupe have become well known through *Saturday Night Live* and the *SCTV* series. Among those who cut their teeth on the Toronto stage are Mike Myers, Dan Aykroyd, Martin Short, Andrea Martin, and Catherine O'Hara. Recent grads Ryan Stiles and Colin Mochrie appear on *Whose Line Is It Anyway?* Weekend shows tend to sell out in summer. The cost is C$21–C$28, or C$53–C$60 for dinner and show. ⊠ *56 Blue Jays Way, Entertainment District* ☏ *416/343-0011 or 800/263-4485* ⊕ *www.secondcity.com.*

Yuk Yuk's Superclub. Part of a Canadian comedy franchise, this giant venue headlines the best stand-ups, with covers usually between C$10 and C$17. Admission is cheaper on Monday and Tuesday, when amateurs and students from the Humber College Comedy School take the stage. Booking a dinner-and-show package guarantees you better seats. ⊠ *260 Richmond St. W, Entertainment District* ☏ *416/967-6425* ⊕ *www.yukyuks.com.*

Dance Clubs

Fez Batik. A twenty- to thirtysomething crowd comes to dine and cut the rug in this popular Moroccan-style club, decorated with Persian carpets, gauzy drapes, and velvety banquettes. Funky patrons get down to DJs spinning underground hip-hop, retro, and other danceable beats.

Parry Farrell has spun records here. The dress code prohibits sweat suits and baseball caps. ⊠ *129 Peter St., Entertainment District* ☎ *416/ 204–9660* ⊕ *www.bandofgypsies.com.*

★ **The Courthouse Chamber Lounge.** With its lofty ceilings, plush couches, and roaring fireplaces, this club above the Courthouse Market Grille more closely approximates a 1940s Hollywood mansion than a courthouse. The cocktail crowd is modern and upscale. The stairs continue up from the restaurant to the dance floor to a lounge that overlooks the scene. The Cell Bar cigar bar is in the basement; it still shows remnants of the actual holding cells from the old courthouse days. ⊠ *57 Adelaide St. E, Old Toronto* ☎ *416/214–9379* ⊕ *www.libertygroup.com.*

The Docks. Far more than just a dance club, this enormous complex on Lake Ontario provides complete entertainment for partygoers, with video games, six beach-volleyball courts, a driving range, a climbing wall, a drive-in movie theater, a swimming pool, 22 outdoor billiard tables, indoor and outdoor dance floors, and even a flying trapeze. There are plenty of places to drink at night. The terrace has spectacular views of Toronto's skyline. ⊠ *11 Polson St., Harbourfront* ☎ *416/469–5655* ⊕ *www.thedocks.com.*

Fodor'sChoice **The Guvernment.** Each of the eight lounges and dance clubs in this in-
★ terlocked complex has its own thematic decor and special events. In the main club, R&B Fridays and Spin Saturdays bring pulsing lasers and clouds of dry ice that float across 22,000 square feet of dance space. The chic rooftop Skybar has one of the city's best skyline views, while the Southeast Asian–influenced Tanja Lounge caters to a mellower crowd. The club gets going after midnight. ⊠ *132 Queen's Quay E, Harbourfront* ☎ *416/869–0045* ⊕ *www.theguvernment.com.*

Inside and Chocolate Lounge. Three levels are decorated in subtle shades of brown and bronze, with expansive space for dancing and lounging. You can warm up to ambient vibe music early on, and then cut loose to livelier house and soul as the hour grows late. Chill out in the VIP basement lounge with bottle service or hit the wildly decorated rooftop patio in the warmer months. The higher-than-average cover charges mean the club tends to attract an older crowd. ⊠ *218 Richmond St. W, Entertainment District* ☎ *416/591–0009.*

★ **joe.** A young crowd comes to dance, drink, and lounge on the three huge levels of this club. Regular theme events, like Friday night's "School Disco," have unusual dress codes, so check what's on before you set out. Weekend covers are usually about C$10. ⊠ *250 Richmond St. W, Entertainment District* ☎ *416/971–6563* ⊕ *www.joeonline.ca.*

Joker. A three-story dance emporium of brooding and ominous proportions, the Joker has a cavelike atmosphere, thanks to its dark decor. Each floor plays different music, but expect high-energy dancing. Saturday night is the most popular—lines start to form as soon as the doors open at 9. Covers range from C$5 to C$10. ⊠ *318 Richmond St. W, Entertainment District* ☎ *416/598–1313* ⊕ *www.jokernightclub.ca.*

System Sound Bar. House, techno, and R&B reverberate throughout this basement-level bar/club. This club is mostly geared to pumped-up electronic music fans in their early twenties. ⊠ *117 Peter St., Entertainment District* ☎ *416/408–3996* ⊕ *www.systemsoundbar.com.*

Tonic Nightclub. Just above the subterranean System Sound Bar, the more sophisticated Tonic attracts a mid-twenties to early thirties crowd. DJs spin house, techno, and R&B. Expect a cover charge of $5 to $10, depending on the night. ⊠ *117 Peter St., Entertainment District* ☏ *416/ 204–9200* ⊕ *www.tonicnightclub.com.*

Velvet Underground. This is the most alternative of Toronto's alternative clubs. The dungeon-esque decor and techno music make it popular among the Goth set, especially on Monday nights. ⊠ *508 Queen St. W, Queen West* ☏ *416/504–6688* ⊕ *www.libertygroup.com.*

Gay & Lesbian

Publications catering to the gay community include *X-Tra,* free at various venues and at paper boxes around town, and *Fab,* a free monthly mag distributed at shops and restaurants. Both have information on nightlife, issues, and events.

Ciao Edie. Have a colorful cocktail and kick back among the retro furnishings at this laid-back lounge. Girls who just wanna have fun can check out the bar's lesbian Here Kitty Kitty night on Sunday, when DJs— including *eye Weekly* sex columnist "Sasha Von Bon Bon"—spin everything from R&B and Latin to classic house and hip-hop. ⊠ *489 College St. W., Little Italy* ☏ *416/927–7774.*

★ **Fly.** Some of the biggest and best DJs from around the world have spun records at the original "Babylon" from television's *Queer As Folk.* An impressive sound sytem, light show, and 10,000 square feet of excellent vibe has won this queer-positive club several Best Dance Club in Toronto awards. ⊠ *12 Gloucester St., between Younge and Church Sts., Downtown* ☏ *416/925–6222* ⊕ *www.flynightclub.com.*

Zipperz–Cell Block. This easygoing gay and lesbian bar caters to mixed age groups. At the piano bar in front, you can join in on classic tunes, from Broadway to Billy Joel, while the dance club in the back rocks with a live DJ on weekends and drag shows weekdays. ⊠ *72 Carlton St., Downtown* ☏ *416/921–0066* ⊕ *www.zipperz-cellblock.ca.*

Latin Dance Clubs

What disco was to the '70s, salsa is to the new millennium. Latin dance clubs have become the hangouts of choice for the club cognoscenti.

Ba-Ba-Lu'U. Truly the best of both worlds, this club in the upscale Yorkville area combines the luxe of a tony lounge—replete with gemcolor stools and polished tables—with the sizzle of sexy Latin rhythms. Novices can sign up for dance lessons; call for times. ⊠ *136 Yorkville Ave., Yorkville* ☏ *416/515–0587.*

Lula Lounge. There's no dress code, but Latin-music lovers of all ages get dressed up to get down to live bands playing Afro-Cuban and Salsa music. Tasty mint-and-lime–spiked *mojitos* get you in the groove. Pop and rock musicians also perform here from time to time; past performances include Sam Phillips and Jonathan Richmond. ⊠ *1585 Dundas St. W., West Toronto* ☏ *416/588–0302* ⊕ *www.lula.ca.*

El Convento Rico Club. A slice of Cuba in the heart of downtown, this club is seedy, steamy, sticky, and the real thing. Toronto's Latin community comes here to play, as do many of the city's gay men. The Saturday night drag show, which features acts like Missy Elliott and Shania

Twain impersonators, is good fun. ✉ *750 College St., Little Italy* ☎ *416/ 588–7800* ⊕ *www.elconventorico.com.*

Lounges

These mellow hotspots serve food and upscale cocktails and usually have comfy seating and relaxed music.

★ **Avenue.** The Four Seasons Toronto hotel's classy lounge combines New York–style sophistication—pale walls, dark wood, rows of tinted glass bottles behind the 20-foot onyx bar—with old-world touches like handmade Italian and French furniture. Drinks, coffees, and teas are all pricey, but what can you expect in one of the most posh hotels in the country? Weekdays attract a business crowd, and weekends bring out the couples. ✉ *21 Avenue Rd., Yorkville* ☎ *416/964–0411.*

Fodor'sChoice **Canoe.** Known for its stellar food and attractive surroundings, this
★ restaurant is on the 54th floor of the Toronto Dominion Centre. Sip a seasonally inspired cocktail such as the autumnal vodka with soaked apples, cranberries, and raisins or something from the extensive wine list. The food menu includes bar bites such as octopus and fiddlehead salad and red chili calamari, while the main menu includes lots of organic and gourmet-worthy ingredients such as organic quail and truffled ricotta gnocci. The food, drink and panoramic view of the lake and the Toronto Islands makes this spot popular with brokers and financial wizards from the neighboring towers, who suit the swank surroundings. ✉ *66 Wellington St. W, Financial District* ☎ *416/364–0054* ⊕ *www. canoerestaurant.com.*

Easy and The Fifth. This is what you get when you cross a New York–style loft with a disco playing Top 10, Latin, and retro tunes. The dark floors, white walls, and high ceilings give the place height, and the crowd of young professionals dressed to the nines in Armani suits and Versace dresses provides the scenery. Couches tucked into corners create cozy conversation areas, while the empty spaces are quickly converted into dance space. A cold buffet of finger foods and dainty sandwiches keeps dancers fueled through the evening. The Easy is busiest Thursday through Saturday nights. Covers range from C$10 to C$14. The Fifth is the restaurant on the fifth floor serving classic French cuisine. ✉ *225 Richmond St. W, Entertainment District* ☎ *416/979–3000* ⊕ *www.easyandthefifth.com.*

Fodor'sChoice **The Paddock.** Glamorous types pack this art deco–style bar throughout
★ the week to drink specialty cocktails and premium beers and sample the above-average fare, which includes local Ontario produce and game such as bison ribs, elk carpaccio, caribou, and lamb. Between 5 and 8 pm, the bar is known as the Saratoga Room, after the original 1940s venue where horse trainers, jockeys and other thoroughbred types commiserated. Patrons can enjoy the retro cocktail menu with $1.50 shrimp cocktails, mini portions of liver paté, and baby filet mignon. A capacious dark-wood bar curves along two walls of the room, while high-backed booths offer a little more privacy. At this writing, live jazz is making an increasingly frequent presence. ✉ *17 Bathurst St., Entertainment District* ☎ *416/504–9997* ⊕ *www.thepaddock.ca.*

The Roof Lounge. Such Canadian literary luminaries as Margaret Atwood and Mordecai Richler used the 18th-floor Roof Lounge as a setting in their writings. It's a quiet and classy bar with dark-wood and marble accents, lined with books and pictures of Canadian writers. Martinis and cosmopolitans are the bar's specialties which go down nicely with selections from their light menu including hamburgers, wraps, and dips. In summer an adjoining patio affords lovely views of the downtown skyline and lake. This remains an important hangout for the upper-middle class, businesspeople, professionals, and, of course, literary types. ⊠ *Park Hyatt Hotel, 4 Avenue Rd., Yorkville* ☎ *416/925–1234.*

Music

Most major international recording companies have offices in Toronto, so the city is a regular stop for top musical performers, ranging from the Rolling Stones to Shania Twain to Justin Timberlake. Most clubs have cover charges that range from $5 to $10.

Each June, Toronto hosts **NorthbyNortheast** (NXNE; ☎ 416/863–6963 ⊕ www.nxne.com), an annual festival that brings over 350 up-and-coming bands to the city. Affiliated with the similar SouthbySouthwest festival in Austin, Texas, it's a good opportunity to track new groups, artists, and trends.

Large Venues
The Air Canada Centre. Flexible seating configurations here suit medium and large rock concerts. Artists who performed here in 2004 include Sting, Madonna, and The Corrs. ⊠ *40 Bay St., Downtown* ☎ *416/815–5500* ⊕ *www.theaircanadacentre.com.*
The Hummingbird Centre for the Performing Arts. This venue plays host to an eclectic mix of pop and world music. ⊠ *1 Front St. E, Old Toronto* ☎ *416/872–2262* ⊕ *www.hummingbirdcentre.com.*
The SkyDome. This huge venue can seat 70,000, so it's home to the biggest shows in town. ⊠ *1 Blue Jays Way, Old Toronto* ☎ *416/341–3663* ⊕ *www.skydome.com.*

Smaller Venues
The Molson Amphitheatre. Pop, rock, and jazz concerts take place at this amphitheater by the lake throughout the summer at modest prices. The view of the skyline and the summer breezes make this one of the loveliest places to hear music in Toronto. ⊠ *Ontario Place, 955 Lakeshore Blvd. W, Harbourfront* ☎ *416/870–8000.*
The Phoenix Concert Theatre. A wide variety of music is presented at this two-room venue. Many nights, music airs live at local radio stations from the Main Room while in the Parlour, every genre from house to retro-rock and live local bands can be enjoyed in a somewhat more intimate setting. Cover charges range from C$5 to C$8 depending on the night. ⊠ *410 Sherbourne St., Cabbagetown* ☎ *416/323–1251* ⊕ *www. libertygroup.com/phoenix/phoenix.html.*

Folk
Free Times Cafe. This restaurant that specializes in vegetarian Middle Eastern food has acoustic and folk music every night of the week, plus a highly popular traditional Jewish brunch, complete with live klezmer music, every Sunday. ⊠ *320 College St., Chinatown* ☎ *416/967–1078.*

Hugh's Room. The biggest names in folk music love to play this venue because the audiences here love to listen. The dinner-folk club offers a full menu at cabaret-style tables, followed by an intimate performance of traditional or modern folk. Many shows sell out, so book early. ✉ *2261 Dundas St. W, Downtown* ☎ *416/531–6604* ⊕ *www.hughsroom.com.*

Jazz & Funk

The Montreal Bistro & Jazz Club. In this former piano factory, the large dining room is to the right and the jazz club is to the left. Dine in the restaurant, with jazz wafting in from the other room, or in the club itself where you can listen more intensely. ✉ *65 Sherbourne St., Old Toronto* ☎ *416/363–0179* ⊕ *www.montrealbistro.com.*

The Orbit Room. At this icon on funky College Street, you can drink by lava lamp at the bar or take a turn on the compact dance floor. Either way, you experience small-club funk and rockabilly at its finest. Lines form at around 10 PM Thursday through Saturday for the first set, and the second set starts at midnight. ✉ *580A College St., Little Italy* ☎ *416/535–0613.*

The Pilot Tavern. Modern mainstream jazz is served up Saturday afternoons, along with good burgers. ✉ *22 Cumberland St., Yorkville* ☎ *416/923–5716* ⊕ *www.thepilot.ca.*

Fodor'sChoice ★ Top O' The Senator. The city's first club devoted exclusively to jazz sits atop the Torch restaurant. With its long wooden bar and dark blue, towering ceilings, this fabulous room exudes a between-the-wars jazz lounge atmosphere. ✉ *249 Victoria St., Old Toronto* ☎ *416/364–7517* ⊕ *www.thesenator.com.*

Pop & Rock

The Cameron Public House. "Alternative" music showcased at this small venue ranges from jazz to hard rock and new country. Because it's close to the Ontario College of Art and Design, the Cameron draws a creative bunch during the week. The suburbanite scene gets heavy on weekends, as do the crowds. ✉ *408 Queen St. W, Queen West* ☎ *416/703–0811* ⊕ *www.thecameron.com.*

★ ¿C'est What? An eclectic mix of local bands plays almost every night at this club in The Esplanade area. You'll also find house beers, 25 other Ontario microbrews, and plain good cooking. ✉ *67 Front St. E, Downtown* ☎ *416/867–9499* ⊕ *www.cestwhat.com.*

Chick 'n Deli. Long one of the great jazz places in Toronto, this club now plays Top 40 music, with cover bands every night. A dance floor, dark wood, and casual friendliness gives the place a neighborhood bar–type atmosphere. ✉ *744 Mount Pleasant Rd., Rosedale* ☎ *416/489–3363* ⊕ *www.chickndeli.com.*

Horseshoe Tavern. Since 1947, this has been known across the city as the tavern with entertainment, especially country music. Charlie Pride, Tex Ritter, Hank Williams, and Loretta Lynn all played here. Now the music is mostly alternative rock, along with some live roots, blues, and rockabilly. Good new bands perform here six nights a week. No food is served, but there's plenty of booze. The place draws lots of young people in their twenties and thirties. ✉ *370 Queen St. W, Queen West* ☎ *416/598–4753* ⊕ *www.horseshoetavern.com.*

Lee's Palace. Rock-and-roll and punk are served up CBGB style at this club on the edge of the University of Toronto campus. Grab a table or watch the show from the sunken viewing area. Shows go from 8 PM on. And dig that crazy graffiti facade! ✉ *529 Bloor St. W, The Annex* ☎ *416/532–7383* ⊕ *www.leespalace.com.*

The Opera House. This venue for live, largely alternative acts is also a dance club. It's a hot place for ravers. ✉ *735 Queen St. E, East Toronto* ☎ *416/466–0313* ⊕ *www.theoperahousetoronto.com.*

The Underground at the Drake Hotel. Talk about so hip it hurts. The Underground fills up every night with young, artsy types with edgy haircuts and indie designers here for the indie bands. At the odd indie-rock "mash-up" night, members of various bands such as The Hidden Cameras and Barcelona Pavilion perform in homemade rock operas. The sound system is great, and the stark walls are usually decorated with art or projections. ✉ *1150 Queen St. W, Queen West* ☎ *416/531–5042.*

Rhythm & Blues

Chicago's Diner. See and hear the blues stars of tomorrow from Monday to Saturday at this real charmer. Good hamburgers are served in a classic tavern downstairs. Check out the red neon sign in the shape of a beer bottle cap. ✉ *335 Queen St. W, Queen West* ☎ *416/977–2904* ⊕ *www.chicagosdiner.ca.*

Grossman's Tavern. Old and raunchy, Grossman's was described in the 1980s by one *Toronto Star* writer as "long established, but never entirely reputable"—which makes it ideal for the blues. There are R&B bands nightly and jazz on Saturday afternoon. ✉ *379 Spadina Ave., The Annex* ☎ *416/977–7000* ⊕ *www.grossmanstavern.com.*

The Silver Dollar Room. Some of the top blues acts around play here. The bar is long and dark, but the blues-loving clientele are friendly, and you stand a good chance of striking up a conversation with the musicians themselves between sets. ✉ *486 Spadina Ave., The Annex* ☎ *416/763–9139* ⊕ *www.silverdollarroom.com.*

Supper Clubs

The past few years have witnessed the rebirth of the supper club in Toronto. The places listed below also have active bars, for those who prefer to limit the evening to drinks and dancing.

Rosewater Supper Club. Blue velvet banquettes for two fill this lovely place that's perfect for a festive night on the town. Modern French cuisine is on the menu. One lounge has a baby grand and a torch singer, and a live three-piece jazz band performs on Thursdays and Saturdays, when those so inclined can take a twirl on the dance floor. ✉ *19 Toronto St., Old Toronto* ☎ *416/214–5888* ⊕ *www.libertygroup.com.*

Ultra Supper Club. At this contemporary and swanky supper club on the hip Queen Street strip, you can relax in the lounge with a fancy cocktail and a little later tuck into lobster and sweetbread ravioli in the dining room. DJs spinning mainstream tunes and new-world styles are on hand Thursdays, Fridays, and Saturdays to get people dancing. On Wednesday (Mingle Night), DJ Jojo Flores and others spin house for a chilled-out, loungey vibe. ✉ *314 Queen St. W, Entertainment District* ☎ *416-263-0330* ⊕ *www.ultrasupperclub.com.*

SPORTS &
THE OUTDOORS

MOST LIKELY ITEM TO IMPRESS A LOCAL
Maple Leaf hockey tickets ⇨*p.111*

BEST REASON TO BUNDLE UP
Ice-skating in Nathan Phillips Square ⇨*p.112*

BEST WAY TO GO WITH THE FLOE
Ice canoeing ⇨*p.112*

ROLL WITH IT
Five-pin bowling ⇨*p.110*

BEST ALTERNATIVE TO CONCRETE
High Park ⇨*p.107*

Updated by
Kirsten
McKenzie

THE CITY OF TORONTO ENJOYS A LOVE-HATE RELATIONSHIP with its professional sports teams, including the Toronto Blue Jays. Fans can sometimes be accused of being fair-weather—except when it comes to hockey. In Toronto the national sport attracts rabid, sellout crowds, whether the Maple Leafs win, lose, or draw.

An extensive network of parks and trails provides opportunities to enjoy outdoor activities in Toronto year-round—biking, boating, hiking, or cross-country skiing. The parks of the Toronto Islands have spectacular views of the city skyline, and the Don Valley Trail System snakes from north of the city all the way down to Lake Ontario.

BEACHES

Lake Ontario is rarely warm enough for sustained swimming, except in late August, and is often too polluted for any kind of dip. Still, it's fun to relax or take a stroll on one of the city's beaches. Once the site of a large, rollicking amusement park, **Sunnyside Beach,** west of downtown, is now a favorite place for a swim in the safe, heated water of the "tank" or a quick snack in the small restaurant inside the handsomely restored 1922 Sunnyside Bathing Pavilion. One of the few remnants of the old amusement park is the Palais Royale dance hall, where you can still catch live swing music most weekends. The park is easily accessible by streetcar at the Queensway intersections at King Street, Queen Street, and Roncesvalle Avenue. Sir Casimir Gzowski Park is a short walk away.

In the east end, **Beaches Park,** south of Queen Street and east of Coxwell Avenue, has a lengthy boardwalk, local canoe club, and public washrooms. A 20-minute streetcar ride east of downtown, along Queen Street, at Coxwell Avenue, is **Woodbine Beach Park.** The city's most pleasing beaches—and certainly the ones with the best views—are on the **Toronto Islands.** The best ones are those on the southeast tip of Ward's Island, the southernmost edge of Centre Island, and the west side of Hanlan's Island. A portion of Hanlan's Beach is clothing-optional.

PARKS

FodorsChoice At close to 400 acres, **High Park** is the city's largest playground; in summer, hordes descend to enjoy the outdoor activities here. Between the manicured rose gardens in the west and the sprawling forest in the east, there are numerous recreational facilities: a large public swimming pool, tennis courts, baseball and soccer fields, fitness trails, and walking paths. In the southwest corner of the park is **Grenadier Pond,** home to thousands of migrating birds. You can fish in its well-stocked waters, either from the shore or from a rented rowboat. In winter, you can ice-skate on its frozen surface. The modest **High Park Zoo** is free to all. The park hosts many summer special events, including professionally staged Shakespeare productions. To get here, take the TTC to the High Park Station and walk south; you can also take the College Street streetcar to the eastern end of the park and walk west. The main entrance is off Bloor Street West at High Park Avenue. ⊠ *Bordered by Bloor St. W,* *the Gardiner Expressway, Parkside Dr., and Ellis Park Rd., Southwest Toronto* ☎ *416/392–1111, 416/392–1748 walking tours.*

The **Highland Creek Ravines** are considered the most beautiful in Toronto. They are ideal for cross-country skiing, biking, and jogging. Both **Colonel Danforth Park** and **Morningside Park** follow Highland Creek. The **Colonel Danforth Trail** begins south of Kingston Road, on the east side of Highland Creek Bridge, and Morningside Park is accessible off Morningside Avenue, between Kingston Road and Ellesmere Avenue. ⊕ *Enter from the grounds of Scarborough College* ⊠ *1265 Military Trail, Northeast Toronto.*

On the west bank of the Humber River, Fred T. James started what is now **James Gardens** in 1908 and finished it in 1948. With a variety of flowers suited to the Canadian climate, stone pathways, and mature trees, James Gardens is a quiet haven at any time of year. A winterized, fully accessible washroom is on the property. ⊠ *Off Edenbridge Dr., east of Royal York Rd., south of Scarlett Mills Park, Southwest Toronto* ☎ *416/ 392–8186* ⊠ *Free* ☉ *Daily dawn–dusk.*

Scarlett Mills Park, north of James Gardens on the west bank of the Humber River, has an appealing wildflower reserve. The park is ideal for picnics, and attracts cross-country skiers in winter. You can watch golfers at play, as the park overlooks Scarlett Woods Golf Course. Pedestrians and cyclists can travel through the park along the **Tommy Thompson Trail.** Note that there are no washrooms in the park. ⊠ *Entrance off Edenbridge Dr., Southwest Toronto* ☉ *Daily dawn–dusk.*

🄲 **Sherwood Park** is a well-kept secret in Toronto, with one of the finest children's playgrounds in the city, a lovely wading pool, and a hill that seems to go on forever. A ravine begins at the bottom of the hill; you can follow it across Blythwood Road, all the way to Yonge Street and Lawrence Avenue. There, subways and buses await you—as do the beautiful rose gardens in **Alexander Muir Park.** Or walk or bike southeast to **Sunnybrook Park,** then head 13 km (8 mi) south along the ravine to the lake. ⊠ *Near Lawrence Ave. E and Mount Pleasant Rd., Northeast Toronto.*

🄲 From **Sir Casimir Gzowski Park** you have marvelous views of the Toronto Islands, Ontario Place, and the downtown skyline. A paved trail—ideal for jogging, biking, and in-line skating—hugs the lakeshore, and there's a boardwalk made of Trex, a product partially derived from recycled plastic garbage bags. The park is accessible by the 501 Queen and 504 King streetcars and is right next to Sunnyside Park. ⊠ *Along Lakeshore Blvd. W, Southwest Toronto.*

SPORTS & FITNESS

Baseball

★ The **Toronto Blue Jays** (⊠ SkyDome, 1 Blue Jays Way, Old Toronto ☎ 416/341–1111, 416/341–1234 for ticket information ⊕ www. bluejays.com) play from April through September. Interest in the team has fallen since they won consecutive World Series championships in

A number of agencies can help you find out more about sports and the outdoors in and around Toronto. **Access Toronto** (✉ City Hall, 100 Queen St. W, Queen West ☎ 416/338–0338 ⊕ www.city.toronto.on.ca/accesstoronto) provides area maps. **Tourism Toronto** (✉ 207 Queen's Quay W, Downtown ☎ 416/203–2500 or 800/363–1990 ⊕ www.torontotourism.com) has information on recreational and professsional sports teams and outdoor recreation.

Toronto and Region Conservation (☎ 416/667–6299 ⊕ www. trca.on.ca) gives out a pamphlet on parks and trails. **Toronto Parks and Recreation** (✉ 55 John St. ☎ 416/392–8186 ⊕ www.city.toronto. on.ca/parks) has maps of park biking and jogging paths and can provide information about public golf courses. The Sports & Rec section of **Toronto Web Sites** ⊕ *www.torontowebsites.com.* links you with information on the city's spectator sports.

5

1992–93. Recent seasons have seen a lot of young players trying to make their mark. The spectacular SkyDome has a fully retractable roof; some consider the dome to be one of the world's premier entertainment centers. Tickets are C$6 to C$56.

Basketball

The city's NBA franchise, the **Toronto Raptors** (✉ Air Canada Centre, 40 Bay St., at Carlton St., Downtown ☎ 416/815–5600, 416/872–5000 for tickets ⊕ www.raptors.com), played its first season in 1995–96. For several years they struggled mightily to win both games and fans in this hockey-mad city. But the Raptors have finally come into their own. Games often sell out, and fans are rabid for high-flying dunkmaster Vince Carter. Tickets run from C$14 to C$500 per game and are available beginning in July; the season is from October through April.

Bicycling

More than 29 km (18 mi) of street bike routes cut across the city, and dozens more follow safer paths through Toronto's many parks. Bike rentals are available in Toronto as well as on the Toronto Islands.

Cyclepath (✉ 1510 Danforth Ave. Southeast Toronto ☎ 416/463–5346) has a selection of bicycles to rent for C$25 to C$40 a day.

The **Don Valley Trail System** begins at Edward's Gardens and runs to the lake. **Humber Valley Parkland** stretches along the Humber River ravine, from north of the city limits (Steeles Avenue) down to where the Humber flows quietly into Lake Ontario, not far from High Park. Its peaceful location away from traffic makes the park ideal for a hiking, jogging, or biking tour. Another option is to rent a bike at the lakeside Sir Casimir Gzowski Park, which is accessible by the 501 Queen and 504

King streetcars. You could ride from the park up the Humber Valley Parkland. The **Martin Goodman Trail** is a 19-km (12-mi) strip that runs along the waterfront all the way from the Balmy Beach Club in the east end out past the beaches southwest of High Park.

Bowling

Toronto has five-pin bowling, a marvelous tradition unknown to most Americans. This sport of rolling a tiny ball down an alley at five fat pins—each with a different numerical value, for a possible score of 450—is perfect for children, even as young as three or four, and for everyone on a rainy day. **Bowlerama** (✉ 2788 Bathurst St., south of Lawrence Ave. W, North York ☎ 416/782–1841 ⊕ www.bowlerama.com ✉ Newtonbrook Plaza, 5837 Yonge St., south of Steeles Ave., North York ☎ 416/222–4657) has lanes all over the city. The Newtonbrook Plaza location is open 24 hours a day.

Canoeing

At Grenadier Pond in High Park, on Centre Island, at Ontario Place, at the Harbourfront Centre, and in most of the conservation areas surrounding Toronto you can rent canoes or punts from April to September.

Harbourfront Canoe and Kayak Centre (✉ 283A Queen's Quay W, Harbourfront ☎ 416/203–2277 ⊕ paddletoronto.com/rentals.htm) rents canoes for C$20 per hour or C$40 per day, single kayaks for C$20 per hour or C$50 pe day, and tandem kayaks for C$30 per hour or C$65 per day.

Canoe Ontario (☎ 416/426–7170 ⊕ canoeontario.ca) has information about one of the world's largest canoeing and rowing regattas, held every July 1 on Toronto Islands' Long Pond.

Car Racing

For three days in mid-July, the **Molson Indy Toronto** (✉ Downtown ☎ 416/872–4639 🖷 416/351–8560 ⊕ molsonindy.com) roars around the Canadian National Exhibition grounds and the major thoroughfare of Lakeshore Boulevard. (Local traffic is diverted.) You can book tickets from late February or early March. About C$250 gets you a three-day "gold" reserved seat (C$170 for silver, and C$90 for bronze), but general admission for the qualification rounds, the practice rounds, and the Indy itself can be considerably less expensive.

Motorcycle and formula racing are held at **Mosport** (✉ Exit 75, Hwy. 401, north of Bowmanville ☎ 905/983–9141 ⊕ www.mosport.com), about 96 km (60 mi) northeast of Toronto. Mosport is a multitrack facility, with a 4-km (2½-mi), 10-turn road course; a 1-km (½-mi) paved oval; a 1-km (½-mi) kart track; and the Mosport Driver Development Centre. Races take place from May to September.

Cricket

The British and Commonwealth influence, though waning, is strong enough to buoy local teams who play in their pristine whites and make moves that those brought up on baseball may find mysterious but fascinating. The **Cricket Association of Ontario** (✉ 81 Lakeshore Rd. E, Mississauga ☎ 416/426–7160 ⊕ http://canada.cricket.ca) has information about finding a game.

Football

The Canadian Football League (CFL) has a healthy following across most of the country, even in Toronto, where the **Toronto Argonauts** (✉ SkyDome, 1 Blue Jays Way, Old Toronto ☎ 416/341–2746 ⊕ www.argonauts.on. ca) have struggled for fans against the Maple Leafs, Raptors, and Blue Jays. Tickets for home games are a cinch to get. Prices range from C$14 to C$41. The season runs from June to late November. American football fans who attend a CFL game discover a faster, more unpredictable and exciting contest than the American version. The longer, wider field means quarterbacks have to scramble more, a nifty thing to watch.

Golf

The golf season lasts only from April to late October.

The top course in Canada, a real beauty designed by Jack Nicklaus, is the 18-hole, par-73 **Glen Abbey** (✉ 1333 Dorval Dr., Oakville ☎ 905/844–1800). The **Canadian Open Championship,** one of golf's Big Five tournaments, is held here in late summer. Cart and greens fees run around C$75 on weekends.

The **Don Valley Golf Course** (✉ 4200 Yonge St., south of Hwy. 401, North York ☎ 416/392–2465) is a par-71, 18-hole municipal course. Greens fees are C$50 Monday to Thursday and C$55 Friday to Sunday; lower twilight rates are available. You can book up to five days in advance.

The **Flemingdon Park Golf Club** (✉ 155 St. Denis Dr., near Don Mills Rd. and Eglinton Ave., North York ☎ 416/429–1740) is a fairly standard, public, nine-hole course. A round is C$24, or C$26 on weekends. The course winds along the Don Valley wall and Taylor Creek, making the city seem far away.

Hockey

Fodor'sChoice ★ The **Toronto Maple Leafs** (✉ Air Canada Centre, 40 Bay St., at Carlton St., Downtown ☎ 416/870–8000 ⊕ www.torontomapleleafs.com) share their venue with the National Basketball Association's Raptors. Whether the Leafs are on a winning or losing streak, their tickets are notoriously the toughest to score of any team in the National Hockey League. Ticket prices range from C$24 to C$390—scalpers often demand up to three times the face value. If you can, plan ahead and book tickets in advance.

Horseback Riding

Central Don Riding Academy (✉ Sunnybrook Park, Park Leslie St. and Eglinton Ave., North York ☎ 416/444–4044) has an indoor arena, an outdoor ring, and riding along nearly 19 km (12 mi) of bridle trails through the Don Valley.

The **Rocking Horse Ranch** (⊠ 11815 Yonge St., Richmond Hill, 35 km [22 mi] north of Toronto ☎ 905/884–3292) leads scenic trail rides year-round.

Horse Racing

Woodbine Race Track (⊠ Hwy. 427 and Rexdale Blvd., Woodbine ☎ 416/675–7223 or 888/675–7223 ⊕ www.woodbineentertainment.com), a 30-minute drive northwest of downtown, near the airport, is the showplace of thoroughbred and harness racing in Canada. Horses run from late April through late October.

Campbellville (⊠ Hwy. 401 and Guelph Line Rd., Campbellville ☎ 416/675–7223 or 888/675–7223 ⊕ www.woodbineentertainment.com), a 30-minute drive west of Toronto, is in the heart of Ontario's standardbred breeding country. The glass-enclosed, climate-controlled grandstand is part of the attractive facilities here. Harness racing is scheduled five nights a week from March through April and September through October.

The **Royal Horse Show** (Royal Winter Fair ⊠ CNE Grounds, Dufferin St., Harbourfront ☎ 416/263–3400 ⊕ www.royalfair.org) is a highlight of Canada's equestrian season each November, with jumping, dressage, and harness-racing competitions.

Fort Erie Race Track (⊠ Bertie St. and Queen Elizabeth Way, Fort Erie, 152 km [95 mi] south of Toronto ☎ 905/871–3200 Toronto, 716/856–0293 Buffalo), in the Niagara region, is beautifully landscaped with willows, manicured hedges, and flower-bordered infield lakes. It has dirt and turf racing, with the year's highlight being the Prince of Wales Stakes, the second jewel in Canada's Triple Crown of Racing. It's open late April to mid-November, Saturday to Tuesday, and some Wednesdays in July and August.

Ice Canoe Racing

★ One of the strangest sports winter has to offer, ice canoeing got its start in Québec more than 100 years ago when teams competed to deliver the mail over the St. Lawrence River. Today there are 36 ice canoeing teams in Canada. Each January, at the Molson Export Ice Canoe Race, five-member teams row through freezing waters over a 3½-km (2-mi) course off **Harbourfront Centre** (⊠ 200–410 Queen's Quay W, Harbourfront ☎ 416/973–4000 ⊕ www.harbourfrontcentre.com), stopping at ice floes to haul their vessels to the next stretch of open water. They compete for C$2,000 in prize money, and of course, honor.

Ice-Skating

★ Toronto operates some 30 outdoor artificial rinks and 100 natural-ice rinks—and all are free. Among the most popular are those in Nathan Phillips Square in front of New City Hall, at Queen and Bay streets; down at Harbourfront Centre (Canada's largest outdoor artificial ice rink); at College Park at Yonge and College streets; on Grenadier Pond within High Park at Bloor and Keele streets; and inside Hazelton Lanes—the classy shopping mall on the edge of Yorkville—on Avenue Road just above Bloor

Street. Rentals are generally available. For details on city ice rinks, call the **Toronto Parks and Recreation Information Line** (☎ 416/392–1111).

Jogging

Good places to jog are the boardwalk of The Beaches in the city's east end, High Park in the West End, the Toronto Islands, and the ravines or other public parks, many of which have jogging paths and trails. Many hotels now provide printed copies of maps showing interesting routes nearby. Toronto is generally safer than most American cities, but it's still wise to use normal prudence and avoid isolated spots. Check with local people on specific parks or routes.

The **Martin Goodman Trail** (Access Toronto ☎ 416/338–0338 for a map) is a 19-km (12-mi) jogging route with an incredible view. The dirt and asphalt trails run along the waterfront from the Balmy Beach Club (end of Beech Avenue) past the western beaches and High Park. It's popular with runners and it's especially busy on weekends. If you get out in the hours before work and after dinner you're likely to catch some spectacular sunrises and sunsets.

Sailing

Sailing on Lake Ontario is especially nice between May and September, but die-hard sailors push the season at both ends. The **Ontario Sailing Association** (✉ 65 Guise St. E, Hamilton ☎ 888/672–7245) is a good resource for sailing on Lake Ontario. The **Royal Canadian Yacht Club** (✉ 141 St. George St., Downtown ☎ 416/967–7245) has its summer headquarters in a beautiful Victorian mansion on Centre Island.

Skiing

Cross-Country

Try Toronto's parks and ravines for cross-country skiing, especially Earl Bales Park, High Park, the lakefront along the southern edge of the city, and best of all, the Toronto Islands. The Kortright Centre, just outside Toronto, has hiking trails, some of which are used for skiing in winter. Most of these places are free. One of the most popular places to rent ski equipment is **Play It Again Sports** (✉ 3456 Yonge St., Downtown ☎ 416/488–6471 ✉ 3055 Dundas St. W, Mississauga ☎ 905/607–2837), which has several locations around Toronto.

Downhill

For more information about ski resorts, see the Side Trips chapter. Call for **lift and surface conditions** (☎ 800/668–2746) in the greater Toronto area.

Glen Eden Ski Area (✉ 5234 Kelso Rd., Milton, 56 km [35 mi] southwest of Toronto ☎ 905/878–5011 ⊕ www.glenelden.on.ca) has a snowboarding half-pipe and quarter-pipe in addition to 12 regular downhill ski runs.

The **Caledon Ski Club** (✉ 17431 Mississauga Rd., Belfountain, 80 km [50 mi] west of Toronto ☎ 519/927–5221 ⊕ www.caledonskiclub.on. ca) has 23 slopes, including 9 for experts.

Two quad chairs serve the 14 runs at the full-service **Hockley Valley Resort** (⊠ R.R. 1, Orangeville, 80 km [50 mi] northwest of Toronto ☎ 519/942–0754 ⊕ www.hockley.com). There's also a hotel, spa, and golf course on-site.

Horseshoe Valley (⊠ R.R. 1, Barrie, 91 km [57 mi] north of Toronto ☎ 705/835–2790 ⊕ www.horseshoeresort.com), one hour from Toronto, has cross-country and downhill skiing, as well as snow-tubing and a top-notch lodge with in-room fireplaces.

Blue Mountain Resort (⊠ R.R. 3, Collingwood, 151 km [93 mi] north of Toronto ☎ 705/445–0231 ⊕ www.bluemountain.ca) has a vertical drop of 720 feet, the province's highest.

Hidden Valley (⊠ Hwy. 60, off Hwy. 400, Huntsville, 281 km [136 mi] north of Toronto ☎ 705/789–1773 ⊕ www.skihiddenvalley.on.ca) has 35 acres of skiable land two hours north of Toronto.

Swimming

Public swimming is available at 16 indoor pools, 12 outdoor pools, and 15 community recreation centers. For the latest information on city pools, call the **Toronto Parks and Recreation Outdoor Pools Hotline** (☎ 416/392–7838). For information about late-night outdoor swimming, call the **Toronto Late-Night Pool Hotline** (☎ 416/392–1899).

★ ☾ **Ontario Place** (⊠ 955 Lakeshore Blvd. W, Harbourfront ☎ 416/314–9900 ⊕ www.ontarioplace.com) lakefront amusement park has an outstanding water park and slide at its Children's Village. If kids tire of the water, they can catch a flick at the Cinesphere movie theater or entertain themselves with other park activities and rides.

Tennis

The city has dozens of courts, all free, many of them floodlit. Parks with courts open daily from 7 AM to 11 PM May to October, including High Park in the West End; Stanley Park on King Street West, three blocks west of Bathurst Street; and Eglinton Park, on Eglinton Avenue West, just east of Avenue Road. Call the **Ontario Tennis Association** (☎ 416/426–7135) for more information on court times, hours, and locations.

The C$45-million **Rexall Centre** (⊠ 1 Shoreham Dr., Downtown ☎ 416/665-9777, 877/283–6647 for tickets ⊕ www.rexallcentre.com) opened in July 2004 on the York University campus as home to the National Tennis Centre. The 12,500-seat stadium hosts big-name tournaments like the Tennis Masters Canada and the Rogers Cup (alternating years with Montréal; it will be held here in 2005).

SHOPPING

Updated by
Ashley
Anderson

TORONTO PRIDES ITSELF on having some of the finest shopping in North America. Indeed, most of the world's name boutiques have branches here, especially in the Yorkville area, where a few choice roads include such designer labels as Hermès, Gucci, and Cartier.

For those a little leaner of wallet, join in one of Torontonians' favorite pastimes: bargain hunting. Locals wear discount threads like badges of honor. A favorable exchange rate means that if you're from out of the country, you land what amounts to an immediate discount on any purchase.

Toronto has a large artistic and crafts community, with numerous art galleries, custom jewelers, clothing designers, and artisans. Objets d'art like sophisticated glass sculpture or Inuit art are ideal as gifts or for your own home.

Music stores all over Toronto stack shelves with international hits as well as homegrown talent like Alanis Morissette, Nickelback, Avril Lavigne, and a host of lesser-known pop, rap, hip-hop, folk, opera, and country artists. Bookstores such as Indigo have lounge areas where you can sip a coffee from the in-store café while perusing books by Canadian authors such as Barbara Gowdy, Ann-Marie McDonald, and Rohinton Mistry.

When it comes to department stores, all roads lead from Holt Renfrew on Bloor Street West, the epicenter of Toronto's designer mecca. A mere block east is the more mid-price department store The Bay. A second Bay can be found across from Eaton Centre, a sprawling shopping complex with multilevel parking in the heart of the city.

Most stores accept credit cards without minimums, though a purchase over C$5 is preferred. U.S. currency generally is accepted, though not always at the most favorable rate of exchange. On Thursday and Friday most stores downtown stay open until 9 PM; on Sunday stores open at noon.

The biggest sale day of the year is Boxing Day, the first business day after Christmas, when nearly everything in the city is half price. In fact, clothing prices tend to drop even further as winter fades. Summer sales start in late June and continue through August.

Bear in mind that the national 7% Goods and Services Tax (GST) is added to the cost of your purchases at the cash register, in addition to the 8% Ontario sales tax. You should save receipts from any major purchases and inquire about rebates on the GST. Ask for the latest refund regulations and forms at Lester B. Pearson International Airport, at visitor-information booths like the one outside Eaton Centre, or at stores.

SHOPPING NEIGHBORHOODS

The Annex

A popular residential area and hangout for students from the nearby University of Toronto, The Annex is Toronto's bohemian refuge. The space that isn't consumed by houses is made up of all things "artsy": cafés and bistros, used-book and -CD stores, and the occasional fashion find, like Risqué, a popular women's clothing store.

Get yourself ready to move around the city by subway and streetcar, and save enough strength to lug all your packages home from these shopping itineraries.

Antiques Whereas Queen Street East from Pape Street to Jones Avenue is for those who enjoy trinkets and kitsch, and King Street East has mostly modern interiors, you have to go elsewhere for more-upscale antiques. Begin at Toronto Antique Center (276 King Street West) in the Entertainment District where you find big-ticket items such as Persian carpets and armoires as well as smaller items such as jewelry and china. Take the streetcar back to the St. Andrew station and pick up the Finch–bound subway. Along Yonge Street, starting from the Rosedale subway stop at Crescent Road and running north to just past the Summerhill stop at Shaftesbury Street, is where you find the best pieces, though not at bargain prices. French bistros punctuate the trip and make great stops for coffee and a croissant.

Queen Street Express One of Toronto's most charming and utilitarian traditions is its streetcars. The Queen Street car traverses the city from The Beaches in the east end, through the antiques stores on Queen Street East, and on to trendy Queen Street West. Start the day by scouring one-of-a-kind gift stores, and wind your way east past clothing stores like Freeway. You can grab a latte at a coffee shop or bakery and walk through Kew Beach Park, on the south side of Queen Street, right down to the lake, where a boardwalk winds along the beach. Hop on the streetcar and continue west to Jones Avenue, where a string of quaint antiques stores begins. Head to Eye Spy (1100 Queen Street East) and Neat Things (1126 Queen Street East) for whimsical '50s nostalgia pieces. Take the streetcar again to Queen Street West, where fashion and funk meet between Simcoe Street (on the east) and Spadina Avenue. It all starts at Price Roman (267 Queen Street West) and Noise (275 Queen Street West, at Simcoe Street) and stretches west with groovy vintage and homespun designer shops. Finish your day at one of the strip's cafés, bistros, or bars.

At the outer corner of The Annex—Bloor Street West and Bathurst—is Honest Ed's, a tacky discount store. It serves as the gateway to Mirvish Village, a one-block assortment of bookstores, antiques shops, and boutiques on Markham Street south of Bloor Street. Local entrepreneur and theater mogul "Honest" Ed Mirvish is the brain behind the area's development.

The Beaches

Queen Street East, starting at Woodbine Avenue, is a great spot for casual clothing stores, gift and antiques shops, and bars and restaurants, all with a resort atmosphere—a boardwalk along the lake is just to the south. To get to The Beaches, take the Queen Street streetcar to Woodbine and walk east. Parking can be a hassle.

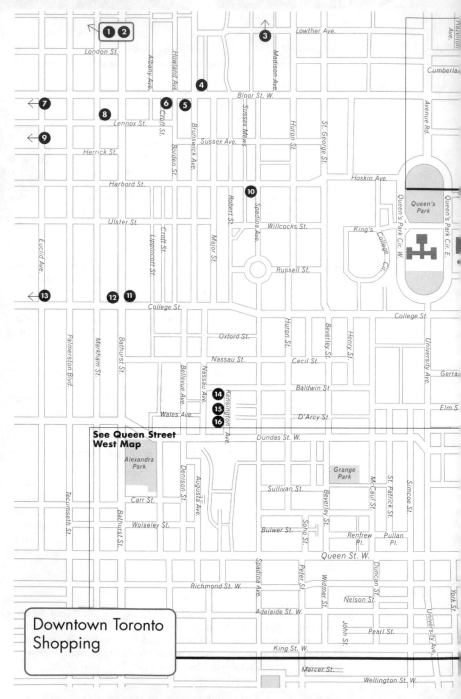

Downtown Toronto Shopping

See Queen Street West Map

Yorkville

In the 1960s Yorkville was Canada's hippie headquarters, a mecca for runaways and folk musicians. Now this area is the place to find the big fashion names, fine leather goods, upscale shoe stores, important jewelers, some of the top private art galleries, specialty bookstores, and crafts and home-decor shops, as well as eateries, from coffee shops to elegant northern Italian restaurants. Streets to explore include Yorkville Avenue and Cumberland Street, running parallel to Bloor Street, and Scollard Street, running north from Yorkville Avenue, east of Avenue Road. These are among the most chichi shopping streets in Canada.

Bloor Street West, from Yonge Street to Avenue Road, is a virtual runway for fashionistas. To lessen the browsing overload, Bloor Street is handily split: the north side has mainstream fare like the Gap, Gap Kids, Banana Republic, and the Body Shop, while the south side plays to fantasy fashion such as Tiffany & Co., Cartier, Royal De Versailles Jewelers, Chanel, and Hermès. The Prada store is a must, if only for the inspired interior design. Women should consider parking their guys at Bay Bloor Radio in the Manulife Centre; it's a stereo mecca and only steps from male-fashion bastions like Eddie Bauer for active wear and Harry Rosen for professional attire. A jolt of java served up at Starbucks in Chapters, a three-story bookstore with lounge areas for adults and a play center for kids, may be just what you need after this shopping experience.

Chinatown & Kensington Market

While the Chinese have made Spadina Avenue their own from Queen Street north to College Street, Spadina's basic bill of fare is still "bargains galore." The street, and the Kensington Market area tucked behind Spadina west to Bathurst Street, between Dundas and College streets, remains a collection of inexpensive vintage clothing stores, Chinese clothing stores, Chinese restaurants, ethnic food and fruit shops, and eateries that give you your money's worth. You find gourmet cheeses, fresh ocean fish, yards of fabric remnants piled high in bins, and designer clothes minus the labels. Be warned—this area can be extraordinarily crowded on weekends, when smart suburbanites head here for bargains. Park your car at the lot just west of Spadina Avenue on St. Andrew's Street (a long block north of Dundas Street), or take the College or Queen streetcar to Spadina Avenue.

King Street East

Furniture heaven is King Street East, beginning at Jarvis Street and continuing almost until the Don River. On King East, sofas and chairs take center stage in productions that involve enormous, brightly lit windows and stark white backdrops, seducing even the most mildly curious. Punctuated between the furniture stores are custom framing shops, art dealers, and cafés to refresh the weary shopper.

Queen Street East

Queen Street East from Pape Street east to Jones Avenue is a bustling thoroughfare noted for its antiques and junk shops. Locals endure the

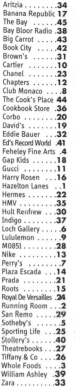

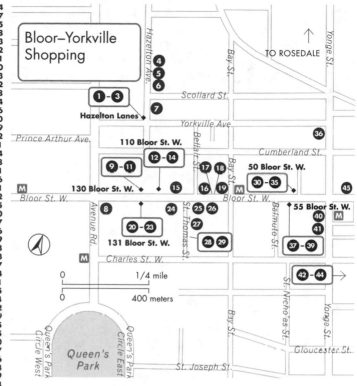

crowds who come here for the exceptional assortment of quality reproduction armoires, bureaus, tables, or garden furnishings. Finish a trip
to the area at Tango Palace, a hot spot for gourmet coffees and decadent desserts at the end of the antiques centered stretch. Parking is at a
premium, but the neighborhood is easily accessible via the Queen Street
streetcar, which passes through every 20 minutes or so.

Queen Street West

If it's funky or fun, it's found on Queen West. The best shops are concentrated on both sides of Queen Street West from University Avenue
to Spadina Avenue, with some fashionable stores as far west as Bathurst
Street. With its collection of vintage stores, Canadian designer boutiques,
and bistros, this strip sets the pace for Toronto's street style. City TV's
headquarters at the corner of Queen and John streets, with Speaker's
Corner (where you can videotape your views for later broadcast on the
station's *Speaker's Corner* show), is a landmark. On Queen West, the
retro stylings of vintage stores like Black Market and Preloved comfortably
coexist with Parade and Fashion Crimes, which both stock Canadian
designs with a bent for the street beat. To really get into the downtown
groove, grab a paper or magazine at Pages and then head into the Second Cup across the street for coffee.

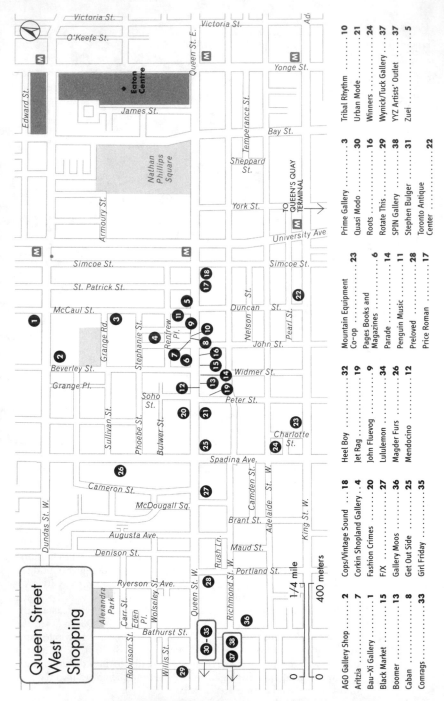

Underground City

Downtown Toronto has a vast underground maze of shopping warrens that burrow between and underneath its office towers. The tenants of the Underground City are mostly the usual assortment of chain stores, with an occasional surprise. Marked PATH walkways (the underground street system) make navigating the subterranean mall easy. The network runs roughly from the Fairmont Royal York hotel near Union Station north to the Atrium at Bay and Dundas, and from Park Road, east of Bloor and Yonge, to Bellair Street and the Manulife Centre.

Midtown

Yonge Street, the longest street in Canada, begins life at Lake Ontario and takes on a multitude of faces before exiting the city. Once you head north from Bloor, you're entering Midtown, which runs approximately from Rosedale to Eglinton. The stretch of Yonge Street that runs from the Rosedale subway stop (at Yonge and Crescent streets) north to just past the Summerhill stop (at Yonge and Shaftesbury streets) is the best place to find the most upscale antiques and interiors shops, such as Absolutely, purveyor of French-provincial wares. If the thought of freight charges dissuades you from serious spending, you can check out the trinkets at tiny shops like French Country and Word of Mouth, which carry every imaginable kitchen device.

DEPARTMENT STORES & SHOPPING CENTERS

The Bay. The modern descendant of the Hudson's Bay Company, which was chartered in 1670 to explore and trade in furs, The Bay carries mid-price clothing, furnishings, housewares, and cosmetics, including designer names as well as The Bay's own lines. The southern end of the Yonge Street store connects to Eaton Centre by a covered skywalk over Queen Street. ⊠ *44 Bloor St. E, Yorkville* ☎ *416/972–3333* ⊠ *176 Yonge St., Downtown* ☎ *416/861–9111.*

Fodor'sChoice **Eaton Centre.** The block-long complex with an exposed industrial style ★ is anchored at its northern end (Dundas Street) by the main branch of what used to be eatons, and is now Sears, and at its southern end by The Bay. Prices at Eaton Centre increase with altitude—Level 1 offers popularly priced merchandise, Level 2 is directed to the middle-income shopper, and Level 3 sells more expensive fashion and luxury goods. Well-lit parking garages are sprinkled around the center, with spaces for nearly 2,000 cars. The complex is bordered by Yonge Street on the east, and James Street and Trinity Square on the west. At this writing, the Eaton Centre's northern end was undergoing a massive facelift, culminating in a Times Square–style media tower on top of a gigantic new anchor store, Sweden's popular H&M. ⊠ *220 Yonge St., Downtown* ☎ *416/598–8560.*

★ **Hazelton Lanes.** The luxury shopping center's 50 stores are a paean to capitalism, with upscale boutiques such as Teatro Verde and TNT Woman and Man, a restaurant with seating in an elegant courtyard, and the natural foods store Whole Foods. ⊠ *55 Avenue Rd., Yorkville* ☎ *416/968–8600.*

Fodor'sChoice **Holt Renfrew.** Housewares and high-end clothing, including couture lines
★ not carried elsewhere in the city, fill this store, which also has its own
product line. ✉ *50 Bloor St. W, Yorkville* ☎ *416/922–2333.*

Queen's Quay Terminal. Incoming ships once unloaded their fishy cargo
at the terminal, which now hosts a collection of unique boutiques,
crafts stalls, food stores, and more. It's a great place to buy gifts. It's an
easy walk from Union Station in summer, and a quick streetcar ride in
winter. Parking is expensive, but discounted with some purchases.
✉ *207 Queen's Quay W, at York St., Harbourfront* ☎ *416/203–0510.*

Sears. This chain store, in Eaton Centre, now fills the space that used
to be occupied by one of Canada's classic department stores, eatons (for
which the center was named). Sears bought the store after eatons filed
for bankruptcy, and now carries lines such as Nike, Kenneth Cole,
Tommy Bahama, and Mexx. An in-store spa, Atelier, offers full services.
✉ *290 Yonge St., Downtown* ☎ *416/343–2111.*

SPECIALTY SHOPS

Antiques & Interiors

Absolutely. A mixture of whimsical trinkets as well as English sideboards and tables are sold at this shop, a famous interiors destination.
There's also an extensive collection of antique boxes made of materials ranging from horn to shagreen. ✉ *1132 Yonge St., Rosedale* ☎ *416/
324–8351* ✉ *1236 Yonge St., Summerhill* ☎ *416/922–6784.*

Belle Époque. Find very French, very *cher* antique and reproduction furnishings here. Specialties include tablecloths, quilts, cushions, handbags,
and hats. ✉ *1066 Yonge St., Rosedale* ☎ *416/925–0066.*

Eye Spy. Retro and contemporary collectibles and furnishings are well
stocked at this boutique. The selection of 1960s Danish pieces is extensive.
✉ *1100 Queen St. E, Queen East* ☎ *416/461–4061.*

French Country. Faience and Verceral dishware and the modern French
tables you put them on are a few of the finds at this quaint shop, which
peddles things food- and wine-related. ✉ *6 Roxborough St. W, Rosedale*
☎ *416/944–2204.*

Orleans. Antiques with interesting pasts wind up here, like sideboards
owned by French peasants during Marie Antoinette's reign. Most items
are mid- to high-priced. ✉ *1096 Yonge St., Rosedale* ☎ *416/966–0005.*

Prince of Serendip Antiques. Visit this shop, full of gilt goodies and restored gold fixtures, when you need a hint of Versailles. The merchandise is pricey, but the pieces are great quality. Custom repairs are
available. ✉ *1073 Yonge St., Rosedale* ☎ *416/925–3760.*

Putti. Sort through European and domestic antiques as well as bath and
garden products at this luxurious store. Prices are a bit steep. ✉ *1104
Yonge St., Rosedale* ☎ *416/972–7652.*

Quasi Modo. Take in this quirky collection of 20th- and 21st-century fur-
niture and design. Here you find Herman Miller lounge chairs and
Noguchi lamps, as well as pottery by Jonathan Adler. ✉ *789 Queen St.
W, Queen West* ☎ *416/703–8300.*

Toronto Antique Center. The complex provides a host of choices for
browsers and shoppers, including about 30 dealers in furniture, dishes,

jewelry, art, and carpets. It's busiest during matinees at nearby theaters, but the market is open Tuesday through Sunday from 10 to 6. ⊠ *276 King St. W, Entertainment District* ☎ *416/345–9941.*

Xit Designs. The postmodern-furnishings boutique focuses on smaller items, such as spa kits and towel racks. In the mix you can find jewelry by such local artists as Richard Wyman. ⊠ *40 Blue Jays Way, Downtown* ☎ *416/778–0823.*

Zig Zag Collectibles. With antiques and trinkets large and small, this place captures the feeling of Grandma's attic. Retro furniture and lighting is circa 1950 to 1970. Prices range from C$20 to C$2,000. ⊠ *1142 Queen St. E, Queen East* ☎ *416/778–6495.*

Art & Crafts Galleries

Toronto is a cosmopolitan art center, with a few hundred commercial art galleries carrying items as varied as glass sculpture, Inuit designs, and contemporary pieces. To find out about special exhibits, check the Saturday edition of the *Globe and Mail* entertainment section, as well as *NOW* and *eye*—free weekly local newspapers on culture distributed on Thursday. *Toronto Life* magazine is also a good source of information on gallery happenings. But to really get a sense of what is available in Toronto, the best thing to do is stroll around areas like Queen Street West and Yorkville. Some buildings are almost entirely dedicated to art galleries, like the building that houses YYZ at 401 Richmond Street West and the recently redesigned Gooderham and Worts complex on Mill Street, just south of Front Street East. Most galleries are open Tuesday to Saturday from 10 to 5 or 6, but call to confirm.

Bau-Xi Gallery. Paul Wong, an artist and dealer from Vancouver, founded this gallery across the street from the Art Gallery of Ontario. The paintings and sculpture are a window on contemporary Canadian art, with a focus on Ontario. Much of the art is affordable. ⊠ *340 Dundas St. W, Downtown* ☎ *416/977–0600.*

Feheley Fine Arts. Browse through Canadian Inuit and Northwest Coast art with a special emphasis on work from the 1950s on. ⊠ *14 Hazelton Ave., Yorkville* ☎ *416/323–1373.*

Gallery Moos. German-born Walter Moos opened his gallery in 1959 to promote Canadian and European art. He's a discerning, reliable dealer who's had Picassos, Chagalls, Mirós, and Dufys, as well as work by such internationally admired Canadians as Gershon Iskowitz, Ken Danby, Sorel Etrog, and Jean-Paul Riopelle. ⊠ *622 Richmond St. W, Queen West* ☎ *416/504–5445.*

Corkin Shopland Gallery. With work by photographers such as André Kertesz and Richard Avedon, this gallery is one of the most fascinating in town. See hand-painted photos, documentary photos, fashion photography, and mixed-media art. ⊠ *55 Mill St., Bldg. 61, Downtown* ☎ *416/304–1050.*

Loch Gallery. The intimate gallery in an old Victorian house almost exclusively exhibits representational and historic Canadian contemporary painting and sculpture. Artists include Jack Chambers, bronze sculptor Leo Mol, and painter John Boyle. ⊠ *16 Hazelton Ave., Yorkville* ☎ *416/964–9050.*

Olga Korper Gallery. Many important artists, such as Lynne Cohen, Paterson Ewen, John McEwen, and Reinhard Reitzenstein are represented by this trailblazing yet accessible gallery, which displays art from the 1960s on. It's a good place for beginning contemporary collectors. ⊠ *17 Morrow Ave., The Annex* ☎ *416/538–8220.*

Prime Gallery. Crafts from across Canada include avant-garde ceramics, wall sculpture, jewelry, and textiles. ⊠ *52 McCaul St., Queen West* ☎ *416/593–5750.*

Sandra Ainsley Gallery. The glass-sculpture gallery within the burgeoning Gooderham and Worts complex on Mill Street has both large and small pieces. Rotating displays have included artists such as Dale Chihuly. ⊠ *55 Mill St., Downtown* ☎ *416/214–9490.*

SPIN Gallery. The trendy latch on to SPIN's innovative sculpture, painting, photography, installation, and new media. Artists such as renowned Canadian artist Charles Pachter and REM lead singer Michael Stipe generate frequent media coverage when they show here. ⊠ *1100 Queen St. W, 2nd fl., Queen West* ☎ *416/530–7656.*

Stephen Bulger. The photography gallery focuses on historical Canadian work, with Canadian and international artists such as Shelby Lee Adams and Larry Towell. ⊠ *1026 Queen St. W, Queen West* ☎ *416/504–0575.*

Wynick/Tuck Gallery. Many of the contemporary Canadian artists displayed here have become well established, attesting to this gallery's influence. The work expresses a wide range of untrendy, often imagistic concerns. ⊠ *401 Richmond W, Queen West* ☎ *416/504–8716.*

YYZ Artists' Outlet. There are two exhibition spaces here: one for visual art and one for time-based conceptions. The visual might contain two- and three-dimensional paintings and sculptures, whereas the time-based area might have performances, films, and videos. ⊠ *401 Richmond St. W, Queen West* ☎ *416/598–4546.*

Auctions

Sotheby's. The Toronto outpost of the international auction house focuses entirely on Canadian art. Auctions happen twice yearly—the end of May and mid-November—at the nearby Ritchie's Auction House on King Street. ⊠ *9 Hazelton Ave., Yorkville* ☎ *416/926–1774 or 800/263–1774.*

Books

Toronto has no shortage of bookstores, from megastores like Chapters and Indigo to secondhand-book shops between the University of Toronto and The Annex.

BMV. BMV (which stands for "Books Magazines Video") carries an impressive selection of new and used books shelved side by side over two floors. The staff is knowledgeable and helpful. ⊠ *2289 Yonge St., Midtown* ☎ *416/482–6002* ⊠ *10 Edward St., Downtown* ☎ *416/977–3087.*

Book City. Find good discounts—especially on publishers' remainders— a knowledgeable staff, and a fine choice of magazines at branches of this late-night Toronto chain, usually open until 10 or 11. Five locations are scattered throughout the city. ⊠ *501 Bloor St. W, The Annex* ☎ *416/*

961–4496 ✉*2350 Bloor St. W, Yorkville* ☎*416/766–9412* ✉*348 Danforth Ave., Yorkville* ☎ *416/469–9997* ✉ *1430 Yonge St., Midtown* ☎ *416/961–1228* ✉ *1950 Queen St. E, Beaches* ☎ *416/698–1444.*

Chapters. The three-story book-lovers' mecca is the gold standard for chain bookstores. There's a Starbucks, lounge areas for reading, and a selection of music CDs. ✉ *110 Bloor St. W, Yorkville* ☎*416/920–9299.*

David Mirvish Books/Books on Art. Quality books and many remainders fill the store, where you get the best price in town for the Sunday *New York Times.* ✉ *596 Markham St., The Annex* ☎ *416/531–9975.*

Indigo. A huge selection of books, magazines, and CDs are stocked at this store, which has a Starbucks and occasional live entertainment. ✉ *55 Bloor St. W, Yorkville* ☎ *416/925–3536* ✉ *2300 Yonge St. Midtown* ☎ *416/544–0049.*

★ **Pages Books and Magazines.** Shelves brim with international and small-press literature, fashion and design books and magazines, and books on film, art, literary criticism, and fiction. ✉ *256 Queen St. W, Queen West* ☎ *416/598–1447.*

This Ain't the Rosedale Library. In addition to stocking a general selection of magazines and books, the store also offers gay and lesbian titles. ✉ *483 Church St., Church & Wellesley* ☎ *416/929–9912.*

SPECIAL-
INTEREST
BOOKSTORES

Ballenford Books. Architecture aficionados visit this store to browse its huge selection of architecture titles. There's even an exhibit displaying architectural drawings by local firms. ✉ *600 Markham St., The Annex* ☎ *416/588–0800.*

Cookbook Store. This store has the city's largest selection of books and magazines on cooking and wine. Book signings are frequently held here. ✉ *850 Yonge St., Yorkville* ☎ *416/920–2665 or 800/268–6018.*

Israel's Judaica Centre. The Centre has the city's best selection of adult and children's books relating to Judaism in English, Hebrew, and Yiddish. Service is excellent. ✉ *870 Eglinton Ave. W, Midtown* ☎*416/256–1010.*

Open Air Books and Maps. More than 10,000 travel books, oodles of atlases and road maps, specialized travel books, and titles on nature and food make this the ideal place to feed your wanderlust. ✉ *25 Toronto St., King East* ☎ *416/363–0719.*

Sleuth of Baker Street. Sleuth of Baker Street is the best place for mysteries and detective fiction, with an extensive collection of titles in both categories. Staff members are detective fiction buffs themselves and can help you sleuth out the elusive noir book for which you've been hunting. The shop also puts out its own newsletter. ✉ *1600 Bayview Ave., Leaside* ☎ *416/483–3111.*

Theatrebooks. An astounding collection of performing-arts books spans theater, film, opera, dance, television, and media studies. ✉ *11 St. Thomas St., Yorkville* ☎ *416/922–7175 or 800/361–3414* ☎*416/922–0739.*

Toronto Women's Bookstore. Titles focus on women and minorities and include the latest fiction by women, feminist works on women's political issues, literary criticism, and lesbian topics. Benches, chairs, and pillows scattered throughout the store make for easy perusing. ✉ *73 Harbord St., The Annex* ☎ *416/922–8744.*

Clothing

Children's Clothing

Babes. It's known for its snowsuits, but you can also score tons of cute indoor wear by Deux par Deux, Hollywood, Blü, and Gumboots for infants up to size 16. ⊠ *2116A Queen St. E, Queen East* ☎ *416/699–6110.*

Gap Kids. Freestanding Gap Kids has plenty of pint-size basics. The downtown location is in the Eaton Centre. ⊠ *80 Bloor St. W, Yorkville* ☎ *416/515–0668* ⊠ *2574 Yonge St., Midtown* ☎ *416/440–0187* ⊠ *Eaton Centre, 220 Yonge St., Downtown* ☎ *416/348–8800.*

Kingly. Subscribing to the belief that boys' clothes should be as interesting as girls, this store carries trendy but practical tot threads (boys' sizes to one year, girls' to four years). Everything is machine-washable. ⊠ *1078 Queen St. W, Queen West* ☎ *416/536–2601* ⊠ *1820 Queen St. E, Queen East* ☎*416/536–8123.*

Men's Clothing

Boomer. One of the best-kept secrets of Toronto men brings together tasteful yet trendy suitings and separates. ⊠ *309 Queen St. W, Queen West* ☎ *416/598–0013.*

Eddie Bauer. Casual wear and sports clothes run to the likes of classic polos and khakis. Outdoor-oriented accessories such as Swiss Army knives and watches are well made, and there's also sturdy luggage. ⊠ *50 Bloor St. W, Yorkville* ☎ *416/961–2525.*

Harry Rosen. The miniature department store is dedicated to the finest men's fashions, with designers such as Hugo Boss, Armani, and Zegna. ⊠ *82 Bloor St. W, Yorkville* ☎ *416/972–0556.*

Moore's, the Suit People. Browse through thousands of discounted Canadian-made dress pants, sport coats, and suits, including many famous labels. You might turn up an all-wool suit for C$250. Sizes run from extra short to extra tall and from regular to oversize; the quality is solid and the service is good. ⊠ *100 Yonge St., Downtown* ☎ *416/363–5442.*

Perry's. These are the suit professionals. Have one custom-made from a broad range of fabrics, or buy off the rack from a collection of some of the finest ready-to-wear suits, which are made by Sanuelsohn and Jack Victor (who are both from Montreal). ⊠ *1250 Bay St., Yorkville* ☎ *416/923–7397.*

Stollerys. From wool to linen to salespeople with round spectacles holding measuring tapes, walking into this department store is like stepping into a tailor shop in 1900s England, only on a grander scale. Choose from four floors of carefully conservative clothing. ⊠ *1 Bloor St. W, Yorkville* ☎ *416/922–6173.*

Tom's Place. Find bargains aplenty on brand-name suits like Calvin Klein, Armani, and DKNY. Tom Mihalik, the store's owner, keeps his prices low. He carries some womens' clothes as well. ⊠ *190 Baldwin St., Kensington Market* ☎ *416/596–0297.*

Men's & Women's Clothing

Banana Republic. Snap up this chain's well-constructed basic separates, suits, and casual wear. Prices are mid-range, but the sales rack has good deals. ⊠ *80 Bloor St. W, Yorkville* ☎ *416/515–0018.*

Club Monaco. The bright and airy flagship store of this successful chain, now owned by Ralph Lauren, has homegrown design basics: mid-price sportswear and career clothes. ⊠ *157 Bloor St. W, Yorkville* ☎ *416/ 591–8837.*

Gucci. Canada's only Gucci boutique sells the label's full range of goods, including ready-to-wear, footwear, and fragrance. ⊠ *130 Bloor St. W, Yorkville* ☎ *416/963–5127.*

Jet Rag. Trendy threads, most by local designers, stock this sliver of a store on the Queen West strip. ⊠ *359 Queen St W, Queen West* ☎ *416/ 979–2677.*

★ **Roots.** Torontonians' favorite leather jackets, bags, and basics come from this flagship store, which also manufactures Olympic uniforms for Canada, the U.S., Barbados, and Great Britain. Branches are in several other Toronto neighborhoods. ⊠ *100 Bloor St. W, Yorkville* ☎ *416/323– 3289* ⊠ *1485 Yonge St., Midtown* ☎ *416/967–4499* ⊠ *2670 Yonge St., Midtown* ☎ *416/482–6773* ⊠ *356 Queen St. W, Queen West* ☎ *416/ 977–0409* ⊠ *Eaton Centre, 220 Yonge St., Downtown* ☎ *416/593–9640.*

M0851 Searching for a *Matrix*-like coat? This is the place to go. Sort through leather and denim jackets, pants, bags, and luggage. You can even have leather furniture, such as chairs and four-seater couches, made to order. ⊠ *23 St. Thomas, Yorkville* ☎ *416/920–4001.*

Sim & Jones. Founding design team Pui Sim and Alarice Jones turn out polished looks for the hip urban professional. They also carry the lines of other local designers and have a line of home accessories. ⊠ *388 College St., Little Italy* ☎ *416/920–2573.*

Urban Outfitters. The young and trendy scan the racks here for the latest "it" piece. Prices are comparatively high considering the clothes' often low quality. Don't miss the quirky, modern housewares and oddball coffee-table books. ⊠ *235 Yonge St. W, Downtown* ☎ *416/214–1466.*

Zara. The Spanish chain consistently attracts crowds craving gorgeous knockoffs of the hottest runway trends. If you see something you like, grab it; it won't be there for long. ⊠ *50 Bloor St. W, Yorkville* ☎ *416/ 916–2401* ⊠ *220 Yonge St., Downtown* ☎ *647/288–0333.*

Zuei. Two levels here hold fascinating items. Designs popular in Japan and funky clothing accessories fill the top floor, while the ground floor houses a bevy of wondrous gadgets and knickknacks. ⊠ *4 St. Patrick St., Queen West* ☎ *416/597–1785.*

Vintage Clothing

Black Market. True vintage buffs hunt through the racks—very thrift shop— to uncover the best bargains. The second-floor shop overlooks Queen Street; a second, larger store across the road houses the biggest discounts. ⊠ *319 Queen St. W, Queen West* ☎ *416/591–7945* ⊠ *256A Queen St. W, Queen West* ☎ *416/599–5858.*

★ **Courage My Love.** The best vintage store in Kensington Market is crammed with the coolest retro stuff, from sunglasses to tuxedos. The in-house cat adds a nice touch. ⊠ *14 Kensington Ave., Kensington Market* ☎ *416/979–1992.*

Preloved. Former models and fashion insiders stock this shop by combing the vintage market and reconstructing their finds into the most unique designs. ⊠ *613 Queen St. W, Queen West* ☎ *416/504–8704.*

Tribal Rhythm. A horde of imported Thai and Indian trinkets, rows of quirky body jewelry, and vintage clothing are part of the charming and eclectic mix at this shop. ⊠ *248 Queen St. W, Queen West* ☎ *416/595–5817.*

Women's Clothing

Aritzia. Young urban woman come here for modern funky pieces by lines such as Miss Sixty, Seven, and the house line Talula. There are other locations throughout the city. ⊠ *280 Queen St. W, Queen West* ☎ *416/ 977–9919* ⊠ *Eaton Centre, 220 Queen St. W, Downtown* ☎ *416/ 204–1318* ⊠ *50 Bloor St. W, Yorkville* ☎ *416/934–0935.*

Chanel. Coco would have loved the largest Chanel boutique in Canada. The lush surroundings showcase most of the line, including the double-C bags and accessories. ⊠ *131 Bloor St. W, Yorkville* ☎ *416/925–2577.*

Comrags. Designers Joyce Gunhouse and Judy Cornish have supplied the city with more than 20 years of smart, sophisticated women's clothing designs. ⊠ *654 Queen St. W, Queen West* ☎ *416/360–7249.*

Corbò Boutique. Some of the most tasteful designers—Miu Miu, Prada, and Costume National, to name a few—are gathered here under one roof, along with some of the finest footwear in town. Did someone say Jimmy Choo or Ann Demeulemeester? This is upscale one-stop shopping. ⊠ *131 Bloor St. W, Yorkville* ☎ *416/928–0954.*

Fashion Crimes. Part old-world romantic, part Queen West funk, this haven of glam party dresses and dreamy designs has a display case packed full of elegant baubles and sparkling tiaras. Designer and owner Pam Chorley also has a pint-size label for girls called Misdemeanours. ⊠ *322½ Queen St. W, Queen West* ☎ *416/592–9001.*

Freeway. The casual clothing at this spot in The Beaches district is in line with the area's Coney Island atmosphere. Here's the place to find lines like Mexx and Dex Brothers—a combination of sporty and sexy. ⊠ *1978 Queen St. E, Queen East* ☎ *416/693–6670.*

F/X. Some call the crinolined skirts, wild colors, and short skirts here masquerade, but the clothes are undeniably fun, especially for evening wear. There's also a variety of quirky knickknacks, as well as cards and candy. ⊠ *515 Queen St. W, Queen West* ☎ *416/504–0888.*

Girl Friday. Designer Rebecca Nixon sells sweet and stylish designs with a retro glam look. ⊠ *776 College St., Little Italy* ☎ *416/531–1036* ⊠ *740 Queen St. W, Queen West* ☎ *416/364–2511.*

Hermès. The Parisian design house caters to the upscale horse- and hound-loving set, selling its famous—and pricey—classic sportswear, handbags (by the names of Kelly and Birkin), and accessories (those luxe silk scarves and ties). ⊠ *131 Bloor St. W, Yorkville* ☎ *416/968–8626.*

Kitsch Boutique. Pick out a loud Betsey Johnson evening dress or punky BCBG suit among these trendy pieces, many of which are imported from Miami, New York, Los Angeles, and France. Swing through the basement, where slow sellers are relegated until they're scooped up at half-price. ⊠ *325 Lonsdale Rd., Midtown* ☎ *416/481–6712* ⊠ *347 Bay St., Downtown* ☎ *416/861–9572.*

Lululemon. The bright and airy store is a perfect Zen match for items such as specialized yoga sports bras, top-of-the-line yoga mats, and stretchy yoga and gym togs. ⊠ *734 Queen W, Queen West* ☎ *416/703–1399*

☒ *130 Bloor W, Yorkville* ☎ *416/964–9544* ☒ *2558 Yonge St., Midtown* ☎ *416/487–1390.*

Mendocino. Score the best of the mid-price, super trendy lines here—the polished looks you find in *In Style* magazine. Slide on a cute miniskirt or wiggle on a quirky tee. Labels include Citizens of Humanity, Trina Turk, and Debbie Schuchat. This great stop if you have a limited amount of time and want to pack a lot in, since you can peruse the day and evening designs of a number of lines here. ☒ *294 Queen St. W, Queen West* ☎ *416/593–1011.*

Parade. The store's Prada-esque designs are whimsical and flirtatious takes on female fashion. ☒ *315 Queen St. W, Queen West* ☎ *416/971–7767.*

Plaza Escada. The spacious store carries the designer Escada line of chic Italian creations. ☒ *110 Bloor St. W, Yorkville* ☎ *416/964–2265.*

Prada. The avant-garde designs are overshadowed only by the brilliant celadon interior of the store and the traffic-stopping window displays. ☒ *131 Bloor St. W, Unit 5, Yorkville* ☎ *416/513–0400.*

Price Roman. Edgy career and evening wear—think bias-cut dresses and asymetrical hemlines—come in surprising fabric choices here, like Asian brocades and various silks. ☒ *267 Queen St. W, Queen West* ☎ *416/979–7363.*

Risqué. Shoppers find trendy clothes by Toronto designers as well as inexpensive accessories at this spot in The Annex. ☒ *404 Bloor St. W, The Annex* ☎ *416/960–3325.*

San Remo. Find that ultrafeminine yet funky piece within this offbeat shop's lavender walls. ☒ *23 St. Thomas St., Yorkville* ☎ *416/920–3195.*

★ **Want.** With their inventory direct from Los Angeles, Want has the goods you probably won't find elsewhere in Toronto. The focus is on dresses, which run from fun and sporty to black-tie. ☒ *1454 Yonge St., Midtown* ☎ *416/934–9268* ☒ *1694 Avenue Rd., Midtown* ☎ *416/256–9268.*

★ **Winners.** Toronto's best bargain outlet has designer lines at rock-bottom prices. The Yonge Street branch, below the elegant Carlu event center, is enormous. ☒ *57 Spadina Ave., Downtown* ☎ *416/585–2052* ☒ *444 Yonge St., Downtown* ☎ *416/598–8800.*

Food

Food Markets

FodorśChoice ★ **Kensington Market.** The outdoor market has a vibrant ethnic mix and charming restaurants, and sells everything from great cheese, coffee, nuts, and spices to natural foods, South American delicacies, and Portuguese baked goods. Vintage-clothing lovers delight in the shops tucked into houses lining the streets. Saturday is the best day to go, preferably by public transit; parking is difficult. ☒ *Northwest of Dundas St. and Spadina Ave., Kensington Market* ☎ *No phone.*

St. Lawrence Market. Nearly 60 vendors occupy the historic permanent indoor market and sell items such as produce, caviar, jewelry, and handmade crafts. The building, on the south side of Front Street, was once Toronto's city hall, and it fronted the lake before extensive landfill projects were undertaken. The best time to visit is early (from 5 AM) on Saturday, when there's a farmers' market (in the building on the north side).

⊠92 Front St. E, at Jarvis St., Downtown ☎416/392–7219 ⊘Tues.–Thurs. 8–6, Fri. 8–7, Sat. 5–5; Farmers' market Sat. 5–5.

Food Shops

All the Best Fine Foods. Stop here for imported cheeses and good local breads as well as high-quality prepared foods and condiments. ⊠ 1099 Yonge St., Rosedale ☎ 416/928–3330.

Big Carrot Natural Food Market. The large and adventurous health-food supermarket carries large selections of organic produce, health and beauty aids, and vitamins. There's a café on-site and freshly prepared foods for takeout. ⊠ 348 Danforth Ave., Danforth ☎ 416/466–2129.

Pusateri's. From its humble beginnings as a produce stand in Little Italy, Pusateri's has grown into Toronto's deluxe supermarket, with a wide range of in-house prepared foods, local and imported delicacies, and desserts and breads from the city's best bakers. It's great for putting together a picnic. ⊠ 1539 Avenue Rd., Midtown ☎ 416/785–9100.

Whole Foods. The gourmet grocery store has both mid- and high-priced items. Salad and pasta bars, freshly baked goods, and an impressive selection of prepared foods line one wall. ⊠ 187 Avenue Rd., Yorkville ☎ 416/944–0500.

Fur

Fur central is Spadina Avenue, from Queen Street north to Dundas Street.

Glen & Paul Magder Furs. Ladies who lunch have bought coats and jackets here for more than two decades. The store also refurbishes fur and does alterations while you wait. ⊠ 202 Spadina Ave., Chinatown ☎ 416/504–6077.

Home Decor & Furnishings

AGO Gallery Shop. The store attached to the Art Gallery of Ontario has an overwhelming selection of curiosities, from books on maximal architecture to colorful dollhouses to prints of celebrated paintings. Adults and kids can shop side by side among the books and fun educational toys. ⊠ 317 Dundas St. W, Downtown ☎ 416/979–6610.

The Art Shoppe. The block-long, two-story shop is chock full of eclectic high-brow furniture. ⊠ 2131 Yonge St., Midtown ☎ 416/487–3211.

★ **Caban.** Club Monaco's flagship home-concept store is bright and big, with themed departments, a listening booth, a kitchen, and a fireplace. You can also buy clothing, books, and music. ⊠ 262–264 Queen St. W, Queen West ☎ 416/596–0386.

Demarco-Perpich. The floral store sells adorable arrangements and garden-inspired accents for the home. ⊠ 1116 Yonge St., Rosedale ☎ 416/ 967–0893.

Hollace Cluny. The shop sells mainly handmade modern furnishings and accents. ⊠ 1070 Yonge St., Rosedale ☎ 416/968–7894.

IKEA. The high-quality, reasonably priced goods make the Swedish home furnishings store worth the crowds and the 45-minute drive from downtown. Pick up pots and pans, picture frames, or an entire living room set. Most furniture requires assembly. ⊠ 15 Provost Dr., North York ☎ 416/222–4532.

Seagull Classics Ltd. Victorian and Tiffany-style lamps as well as art deco–inspired forms are among this store's unusual selection of lighting. ⊠ *1974 Queen St. E, Queen East* ☎ *416/690–5224.*

Urban Mode. Modern and trend-oriented home accessories here include colorful plastic desk accessories in interesting shapes and funky wine racks and CD stands. Most are Canadian-designed. ⊠ *389 Queen St. W, Queen West* ☎ *416/591–8834 or 877/265–5895.*

Jewelry

Cartier. The famous jewel box caters to Toronto's elite and has a good selection of the jewelry designer's creations, including the famous triple-gold-band Trinity Ring and the diamond-studded Torture watch. ⊠ *130 Bloor St. W, Yorkville* ☎ *416/413–4929.*

Royal De Versailles. Don't let the front-door security scare you away from some of the most innovatively classic jewelry designs in town. ⊠ *101 Bloor St. W, Yorkville* ☎ *416/967–7201.*

Tiffany & Co. Tiffany is perfect for breakfast or anytime. It's still the ultimate for variety and quality in classic jewelry. ⊠ *85 Bloor St. W, Yorkville* ☎ *416/921–3900.*

Kitchenware & Tabletop

The Cook's Place. Even the most cosmopolitan chef should find something to take home among this immense selection of cookware, including baking pans and hard-to-find gadgets and utensils. Don't miss the fascinating "wall of stuff." ⊠ *488 Danforth Ave., Danforth* ☎ *416/461–5211.*

Give It a Stir. The amount of polished chrome is mesmerizing and comes in a variety of modern kitchen utensils and appliances, like Dualit toasters, Wusthof knives, and a plethora of Gaggia espresso machines. The size of the store alone may tickle a cook's fancy. ⊠ *1560 Yonge St., Rosedale* ☎ *416/920–7447.*

William Ashley. Ashley's has an extensive collection of china patterns and can often secure those they don't carry. Crystal and china are beautifully displayed, and prices are decent on expensive names such as Waterford. ⊠ *55 Bloor St. W, Yorkville* ☎ *416/964–2900.*

Word Of Mouth. High-end kitchen appliances, accessories, and tools are priced very competitively, since this store imports directly. ⊠ *1134 Yonge St., Rosedale* ☎ *416/929–6885.*

Music & Stereo Equipment

Bay Bloor Radio. The stereo haven has the latest equipment and sound-sealed listening rooms that allow the connoisseur to test-drive equipment. ⊠ *Manulife Centre, 55 Bloor St. W, Yorkville* ☎ *416/967–1122.*

Cops/Vintage Sounds. The well-known and well-frequented shop combo is revered as the best used-CD store in the city. Upstairs, Vintage Sounds sells vinyl, 45s, LPs, and CDs from the '50s to '80s, while the downstairs Cops is more contemporary, with reggae, hip hop, jazz, and soul. The stores are independently owned, but you must walk through Cops to get to Vintage. ⊠ *229 Queen St. W, Queen West* ☎ *416/598–4039.*

Ed's Record World. Ed's Record World and its CD Replay branches are about as *High Fidelity* (minus the vinyl) as they come. The staff is knowledgeable and there are frequent deals on older CDs. Both sell new and used CDs and DVDs. ✉ *2283 Yonge St., Midtown* ☎ *416/489–1144* ✉ *762 Yonge St., Yorkville* ☎ *416/513–1144* ✉ *523 Bloor St. W, Yorkville* ☎ *416/516–0606.*

HMV. The megastore has the largest selection of CDs in the city, in all categories. In-store listening stations allow consumers to sample any CD prior to purchase. ✉ *50 Bloor St. W, Yorkville* ☎ *416/324–9979* ✉ *333 Yonge St., Downtown* ☎ *416/596–0333.*

Penguin Music. The slender little store packs a mighty wallop. Choose from a plethora of used indie-label CDs. ✉ *2 McCaul St., Downtown* ☎ *416/597–1687.*

Rotate This. Record buyers in the know come here for underground and independent music from Canada, the United States, and beyond. The store has CDs as well as LPs, some magazines, concert tickets, and other treats. ✉ *620 Queen St. W, Queen West* ☎ *416/504–8447.*

Sam the Record Man. The Toronto institution has occupied the corner of Yonge and Gould streets since 1961, but it's been around since the 1930s. A wide assortment of music is stocked, and the bargain bins are always overflowing. ✉ *347 Yonge St., Downtown* ☎ *416/646–2775.*

Soundscapes. Crammed with pop, rock, jazz, blues, folk, ambient, psychedelic, garage, avant-garde, and electronic titles, this shop satisfies the hip as well as fans of early Americana. Selections and organization reflect a love of music and its ever-expanding history. ✉ *572 College St., Little Italy* ☎ *416/537–1620.*

Shoes

Brown's. The excellent selection of shoes can make your heart race. At the Bloor store, you can find the latest punky Steve Madden next to a vampish Manolo Blahnik. Brown's also carries a broad range of handbags and boots. ✉ *Eaton Centre, Downtown* ☎ *416/979–9270* ✉ *Holt Renfrew, 50 Bloor St. W, Yorkville* ☎ *416/960–1174.*

David's. The collection is always elegant, if somewhat subdued—designers usually include Hugo Boss, Taryn Rose, and Lorenzo Banfi. ✉ *66 Bloor St. W, Yorkville* ☎ *416/920–1000.*

Get Out Side. Get your funky street wear fix here. There are styles for men and women, as well as an entire wall of sneakers. ✉ *437 Queen St. W, Queen West* ☎ *416/593–5598.*

Heel Boy. A number of well-known brand-name lines and a few edgier ones make this a popular shoe-shopping spot. ✉ *682 Queen St. W, Queen West* ☎ *416/362–4335.*

John Fluevog. Fluevog began in Vancouver, infusing good quality with fun, flair, and cutting-edge design. Now an international shoe star, Fluevog can be found all over the U.S., in Australia, and luckily, also on Queen Street West. ✉ *242 Queen St. W, Queen West* ☎ *416/581–1420.*

Mephisto Boutique. These fine walking shoes have been around since the 1960s and are made entirely from natural materials. Passionate walkers swear by these shoes and claim they never, ever wear out—even on cross-Europe treks. ✉ *1177 Yonge St., Rosedale* ☎ *416/968–7026.*

Pegabo. Here's where to score knockoff versions of designer shoes. ⊠ *91 Bloor St. W, Yorkville* ☎ *416/323–3722.*

Zola. The store is tiny, but it's what's inside—a selection of women's shoes that includes the likes of Sigerson Morrison and Emma Hope—that counts. ⊠ *1726 Avenue Rd., Midtown* ☎ *416/783–8688.*

Sporting Goods

Fodor'sChoice **Mountain Equipment Co-op.** MEC, the much-beloved Toronto spot for any-
★ one remotely interested in camping, sells wares for minor and major ex-peditions. A baffling assortment of backpacks allows you to choose anything from a schoolbag to a globe-trotting sack, and a rock-climb-ing wall allows you to try out the rappelling goods. ⊠ *400 King St. W, Downtown* ☎ *416/340–2667.*

★ **Nike.** The store's two floors display everything the famous brand name has to offer, from athletic equipment to sneakers. ⊠ *110 Bloor St. W, Yorkville* ☎ *416/921–6453.*

Puma. There was a big to-do when Puma moved into the Yonge and Eglin-ton neighborhood, with people scrambling to own some apparel em-broidered with the cat. Two floors have workout wear, bags, and sneakers. ⊠ *2532 Yonge St., Midtown* ☎ *416/486–7862.*

The Running Room. The knowledgeable staff can guide you to the perfect pair of running shoes, taking into consideration your foot type and ap-propriate level of material breathability. The Running Rooms have spawned a running community and shops have sprouted up all over the country; group runs commence every Wednesday evening and Sunday morn-ing. ⊠ *55 Avenue Rd., in Hazelton Lanes, Yorkville* ☎ *416/960–3910.*

Sporting Life. The first off the mark with the latest sportswear trends, this is the place to get couture labels like Juicy, La Coste, and Burberry—or to snag snowboard gear and poll the staff for advice on where to go to use it. A second "bikes and boards store" is down Yonge Street, and a third and much smaller store at Yorkville focuses on athletics. ⊠ *2665 Yonge St., Midtown* ☎ *416/485–1611* ⊠ *2454 Yonge St., Midtown* ☎ *416/485–4440* ⊠ *95 Bloor St. W, Yorkville* ☎ *416/485–2787.*

SIDE TRIPS
FROM TORONTO

Updated by
Ilona
Kauremszky,
Bruce Bishop,
and Vernon
O'Reilly-
Ramesar

THE RUSH OF 700,000 GALLONS OF WATER A SECOND. The devastatingly sweet, crisp taste of ice wine. The tug of a fish hooked under a layer of ice. Sure, the big-city scene in Toronto delivers the hustle and bustle you came for—but escaping the city can transport you to mesmerizing and deservedly hyped Niagara Falls, acres of local vineyards in Niagara-on-the-Lake and the surrounding Wine Region, or the whimsical Cottage Country, with its quiet towns, challenging ski slopes, and lakefront resorts. Have an itch for the stage? Two major theater events, the Stratford Festival and the Shaw Festival, have long seasons with masterfully orchestrated plays by the bards, Will and George Bernard. You can hit the outdoors on Bruce Trail, Canada's oldest and longest footpath, which winds from Niagara Falls to Tobermory.

If you are driving to your destination, the best time to leave Toronto is early- to mid-week; however, you should avoid the weekday rush hours of 7 to 9:30 AM and 4 to 6:30 PM. Toll highways and bridges are rare.

Exploring Ontario

About the Restaurants

George Bernard Shaw once said, "No greater love hath man than the love of food," and Niagara-on-the-Lake, which hosts a festival devoted to the playwright, is a perfect place to indulge your epicurean desires. Many eateries serve fine produce and wines from the verdant Niagara Peninsula. In fact, Niagara wines make appearances on menus provincewide; try the sweet ice wine with dessert. Though the town appears to have changed little from its turn-of-the-20th-century style, the rebuilding and renovation of historical inns have brought this sleepy town into the first-class hospitality arena.

Expect a variety of cuisines across the province: fresh-caught fish in Cottage Country, great home-style French-Canadian fare in small-town inns, or haute Canadian in Niagara Wine Region restaurants. Thanks to a long-standing British influence, there's plenty of roast beef, shepherd's pie, and rice pudding, especially in the English-dominated enclaves of London, Stratford, and Hamilton. Reservations at medium-price and upscale restaurants are recommended, particularly during peak season in the ski and festival towns; the same advice applies to Niagara Falls. Ontarians crave Tim Horton's doughnuts, found at franchise shops in virtually every city.

About the Hotels

Reservations are strongly recommended everywhere during summer, especially in Ottawa, Toronto, and Niagara Falls. The small inns of Stratford and Niagara-on-the-Lake fill up during the summer cultural festivals. Prices are comparable to those in the U.S.—although in Canadian dollars. All types of accommodations tend to be more expensive in tourist venues. In Niagara Falls, for example, hotel and motel rates are determined by proximity to the famous waterfall. Taxes are seldom included in quoted prices, but rates sometimes include food, especially in areas such as Muskoka and Haliburton, where many resorts offer meal plans.

Most major cities have bed-and-breakfast associations.

What it Costs

WHAT IT COSTS in Canadian dollars				
	$$$$	$$$	$$	$	¢
RESTAURANTS	over $30	$20–$30	$12–$20	$8–$12	under $8
HOTELS	over $250	$175–$250	$125–$175	$75–$125	under $75

Restaurant prices are per person for a main course at dinner. Hotel prices are for two people in a standard double room in high season, excluding 7% GST and 5% room tax.

NORTH OF TORONTO TO THE LAKES

Outcroppings of pink and gray granite mark the rustic area in the Canadian Shield known to locals as Cottage Country. Drumlins of conifer and deciduous forest punctuate 100,000 freshwater lakes formed from glaciers during the Ice Age. Names of towns and places such as Orillia, the Muskokas, Gravenhurst, Haliburton, and Algonquin reveal the history of the land's inhabitants, from Algonquin tribes to European explorers to fur traders. The area became a haven for the summering rich and famous during the mid-19th century, when lumber barons who were harvesting near port towns set up steamship and rail lines, making travel to the area possible. Since then, Cottage Country has attracted urbanites who make the pilgrimage to hear the call of the loon or swat incessant mosquitoes and black flies. "Cottages" is a broadly used term that includes log cabins as well as palatial homes that wouldn't look out of place in a wealthy urban neighborhood. For the cottageless, overnight seasonal camping is an option in one of the provincial parks.

To reach this area, take Highway 400 north, which intersects with Cottage Country's highly traveled and often congested Highway 11. Highway 60 is less traveled and cuts across the province through Algonquin Provincial Park.

Barrie

90 km (56 mi) north of Toronto on Hwy. 400.

Barrie is on the shore of Lake Simcoe and was originally a landing place for the area's aboriginal inhabitants and, later, for fur traders. Today, it's an attractive city serving as the gateway to the popular ski resorts and northern Huronia summer vacation lands. Barrie has events year-round. The town's annual **Winterfest** (☎ 705/739–9444 or 800/668–9100 ⊕ www.city.barrie.on.ca), in early February, has ice fishing, dogsledding, ice sculptures, ice motorcycling, hot-air ballooning, and other colorful activities. From late June through Labor Day, informal drama productions spotlight Canadian playwrights at the **Gryphon Theatre** (✉ Georgian College, Georgian Dr. and Bell Farm Rd. ☎ 705/728–4613 ⊕ www.gryphontheatre.com). You can watch harness racing at **Georgian Downs Racetrack** (☎ 705/726–9400 or 866/915–9400 ⊕ www.georgiandowns.com). On the August Simcoe Day long weekend (usually the first full weekend of the month), **Kempenfest Waterfront Festival** (☎ 705/739–

Fruit-Picking
Many fruit farms on the Niagara Peninsula offer roadside stands and/or pick-your-own options (☎ 800/263–2988 for information). Here and around Stratford you find an abundant choice of such fruit as blueberries, peaches, and cherries, as well as late-summer vegetables like corn and field tomatoes.

Hiking
The Bruce Trail, a posted hiking path, starts in the Niagara region and follows the Niagara Escarpment north about 240 km (150 mi) to Lake Huron. The Niagara Parkway, which runs 56 km (35 mi) along the Niagara River, has easy walks and great water views. Many pleasant hiking trails can be found outside Stratford proper.

7

Skiing
Blue Mountain, near Barrie, is popular, with 32 downhill trails and Ontario's largest ski resort, the Blue Mountain Inn. Horseshoe Valley Resort, also near Barrie, offers downhill skiing (it has 22 alpine runs), as well as cross-country skiing, though skiers interested in lodge-to-lodge packages will want to check out Haliburton.

Theater
A couple of long-dead British playwrights have managed to make two Ontario towns boom from May through October. The Shakespeare festival in Stratford and the Shaw festival in Niagara-on-the-Lake both enjoy great popular success as well as critical acclaim.

Wineries
One of the three best regions for wine production in Canada (Point Pelee, also in Ontario, and British Columbia are the others), the Niagara Peninsula has an unusually good microclimate for growing grapes. More than 20 small, quality vineyards produce fine wines in the area near St. Catharines; most of them offer tastings and tours.

4216 ⊕ www.kempenfest.com) transforms about 2½ km (1 mi) of Barrie's waterfront into an arts-and-crafts fair. The event includes live entertainment on two stages, antiques shows, and specialty-food samplings, and draws some 200,000 visitors.

Where to Stay & Eat

$$-$$$
Fodor'sChoice
★
✕⊡ **Blue Mountain Resort.** In addition to being the largest ski resort in Ontario, this acclaimed lodge 71 km (44 mi) outside of Barrie has an outstanding 18-hole golf course and a faux alpine village flanked with shops and restaurants. Rooms are at the **Blue Mountain Inn;** suites have kitchens and fireplaces. The inn's Pottery dining room ($$–$$$$) serves Continental interpretations of Canadian standards. ⊠ *R.R. 3, Collingwood L9Y 3Z2* ☎ *705/445–0231 or 877/445–0231* 🖷 *705/444–1751* ⊕ *www.bluemountain.ca* ✍ *95 rooms, 2 suites* ♿ *7 restaurants, room service, some in-room hot tubs, cable TV with movies and video games, 9 tennis courts, indoor pool, gym, 6 outdoor hot tubs, 6 saunas, spa, beach, squash, 2 lounges, shop, Internet* ⊟ *AE, DC, MC, V.*

$$-$$$
Fodor'sChoice
★
✕⊡ **Horseshoe Resort.** Modern guest rooms at this top-drawer lodge have down comforters, and many suites have sunken living rooms, fireplaces, and whirlpool baths. Dining options include the distinctive Continen-

tal menu of the formal Silks Fine Dining ($$$–$$$$), the casual Santa Fe–style Go West Grill ($), and the hearty bar fare at Crazy Horse Saloon ($–$$). ⌂ *Horseshoe Valley Rd., R.R. 1, Box 10, L4M 4Y8* ☏ *705/835–2790 or 800/461–5627* 📠 *705/835–6352* ⊕ *www. horseshoeresort.com* ⤶ *54 rooms, 48 suites* 🏃 *3 restaurants, café, 2 18-hole golf courses, 2 tennis courts, 2 pools (1 indoor), gym, hot tub, spa, mountain bikes, hiking, squash, cross-country skiing, downhill skiing, lounge* ▭ *AE, DC, MC, V.*

$–$$ ✕🏠 **Talisman Mountain Resort.** Rooms at this year-round resort have views of either the Beaver Valley or Talisman Mountain and are done in floral patterns or warm gold tones. Outdoor hot tubs, a spa, and yoga classes can help you relax after hitting the ski slopes. The Tyrolean Restaurant ($$–$$$$) serves Canadian dishes such as Alberta steak or local trout. ✉ *150 Talisman Dr., Kimberley N0C 1G0* ☏ *519/599–2520 or 800/ 265–3759* 📠 *519/599–3186* ⊕ *www.talisman.ca* ⤶ *85 rooms, 8 suites* 🏃 *Restaurant, cafeteria, 9-hole golf course, tennis, pool, 3 outdoor hot tubs, exercise equipment, sauna, spa, bicycles, cross-country skiing, downhill skiing, ice-skating, sleigh rides* ▭ *AE, D, MC, V.*

Skiing & Snowboarding

The province's highest vertical drop, of 720 feet, is at **Blue Mountain Resort** (✉ R.R. 3, Collingwood ☏ 705/445–0231, 416/869–3799 from Toronto 📠 705/444–1751 ⊕ www.bluemountain.ca), 11 km (7 mi) west of Collingwood, off Highway 26. Ontario's most extensively developed and heavily used ski area has 37 pistes served by a high-speed quad lift, three triple chairs, four double chairs, and three rope tows. One of the few resorts to offer snowboarding, tubing, and cross-country and downhill skiing trails and facilities is **Horseshoe Valley Resort** (⌂ Horseshoe Valley Rd., R.R. 1, Box 10 ☏ 705/835–2790 or 800/461–5627 📠 705/835–6352 ⊕ www.horseshoeresort.com), 50 km (31½ mi) north of Barrie, off Highway 400. The resort has 22 alpine runs, 14 of which are lit at night, served by seven lifts. The vertical drop is only 308 feet, but several of the runs are rated for advanced skiers.

☺ Skiers and snowboarders can take advantage of 36 runs at **Mount St. Louis Moonstone** (✉ R.R. 4, Coldwater L0K 1E0 ☏ 705/835–2112 or 416/368–6900 📠 705/835–2831 ⊕ www.mslm.on.ca), 30 km (18 mi) north of Barrie. The majority of slopes are for beginner and intermediate skiiers, though there's a sprinkling of advanced runs. The resort's Kids Camp, a daycare and ski school combination, attracts families. Inexpensive cafeterias within the two chalets serve decent meals. No overnight lodging is available. Nestled at the base of Mt. Talisman in the heart of Beaver Valley is the Tirolean-inspired ☺ **Talisman Mountain Resort** (✉ 150 Talisman Dr., Kimberley ☏ 519/599–2520 or 800/265–3759 ⊕ www.talisman. ca). Families like the resort for its popular Kids Klub, a program in which children are placed into age-based ski groups for daily activities.

Penetanguishene & Midland

47 km (29 mi) north of Barrie on Hwys. 400 and 93.

The quiet towns of Penetanguishene (known locally as Penetang) and Midland occupy a small corner of northern Simcoe County known as

SKIING AT A GLANCE

These are the Ontario hills with the best snow conditions.

Blue Mountain (☎ 705/445–0231 ⊕ www.bluemountain.ca), Ontario's largest four-season resort, in Collingwood.

Horseshoe Valley (☎ 705/835–2790, 416/283–2988 from Toronto, 800/461–5627 ⊕ www.horseshoeresort.com), one hour north of Toronto.

Mount St. Louis Moonstone (☎ 705/835–2112, 416/368–6900 from Toronto ⊕ www.mslm.on.ca), north of Barrie.

Sir Sam's Ski Area (☎ 705/754–2298 ⊕ www.sirsams.com), in Haliburton.

Talisman Mountain Resort (☎ 519/599–2520 or 800/265–3759 ⊕ www.talisman.ca), two hours north of Toronto in Kimberley.

Huronia. Both towns sit on a snug harbor at the foot of Georgian Bay's Severn Sound.

★ **Sainte-Marie among the Hurons,** 5 km (3 mi) east of Midland on Highway 12, is a reconstruction of the Jesuit mission that was originally built on this spot in 1639. The village, which was once home to a fifth of the European population of New France, was the site of the European settlers' first hospital, farm, school, and social service center in Ontario. Villagers also constructed a canal from the Wye River. A combination of disease and Iroquois attacks led to the mission's demise. Twenty-two structures, including a native longhouse and wigwam, have been faithfully reproduced from a scientific excavation. The canal is working again, and staff members in period costume saw timber, repair shoes, sew clothes, and grow vegetables—keeping the working village alive. ✉ Hwy. 12 E ☎ 705/526 7838 ⊕ www.saintemarieamongthehurons. on.ca ✇ $C11 ✆ Mid-May–mid-Oct., daily 10–5 (last entry at 4:45).

On a hill overlooking Sainte-Marie among the Hurons is the **Martyrs' Shrine,** a twin-spired stone cathedral built in 1926 to honor the eight missionaries who died in Huronia; in 1930, five of the priests were canonized by the Roman Catholic Church. The grounds include a theater, a souvenir shop, a cafeteria, and a picnic area. ✉ Off Hwy. 12 E ☎ 705/526–3788 ⊕ www.martyrs-shrine.com ✇ C$3 ✆ Mid-May–mid-Oct., daily 8:30 AM–9 PM.

The best artifacts from several hundred archaeological digs in the area are displayed at the **Huronia Museum** in Little Lake Park, Midland. Behind the museum and gallery building is **Huron-Ouendat Village,** a full-scale replica of a 16th-century Huron settlement. ✉ Little Lake Park ☎ 705/526–2844 or 800/263–7745 ⊕ www.huroniamuseum.com ✇ Museum and village C$6 ✆ May–June, daily 9–5; July–Aug., daily 9–6; Sept.–Apr., Mon.–Sat. 9–5.

Cruises leave from the town docks in Midland and Penetang to explore the 30,000 Islands region of Georgian Bay from May through October. The 300-passenger *Miss Midland* (☎888/833–2628 ⊕www.midlandtours. com) leaves from the Midland town dock and offers 2½-hour sightseeing cruises daily (C$20) mid-May to mid-October. From the Penetang town dock, the 200-passenger **MS *Georgian Queen*** (☎ 705/549–7795 or 800/ 363–7447 ⊕www.georgianbaycruises.com) takes passengers on three-hour tours (C$20) of the islands. These cruises depart from one to three times daily, mid-May to mid-October; call ahead for times.

Where to Stay

$$–$$$$ 🏨 **Best Western Highland Inn and Conference Centre.** An enormous atrium anchors this completely self-contained hotel-motel-resort. Honeymoon suites have cherry-red, heart-shape tubs or fireplace rooms with sunken hot tubs. Sunday brunches by the pool in the Garden Atrium Café are popular; there are two other dining areas (reserve ahead) as well. ⊠ *924 King St., at Hwy. 12, Midland L4R 4L3* ☎ *705/526–9307 or 800/461– 4265* 🖨 *705/526–0099* ⊕ *www.bestwesternmidland.com* ⇒ *122 rooms, 16 suites* ♿ *2 restaurants, indoor pool, gym, hot tub, sauna, laundry facilities, lounge* ⊟ *AE, D, DC, MC, V.*

Parry Sound

117 km (73 mi) north of Penetanguishene and Midland via Hwys. 400 or 12 and 69.

Parry Sound has two big claims to fame: it's the home of hockey legend Bobby Orr, and it has Canada's largest sightseeing cruise ship, accommodating 550 passengers. The *Island Queen* offers an extensive three-hour cruise around the narrow channels and shallow waterways known as the 30,000 Islands of Georgian Bay. Tours run once or twice daily, depending on the season. There's free parking at the town dock. ⊠ *9 Bay St.* ☎ *705/746–2311 or 800/506–2628* ⊕ *www.island-queen. com* 🎫 *C$25* ☉ *June–mid-Oct., daily; call for cruise times.*

Groove to jazz, folk, and classical music during **Festival of the Sound** (☎ 705/746–2410 or 866/364–0061 ⊕ www.festivalofthesound.on. ca), which runs from mid-July to mid-August. Performances take place daily at the state-of-the-art Charles W. Stockey Centre for the Performing Arts, the Bobby Orr Hall of Fame & Entertainment Centre, and the decks of the *Island Queen.*

Orillia

98 km (61 mi) southeast of Parry Sound on Hwy. 69, 35 km (22 mi) northeast of Barrie on Hwy. 11.

A former lumber town shoehorned between Lake Simcoe and Lake Couchiching in central Ontario, Orillia (which means riverbank in Spanish) developed into a summer-cottage haven at the turn of the 20th century. The year-round cottage town has 30,000 residents and is known as the home of humorist Stephen Leacock.

The redbrick, turreted **Orillia Opera House** was built in 1873 and renovated in 1917 after a fire destroyed much of it. Though some details were changed, such as the design of the roof, the opera house still looks similar to its original design and has been named an Ontario Heritage site. The **Sunshine Festival Theatre Company** (⊕ www.sunshinefestival. ca) performs classic plays and Broadway shows at the opera house from May to October. ⊠ *West St. and Mississaga St.* ☎ *800/683–8747* ⊕ *www.operahouse.orillia.on.ca.*

★ Readers of Canada's great humorist Stephen Leacock may recognize Orillia as "Mariposa," the town he described in *Sunshine Sketches of a Little Town.* Leacock's former summer home is now the **Stephen Leacock Museum,** a National Historic Site. Among the rotating exhibits are books, manuscripts, and photographs depicting Leacock and the region that inspired his writings. In the Mariposa Room, characters from the book are matched with the Orillia residents who inspired them. ⊠ *50 Museum Dr., off Hwy. 12B* ☎ *705/329–1908* ⊕ *www.leacockmuseum. com* ⊠ *C$5* ۞ *May and Sept., weekdays 10–5; June–Aug, daily 10–5.*

For the past few years, **Casino Rama,** the largest First Nations–run gambling emporium in Canada, has lured thousands of visitors to the Orillia area. The 192,000-square-foot complex 5 km (3 mi) north of town has 2,300 slot machines, more than 120 gambling tables, 9 restaurants, an entertainment lounge, an adjoining 300-room all-suites luxury hotel, and a gift shop. ⊠ *R.R. 6, Rama Reserve* ☎ *705/329–3325 or 800/832–7529* ⊕ *www.casino-rama.com.*

Gravenhurst

38 km (24 mi) north of Orillia on Hwy. 11.

North along Highway 11, rolling farmland suddenly changes to lakes and pine trees amid granite outcrops of the Canadian Shield. This region, called Muskoka, is a favorite playground of people who live in and around Toronto. Gravenhurst is a town of approximately 10,000 and the birthplace of Norman Bethune, regarded as a Canadian hero.

Bethune Memorial House, an 1880-vintage frame structure, is a National Historic Site that honors the heroic efforts of field surgeon and medical educator Norman Bethune, who worked in China during the Sino-Japanese War in the 1930s and trained thousands to become medics and doctors. There are period rooms and an exhibit tracing the highlights of his life. The house has become a shrine of sorts for Chinese diplomats visiting North America. ⊠ *235 John St. N, P1P 1G4* ☎ *705/687–4261* ⊕ *www.parkscanada.gc.ca/bethune* ⊠ *C$3.50* ۞ *June–Oct., daily 10–4; Nov.–May, weekdays 1–4.*

★ From mid-June to mid-October, the **Muskoka Lakes Navigation and Hotel Company** runs cruises which tour the Muskoka Lakes. Excursions range from 90 minutes to two days in length (passengers dine aboard but sleep in one of Muskoka's grand resorts). Reservations are required. The **RMS Segwun** (the initials stand for Royal Mail Ship) is the sole survivor of a fleet of steamships that provided transportation through the Muskoka Lakes. The 128-foot-long, 99-passenger boat was built in 1887 and restored in 1970. The 200-passenger *Wenonah II* is a 1907-inspired vessel with modern technology. The 1915 *Wanda III* steam yacht is available for private cruises only. ⊠ *820 Bay St., Gravenhurst* ☎ *705/687–6667* ⊕ *www.segwun.com.*

Where to Stay & Eat

$$$$
Fodor'sChoice
★

✕⊡ **Taboo Resort, Golf and Conference Centre.** A magnificent 1,000-acre landscape of rocky outcrops and windswept trees typical of the Muskoka region surrounds this year-round luxury resort, which was built in 1926. All kinds of diversions are available, including a highly rated golf course, an outdoor ice-skating rink, and canoeing or windsurfing on Lake Muskoka. The exterior resembles a traditional northern Canadian lodge, but rooms have a sleek, modern design, with such touches as wrought-iron furniture and crisp, white linens. Lodge rooms offer forest and lake views. Suites and chalets have wood-burning fireplaces. The lakeside Wildfire dining room ($$–$$$$) serves Asian-inspired fare. ⊠ *Muskoka Beach Rd., P1P 1R1* ☎ *705/687–2233 or 800/461–0236* ⊟ *705/687–7474* ⊕ *www. tabooresort.com* ➳ *80 rooms, 22 suites, 56 condos* ⚹ *5 restaurants, some in-room hot tubs, some kitchens, some microwaves, refrigerators, in-room VCRs, 18-hole golf course, 9-hole golf course, 5 tennis courts, 5 pools (1 indoors), health club, spa, boating, jet skiing, parasailing, mountain bikes, hiking, horseback riding, cross-country skiing, ice-skating, snowmobiling, 3 bars, babysitting, children's programs (ages 3–12), playground, meeting rooms; no smoking* ⊟ *AE, DC, MC, V.*

☼ **$$–$$$**
⊡ **Bayview-Wildwood Resort.** The complex, a 15-minute drive south of Gravenhurst, dates to 1898 and is particularly geared to outdoor types and families. Canoeing and kayaking are popular; floatplane excursions and golf can also be arranged. Some guest rooms have fireplaces, whirlpool baths, and views over the lake. You must book a family vacation, conference package, or weekend package to stay here. ⊠ *1500 Port Stanton Pkwy., R.R. 1, Severn Bridge P0E 1N0* ☎ *705/689–2338 or 800/ 461–0243* ⊟ *705/689–8042* ⊕ *www.bayviewwildwood.com* ➳ *34 rooms, 26 suites, 17 cottages* ⚹ *Dining room, some in-room hot tubs, some kitchens, 2 tennis courts, 2 pools (1 indoors), gym, boating, fishing, biking, billiards, boccie, Ping-Pong, shuffleboard, squash, cross-country skiing, snowmobiling; no smoking* ⊟ *AE, DC, MC, V* ⍟*FAP.*

Haliburton

90 km (56 mi) northeast of Gravenhurst via Hwy. 11 and Hwy. 118, 250 km (155 mi) northeast of Toronto.

Pink granite outcroppings left by the Canadian Shield, rushing rivers, groves of sugar maples, and jack pines speckle the topography of Haliburton. Once the stomping ground of the Huron, Mississauga, and Ojibwa tribes, explorers, fur traders, and loggers, Haliburton's rugged environment now attracts snowmobilers, skiers, mountain bikers, canoers, kayakers, and hikers. The all-season destination is close to Algonquin Provincial Park and less congested than its neighbors (the Muskokas and the Kawarthas).

Where to Stay

★ **$$$–$$$$**
⊡ **Sir Sam's Inn.** The restored inn from 1910 has hints of grandeur, such as a massive stone fireplace, hand-hewn beams, and floor-to-cathedral-ceiling windows overlooking Eagle Lake. Lakeside rooms have wood-burn-

ing fireplaces and whirlpool baths. In winter you have access to Sir Sam's ski area, which has 12 runs and six lifts, including two quad chairs. A nearby pine-and-hardwood forest is an inviting setting for summer strolls. The dining room serves northern specialties—caribou (with wine and blueberry sauce) and fresh game hen. ⌖ *Box 156, Eagle Lake P.O., K0M 1M0* ☎ *705/ 754–2188 or 800/361–2188* 🖷 *705/754–4262* ⊕ *www.sirsamsinn.com* 🛏 *25 rooms* ⚒ *Restaurant, fans, some in-room hot tubs, tennis court, pool, lake, sauna, windsurfing, boating, waterskiing, fishing, mountain bikes, hiking, cross-country skiing, downhill skiing, ice-skating, snowmobiling, no-smoking rooms; no a/c, no kids under 12* ☰ *AE, DC, MC, V.*

★ $$$ 🖿 **Domain of Killien.** A haven of year-round relaxation, Killien offers exclusive access to 5,000 acres of private forest, streams, and lakes near Algonquin Provincial Park. Rooms in the main lodge have whirlpool tubs, cedar dressing rooms, and views of the lake. Cabins have fireplaces and decks overlooking the lake. Fine wines are served with sophisticated dishes that showcase local ingredients: wild game in fall, organically grown herbs and vegetables in spring, house-smoked duck and salmon year-round. The trout and bass are fresh from local lakes, and even the maple syrup is homemade. ⌖ *Carrol Rd., Box 810, K0M 1S0* ☎ *705/ 457–1100 or 800/390–0769* 🖷 *705/457–3853* ⊕ *www.domainofkillien. com* 🛏 *5 rooms, 7 cabins* ⚒ *Restaurant, some in-room hot tubs, 2 tennis courts, boating, hiking, cross-country skiing, ice-skating; no a/c, no room TVs, no smoking* ☰ *AE, DC, MC, V* ⦿ *MAP.*

Sports & the Outdoors

SKIING LODGE-
TO-LODGE   More than 500 km (200 mi) of groomed wilderness trails weave throughout Haliburton County. Three- and four-night guided lodge-to-lodge cross country ski packages are available along the Haliburton Nordic Ski Trail system. There are groups for skiers of all levels, and the trips cover 8 km to 25 km (5 mi to 16 mi) per day, depending on the group's abilities. Six lodges participate in the program, and skiers stay and dine at a different lodge each night. Packages include all meals, trail passes, and a guide. For information about ski packages, contact **Haliburton Highlands Trails and Tours** (⌖ General Delivery, Carnarvon K0M 1J0 ☎ 705/ 489–4049 ⊕ www.trailsandtours.com).

SNOWMOBILING   **C Mac Snow Tours** (☎ 519/887–6686 or 800/225–4258 ⊕ www. cmacsnowtours.ca) has five- and six-night all-inclusive snowmobile excursions in Haliburton Highlands–Algonquin Provincial Park. In the 50,000-acre, privately owned **Haliburton Forest** (✉ R.R. 1, K0M 1S0 ☎ 705/754–2198 ⊕ www.haliburtonforest.com) there are 300 km (186 mi) of well-developed snowmobile trails, plus a shelter system. The day-use trail fee is C$30. Machine and cottage rentals are available; call for rates.

Bracebridge

23 km (14 mi) north of Gravenhurst on Hwy. 11.

Holiday cheer brightens Bracebridge in summer with Christmas-oriented amusements. The Bracebridge Falls on the Muskoka River are a good option for those who prefer a more peaceful excursion. Youngsters can ride the Kris Kringle River Boat, Rudolph's Sleigh Ride Roller Coaster, the Candy Cane Express Train, bumper boats, paddleboats, ponies, and more at **Santa's Village**. At the same location, **Sportsland** (☒ C$3 per ticket, rides cost one or two tickets each ⊙ Mid-June–early Sept., Mon.–Sat. 10–9, Sun. 10–6), for children 12 and older, has go-carts, batting cages, in-line skating, 18-hole miniature golf, laser tag, and an indoor activity center with video games. ⊠ *Santa's Village Rd. west of Bracebridge* ☎ *705/645-2512* ⊕ *www.santasvillage.on.ca* ☒ *C$20* ⊙ *Mid-June–early Sept., daily 10–6.*

Where to Stay & Eat

★ $–$$ ✕☒ **Inn at the Falls.** Look out at the magnificent Bracebridge Falls from this Victorian inn, built in 1876, and its annex of motel-style rooms. A few rooms have fireplaces, balconies, and whirlpool tubs, and all are individually decorated in period style. A ghost, said to live in one room, is somewhat of an attraction. The outdoor pool is heated. The main dining room ($$–$$$) and pub offer food and live entertainment; there's an outdoor patio as well. Try the steak-and-kidney pie. ⌂ *1 Dominion St., Box 1139, P1L 1V3* ☎ *705/645-2245 or 877/645-9212* ☐ *705/645-5093* ⊕ *www.innatthefalls.net* ⌥ *42 rooms, 2 cottages* ⌂ *Restaurant, some in-room hot tubs, some minibars, pool, pub; no a/c in some rooms, no smoking* ☐ *AE, DC, MC, V* ⦿ *CP.*

Dorset

48 km (30 mi) northeast of Bracebridge via Hwys. 11 and 117.

Dorset is a handsome village on Lake of Bays. In summer the self-guided trails at the defunct **Leslie M. Frost Natural Resources Center** (⊠ Hwy. 35 at St. Nora's Lake, Dorset) are a great way to explore Ontario's wildlife. Though the washroom facilities and information center are closed, the trails are open. **Robinson's General Store** (⊠ Main St. ☎ 705/766–2415) has been in business since 1921. Look for the moose-fur hats and pine furniture. The 82-foot-high **Dorset Tower** (⊕ www.dorset-tower.com), open mid-May to October 31, allows you to see across the lake and over the forested landscape from its lookout (C$2 per car or C$10 seasonal pass). You can circle back to Toronto on scenic Highway 35 or make Dorset a stop on a tour from Huntsville around Lake of Bays.

Huntsville

34 km (21 mi) north of Bracebridge on Hwy. 11, 215 km (133 mi) north of Toronto on Hwys. 400 and 11.

The Huntsville region is filled with lakes and streams, strands of virgin birch and pine, and deer that browse along its trails. Because the area is part of Toronto's Muskoka region, there's no shortage of year-round resorts. The Huntsville area is usually the cross-country skier's best bet for an abundance of natural snow in southern Ontario. All resorts have trails.

Where to Stay & Eat

$$–$$$$ ✕☒ **Deerhurst Resort.** The ultradeluxe resort spread along Peninsula Lake
FodorsChoice is an 800-acre, self-contained community. The flavor is largely modern,
★ although the rustic main lodge dates from 1896. The resort's Pavilion wing

is four stories high, embellished with an octagonal tower and decorative gables; its rooms are done in a floral-and-stripe combination and have large windows with views of the grounds and lakefront. Steamers restaurant ($$–$$$) specializes in steaks prepared with a choice of marinades and imaginative sauces. Eclipse Dining Room ($$$–$$$$) serves Canadian specialties, such as Ontario lamb, Alberta beef, and rainbow trout. ⊠ *1235 Deerhurst Dr., P1H 2E8* ☎ *705/789–6411 or 800/461–4393* 🖷 *705/789–5204* ⊕ *www.deerhurstresort.com* 📞 *412 rooms* ♿ *3 restaurants, 2 18-hole golf courses, tennis court, indoor pool, gym, spa, windsurfing, boating, horseback riding, racquetball, squash, cross-country skiing, snowmobiling, sleigh rides, lounge, no-smoking rooms* ☰ *AE, D, DC, MC, V.*

$$–$$$$ ✕🖭 **Norsemen Restaurant and Resort.** Rustic two- and three-bedroom cottages overlook Walker Lake at this resort. In summer cottages are rented by the week only. Even more famous than the charming lakeside lodgings, however, is the resort's dining room. The Norsemen Restaurant ($$$–$$$$) has earned generations of devotees by serving a tempting Canadian harvest—including fresh Atlantic salmon, breast of pheasant, and medallions of caribou—prepared with European flair. It's open for dinner only (seatings from 6 to 8:30) Tuesday through Sunday in summer, and Thursday through Sunday in winter. ⊠ *1040 Walker Lake Dr., R. R. 4, P1H 2J6* ☎ *705/635–2473, 800/565–3856 in Canada* 🖷 *705/ 635–9370* ⊕ *www.norsemen.ca* 📞 *7 cottages* ♿ *Restaurant, fans, kitchenettes, boating, fishing, cross-country skiing; no a/c, no room phones, no room TVs* ☰ *AE, MC, V.*

$–$$ 🖭 **Portage Inn.** Stay near pine trees, ski runs, and snowmobile trails at this country style 1889 home, which is open year-round. Rooms have great views of the surrounding forested hills and lake; the king bedroom has an ensuite hot tub. The inn has snowshoeing in winter and canoeing and kayaking in summer. ⊠ *1563 N. Portage Rd., P1H 2J6* ☎ *705/788–7171 or 888/ 418–5555* 🖷 *705/788–7070* ⊕ *www.discovermuskoka.ca⁄portageinn* 📞 *6 rooms, 2 cottages* ♿ *Fans, some in-room hot tubs, cable TV in some rooms, some in-room VCRs, tennis court, hot tub, boating, mountain bikes, volleyball; no a/c, no TV in some rooms* ☰ *MC, V* 🍽 *CP.*

Algonquin Provincial Park

★ *35 km (23 mi) east of Huntsville on Hwy. 60.*

Algonquin Provincial Park stretches across 7,725 square km (2,983 square mi), containing more than 1,000 lakes and 1,000 species of plants, and encompassing forests, rivers, and cliffs. The typical visitor is a hiker, canoeist, camper—or all three. But don't be put off if you're not the athletic or outdoorsy sort. About a third of Algonquin's visitors come for the day to walk one of the 17 interpretive trails, or enjoy a swim or a picnic. Swimming is especially good at the Lake of Two Rivers, halfway between the west and east gates along Highway 60. A morning drive through the park in May or June is often rewarded by moose and deer sightings. Park naturalists give talks on area wildflowers, animals, and birds, and you can book a guided hike or canoe trip. Expeditions to hear wolf howling take place in late summer and early autumn. The **visitor center,** near the east side of the park, has information on park programs, a bookstore, a restaurant, and a panoramic-viewing deck. The park's **Al-**

gonquin Logging Museum (⊙ Late May–mid Oct., daily 9–5) depicts life at an early Canadian logging camp. ⊠ *Hwy. 60; the main and east gate is west of the town of Whitney; the west gate is east of the town of Dwight* ⊕ *Box 219, Whitney K0J 2M0* ☏ *705/633–5572* ⊕ *www.algonquinpark. on.ca* ⊠ *C$12 per vehicle* ⊙ *Park daily 8 AM–10 PM.*

The **Radcliffe Hills** resort, south of the park on Highway 60, has a vertical drop of 450 feet and a tubing run with a tube lift. ⊠ *Hwy. 62, 50 km (31 mi) east of Algonquin Park's main entrance* ⊕ *Box 188, Barry's Bay K0J 1B0* ☏ *613/756–2931 or 800/668–8249* ⊕ *www.radhills.ca.*

Where to Stay & Eat

$$$–$$$$
Fodor'sChoice
★

✕▦ **Arowhon Pines.** The stuff of local legend, Arowhon is a family-run resort in Algonquin Provincial Park known for unpretentious luxury and superb dining. Two- to twelve-bedroom log cabins are decorated with antique pine furnishings and have lounges. The waterside suites have fireplaces and private decks. Room rates include three daily meals in the teepee-style dining hall, which has lake and forest views. The fare focuses on Ontario's seasonal ingredients and might include pancakes with maple syrup or Welsh rarebit with Canadian bacon for breakfast, and Ontario wild rice salad and maize-fed-chicken breast for dinner. Non-lodgers can reserve prix-fixe meals ($$$$). If you'd like wine with dinner, bring your own: park restrictions prohibit its sale here. Swimming, sailing, hiking, and birding are all possible. ⊠ *Off Hwy. 60, Box 10001, Algonquin Park, Huntsville P1H 2G5* ☏ *705/633–5661 or 416/483– 4393* ☒ *705/633–5795* ⊕ *www.arowhonpines.ca* ⟿ *50 rooms in 13 cabins* ⚐ *Restaurant, fans, boating, hiking, lake; no a/c, no room phones, no room TVs* ▤ *MC, V* ⊙ *Closed mid-Oct.–May* ⟨⟩*I FAP.*

★ $$–$$$

✕▦ **Bartlett Lodge.** A short boat ride on Cache Lake, to about halfway through Algonquin Provincial Park along Highway 60, transports you to this 1917 resort. The immaculate cabins have gleaming hardwood floors and king-size beds or two singles. Quiet reigns: no waterskiing, jet skiing, or motors over 10 horsepower are allowed on the lake (but you can take out a canoe); and you won't find radios, phones, or TVs in the cabins. The Algonquin-style dining room, with exposed beams, offers a choice of traditional Canadian breakfast and table d'hôte menus. Non-lodgers are welcome for dinner ($$$$). No wine is sold, but you're welcome to bring your own. ⊕ *Box 10004, Algonquin Park, Huntsville P1H 2G8* ☏ *705/633–5543, 905/338–8908 in winter* ☒ *705/633–5746* ⊕ *www.bartlettlodge.com* ⟿ *12 cabins* ⚐ *Restaurant, some minibars, boating, mountain bikes, shop, business services; no a/c, no room phones, no room TVs* ▤ *MC, V* ⊙ *Closed mid-Oct.–May* ⟨⟩*I MAP.*

CAMPING Camping is available in three categories. Along the Park Corridor, a 56-km (35-mi) stretch of Highway 60, are eight organized campgrounds. Within the park's vast interior, you won't find any organized campsites (and the purists love it that way). In between these extremes are the lesser-known peripheral campgrounds—Kiosk, Brent, and Achray—which you reach by long, dusty roads. These have only firewood and non-flushing pit toilets; the organized campsites have showers, picnic tables, and in some cases, RV hook-ups. All organized campsites must be reserved; call **Ontario Parks** (☏ 800/688–7275 ⊕ www.ontarioparks.com). You need permits (C$12) for interior camping, available at the Canoe Centre adjacent to the Portage Store or from Ontario Parks.

Outfitters

Algonquin Outfitters (✉ R.R. 1, Dwight P0A 1H0 ☎ 705/635–2243 ⊕ www.algonquinoutfitters.com) has four store locations in and around the park—Oxtongue Lake, Huntsville, Opeongo Lake, and Brent Base on Cedar Lake—specializing in canoe rentals, outfitting and camping services, sea kayaking, and a water taxi service to the park's central areas. Call when you arrive to confirm equipment rentals and tour availability.

If you plan to camp in the park, you may want to contact the **Portage Store** (✉ Hwy. 60, Box 10009, Huntsville P1H 2H4 ☎ 705/663–5622 in summer, 705/789–3645 in winter ⊕ www.portagestore.com), which provides extensive outfitting services. They have packages that might include permits, canoes, and food supplies, as well as maps and detailed information about routes and wildlife.

THE NIAGARA PENINSULA

Within this small expanse of land, bordered by Lake Ontario to the North and Lake Erie to the South, you can stumble across a roadside fruit stand on a tour through rustic vineyards or gamble to your heart's content alongside one of nature's most beautiful displays of water. The Niagara Peninsula's various flavors make it a good place to entertain both high- and low-brow interests. Niagara Falls, with its daring adventure tours, wax museums, and honeymoon certificates—not to mention its wildly popular water attraction—has a certain kitschy-and-glitzy quality. Niagara-on-the-Lake, which draws theatergoers to its annual Shaw Festival, is a more tasteful, serene town. Niagara is also one of Canada's three best regions for wine production (Point Pelee, also in Ontario, and the province of British Columbia are the others). More than 55 small vineyards produce fine wines, and most of them offer tastings and tours.

Niagara Falls

130 km (81 mi) south of Toronto via the Queen Elizabeth Way.

Fodor'sChoice   Although cynics have had a field day with **Niagara Falls**—calling it every-
★   thing from "water on the rocks" to "the second major disappointment of American married life" (Oscar Wilde)—most visitors are truly impressed. Missionary and explorer Louis Hennepin, whose books were widely read across Europe, described the falls in 1678 as "an incredible Cataract or Waterfall which has no equal." Nearly two centuries later, Charles Dickens declared, "I seemed to be lifted from the earth and to be looking into Heaven." Henry James recorded in 1883 how one stands there "gazing your fill at the most beautiful object in the world."

These rave reviews lured countless daredevils to the falls. In 1859, 100,000 spectators watched as the French tightrope walker Blondin successfully crossed Niagara Gorge, from the American to the Canadian side, on a 3-inch-thick rope. From the early 18th century, dozens went over in boats and barrels. Nobody survived until 1901, when schoolteacher

Annie Taylor emerged from her barrel and asked, "Did I go over the falls yet?" The stunts were finally outlawed in 1912.

The waterfall's colorful history began more than 10,000 years ago as a group of glaciers receded, diverting the waters of Lake Erie northward into Lake Ontario. The force and volume of the water as it flowed over the Niagara Escarpment created the thundering cataracts now known so well. The lure of Niagara Falls hasn't dimmed for those who want to marvel at a premier natural wonder; Niagara Falls, on the border of the United States and Canada, is one of the most famous tourist attractions in the world, and one of the most awe-inspiring.

The falls are actually three cataracts: the American and Bridal Veil Falls in New York State, and the Horseshoe Falls in Ontario. In terms of sheer volume of water—more than 700,000 gallons per second in summer—Niagara is unsurpassed in North America.

On the American side, you can park in the lot on Goat Island near the American Falls and walk along the path beside the Niagara River, which becomes more and more turbulent as it approaches the big drop-off of just over 200 feet.

After experiencing the falls from the U.S. side, you can walk or drive across Rainbow Bridge to the Canadian side, where you can get a far view of the American Falls and a close-up of the Horseshoe Falls. You can also park your car for the day in any of several lots on the Canadian side, and hop onto one of the People Mover buses, which run continuously to all the sights along the river. If you want to get close to the foot of the falls, the *Maid of the Mist* boat takes you close enough to get soaked in the spray.

The amusement parks and tacky souvenir shops that surround the falls attest to the area's history as a major tourist attraction. Most of the gaudiness is contained on Clifton Hill, Niagara Falls's toned-down Times Square. Despite these garish efforts to attract visitors, the landscaped grounds around the falls are lovely and the beauty of the falls remains untouched.

Niagara Falls Tourism (⊠ 5515 Stanley Ave., main center ☎ 905/356–6061 or 800/563–2557 ⊕ www.discoverniagara.com) can help plan your trip and distributes information at its main center. Phone lines are open from 8 to 6 daily.

★ If you're here in winter, the **Winter Festival of Lights** (⊕ www. niagarafallstourism.com/wfol) is a real stunner. Seventy trees are illuminated with 34,000 lights in the parklands near the Rainbow Bridge. The falls are illuminated nightly from 5 to 11 from late November to mid-January.

❶ The **Niagara Parks Botanical Gardens and School of Horticulture** has been graduating professional gardeners since 1936. The art of horticulture is celebrated by its students with 100 acres of immaculately maintained gardens. Within the Botanical Gardens is the **Niagara Parks Butterfly Conservatory** (☎ 905/356–8119 ⊡ C$10), housing one of North America's largest collections of free-flying butterflies—at least 2,000 are protected

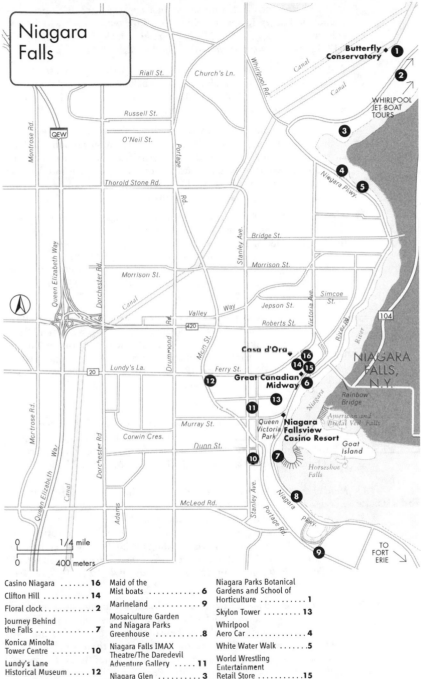

Niagara Falls

Riall St.

Church's Ln.

Russell St.

O'Neil St.

Thorold Stone Rd.

Morrison St.

Montrose Rd.

QEW

Portage Rd.

Dorchester Rd.

Queen Elizabeth Way

Canal

Valley Way

420

Lundy's La.

20

Main St.

Drummond Rd.

Ferry St.

Murray St.

Corwin Cres.

Dunn St.

Adams

McLeod Rd.

Montrose Way

Queen Elizabeth Way

Canal

Dorchester Rd.

Stanley Ave.

Bridge St.

Morrison St.

Jepson St.

Roberts St.

Simcoe St.

Victoria Ave.

River Rd.

104

Butterfly Conservatory ◆ ❶

❷

WHIRLPOOL JET BOAT TOURS

❸

Niagara Pkwy.

❹

❺

Whirlpool Rd.

Canal

Canal

NIAGARA FALLS, N.Y.

Casa d'Oro ◆ ❶❻
❶❹❶❺

Great Canadian Midway ❻

❶❷

❶❸

❶❶

Queen Victoria Park

Niagara Fallsview Casino Resort ◆ ❼

Niagara River

Rainbow Bridge

American and Bridal Veil Falls

Goat Island

Horseshoe Falls

❽

❾

TO FORT ERIE →

0 — 1/4 mile
0 — 400 meters

in a climate-controlled, rain-forest–like conservatory. It's open year-round and houses 50 species from around the world, each with its own colorful markings. ✉ *2405 N. Niagara Pkwy.* ☎ *905/356–8119 or 877/642–7275* ⊕ *www.niagaraparks.com/attractions* ✆ *Free* ⊙ *Daily 9–6.*

② A short distance (downriver) on the Niagara Parkway from the Botanical Gardens and School of Horticulture is a **floral clock,** one of the world's largest, comprising 20,000 small plants. Its "living" face is planted in a different design twice every season.

③ There are trails maintained by the National Parks Commission (NPC) in the **Niagara Glen** (⊕ www.discoverniagara.com/attractions). A bicycle trail that parallels the Niagara Parkway from Fort Erie to Niagara-on-the-Lake winds between beautiful homes on one side and the river, with its abundant bird life, on the other. The terrain can be steep and rugged, so be sure to pack proper footwear.

★ ④ The **Whirlpool Aero Car,** in operation since 1916, is a cable car that crosses the Whirlpool Basin in the Niagara Gorge. This trip is not for the faint-hearted, but there's no better way to get an aerial view of the gorge, the whirlpool, the rapids, and the hydroelectric plants. ✉ *Niagara Pkwy., 4½ km (3 mi) north of the falls* ☎ *905/371–0254 or 877/642–7275* ⊕ *www.niagaraparks.com* ✆ *C$10* ⊙ *Mid-June–early Sept., weekdays 10–5, weekends 9–5.*

⑤ The **White Water Walk** involves taking an elevator to the bottom of the Niagara Gorge, the narrow valley created by the Niagara Falls and River, where you can walk on a boardwalk beside the torrent of the Niagara River. The gorge is rimmed by sheer cliffs as it enters the giant whirlpool. ✉ *Niagara Pkwy., 3 km (2 mi) north of falls* ☎ *905/371–0254 or 877/642–7275* ⊕ *www.niagaraparks.com* ✆ *C$7.50* ⊙ *Mid-Apr.–Oct., daily 9–5.*

need a break? **Riverview Market Eatery.** Duck into the lower level of Queen Victoria Place, between the American Falls and the Horseshoe Falls, for good sandwiches or burgers at this market-style cafeteria. The salad bar is especially popular. ✉ *6345 Niagara River Pkwy.*

⑥ Fodor'sChoice ★ *Maid of the Mist* boats have been operating since 1846, when they were wooden-hulled, coal-fired steamboats. Today boats tow fun-loving passengers on 30-minute journeys to the foot of the falls, where the spray is so heavy that raincoats must be distributed. From the observation areas along the falls, you can see those boarding the boats in their yellow slickers. ✉ *Tickets and entrance at foot of Clifton Hill* ☎ *905/358–0311* ⊕ *www.maidofthemist.com* ✆ *C$13* ⊙ *May–mid-Oct., daily 9:45–4:45. Call for departure times.*

★ ⑦ At **Journey Behind the Falls** your admission ticket includes use of rubber boots and a hooded rain slicker. An elevator takes you to an observation deck that provides a fish's-eye view of the Canadian Horseshoe Falls and the Niagara River. From there a walk through three tunnels cut into the rock takes you behind the wall of crashing water. ✉ *Tours begin at Table Rock House, Queen Victoria Park* ☎ *905/371–0254 or 877/*

642–7275 ⊕ *niagaraparks.com* ✉ *C$10* ⊙ *Mid-June–early Sept., daily 9 AM–11 PM; early Sept.–mid-June, daily 9–5.*

⑧ Mosaiculture Garden and Niagara Parks Greenhouse house thousands of living plants, sculpted into life-size creatures, including moose, bears, and geese in flight. ✉ *Niagara Pkwy., ¼ mi south of the Horseshoe Falls* ☎ *905/371–0254 or 877/642–7275* ⊕ *www.niagaraparks.com* ✉ *C$4.50* ⊙ *Mid-June–Oct., daily 9:30–dusk.*

ᗺ ⑨ Marineland, a theme park with a marine show, wildlife displays, and rides, is 1½ km (1 mi) south of the falls. The daily marine show includes performing killer whales, dolphins, harbor seals, and sea lions. Three separate aquariums also house sharks, an ocean reef, and freshwater fish from around the world. Children can pet and feed members of a herd of 500 deer and get nose-to-nose with North American freshwater fish. Among the many rides is Dragon Mountain, the world's largest steel roller coaster. Marineland is signposted from Niagara Parkway or reached from the Queen Elizabeth Way by exiting at McLeod Road (Exit 27). ✉ *8375 Stanley Ave.* ☎ *905/356–9565* ⊕ *www.marinelandcanada.com* ✉ *C$33.95* ⊙ *Late June–early Oct., daily 9–6; shows at regular intervals.*

⑩ Konica Minolta Tower Centre, 525 feet above the base of the falls, affords panoramic views of the Horseshoe Falls and the area. ✉ *6732 Fallsview Blvd.* ☎ *905/356–1501 or 800/461–2492* ⊕ *www.infoniagara.com* ✉ *C$6.95* ⊙ *9 AM until lights go off at the falls (as late as midnight in summer).*

⑪ Niagara Falls IMAX Theatre/The Daredevil Adventure Gallery. You can see the falls up close and travel back in time for a glimpse of its 12,000-year-old history with *Niagara: Miracles, Myths and Magic,* on the six-story IMAX screen. The Daredevil Adventure Gallery chronicles the expeditions of those who have tackled the falls. ✉ *6170 Fallsview Blvd.* ☎ *905/374–4629* ⊕ *www.imaxniagara.com* ✉ *C$12* ⊙ *Daily 9–9; movies run every hr on the hr.*

★ ⑫ On the site of one of the fiercest battles in the War of 1812 is **Lundy's Lane Historical Museum,** in a limestone building dating to 1874. There are displays of the lives of settlers during the war period, native artifacts, and military attire. ✉ *5810 Ferry St.* ☎ *905/358–5082* ⊕ *www. lundyslanemuseum.com* ✉ *C$2* ⊙ *May–Nov., daily 9–4; Dec.–Apr., weekdays noon–4.*

★ ᗺ ⑬ Rising 775 feet above the falls, **Skylon Tower** offers the best view of both the great Niagara Gorge and the entire city. An indoor-outdoor observation deck, with visibility up to 130 km (80 mi) on a clear day, facilitates the view. Amusements for children plus a revolving dining room are other reasons to visit. The lower level has a gaming arcade, and there's a 3-D/4-D theater within the compound. ✉ *5200 Robinson St.* ☎ *905/ 356–2651 or 800/814–9577* ⊕ *www.skylon.com* ✉ *C$10.50* ⊙ *Mid-June–early Sept., daily 8 AM–midnight; early Sept.–mid June, daily 10–10.*

ᗺ ⑭ Clifton Hill is the most crassly commercial district of Niagara Falls. Sometimes referred to as "Museum Alley," this area includes more wax museums than one usually sees in a lifetime—and a House of Frankenstein

Burger King. Attractions are typically open late (11 PM), with admission ranging from C$7 to C$13. They include the **Guinness Museum of World Records** (☎ 905/356–2299 ⊕ www.guinnessniagarafalls.com); Ripley's Believe It or Not Museum and **Ripley's Moving Theatre** (☎ 905/356–2261 ⊕ www.ripleysniagara.com), a 3-D movie with 4-D effects, where you actually move with the picture (seats move in 8 directions); and **Movieland Wax Museum** (☎ 905/358–3676 ⊕ www.infoniagara.com/attractions/movieland.html), with such lifelike characters as Indiana Jones and Snow White. A six-story-high chocolate bar, at the base of Clifton Hill, marks the entrance to the **Hershey's World of Chocolate** (⊠ 5685 Falls Ave. ☎ 800/468–1714). Inside are 7,000 square feet of milk shakes, fudge, truffles, cookbooks, and those trademark Kisses. Lots of free samples are doled out and fudge-making demonstrations are held hourly.

⑮ Canada's first **World Wrestling Entertainment Retail Store** is filled to its rafters with official WWE clothing, coffee mugs, and memorabilia. A big draw is the dazzling laser light show. You can also take the plunge on the *Pile Driver* (open mid-May through September 30), a ride that takes you up 220 feet for a seconds-long stomach-dropping plummet. ⊠ *Clifton Hill and Falls Ave.* ☎ *905/354–7256 or 800/263–7135* ⊕ *www.fallsavenue. com/wwe.html* 🎟 *Free, Pile Driver C$9* ☉ *Sept.–June, daily 11–11; July–Aug., 11 AM–1 AM.*

⑯ **Casino Niagara,** in a setting reminiscent of the 1920s, has slot machines, video poker machines, and gambling tables, where games such as blackjack, roulette, and baccarat are played. Within the casino are several lounges and all-you-can-eat buffet restaurants. Valet parking and shuttle service are available. ⊠ *5705 Falls Ave.* ☎ *905/374–3598 or 888/946–3255* ⊕ *www.discoverniagara.com* ☉ *Daily 24 hrs.*

Where to Stay & Eat

The walk from most hotels down to the falls is a steep one. You might want to take a taxi back up, or hop aboard the Falls Incline Railway, which operates between Portage Street (at the rear of the **Niagara Fallsview Casino Resort**) and the Niagara Parkway (across from the Canadian Falls). The trip takes about one minute and costs C$3.

$$$$ ✗ **Skylon Tower.** The view from the Revolving Dining Room, perched at 775 ft overlooking the Horseshoe Falls, is breathtaking, and the food is good, too. Traditionally prepared rack of lamb, baked salmon, teak, and chicken make up the list of entrées. The crowd tends toward the eclectic, with people in cocktail wear and casual clothes seated side-by-side. Even with a reservation, there may be a short wait. An "early bird" (4:30 to 6:30) prix-fixe menu is C$35; otherwise, plan on spending at least C$40 per person to dine in the tower. ⊠ *5200 Robinson St.* ☎ *905/356–2651 or 800/814–9577* ⊕ *www.skylon.com* ⚑ *Reservations essential* ▤ *AE, DC, MC, V.*

$$$–$$$$ ✗ **Table Rock.** The view's the thing here. Table Rock, run by Niagara Parks, serves standard U.S.–Canadian fare, but the setting is extraordinary—you sit perched at the edge of the Horseshoe Falls. The dining room, in the rear of a two-story souvenir shop, has familiar food, such as Caesar salads and prime rib. Window seats can't be reserved. ⊠ *6650*

Niagara Pkwy., just above Journey Behind the Falls ☎ *905/354–3631* ⊕ *www.niagaraparks.com* ▤ *AE, DC, MC, V.*

★ **$$$–$$$$**   ✗ **21 Club.** Whether you come to the casino for baccarat or the slots, dining at this elegant restaurant is no gamble. The menu has high-end steakhouse fare and some Italian dishes. The insulated dining room is away from the crowds and is a quiet setting in which to appreciate shrimp cocktail or lobster *lasagnetta,* fresh pasta wrapped around sautéed lobster, shallots, and basil. You'd have to search far to find a more delectably grilled 24-ounce Canadian porterhouse steak. ☒ *Casino Niagara, 5705 Falls Ave.* ☎ *905/374–3598* ▤ *AE, DC, MC, V.*

$$–$$$$ ✗ **Casa d'Oro.** It looks a little like a Disney version of a Venetian castle, but the ornate wall sconces, fireplaces, wine casks, and huge faux-marble and bronze sculptures are somehow not out of place in Niagara Falls. Run by the Roberto family for 30 years, the Italian restaurant draws diners with its gigantic portions of prime rib, T-bones, and the hefty Lasagna Roberto. After dinner, you can cross a painted bridge that spans a water-filled moat to the Rialto nightclub's raised dance floor. ☒ *5875 Victoria Ave.* ☎ *905/356–5646* ⊕ *www.thecasadoro.com* ▤ *AE, D, DC, MC, V.*

★ **$$–$$$$**   ✗ **Casa Mia.** All the pasta is kitchen-made at this lovely off-the-tourist-track Italian villa, 10 minutes from the falls. Fresh-grated beets impart a shocking pink color to the gnocchi, divine with Gorgonzola sauce. If you've ever wondered what fresh cannelloni is like, try these light pasta pancakes, filled with coarse-ground veal and spinach. The veal chop is pan-seared with sage and truffle oil. Heart-smart menu selections are indicated, and even desserts, particularly the *cassata* (a light cake with homemade-ice-cream terrine) are not overly heavy. Weekends bring live music to the piano lounge. ☒ *3518 Portage Rd.* ☎ *905/356–5410* ⊕ *www.casamiaristorante.com* ▤ *AE, MC, V.*

$–$$ ✗ **Capri.** The family-owned restaurant serves huge, Italian-style platters such as linguine with chicken cacciatore. The three dining rooms, decorated in dark-wood paneling, draw families daily because of the half-dozen specially priced children's dishes and a something-for-everyone menu. ☒ *5438 Ferry St. (Hwy. 20), about 1 km (½ mi) from the falls* ☎ *905/354–7519* ▤ *AE, DC, MC, V.*

$–$$ ✗ **Yukiguni.** Reasonable lunch specials, which include miso soup, fresh salad, and such entrées as juicy pepper-flavored chicken skewers, make this a popular spot. Other menu options include tempura soba, thin buckwheat noodles that come with shrimp and vegetable tempura; and steamed smoked eel, served on rice in a round stacked lacquer box. Chicken and salmon teriyaki leave an aromatic trail as they are carried aloft on sizzling iron plates. ☒ *5980 Fallsview Blvd.* ☎ *905/354–4440* ▤ *AE, DC, MC, V.*

★ **$$–$$$$**   ✗⊞ **Sheraton Fallsview Hotel and Conference Centre.** Most of the over-size guest rooms and suites in this upscale, high-rise hotel have breathtaking views of the falls, and even basic family suites have wide floor-to-ceiling window bays which overlook the cascades. Loft Suites are spacious, and the Whirlpool Rooms have open whirlpool baths that look out to the bedroom and the falls beyond. The fine dining room ($$–$$$$) offers a bargain-price weekend buffet (C$19 from 5:30 to 7:30 PM); à la carte diners can choose from a French menu that might include tournedos with a three-peppercorn sauce. There's a two-night minimum stay on weekends. ✉ *6755 Fallsview Blvd., L2G 3W7* ☎ *905/ 374–1077 or 800/267–8439* 🖶 *905/374–6224* ⊕ *www.fallsview.com* 🛏 *295 rooms ᎕ 3 restaurants, pool, hot tub, sauna, spa, lobby lounge, convention center, meeting rooms* ☰ *AE, D, DC, MC, V.*

$$$$ 🏨 **Niagara Fallsview Casino Resort.** The C$1-billion price tag of this casino-resort means there are touches of luxury everywhere: natural light streams through glass domes and floor-to-ceiling windows, chandeliers hang in grand hallways, and wall and ceiling frescoes lend an aristocratic feel. All bright and colorful rooms in this 30-story hotel tower have views of either the Canadian or American Falls. VIP rooms have extra-large whirlpool tubs. Murals depict Niagara scenes in the full casino. Performers such as Alanis Morissette and Wynona Judd have headlined shows in the performing arts center. The lavish buffet is excellent and reasonable (C$20 for dinner); a lobby bistro, The Famous, is equally good. ✉ *6380 Fallsview Blvd., L2G 7X5* ☎ *905/358–3255 or 888/946– 3255* 🖶 *905/371–7952* ⊕ *www.discoverniagara.com* 🛏 *283 rooms, 85 suites* ☰ *AE, MC, V ᎕ 3 restaurants, café, cable TV, in-room safes, some in-room hot tubs, some kitchens, indoor pool, gym, sauna, spa, casino, showroom, shops, laundry services, concierge, concierge floor, Internet, business services, convention center, no-smoking rooms.*

$$$–$$$$ 🏨 **Renaissance Fallsview Hotel.** Many rooms overlook the falls at this luxuriously appointed hotel, about ½ km (¼ mi) from the mighty cataracts. The elegant rooms have floor-to-ceiling mirrors, wingback chairs with puffy throw pillows, and a flood of sunlight streaming in. The Jacuzzi rooms, where bath and bed are separated only by cherry-red drapes, can be romantic. In Mulberry's Dining Room ($–$$), you can sample the artistry of executive chef Michael Heeb. There are lots of recreational facilities on the premises and golf and fishing nearby. ✉ *6455 Buchanan Ave., L2G 3V9* ☎ *905/357–5200 or 800/363–3255* 🖶 *905/357–3422* ⊕ *www.renaissancefallsview.com* 🛏 *262 rooms ᎕ 2 restaurants, indoor pool, gym, hot tub, sauna, racquetball, squash, lounge, business services, meeting rooms* ☰ *AE, D, DC, MC, V.*

$$–$$$$ 🏨 **Quality Inn Clifton Hill.** Very near the falls and not far from a golf course, this chain-run inn is on nicely landscaped grounds, which can be viewed from a pleasant patio. The hotel's basic rooms are clean and comfortable; some suites have hot tubs. The hotel has an eye toward families, with two dragon waterslides, a playground, and rooms with three beds. ✉ *4946 Clifton Hill, Box 60, L2E 6S8* ☎ *905/358–3601 or 800/263–7137* ⊕ *www.qualityniagara.com* 🛏 *263 rooms ᎕ Restaurant, some in-room hot tubs, cable TV, 2 pools, hot tub, lobby lounge, playground* ☰ *AE, D, MC, V.*

★ $$–$$$ 🏨 **Brock Plaza Hotel.** Since its opening in the 1920s, this grande dame of Niagara hotels has hosted royalty, prime ministers, and Hollywood stars. Now completely renovated but with glamorous details intact, the imposing, stone-walled Brock is part of the Casino Niagara complex, with indoor access to gaming facilities, the Hard Rock Café, and the Rainbow Grill Restaurant overlooking the falls. White wainscoting and brass fixtures blend with expansive windows that offer views of the falls from nearly every room. ✉ *5685 Falls Ave., L2E 6W7* ☎ *905/374–4444 or 800/263– 7135* 🖶 *905/371–8347* ⊕ *www.niagarafallshotels.com* 🛏 *234 rooms*

♿ *Restaurant, coffee shop, dining room, indoor pool, hot tub, sauna, lounge* ☰ *AE, D, DC, MC, V.*

$ 🖵 **Villager Premiere.** The two-story motel offers good, basic accommodations. Some rooms have whirlpool tubs while others have heart-shaped tubs; the two efficiency suites have small kitchens. ✉ *7600 Lundy's La., L2H 1H1* ☎ *905/374–7010, 905/354–2211 reservations, 800/572–0308* 🖨 *905/358–0696* 🛏 *50 rooms* ♿ *Restaurant, some in-room hot tubs, pool* ☰ *AE, DC, MC, V.*

Guided Tours

Double Deck Tours (✉ 3957 Bossert Rd. ☎ 905/374–7423 ⊕ www. doubledecktours.com) operates 4½- to 5-hour tours in double-decker English buses. Tours operate daily from mid-May through October and include most of the major sights of Niagara Falls. The C$56.25 fare includes admission to Journey Behind the Falls, *Maid of the Mist,* and a trip in the Whirlpool Aerocar. Tours depart from the *Maid of the Mist* building at the foot of Clifton Hill.

From late April to mid-October, Niagara Parks operates a **People Mover System** (☎ 905/357–9340) in which air-conditioned buses travel on a loop route between its public parking lot above the falls at Rapids View Terminal (well marked) and the Whirlpool Aerocar parking lot about 8 km (5 mi) downriver. A day pass, which is available at any booth on the system for C$7.50 and includes parking and a People Mover ticket for everyone in the car, allows you to get on and off as many times as you wish at the well-marked stops along the route.

★ **Niagara Helicopters Ltd.** (✉ 3731 Victoria Ave. ☎ 905/357–5672 or 800/ 281–8034 ⊕ www.niagarahelicopters.com ☰ AE, MC, V) takes you on a nine-minute flight over the giant whirlpool, up the Niagara Gorge, and past the American Falls, then banks around the curve of the Horseshoe Falls. Daily trips run year-round (weather permitting). It costs C$100 per person; family rates are available. Reservations are not accepted.

Wet and wild **Whirlpool Jet Boat Tours** (✉ 61 Melville St., Niagara-on-the-Lake ☎ 905/468–4800 or 888/438–4444 ⊕ www.whirlpooljet. com) veer around and hurdle white-water rapids on a one-hour thrill ride that follows Niagara canyons up to the wall of rolling waters, just below the falls. Children under six are not permitted. The tour departs from Niagara-on-the-Lake and Queenston, Canada, and Lewiston, New York. Tours run from May through October, daily, and cost C$54, although discounts are available when you book online.

Biking & Hiking

The **Niagara Parks Commission** (☎ 905/371–0254 or 877/642–7275 ⊕ www.niagaraparks.com) maintains 56 km (30 mi) of **bicycle trails** along the Niagara River between Fort Erie and Niagara-on-the-Lake. It also has information on nearby hiking trails, local parks, and the Niagara Gorge.

★ The 800-km (496-mi) **Bruce Trail** (✉ Box 857, L8N 3N9 ☎ 905/529– 6821 or 800/665–4453 ⊕ www.brucetrail.org) stretches northwest along the Niagara Escarpment from the orchards of the Niagara Peninsula to the craggy cliffs and bluffs at Tobermory, at the end of the Bruce Peninsula. The Escarpment is a UNESCO World Biosphere Reserve (one of 12 in Canada). You can access the hiking trail at just about any point along the route, so your hike can be any length you wish. **Hike Ontario** (☎ 416/426–7362 ⊕ www.hikeontario.com) has information and maps about hikes in the province.

Niagara Wine Region

Niagara Pkwy. between Niagara Falls and Niagara-on-the-Lake and on Hwy. 55

Some of the Niagara Peninsula's 55 wineries are on the Niagara Parkway between Niagara Falls and Niagara-on-the-Lake, or on Highway 55 from the Queen Elizabeth Way. As the quality of Ontario wines continues to improve and excel in international competitions, wine makers here have caught the attention of a growing number of wine lovers. The majority of area wineries have tastings and tours, in addition to selling their products on-site; call ahead for exact times.

The **Niagara Grape & Wine Festival** (☎ 905/688–0212 ⊕ www.grapeandwine.com) celebrates its 54th anniversary in 2005 and oversees several annual festivals and events that honor Niagara's wine-making history. Wine was first produced in the region in 1869 and quality estate wineries started business in 1972. In mid-January the Niagara wine industry celebrates its treasured liquid libation with the **Niagara Ice Wine Festival,** when thousands of visitors take the 10-day Wine Route with a Festival Ice Wine Touring Passport for access to tours, tastings, and winery events. The wine-related event with the biggest buzz is held in

★ late September: the **Niagara Wine Festival** honors the annual grape harvest and is one of Canada's largest annual celebrations, presenting over 100 wine and culinary events, and attracting over 500,000 people to the host city of St. Catharines and the adjoining Niagara Region. Taking place in mid-June, the **New Vintage Niagara Festival** celebrates Ontario's first taste of the previous year's harvest with wine galas. A Festival Touring Pass offers tours, generous samplings, and special events at 35 participating wineries across the Niagara Region.

Fodor'sChoice The **Wine Route,** so named for the wineries it passes, takes you on a well-
★ marked strip of highway between Hamilton and Niagara Falls, onto some secondary roads passing the region's attractive scenery, and through postcard-perfect small towns and villages.

From Toronto, take the QEW west and follow the signs for Niagara Falls until just past Hamilton. Exit the QEW at Fifty Road and follow it south, turning east onto Highway 8, which becomes Regional Road 81. This route takes you past wineries, large and small, through the towns of Grimsby, Beamsville, and the appropriately named town of Vineland, as it climbs the Niagara Escarpment past woods and vineyards to the hamlet of Jordan (in addition to the wineries here, there are antiques and specialty shops housed in historic buildings). East of Jordan, the Wine Route turns south on 5th Street and then goes east on 8th Avenue to join Regional Road 89, which goes through the city of St. Catharines before swinging north again on Four Mile Creek towards Niagara-on-the-Lake. There are plenty of wineries to visit here.

Several wineries, including Peller Estates Winery and Strewn Winery, have full-service upscale restaurants. Some establishments have patio wine bars and picnic facilities. For a map including locations of wineries and details of summer events, contact the **Wine Council of Ontario** (✉ 110 Hanover Dr., Suite B205, St. Catharines L2W 1A4 ☎ 905/684–8070 ⊕ www.wineroute.com).

Hillebrand Estates Winery. With over 300 wine awards, this is a must-see winery that produces many excellent varieties—a small batch of pinot noir, chardonnay, ice wine, and more. After the half-hour cellar and vine-yard tour are tastings of this vintner's latest achievements (two complimentary tastings on the winery tour). The café serves terrific meals ($$$–$$$$). Between May and October you can attend seminars on decanting, vintage wine tastings, and proper aging of wines (C$5 per seminar). Daily twilight tours are offered July through September at 7 and 8 PM. ✉ *1249 Niagara Stone Rd., Niagara-on-the-Lake L0S 1J0* ☎ *905/ 468–7123 or 800/582–8412* ⊕ *www.hillebrand.com* ☉ *Oct.–May, daily 10–5; June–Sept., daily 10–6. Tours every hr on the hr.*

The visitor center of **Inniskillin Wine** is housed in a restored 1920s barn, set among acres of lush vineyards. This large winery specializes in producing premium Vintners Quality Alliance (VQA) wines, including top-notch pinot noir, chardonnay, and cabernet blanc. Be sure to go on the self-guided tour, which includes one tasting of white wine and one red variety; samplings cost up to C$4. ✉ *Line 3 at Niagara Pkwy., Niagara-on-the-Lake L0S 1J0* ☎ *905/468–2187 or 888/466–4754, Ext. 325* ⊕ *www.inniskillin.com* ☉ *May–Oct., daily 10–6, tasting bar 11–5:30; Nov.–Apr., daily 10–5, tasting bar 11–4:30. Tours May–Oct., daily at 10:30 and 2:30; Nov.–Apr., weekends at 10:30 and 2:30.*

Jackson-Triggs Niagara Estate Winery is an ultramodern facility that blends state-of-the-art wine-making technology with age-old, handcrafted enological savvy. In 2004 the winery received the Best Canadian Winery award at the Vinitaly International Wine competition in Italy, and more accolades at the San Francisco International Wine Competition, including a double gold award for its Grand Reserve Riesling ice wine. Its premium VQA wines can be sipped in the tasting gallery (three complimentary tastings on the winery tour), and purchased in the retail boutique. ✉ *2145 Niagara Stone Rd., Niagara-on-the-Lake L0S 1J0* ☎ *905/468–4637 or 866/589–4637* ⊕ *www.jacksontriggswinery.com* ☉ *May–Oct., daily 10:30–6:30; Nov.–Apr., daily 10:30–5:30. Tours daily 10:30–5:30.*

An ice-wine producer with over 220 medals in domestic and international competitions, **Pillitteri Estates Winery** is also famous for its wine master, Sue-Ann Staff, who was named Ontario's Winemaker of the Year (2002)— the first woman so honored. The winery's ice wine is unique in that its grapes are harvested far later in winter than those of most other producers. When pressed, these handpicked, frozen grapes yield a juice with an intense concentration of sugars, acids, flavors, and aromas. Tours include two complimentary tastings. ✉ *1696 Niagara Stone Rd., Niagara-on-the-Lake L0S 1J0* ☎ *905/468–3147* ⊕ *www.pillitteri.com* ☉ *May 15–Oct. 15, daily 10–8; Oct. 16–May 14, daily 10–6. Tours daily at noon and 2.*

CloseUp

SWEET SIPPINGS: ONTARIO'S ICE WINES

O NTARIO IS THE WORLD'S LEADING PRODUCER OF *ice wine, a product inspired by Niagara's hot late summers and bracing winters. Ice wine is produced from ripe grapes left on the vine into the winter. When the grapes start to freeze, most of the water in them turns solid, resulting in a fructose-laden, aromatic, and flavorful center. (Temperatures must be -8°C [18°F]) for at least 24 hours for this process to occur.) Ice wine grapes must be picked at freezing temperatures before sunrise and basket-pressed immediately to assure best results. The juice is allowed to settle for three to four days. Then it is clarified and slowly fermented using specially cultivated yeasts. By nature ice wine is sweet, but when well made this nectar smells of dried fruits, apricots, and honey, and finishes with a long, refreshing aftertaste.*

For ice wine most Ontario wine makers prefer Vidal grapes, due to their thick skin and resistance to cracking in subzero temperatures. The thin-skinned Riesling yields better results but is susceptible to cracking and ripens much later than Vidal. Niagara wineries specializing in ice wine also use gewürztraminer, pinot noir, pinot gris, cabernet franc, chardonnay, gamay, merlot, and Kerner.

Canadian ice wines sell for about C$45 per 375-ml bottle. The higher prices commanded by ice wine reflect the precariousness involved in its production and its scarcity. Production is relatively small, with Ontario vintners producing about 65,000 cases each season. Look for ice wine that has an official mark of the Vintners Quality Alliance (VQA) Canada.

★ Known as one of Ontario's most beautiful wineries, the 75-acre **Vineland Estates Winery** dates to 1845, when it was a Mennonite homestead. The original buildings have been transformed into the visitor center and production complex. Tour fees are C$6 per person, which includes three free tastings; additional samplings of Vineland's exquisite dry and semidry Rieslings are just 50¢ each. The excellent Italian Vineland Estates Winery Restaurant ($$$–$$$$), open daily for lunch and dinner, is also quite a draw. ⊠ *3620 Moyer Rd., Vineland L0R 2C0* ☎ *905/ 562–7088 or 888/846–3526* ⊕ *www.vineland.com* ☉ *May–Oct., daily 10–6. Public tours (C$6) May–Oct., daily at 11 and 3; Nov.–Apr., weekends at 3. Private tours by request.*

Where to Stay & Eat

$$$–$$$$
Fodor'sChoice
★

✕ **Vineland Estates Winery Restaurant.** Exquisite Italian food and venerable wines are served by an enthusiastic staff on the wine deck or in the glassed-in restaurant, with a panoramic view of the vineyard and lake. The fresh lemon poppy-seed baguette is served warm, and the pasta is homemade (try the inch-thick pappardelle noodles tossed with Niagara hazelnuts, arugula, cremini mushrooms, and Montasio cheese). Feeling carnivorous? The chef pan-roasts local venison and partners it with parsnip-potato puree, leeks, and blueberry jus. Desserts are a happy marriage of local fruits and an imaginative pastry chef. ✉ *3620 Moyer Rd., Vineland* ☎ *905/562–7088 or 888/846–3526* ⊕ *www.vineland.com* ▤ *AE, D, MC, V.*

$$–$$$$
Fodor'sChoice
★

✕▦ **Inn on the Twenty.** The inn is part of Leonard Pennachetti's Cave Spring Cellars winery in the village of Jordan, a 30-minute drive from Niagara-on-the-Lake. Rooms have elegant 1920s mahogany headboards, whirlpool baths, and fireplaces. The sophisticated resturant On the Twenty ($$$–$$$$) has top-notch cuisine that emphasizes regional specialties. Dine on signature Shorthills trout in Riesling-rhubarb butter, or partridge in hazelnut chardonnay sauce. You can tour and sample the wines of Cave Spring Cellars across the street. The restaurant is closed some days in January, so call ahead. ✉ *3845 Main St., Jordan L0R 1S0* ☎ *905/562–5336, 905/562–7313 restaurant, 800/701–8074* 🖷 *905/562–0009* ⊕ *www.innonthetwenty.com* 🛏 *29 rooms* ⚄ *Restaurant, in-room data ports, in-room hot tubs, some refrigerators, no-smoking rooms* ▤ *AE, DC, MC, V* �'◎' *CP.*

Bicycle Tours

Biking through the Niagara Region in any direction brings a touch of adventure as well as the opportunity to linger a while longer at each stop along the Wine Route. Remember to bring along sunscreen and sunglasses, and always dress for the season. Stiff-sole running shoes for hard pedaling and occasional hiking over rough terrain are recommended.

Niagara Wine Tours International (☎ 905/892–9770 ✉ 2755 Hurricane Rd., R.R. 2, Welland L3B 5N5 ⊕ www.niagarawinetours.com) leads guided bike tours along the Wine Route. A leisurely afternoon cycle includes wine tastings at three wineries for C$55. The Jordan Wine Country Tour has tastings at four wineries and includes lunch; it costs C$120.

Steve Bauer Bike Tours (⌖ 4979 King St., Box 342, Beamsville L0R1B0 ☎ 905/563–8687 🖷 905/563–9697 ⊕ www.stevebauer.com) specializes in unique one- or multi-day bike tours. Niagara Getaway trips are organized from May through September; the all-inclusive two-night package covers accommodations, full breakfasts, lunch and dinner, wine-tasting stops, spa treatments at a local resort, along with fruits and snacks en route, and costs C$699. All tours are fully guided with van support.

Niagara-on-the-Lake

15 km (9 mi) north of (downriver from) Niagara Falls via the Niagara Pkwy. and Hwy. 55.

Since 1962 Niagara-on-the-Lake has been considered the southern outpost of fine summer theater in Ontario because of its acclaimed Shaw Festival. But it offers far more than Stratford, its older theatrical sister to the west: as one of the country's prettiest and best-preserved Victorian towns, Niagara-on-the-Lake has architectural sights, small shops, flower-lined streets in summer, and quality theater nearly year-round. The town of 14,000 is worth a visit at any time of the year for its inns, restaurants, and proximity to the wineries, but the most compelling time to visit is from April through November, when the Shaw Festival is in full swing.

Niagara-on-the-Lake remained a sleepy town until 1962, when local lawyer Brian Doherty organized eight weekend performances of two

George Bernard Shaw plays, *Don Juan in Hell* and *Candida*. The next year he helped found the festival, whose mission is to perform the works of Shaw and his contemporaries.

The three theaters used by the Shaw Festival present quality performances, but what's also special are the abundant orchards and flower gardens, sailboats, and the utterly charming town of Niagara-on-the-Lake itself.

★ This is a very small town that can easily be explored on foot. **Queen Street** is the core of the commercial portion; walking east along that single street, with Lake Ontario to your north, you get a glimpse of the town's architectural history. At No. 209 is the handsome *Charles Inn*, built in about 1832 for a member of Parliament, with later additions at the end of the 19th century. No. 187 dates from 1822, with later Greek Revival improvements. A veteran of the 1814 Battle of Lundy's Lane in Niagara Falls once occupied No. 165, an 1820 beauty. For decades, No. 157, built in 1823, was occupied by descendants of the Rogers-Harrison family, prominent since the early 19th century in church and town affairs. McClelland's, a store at No. 106, has been in business in Niagara-on-the-Lake since the War of 1812. The huge "T" sign means "provisioner."

Grace United Church, built in 1852, is a collage of architectural styles, including Italianate and Norman. Stained-glass windows dedicated to the memory of Canadians killed in World War I were installed in the 1920s. The church was commissioned by a congregation of "Free Kirk" Presbyterians, but was later sold to Methodists and now serves a congregation of the United Church (a merger of Presbyterians, Methodists, and Congregationalists). ✉ *222 Victoria St.* ☎ *905/468–4044.*

The **Niagara Apothecary** was built in 1866 and restored in 1971. The museum has exquisite walnut and butternut fixtures, crystal pieces, and a rare collection of apothecary glasses. ✉ *5 Queen St.* ☎ *905/468–3845* ☒ *Free* ⊙ *Mid-May–early Sept., daily noon–6.*

The **Niagara Historical Society & Museum,** one of the oldest (established 1895) museums of its kind in Ontario, has an extensive collection relating to the often colorful history of the Niagara Peninsula from earliest times through the 19th century. The museum has a gift shop and offers guided tours of the town. ✉ *43 Castlereagh St.* ☎ *905/468–3912* ⊕ *niagara.com/~nhs* ☒ *C$5* ⊙ *May–Oct., daily 10–5:30; Nov.–Apr., daily 1–5.*

⟳ On a wide stretch of parkland south of town sits **Fort George National His-**
Fodor'sChoice **toric Park.** The fort was built in the 1790s, but was lost to the Yankees
★ during the War of 1812. It was recaptured after the burning of the town in 1813, and largely survived the war, only to fall into ruins by the 1830s. It was reconstructed a century later, and you can explore the officers' quarters, the barracks rooms of the common soldiers, the kitchen, and more. Like many other historic sites in Ontario, the town is staffed by people in period uniform who conduct tours and reenact 19th-century infantry and artillery drills. ✉ *Queens Parade, Niagara Pkwy.* ☎ *905/468–4257* ⊕ *www.niagara.com/~parkscan* ☒ *C$6* ⊙ *Apr.–Oct., daily 10–5.*

Guided Tours
Queens Royal Tours (✉ 128 Anne St., Box 42 ☎ 905/468–1008 ⊕ www.queensroyal.com) conducts year-round tours in and around Niagara-

Niagara-on-the-Lake

on-the-Lake. Half-hour horse-and-carriage rides are C$50, and one-hour rides are C$90. Wine tours lead from a vintage car cost C$50 per person for three wineries, tasting included.

Where to Stay & Eat

The area has some lovely restaurants and inns, both within town and outside it; a number of wineries here have restaurants and inns as well. Especially during summer, make reservations whenever possible.

$$$–$$$$ ✕**Buttery Theatre Restaurant.** At Margaret Niemann's authentic British pub–café, the wood-beam ceiling, beaten copper tabletops, and china and pewter all bear the patina of age. Lively Tudor-style banquets and feasts are held every Friday and Saturday (prix fixe C$55), and the tavern menu includes good pâtés and Cornish pasties (beef-filled pastry). The chef bakes chicken with fresh lemons and roasts leg of lamb. The roast duckling on the weekday prix-fixe menu (C$26) is an excellent choice. Afternoon tea is served daily from 2 to 5. ✉ *19 Queen St.* ☎ *905/468–2564* ✆ *www. thebutteryrestaurant.com* ▭ *AE, MC, V* ☾ *Closed Sun.*

★ **$$$–$$$$** ✕**Hillebrand Vineyard Café.** After a complimentary winery tour and tasting, you can settle down to a superb meal created by Chef Tony di Luca. Culinary masterpieces include goat cheese truffles on grilled vegetables, and wild mushroom soufflé with foie gras toast. The tossed salad is a beautiful relationship between organic greens, sun-dried blueberries, and roasted crisp garlic. The pastry chef composes incredible desserts: a bittersweet chocolate cup is filled with vanilla ice cream and topped with candied hazelnuts. ⊠ *1249 Niagara Stone Rd., at Hwy. 55* ☎ *905/468–7123 or 800/582–8412* ⊕ *www.hillebrand.com* ⊟ *AE, D, MC, V.*

$$$–$$$$ ✕ **Ristorante Giardino.** Italian marble combines with stainless steel and rich colors to create a contemporary Italian setting on 19th-century Queen Street. Chefs recruited from Italy produce antipasti such as Parma ham served with melon, smoked salmon terrine, or marinated swordfish with herbs. There's always grilled fresh fish or oven-roasted chicken and lamb. Make time to indulge in the kitchen's classic Italian desserts and fresh Niagara fruits. The long wine list is worth a careful read. ⊠ *Gate House Hotel, 142 Queen St.* ☎ *905/468–3263* ⊕ *www.gatehouse-niagara.com* ⊟ *AE, DC, MC, V* ☾ *Closed Jan. and Feb.*

$$ ✕ **Fans Court.** Delicate Cantonese cuisine is prepared in a lovely, antiques-filled restaurant in a courtyard between an art gallery and a greenhouse. Mature jade trees in urns stand at the entrance. In summer you can sit outdoors and sample such favorites as lemon chicken, black-pepper-and-garlic beef, and fried rice served in a pineapple. ⊠ *135 Queen St.* ☎ *905/468–4511* ⊟ *AE, MC, V.*

★ $$$$ ✕🖭 **Pillar and Post Inn, Spa and Conference Center.** This hotel, six long blocks from the heart of town, has been a cannery, barracks, and basket factory. Most rooms have handcrafted early American pine furniture, patchwork quilts, and such modern amenities as hair dryers. The 100 Fountain Spa has soothing body treatments. The casual Vintages Wine Bar and Lounge serves regional cuisine and wines. The Cannery & Carriages Dining Room menu ($$$–$$$$) is inspired by what the market has to offer like pesto encrusted Atlantic salmon or sea bass with summer squash. ⊠ *48 John St., L0S 1J0* ☎ *905/468–2123 or 888/669–5566* 🖶 *905/468–3551* ⊕ *www.vintageinns.com* ⌨ *123 rooms* ♿ *2 restaurants, 2 pools (1 indoors), health club, sauna, spa, lobby lounge, business services* ⊟ *AE, D, DC, MC, V.*

$$$$
Fodor's Choice
★
✕🖭 **Prince of Wales Hotel.** A visit from the Prince of Wales in the early 1900s inspired the name of this venerable hostelry. Plenty has changed since then. The improved Prince of Wales has been designed in the style of an upper-crust English manor house, Victorian in flavor and complete with its own tearoom (where the Queen herself might feel at home). Exquisite wall treatments, antique furnishings, and fresh flowers meet the eye at every turn. The Escabèche restaurant ($$$–$$$$) serves eclectic cuisine such as Arctic Char fillet with spinach and artichokes in lemon-caper butter. At the Churchill Lounge, lighter and less-expensive meals such as salads and wild-mushroom risotto are served. ⊠ *6 Picton St., Box 46, L0S 1J0* ☎ *905/468–3246 or 888/669–5566* 🖶 *905/468–5521* ⊕ *www.vintageinns.com* ⌨ *114 rooms* ♿ *Dining room, tea shop, indoor pool, health club* ⊟ *AE, D, DC, MC, V.*

★ $$$$ ✕🖭 **Queen's Landing Inn.** Many rooms at this inn have knockout views of historic Fort George and the marina—be sure to ask for one when making a reservation. A smattering of antiques and canopy beds make rooms elegant; many have working fireplaces and modern whirlpool baths. The Tiara Dining Room ($$$–$$$$) has an outstanding regional menu in a room flattered by stained glass and a full view of the lake. The kitchen provides a blend of Asian spicing and excellent local meats and produce. Main courses such as cinnamon-roasted veal tenderloin and parsley-crusted breast of chicken with buckwheat risotto show the skill and imagination of the chef, who also prepares a vegetarian tasting menu. ⬠ *155 Byron St., Box 1180, L0S 1J0* ☎ *905/468–2195 or 888/669–5566* 🖷 *905/ 468–2227* ⊕ *www.vintageinns.com* ⟿ *144 rooms* ⬥ *Dining room, cable TV, indoor pool, gym, hot tub, sauna, lounge* ☰ *AE, D, DC, MC, V.*

$$$–$$$$ ✕⊡ **Oban Inn.** Take in views of Lake Ontario at this elegant country inn, which was built in 1869. Each room is distinct, embellished with antiques for a British tone; some have fireplaces. You can while away the day on the inn's broad verandas or in its beautifully manicured gardens. The popular dining room ($$) spotlights Canadian beef; the poached salmon is a favorite in summer. The lounge offers an all-day menu of traditional fish-and-chips, steak-and-ale pie, sandwiches, and appetizers. On Sunday a brunch of whole turkey, ham, and prime rib brings out the locals. ✉ *160 Front St., L0S 1J0* ☎ *905/468–2165 or 888/669–5566* 🖷 *905/ 468–4165* ⊕ *www.vintageinns.com* ⟿ *25 rooms, 1 suite* ⬥ *Restaurant, cable TV, bicycles, pub, library, babysitting, concierge, meeting rooms, airport shuttle, some pets allowed (fee)* ☰ *AE, D, DC, MC, V.*

$$–$$$$ ✕⊡ **The Charles Inn.** An air of old-fashioned civility permeates this 1852 Georgian gem. You can enjoy a summer evening playing board games on the outdoor patio and dining on some of the best food to be found in the area. Fireplaces, claw-footed bathtubs, and a mixture of 19th-century antique and reproduction furniture add to the period charm of the large, bright rooms. Many rooms have doors onto the upper veranda.

★ In the Old Towne Dining Room ($$$), chef William Bunyansky crafts exquisite dishes, avoiding overpowering sauces and focusing instead on the natural flavors of his fresh ingredients. Many dishes, such as pan-seared pickerel with grilled vegetables, draw from the produce of the area. ✉ *209 Queen St., L0S 1J0* ☎ *905/468–4588* ⊕ *www.charlesinn. ca* ⟿ *10 rooms, 2 suites* ⬥ *Restaurant, room service, cable TV, massage, laundry services; no smoking* ☰ *AE, MC, V.*

$$$ ✕⊡ **White Oaks Conference Resort & Spa.** Though the exterior of this hotel looks rather institutional, the interior is anything but. Sleek, modern room furnishings in woodsy earth tones convey rest and relaxation. The fitness club contains a wide variety of top-of-the-line equipment. The luxury resort has many activities, such as squash, racquetball, tennis, and fitness classes. Golf carts whisk you from the hotel's front door to the Royal Niagara golf course, a first-class facility across the street. The sleek Liv Restaurant ($$$–$$$$) has chic menu items such as grilled sea scallops with crawfish tails accompanied by cilantro and coconut-milk rice. ✉ *253 Taylor Rd., L0S 1J0* ☎ *905/688–2550 or 800/263–5766* 🖷 *905/ 688–2220* ⊕ *www.whiteoaksresort.com* ⟿ *198 rooms, 22 suites* ⬥ *2 restaurants, 8 indoor tennis courts, indoor pool, health club, hot tub, sauna, racquetball, squash, lobby lounge, business services* ☰ *AE, D, MC, V.*

★ **$$–$$$** ✕⊡ **Olde Angel Inn.** Though established in 1779, the current incarnation of the lemon-yellow, green-shuttered coach house dates to 1816, when it was rebuilt after it burned down during the War of 1812. Some of this history remains alive; a resident ghost—some say he's a soldier who had gone AWOL and was killed here—is believed to walk the cellar. Rooms have canopy beds. The English-style tavern sets out pub fare such as steak, Guinness, and oyster pie on antique wooden refectory tables. Entrées on the dining room menu ($$$–$$$$) include prime rib of beef au jus and rack of lamb with mint sauce. Even if you don't stay here, be sure to stop in for a meal. ☒ *224 Regent St., L0S 1J0* ☎ *905/ 468–3411* ⊕ *www.angel-inn.com* ⤳ *5 rooms, 3 cottages* ♿ *Restaurant, pub, wine bar; no smoking* ▭ *AE, D, DC, MC, V.*

$$$$ ⊞ **Harbour House.** A classy nautical theme pervades this Eastern Seaboard–style boutique hotel on the Niagara River. The building's 1880s maritime look is topped off with a cedar shingle roof. Spacious rooms have cozy touches like electric fireplaces, feather-top beds, and Frette robes, as well as DVD and CD players and a library of disks. You can sample local preserves, homemade pastries, and exotic teas at breakfast and attend wine and cheese tastings in the afternoon. Wineglasses, an ice bucket, and a corkscrew are in each guestroom, in case you pick up a local bottle. This is a good alternative to the myriad of B&Bs in town. ☒ *85 Melville St., L0S 1J0* ☎ *905/468–4683* 🖷 *905/468–0366* ⊕ *www.harbourhousehotel.ca* ⤳ *29 rooms, 2 suites* ♿ *Dining room, some in-room hot tubs, cable TV, massage, Internet, meeting room, some pets allowed; no smoking* ▭ *AE, MC, V* ⦿l *BP.*

$$$–$$$$ ⊞ **Riverbend Inn & Vineyard.** A vineyard surrounds the restored palatial 1860s Georgian mansion, which feels sublimely isolated from the hustle and bustle of town. Though the vineyard hasn't started to produce, it still creates the intended impression of rusticity. The mansion's atrium aims for grandness, with a chandelier and small display case of archaeological relics found on-site; reproduction Renoirs hung around the lobby area fall flat in comparison. Spacious rooms might be painted bright yellow or sage green, and have dark-wood furniture and small chandeliers. Those overlooking the lobby have tall ceilings, but voices from the lobby can carry into the rooms at night; quieter rooms are down the hall. ☒ *16104 Niagara River Pkwy., L0S 1J0* ☎ *905/468–8866* 🖷 *905/ 468–8829* ⊕ *www.riverbendinn.ca* ⤳ *19 rooms, 2 suites* ♿ *Restaurant, room service, cable TV, bar, Internet, business services; no smoking* ▭ *AE, DC, MC, V* ⦿l *MAP.*

$–$$ ⊞ **Moffat Inn.** This charmer has individually appointed rooms, some with original 1835 fireplaces, outdoor patios, brass beds, and wicker furniture. The independent on-site restaurant Tetley's serves an imaginative variety of dishes including sushi, fondue, and meats cooked on hot granite rocks. ☒ *60 Picton St., L0S 1J0* ☎ *905/468–4641* ⊕ *www.moffatinn. com* ⤳ *22 rooms* ♿ *Restaurant; no smoking* ▭ *AE, MC, V.*

Nightlife & the Arts

FodorśChoice ★   The **Shaw Festival** began modestly back in the early 1960s with a single play and a premise: to perform the plays of George Bernard Shaw and his contemporaries, who include Noël Coward, Bertolt Brecht, J. M. Barrie, and J. M. Synge. The season now runs from April through December with close to a dozen plays. The festival operates in three buildings within a few blocks of one another. The handsome **Festival Theatre,** the largest of the three, stands on Queen's Parade near Wellington Street and houses the box office. The **Court House Theatre,** on Queen Street between King and Regent streets, served as the town's municipal offices until 1969. At the corner of Queen and Victoria streets is the slightly smaller **Royal George Theatre,** the most intimate of the three. Tickets (which can also be ordered online) cost C$20 to C$77. ⌖ *Shaw Festival Box Office, Box 774, 10 Queen's Parade L0S 1J0* ☎ *905/468-2172 or 800/511-7429* 🖷 *905/468-3804* ⊕ *www.shawfest.com.*

en route

The Niagara Peninsula is Ontario's fruit basket. From midsummer to late fall, fruit and vegetable stands proliferate along the highways and byways, and several farmers' markets are scattered along Queen Elizabeth Way (QEW) between Niagara Falls and Hamilton. Some of the best stands are on Highway 55, between Niagara-on-the-Lake and the QEW, as well as along Lakeshore Road, between Niagara-on-the-Lake and St. Catharines. **Harvest Barn Market** (⌖ Hwy. 55, Niagara-on-the-Lake ☎ 905/468-3224), marked by a red-and-white-stripe awning, not only sells regional fruits and vegetables but also tempts with its baked goods: sausage rolls, tiny loaves of bread, and fruit pies. You can test the market's wares at the picnic tables, where knowledgeable locals have lunch. **Greaves Jams & Marmalades** (⌖ 55 Queen St. ☎ 905/468-3608 or 800/515-9939 ⊕ www. greavesjams.com) makes jams, jellies, and marmalades from mostly local produce using family recipes, some of which have been around since the company began in 1927. The spreads don't have any preservatives, pectin, or additives, and are an Ontario favorite.

STRATFORD

45 km (28 mi) west of Kitchener on Hwys. 7 and 8.

In July 1953, Alec Guinness, one of the world's greatest actors, joined with Tyrone Guthrie, probably the world's greatest Sakespearean director, beneath a hot, stuffy tent in a backward little town about 145 km (90 mi) and 90 minutes from Toronto. This was the birth of the Stratford Festival of Canada, which runs from April to early November and is one of the most successful, most widely admired theaters of its kind. It's ensured Stratford a place on Canada's cultural map.

The origins of Ontario's Stratford are modest. After the War of 1812, the British government granted a million acres of land along Lake Huron to the Canada Company, headed by a Scottish businessman. When the surveyors came to a marshy creek surrounded by a thick forest, they named it "Little Thames" and noted that it might make "a good mill-site." It was Thomas Mercer Jones, a director of the Canada Company, who decided to rename the river the Avon, and the town Stratford. The year was 1832, 121 years before the concept of a theater festival would take flight and change Canadian culture.

For many years Stratford was considered a backwoods hamlet. Then came the first of two saviors of the city, both of them (undoubting) Thomases. In 1904 an insurance broker named Tom Orr transformed Stratford's riverfront into a park. He also built a formal English garden, where every flower mentioned in the plays of Shakespeare—monkshood to sneeze-wort, bee balm to bachelor's button—blooms grandly to this day.

Next, Tom Patterson, a fourth-generation Stratfordian born in 1920, looked around, saw that the town wards and schools had names like Hamlet, Falstaff, and Romeo, and felt that some kind of drama festival might save his community from becoming a ghost town. The astonishing story of how he began in 1952 with C$125 (a "generous" grant from the Stratford City Council), tracked down the directorial genius Tyrone Guthrie and the inspired stage and screen star Alec Guinness, obtained the services of the brilliant stage designer Tanya Moiseiwitsch, and somehow pasted together a long-standing theater festival in a little over one year is recounted in Patterson's memoirs, *First Stage—The Making of the Stratford Festival.*

The festival is now moving into middle age, having celebrated its 52nd season in 2004, but it has had its ups and downs. Soon after it opened and wowed critics from around the world with its professionalism, costumes, and daring thrust stage, the air was filled with superlatives that had not been heard in Canada since the Great Blondin walked across Niagara Falls on a tightrope.

The early years brought giants of world theater to the tiny town of some 20,000: James Mason, Alan Bates, Christopher Plummer, Jason Robards Jr., and Maggie Smith. But the years also saw an unevenness in productions and a tendency to go for flash over substance. Many never lost faith in the festival; others, such as Canada's greatest theater critic, the late Nathan Cohen of the *Toronto Star,* have bemoaned the fact that Stratford has become Canada's most sacred cow.

Sacred or not, Stratford's offerings are still among the best of their kind in the world, with at least a handful of productions every year that put most other summer arts festivals to shame. The secret to deciding which ones to see is to try to catch the reviews of the plays. The *New York Times* always runs major write-ups, as do newspapers and magazines in many American and Canadian cities.

Today Stratford is a city of 30,000 that welcomes over 650,000 annual visitors, drawn like moths to the theater's flame. There are quieter things to do in Stratford when the theaters close. Art galleries remain open throughout winter. Shopping is good off-season, and those who love peaceful walks can stroll along the Avon. Many concerts are scheduled in the off-season, too.

Gallery Stratford has regular exhibits of Canadian visual art (some for sale) and, in summer, of theater arts. ⊠ *54 Romeo St.* ☎ *519/271–5271* ⊕ *www.gallerystratford.on.ca* ✉ *May–early Sept., C$8; mid-Sept.–Apr., C$5* ☉ *Tues.–Fri. and Sun. 1–4, Sat. 10–4.*

★ You can brush up on Stratford and Perth County history at the **Stratford Perth Museum.** Watch demonstrators crank the working printing press from 1827, or browse through the other displays, which cover such topics as hockey in Stratford, the city's railroad, and the settlement of the area in the early 1800s. An exhibit on some of Canada's firsts includes the story of Dr. Jenny Trout, Canada's first female physician. ⊠ *270 Water St.* ☎ *519/271–5311* ⊕ *www.cyg.net/~spmuseum* ✉ *Donation* ☉ *May–Oct., Tues.–Sat. 10–5, Sun. and Mon. noon–5; call for reduced hrs Nov.–Apr.*

Where to Stay & Eat

★ $$$$ ✕ **Church Restaurant and Belfry.** It was constructed in 1873 as a Congregational church, but today white tablecloths gleam in the afternoon light that pours through the stained glass windows. Meals here, whether prix-fixe or à la carte, are production numbers. Licorice-dusted diver scallops are topped with candied fennel and citrus, and elk strip steak is pan-roasted. The roast Ontario lamb with garlic custard and eggplant flan is outstanding. Upstairs the Belfry ($$–$$$$) uses the same excellent kitchen, but the setting is casual, and the dishes are lighter. ✉ 70 *Brunswick St.* ☎ *519/273–3424* ⊕ *www.churchrestaurant.com* ✍ *Reservations essential* ☰ *AE, DC, MC, V* ⊗ *Closed Mon. and Jan.–Mar.*

$$$$ ✕ **Rundles Restaurant.** The look here is Venetian, in a theatrical Strat-
Fodor'sChoice ford way. Flowing white silk scarves hang from primitive stone masks
★ in this sophisticated, calm space. Several three-course prix-fixe menus and a wine-with-dinner menu offer plenty of choices. The Tasmanian ocean trout, flavored with lemongrass and served with sliced fingerling potatoes and a delicately balanced lobster bouillon, is an example of the considerable artistry chef Neil Baxter lavishes on both the preparation and presentation of his dishes. ✉ *9 Cobourg St.* ☎ *519/271–6442* ⊕ *www.rundlesrestaurant.com* ☰ *AE, DC, MC, V* ⊗ *Closed Mon. and Nov.–mid-May. No lunch Tues., Thurs., and Fri.*

$$$–$$$$ ✕ **Bijou.** Stratford residents flock to this small, self-professed "culinary gem," whose menu changes seasonally. You might have five-spiced quail with organic shiitake mushrooms in a honey, lime, and ginger sauce for your main course. For dessert, there might be a banana terrine with caramelized banana, crème fraîche, and caramel. ⊠ *105 Erie St.* ☎ *519/273–5000* ⊕ *www.bijourestaurant.com* ☰ *AE, MC, V* ◔ *Closed Mon. No lunch Tues.–Thurs.* ◖ *Reservations essential.*

$$$–$$$$ ✕ **Old Prune.** A converted Victorian house holds a number of charming dining rooms and a glass-enclosed conservatory surrounded by a tidy sunken garden. Chef Bryan Steele coaxes fresh local ingredients into innovative dishes: smoked rainbow trout with apple radish and curry oil, vegetable lasagna with roasted tomato sauce, or, with a nod to the East, chicken seasoned with coriander and cumin. Desserts are baked fresh for each meal and come straight from the oven. ⊠ *151 Albert St.* ☎ *519/271–5052* ⊕ *www.oldprune.on.ca* ☰ *AE, MC, V* ◔ *Closed Nov.–mid-May and Mon. No lunch Tues.*

$$ ✕ **Down the Street Bar and Café.** Funky and informal, this bistro with live jazz and food by Stratford Chefs School graduates is the hottest place in town. Thrilling grills of Thai chicken, Moroccan lamb, and Black Angus sirloin make for delicious casual dining. An inspirational late-night menu includes options such as spicy spring rolls, steamed Prince Edward Island mussels, and a classic cheeseburger with the works. A comprehensive selection of imported and microbrew beers are on tap. ⊠ *30 Ontario St.* ☎ *519/273–5886* ☰ *AE, MC, V* ◔ *No lunch Mon.*

$–$$ ✕ **Bentley's Inn.** The well-stocked bar at this long and narrow British-style pub divides the room into two equal halves. There's an unspoken tradition: the actors have claimed one side, and the locals the other. The pub fare has staples such as good fish-and-chips, grilled steak and fries, and steak-and-mushroom pie. Regulars to this watering hole say they come for the imported, domestic, and microbrew beers, 15 of which are draft—the easygoing clientele and camaraderie are bonuses. ⊠ *99 Ontario St.* ☎ *519/271–1121* ⊕ *www.bentleys-annex.com* ☰ *AE, MC, V.*

¢–$$ ✕ **Boomer's Gourmet Fries.** No time for leisurely dining? Boomer's quickly serves fries of every ilk (no preservatives, cooked in canola oil) and scrumptious fish-and-chips year-round. Try a *poutine*, a Canadian pairing of fries, cheese curds, and gravy. ⊠ *26 Erie St.* ☎ *519/275–3147* ⊕ *www.boomersgourmetfries.com* ☰ *MC, V.*

★ **¢–$$** ✕ **York Street Kitchen.** Locals favor the signature thick and juicy sandwiches and homemade comfort dishes here, such as meat loaf and mashed potatoes and sweet-and-sour beef short ribs. You can visit the takeout window for lunch and dinner express service or eat in the funky dining room, with exposed-brick walls painted an eye-popping green, for breakfast, lunch, and dinner. During festival season the lines form early at this year-rounder. ⊠ *41 York St.* ☎ *519/273–7041* ⊕ *www.yorkstreetkitchen.com* ☰ *MC, V.*

★ **$** ✕ **Principal's Pantry.** Generously sized sandwiches and a selection of gluten-free, lactose-free, vegan, and organic foods are served at this unpretentious, cafeteria-style eatery. You can also select one of the Ontario wines and beers listed on the menu board. Although the restaurant is in an industrial-looking Victorian building, the interior is bright and cheerful. ✉ *Discovery Centre, 270 Water St.* ☎ *519/272–9914* ⊕ *www. principalspantry.com* ☰ *AE, MC, V* ✹ *Closed Sun. and Mon.*

★ $–$$$ ⨯🖭 **Queen's Inn at Stratford.** The hotel dates to 1858, though a 1905 remodeling gave it its present-day stone facings and exterior ornamental tinwork. It retains a small-town feel and is still family owned and operated. The restaurant, Henry's ($$–$$$), serves such traditional English fare as beef tenderloin and rack of lamb at reasonable prices. The Boar's Head is a popular pub-lounge with light snacks and great brews. ✉ *161 Ontario St., N5A 3H3* ☎ *519/271–1400 or 800/461–6450* 🖷 *519/271–7373* ⊕ *www.queensinnstratford.ca* ⤴ *32 rooms, 3 suites* ⚴ *Restaurant, some in-room hot tubs, cable TV, lounge, meeting rooms, no-smoking rooms* ☰ *AE, MC, V* ¶◎ *CP.*

$$ ⨯🖭 **The Victorian Inn on the Park.** Tucked among the pines and towering century-old maples along the Avon River, this year-round inn has some suites with Jacuzzi tubs and fireplaces to take the chill out of the fresh countryside air. Many rooms have balconies. The garden patio, on the other hand, is a good place to breathe in some of that fresh air. The walk to the theaters and restaurants in town takes 15 minutes, but the inn's Sawyers on the River restaurant ($$–$$$) has a reputation for the juiciest Canadian beef served in the area. Packages with room, breakfast, and dinner are a good deal. ✉ *10 Romeo St. N., N5A 5M7* ☎ *519/271–4650 or 800/ 741–2135* 🖷 *519/271–2030* ⊕ *www.victorian-inn.on.ca* ⤴ *115 rooms* ⚴ *Restaurant, some microwaves, some refrigerators, indoor pool, bar, no-smoking rooms* ☰ *AE, D, DC, MC, V.*

$$$$ 🖭 **XIS.** A married couple whose backgrounds are in accounting and pharmacy transformed this former downtown bank building into an exquisite, ultra chic inn. White leather chairs, feather beds and duvets, and sleek, shoji-like wood-and-glass panels in rooms might help you sink into a Zen-like mood. You can pamper yourself with Bulgari bath products and Frette linens or treat yourself to cashews, Evian water, and crisp green apples. Coffee, tea, and ice are delivered upon request. The homemade Continental breakfast has aged cheeses. XIS (pronounced *zees*) opened in May 2004 and will perhaps be the most sought-after accommodation in Stratford when word spreads. ✉*6 Wellington St., N5A 2L2* ☎*519/273–9248* 🖷*519/273–4872* ⊕ *www.xis-stratford.com* ⤴ *6 rooms* ⚴ *In-room safes, cable TV, lounge; no smoking* ☰ *AE, MC, V* ✹ *Closed mid Nov.–mid-Apr.* ¶◎ *CP.*

FodorsChoice ★

★ $$ 🖭 **Foster's Inn.** The hotel's street-level bar and restaurant, two doors away from the Avon Theatre, attracts a lively mix of locals, visitors, and theater aficionados. The brick building dates to 1906 and has a bit of history—it once housed the International Order of Odd Fellows, a fraternal organization that started in the United Kingdom. Brightly painted rooms, on the 2nd and 3rd floors, are comfortable if basic, with queen-size beds and wood floors. Though they're above the bar and restaurant, noise isn't a problem. The dining room's artsy waitstaff deliver good-size portions from an open kitchen. Room rates are discounted substantially in winter. ✉ *111 Downie St., N5A 6S3* ☎ *888/728–5555* ⊕ *www.fostersinn.com* ⤴ *9 rooms* ⚴ *Restaurant, cable TV, bar; no smoking* ☰ *AE, D, DC, MC, V.*

$–$$ 🖭 **Deacon House.** Dianna Hrysko and Mary Allen are the well-traveled hosts of this elegant, Edwardian-style home built in 1907. They have created a pleasant, cheery setting in a central location; the long porch is perfect for lounging with a book. Lots of antique country Canadiana fill the guest rooms and the two sitting rooms, and most rooms run to floral patterns and shades of pinks. The full buffet breakfast includes scrumptious scones and muffins and homemade sausages. ⊠ *101 Brunswick St., N5A 3L9* ☎ *519/273–2052* 🖷 *519/273–3784* ⊕ *www.bbcanada.com/1152.html* ⤴ *6 rooms* ⚱ *Dining room, fans; no kids, no smoking* ⊟ *MC, V* ⦿*BP.*

$–$$ 🏨 **Festival Inn.** An old-English atmosphere has survived modernization of this fairly large hotel on the eastern outskirts of town, only a short drive from the theaters. All rooms at this year-round inn have refrigerators and coffeemakers, and four have double whirlpool baths. ⌂ *1144 Ontario St., Box 811, N5A 6W1* ☎ *519/273–1150 or 800/463–3581* 🖷 *519/273–2111* ⊕ *www.festivalinnstratford.com* ⤴ *182 rooms* ⚱ *Restaurant, refrigerators, some in-room hot tubs, cable TV with movies, indoor pool, hot tub, sauna, lobby lounge, business services, meeting rooms, no-smoking rooms* ⊟ *AE, MC, V.*

$–$$ 🏨 **23 Albert Place.** Since this three-story, brick-front building was opened in 1876 as the Windsor Arms, it has been refurbished a few times; no elevator was ever installed, however, so prepare to walk up one or two flights to your room. The hotel is at the heart of the downtown shopping area, just a few hundred yards from the Avon Theatre. Some suites have minirefrigerators and VCRs. ⊠ *23 Albert St., N5A 3K2* ☎ *519/273–5800* 🖷 *519/273–5008* ⤴ *29 rooms, 5 suites* ⚱ *Restaurant, some refrigerators, cable TV, some in-room VCRs, lobby lounge* ⊟ *AE, MC, V.*

$ 🏨 **Swan Motel.** This unassuming brick motel, 3 km (2 mi) south of the Avon Theatre, is known for the flower beds on its generous grounds. Free coffee and muffins await guests in the morning. The Swan can book guests at nearby golf courses. ⊠ *959 Downie St. S, N5A 6S3* ☎ *519/271–6376* 🖷 *519/271–0682* ⊕ *www.swanmotel.on.ca* ⤴ *24 rooms* ⚱ *In-room data ports, refrigerators, cable TV, pool; no smoking* ⊟ *MC, V* ⊘ *Closed Dec.–late Apr.* ⦿ *CP.*

The Arts

Fodor'sChoice The **Stratford Festival** performances—now a mix of Shakespeare, works
★ by other dramatists, and popular musicals—take place in four theaters, each in its own building and each with particular physical aspects (size, stage configuration, technical support) that favor different types of productions. This also means that at the height of the season (July and August) you may have the flexibility of choosing among four simultaneous performances, and a weekend menu including up to 12 different productions.

The **Festival Theatre** (⊠ 55 Queen St.), the original and the largest, has a thrust stage that brings the action deep into the audience space. Try for fairly central seats in this theater. **The Avon** (⊠ 100 Downie St.) has a traditional proscenium stage, good sight lines, elevators to each level, and a theater store. The **Tom Patterson Theatre** (⊠ 111 Lakeside Dr.) is the most intimate of the festival venues. It has a modified thrust stage. The **Studio Theatre** (⊠ George St. and Waterloo St.) specializes in experimental and new works.

The Festival and the Avon theaters are open from late April to early November. The Tom Patterson and Studio productions start in May and close by the end of September. Matinee and evening performances run Tuesday through Saturday; Sunday has regular matinee and occasional evening shows. Theaters are closed Monday.

Regular tickets are C$50 to C$110, but there are many ways to pay less. Spring previews and select fall performances are discounted 30%. Tickets for designated student and senior matinees and performances can run 50% lower than normal prices; these shows require advance booking. Theatergoers aged 30 and under can buy seats online for C$20 two weeks prior to performances.

For tickets, information, and accommodations, contact the **Stratford Festival** (⌂ Box Office, Box 520, N5A 6V2 ☎ 519/273–1600 or 800/567–1600 ⊕ www.stratfordfestival.ca).

Shopping
Stratford's downtown area invites browsing with numerous clothing boutiques, antiques stores, garden shops, music stores, fine furniture and tableware shops, arts-and-crafts studios, galleries, and bookshops. The Theatre Stores, in the lobbies of the Festival and Avon theaters and at 100 Downie Street, offer exclusive festival-related gifts, original costume sketches, and play-related books and music, plus art books, literature, and children's classics.

Visitor Information
The **Stratford Festival** (☎ 519/273–1600 or 800/567–1600 ⊕ www.stratfordfestival.ca) has an accommodations bureau that can help you book a room if you're buying tickets, and lots of festival-related information. **Tourism Stratford** (✉ 47 Downie St., N5A 1W7 ☎ 519/271–5140 or 800/561–7926 ⊕ www.city.stratford.on.ca) has information on all area goings-on.

SIDE TRIPS A TO Z

To research prices, get advice from other travelers, and book travel arrangements, visit www.fodors.com.

AIRPORTS
Toronto, the province's largest city, serves most major airlines at Pearson International Airport. Ottawa International Airport is the gateway to Ontario's Capital Region. The Niagara Falls International Airport in Niagara Falls, New York, is the closest air link to Niagara Falls, Ontario, and its popular attractions.

🛈 Niagara Falls International Airport ☎ 716/297–4494 ⊕ www.nfta.com. **Ottawa International Airport** ☎ 613/248–2000 ⊕ www.ottawa-airport.ca. **Toronto Pearson International Airport** ☎ 416/776–3000 ⊕ www.gtaa.com.

BOAT TRAVEL
The Breeze high-speed ferry service, which debuted in 2004, connects Rochester, New York, with Toronto twice daily. The trip takes about two hours and 15 minutes.

🛈 **The Breeze** ✉ 8 Unwin Ave., Toronto ☎ 877/825–3774 ⊕ www.thebreeze.com.

BUS TRAVEL
About 20 intercity bus lines connect communities all over Ontario; many are run by Greyhound Canada and its affiliates. Ontario Northland serves Toronto, Central Ontario, and Northern Ontario. Penetang-Midland Coach Lines serves Toronto and Central Ontario. Trentway-Wagar Coach Canada

serves Niagara Falls, Hamilton, Toronto, and Kingston. Ontario Tourism can provide details on intercity bus routes, contacts, and schedules. ⚡ **Greyhound Canada & Voyageur Colonial Bus Lines** ☎ 800/661-8747 or 800/668-4438 ⊕ www.greyhound.ca. **Ontario Northland** ☎ 800/461-8558 ⊕ www.webusit.com. **Penetang-Midland Coach Lines** ☎ 800/461-1767 ⊕ www.greyhoundtravel.com/charter/pmcl. **Trentway-Wagar Coach Canada** ☎ 416/393-7911 or 800/461-7661 ⊕ www.coachcanada.com. **Ontario Tourism** ✉ Queen's Park, Toronto M7A 2E1 ☎ 905/282-1721 or 800/668-2746 ⊕ www.ontariotravel.net.

CAR TRAVEL

The Macdonald-Cartier Freeway, known as Highway 401, is Ontario's major highway link. It runs from Windsor in the southwest through Toronto, along the north shore of Lake Ontario, and along the north shore of the St. Lawrence River to the Québec border west of Montréal.

The Queen Elizabeth Way (QEW), named for the wife of King George VI, the late Queen Mother, runs from the U.S. border through the Niagara Region to Toronto. The four- to eight-lane freeway traverses Fort Erie, Niagara Falls, St. Catharines, and Hamilton, and ends in Toronto.

Highway 400 is the main north–south route between Toronto and the Cottage Country (Muskoka Region).

ROAD CONDITIONS Call for 24-hour road-condition information anywhere in Ontario. ⚡ **Road-condition information** ☎ 416/235-1110 or 800/268-1376.

RULES OF THE ROAD Ontario is a no-fault insurance province and minimum liability insurance is C$200,000. If you're driving across the Ontario border, bring the policy or the vehicle registration forms and a free Canadian Non-Resident Insurance Card from your insurance agent. If you're driving a borrowed car, also bring a letter of permission signed by the owner.

Driving motorized vehicles while impaired by alcohol is taken seriously and results in heavy fines, loss of license, vehicle impoundment, or imprisonment. You can be arrested for refusing to take a Breathalyzer test. Radar warning devices are illegal in Ontario even if they are turned off. Police can seize them on the spot, and heavy fines may be imposed.

Studded tires and window coatings that do not allow a clear view of the vehicle interior are forbidden. Right turns on red lights are permitted unless otherwise noted. Pedestrians crossing at designated crosswalks and traffic lights have the right of way.

EMERGENCIES
⚡ **Ambulance, fire, police** ☎ 911.

WHERE TO STAY

BED-AND-BREAKFASTS Some cities and towns have local B&B associations; ask regional and municipal visitor-information offices for more information. A comprehensive B&B guide listing about 200 establishments is published by the Federation of Ontario Bed and Breakfast Accommodations. Bed and Breakfast Online Canada can help you locate a B&B and reserve a room. ⚡ **Reservation Services Bed and Breakfast Online Canada Inc.** ☎ 800/239-1141 ⊕ www.bbcanada.com. **Federation of Ontario Bed and Breakfast Accommodations** ☎ 416/515-1293 ⊕ www.fobba.com.

COTTAGE RENTALS Cottage rentals are available through local real-estate agents or by consulting *Tyler's Cottage Rental Directory*, available in regional bookstores. Tyler's also has a Web site and a phone number, both of which you can use to book a cottage; these options require a C$17 membership fee, which is good for one year.
🚩 **Cottage Rentals** *Tyler's Cottage Rental Directory* ☎ 705/726-6015 or 800/461-7585 ⊕ www.tylers.ca.

SPORTS & THE OUTDOORS

CAMPING Peak season in Ontario parks is June through August, and it is advised that you reserve a campsite if reservations are accepted; sites can be guaranteed by phone, by mail, by Internet, or in person by using a debit card, Visa card, or MasterCard. All provincial parks that offer organized camping have some sites available on a first-come, first-served basis. In an effort to avoid overcrowding on canoe routes and hiking or backpacking trails, daily quotas have been established governing the number of people permitted in the parks. Permits can be obtained ahead of time. The cost per person is C$12. For detailed information on parks and campgrounds province-wide, contact Ontario Parks for the *Ontario Parks Guidebook* or Ontario Tourism for a free outdoor-adventure guide.
🚩 **Ontario Parks** ☎ 800/668-7275 ⊕ Box 25099, 370 Stone Rd. W, Guelph N1G 4T4 ⊕ www.ontarioparks.com. **Ontario Tourism** ✉ Queen's Park, Toronto M7A 2E1 ☎ 905/282-1721 or 800/668-2746 ⊕ www.ontariooutdoor.com.

DOGSLEDDING Winterdance Dogsled Tours take you on afternoon, multiday, and moonlit run adventures in Haliburton and Algonquin Provincial Park. Voyageur Quest provides Canadian wilderness trips year-round in Algonquin Park and throughout northern Ontario.
🚩 **Voyageur Quest** ☎ 416/486-3605 or 800/794-9660 ⊕ www.voyageurquest.com. **Winterdance Dogsled Tours** ☎ 705/457-5281 ⊕ www.winterdance.com.

FISHING Licenses are required for fishing in Ontario and may be purchased from Ministry of Natural Resources offices and from most sporting-goods stores, outfitters, and resorts. Seasons and catch limits change annually, and some districts impose closed seasons. Restrictions are published in *Recreational Fishing Regulations Summary*, free from the Ministry.

There are about 500 fishing resorts and lodges listed in the catalog of fishing packages available free from Ontario Tourism. The establishments are not hotels near bodies of water that contain fish but businesses designed to make sportfishing available to their guests. Each offers all the accoutrements, including boats, motors, guides, floatplanes, and freezers. Rates at these lodges are hefty.
🚩 **Ministry of Natural Resources** ✉ 300 Water St., Peterborough K9J 8M5 ☎ 705/755-2001 or 800/667-1940 ⊕ www.mnr.gov.on.ca/mnr/fishing. **Ontario Tourism** ✉ Queen's Park, Toronto M7A 2E1 ☎ 905/282-1721 or 800/668-2746 ⊕ www.ontariotravel.net.

MULTIACTIVITY SPORTS Call of the Wild offers guided trips of different lengths—dogsledding and cross-country skiing in winter, canoeing and hiking in summer—in Algonquin Provincial Park and other areas in southern Ontario. Prices include transportation from Toronto.
🚩 **Call of the Wild** ☎ 905/471-9453 or 800/776-9453 ⊕ www.callofthewild.ca.

RAFTING A growing number of companies in eastern Ontario offer packages ranging from half-day to weeklong trips from May through September.

Esprit Rafting Adventures offers trips on the Ottawa River, canoeing in Algonquin Provincial Park, or mountain biking in the Upper Ottawa Valley. Owl Rafting conducts half-day excursions on the nearby Ottawa and Madawaska rivers. RiverRun, in Beachburg, a 90-minute drive west of Ottawa, has one-day and multiday tours on the Ottawa River. **⁊ Esprit Rafting Adventures** ☎ 819/683-3241 or 800/596-7238 ⊕ www.espritrafting. com. **Owl Rafting** ☎ 613/646-2263, 613/238-7238, or 800/461-7238 ⊕ www.owl-mkc. ca. **RiverRun** ☎ 613/646-2501 or 800/267-8504 ⊕ www.riverrunners.com.

SKIING   Ski Ontario and snow report have information on the condition of slopes across the province. **⁊ Ski Ontario** ☎ 705/443-5450 ⊕ www.skiontario.on.ca. **Snow report** ☎ 905/282-1721 or 800/668-2746.

SNOWMOBILING   Ontario has 46,000 km (28,580 mi) of trails, and many outfitters and guided excursions are available from Haliburton Highlands–Algonquin Provincial Park to Kenora in the province's far northwest. Halley's Camps has guided excursions on wilderness trails to outpost camps for three to six nights. **⁊Halley's Camps** ☎ 807/224-6531, 800/465-3325 in Ontario ⊕ www.halleyscamps.com.

TRAIN TRAVEL
Ontario is served by cross-Canada VIA Rail, which stops in towns and cities across the southern sector of the province. VIA Rail connects with Amtrak service at Niagara Falls (New York) and Fort Erie (Buffalo, New York). Ontario Northland Rail Services provides four routes throughout Ontario, with service to and from Toronto. **⁊ Amtrak** ☎ 800/872-7245 ⊕ www.amtrak.com. **Ontario Northland Rail Services** ☎ 705/472-4500 or 800/268-9281 ⊕ www.ontc.on.ca. **VIA Rail** ☎ 416/236-2029 or 888/842-7245 ⊕ www.viarail.ca.

VISITOR INFORMATION
There are a number of tourism bureaus with excellent, free information. Ontario Tourism provides detailed guides about a variety of travel interests, from cruising rivers and lakes to big-city adventures, and can help you find information about nearly every corner of the province. **⁊ Georgian Bay Tourism** ✉ 208 King St., Midland L4R 3L9 ☎ 705/526-7884 or 800/263-7745 ⊕ www.georgianbaytourism.on.ca. **Muskoka Tourism** ✉ 1342 Hwy. 11 N, R. R. 2, Kilworthy P0E 1G0 ☎ 705/689-0660 or 800/267-9700 ⊕ discovermuskoka.ca. **Niagara Economic and Tourism Corp.** ✉ 424 S. Service Rd., Grimsby L3M 5A5 ☎ 905/945-5444 or 800/263-2988 ⊕ www.tourismniagara.com. **Niagara-on-the-Lake Chamber of Commerce and Visitor & Convention Bureau** ☎ 905/468-1950 ⊕ www.niagaraonthelake.com. **Ontario Tourism** ✉ Queen's Park, Toronto M7A 2E1 ☎ 905/282-1721 or 800/668-2746 ⊕ www.ontariotravel.net.

UNDERSTANDING TORONTO

TORONTO AT A GLANCE

TORONTO AT A GLANCE

Fast Facts

Nickname: Hogtown, T.O., T-Dot, the Big Smoke
Type of government: Mayor and 44 city councillors, democratically elected every three years in November
Population: 2.4 million (city), 4.9 million (metro)
Population Density: 3,744 people per square km (9,717 people per square mi)
Median age: 31
Crime rate: Down 1.4% in 2002; the second lowest among Canada's big cities

Language: English, French (both official)
Ethnic groups: White 63%; south Asian 10%; Chinese 9%; black 7%; Filipino 3%; Arab/West Asian 2%; Latin American 2%; other 2%; Korean 1%; southeast Asian 1%
Religion: Catholic 34%; Protestant 24%; unaffiliated 17%; Christian Orthodox 4%; Christian 3%; Muslim 5%; Jewish 4%; Buddhist 2%; Hindu 4%; Sikh 2%

Geography & Environment

Latitude: 43° N (same as Bucharest, Romania; Marseilles, France; Sapporo, Japan)
Longitude: 79° W (same as Panama City, Panama; Guayaquil, Ecuador)
Elevation: 105 meters (347 feet); highest point is 209 meters (686 feet) at intersection of Steeles Avenue West and Keele Street
Land area: 641 square km (247 square mi) (city); 5,903 square km (2,279 square mi) (metro)

Parkland: 8,000 hectares (19,768 acres) in 1,500 parks; 18.1 per cent of city's area
Terrain: Low lake and river shores, with Lake Ontario to the south, Etobicoke Creek to the west and the Rouge River to the east, with the metro area bounded by the rolling hills and river valleys of the Oak Ridges Moraine and the cliffs of the Niagara Escarpment
Natural hazards: Fires, floods, severe storms, tornados

Economy

Per capita income: C$38,598 (US$28,166)
Unemployment: 7.7%
Work force: 2.6 million; manufacturing 16%; retail trade 11%; professional, scientific, and technical services 10%; health care and social assistance 8%; finance and insurance 7%; wholesale trade 6%; educational services 6%; accommodation and food services 6%; transportation and warehousing 5%; administrative and support, waste management, and remediation services

5%; construction 5%; information and cultural industries 4%; other services (except public administration) 4%; public administration 3%; real estate and rental and leasing 2%; arts, entertainment, and recreation 2%; utilities 1%
Major industries: Aircraft, banking, distribution, printing and publishing, electrical machinery, farm implements, high-tech, metal products, shipping, slaughtering and meatpacking, tourism, wholesale

Did You Know?

• There's some debate among anthropologists over the origin of the word Toronto. It's agreed that the city name is a French adaptation of a Native American term. Beyond that, a popular theory claims that the city's name stems from the Huron *toronton,* or "place of meeting," referring to the city's beginning role as a trading post. A second theory traces it to the Mohawk *tkaronto* which means "where there are trees in the water," named so because of wood pens placed in the Atherley Narrows north of Toronto to catch fish.

• Toronto hosted the largest bingo game ever on August 19, 1983. 15,756 players hunted for numbers and letters for $165,563 in cash, with one winner taking home a record payout of $66,225.

• Toronto was the name of a successful rock band from the city in the 1980s. They opened for Robert Palmer and Ted Nugent on U.S. tours. The song "What About Love?" recorded by the band Heart was written by Toronto's guitarists.

• The CN Tower is the tallest freestanding tower in the world. It was originally planned only to be an antenna, to improve TV reception for residents in fast-growing Toronto, but builders added tourist facilities late in the design process. Now more than 2 million people visit each year. The 130,000-ton reinforced concrete tower was finished in 1975, stands 1,815 feet 5 inches tall, and would have 185 floors if it were an office or apartment building.

• If 16 miles and 1,368 yards of underground shopping sounds like fun to you, head for the PATH Walkway in Toronto. It's the largest of its kind in the world.

• Toronto instantly became North America's fifth largest city in 1998, when the cities of Toronto, York, East York, North York, Etobicoke, and Scarborough merged.

INDEX

Necropolis Cemetery, 40
Neill-Wycik College Hotel ⊟,
F23, 80-81
New Vintage Niagara Festival,
158
New Year's Eve at City Hall,
F20
Niagara Apothecary
(museum), 162
Niagara Falls, 149-158
children, attractions for,
153-154
dining, 154-156
exploring, 149-150, 152-154
festival, 150
guided tours, 157-158
lodging, 155-157
transportation, 173-174, 176
visitor information, 176
Niagara Falls Festival of
Lights, F20, 150
Niagara Falls IMAX Theatre/
The Daredevil Adventure
Gallery, 153
Niagara Fallsview Casino
Resort ⊟, 154, 156
Niagara Glen, 152
Niagara Grape & Wine
Festival, 158
Niagara Helicopter Ltd., 157
Niagara Historical Society
Museum, 162
Niagara Ice Wine Festival,
158
Niagara-on-the-Lake,
161-167
children, attractions for, 162
dining, 163-165
guided tours, 162-163
lodging, 164-166
nightlife and the arts, 166-167
Niagara Parks Botanical
Gardens and School of
Horticulture, 150, 152
Niagara Parks Butterfly
Conservatory, 150, 152
Niagara Peninsula, 149-167
Niagara Wine Festival, 158
Niagara Wine Region,
158-161
Nightlife, F24, 97-105
Niagara-on-the-Lake, 166-167
Stratford, 172
Nike (shop), 135
Norsemen Restaurant and
Resort ✕⊟, 147
North 44 ✕, 63
North of Toronto to the Lakes,
138-149

NorthbyNortheast (music
festival), F21, 103
Northeast, 81-82
Novotel Toronto Centre ⊟ 78

O

Oban Inn ✕⊟, 165
Observation decks, CN Tower,
15
Old City Hall, 20, 27
Old Mill Inn, The, ⊟, F23, 82
Old Prune ✕, 170
Old Toronto, F10, 4-9,
44-47, 50-51
Old Town Dining Room ✕,
165
Olde Angel Inn ✕⊟,
165-166
Ontario College of Art and
Design Gallery, 20, 27
Ontario Legislative Building,
29, 32
Ontario Place, 14, 17-18,
114
Ontario Sailing Association,
113
Ontario Science Centre, 43
Ontario Tennis Association,
114
Opera, 85
Opera House (rock club),
105
Orbit Room (jazz club), 104
Orillia, 142-143
Orillia Opera House,
142-143
Outdoor activities and sports,
F22, 107-114, 175
Niagara Falls, 157-158
North of Toronto to the Lakes,
140, 141, 145, 149-150
Over Easy ✕, F24, 58

P

Packing tips, F43-F44
Paddock, The (lounge), F24,
102
Pages Books and Magazines
(shop), 127
Palmerston Inn Bed &
Breakfast ⊟, 78-79
Pan-Asian restaurants, 55, 57,
60-61
Pangaea ✕, 58
Pantages Hotel ⊟, 72
Paramount (cinema), 94
Paramount Canada's
Wonderland, 43
Park Hyatt Toronto ⊟, 72

Parks, gardens, and ravines,
F22, 107-108
Alexander Muir Park, 108
Algonquin Provincial Park,
147-149
Bay-Adelaide Park, 10-11
Beaches Park, 107
camping in, 86, 148-149, 175
Centreville, 19
Edwards Gardens, 41
Fort George National Historic
Park, 162
Harbourfront Centre, 14, 17
High Park, 42, 107-108
Highland Creek Ravines, 108
Humber Valley Parkland, 109
James Gardens, 116
Marineland, 153
Morningside Park, 108
Mosaiculture Garden and
Niagara Parks Greenhouse,
153
Music Garden, 17
Niagara Glen, 152
Niagara Parks Botanical
Gardens and School of
Horticulture, 150, 152
Ontario Place, 14, 17-18, 114
Paramount Canada's
Wonderland, 43
Queen's Park, F10, 28-34
Scarlett Mills Park, 108
Sherwood Park, 108
Sir Casimir Gzowski Park, 108
Sunnyside Park, 108
Wellesley Park, 40
Woodbine Beach Park, 107
Parliament Street, 35, 36-37
Parry Sound, 142
Passports, F44-F45
Pastis Express ✕, 63
Pegasus on Church (bar), 99
Penetanguishene, 140-142
Pet emergency service, F39
Pharmacies, F30
Philomena and Dave Bed &
Breakfast ⊟, 81
Phoenix Concert Theatre, 103
Photo help, F31
Pillar and Post Inn, Spa and
Conference Centre ✕⊟,
164
Pillitteri Estates Winery, 159
Pilot Tavern (jazz club), 104
PJ O'Brien ✕, 51
Play It Again Sports, 113
Pop and Rock concerts,
104-105
Portage Inn ⊟, 147

NOTES

FODOR'S KEY TO THE GUIDES

America's guidebook leader publishes guides for every kind of traveler.
Check out our many series and find your perfect match.

FODOR'S GOLD GUIDES
America's favorite travel-guide series offers the most detailed insider reviews of hotels, restaurants, and attractions in all price ranges, plus great background information, smart tips, and useful maps.

COMPASS AMERICAN GUIDES
Stunning guides from top local writers and photographers, with gorgeous photos, literary excerpts, and colorful anecdotes. A must-have for culture mavens, history buffs, and new residents.

FODOR'S CITYPACKS
Concise city coverage in a guide plus a foldout map. The right choice for urban travelers who want everything under one cover.

FODOR'S EXPLORING GUIDES
Hundreds of color photos bring your destination to life. Lively stories lend insight into the culture, history, and people.

FODOR'S TRAVEL HISTORIC AMERICA
For travelers who want to experience history firsthand, this series gives in-depth coverage of historic sights, plus nearby restaurants and hotels. Themes include the Thirteen Colonies, the Old West, and the Lewis and Clark Trail.

FODOR'S POCKET GUIDES
For travelers who need only the essentials. The best of Fodor's in pocket-size packages for just $9.95.

FODOR'S FLASHMAPS
Every resident's map guide, with dozens of easy-to-follow maps of public transit, restaurants, shopping, museums, and more.

FODOR'S CITYGUIDES
Sourcebooks for living in the city: thousands of in-the-know listings for restaurants, shops, sports, nightlife, and other city resources.

FODOR'S AROUND THE CITY WITH KIDS
Up to 68 great ideas for family days, recommended by resident parents. Perfect for exploring in your own backyard or on the road.

FODOR'S HOW TO GUIDES
Get tips from the pros on planning the perfect trip. Learn how to pack, fly hassle-free, plan a honeymoon or cruise, stay healthy on the road, and travel with your baby.

FODOR'S LANGUAGES FOR TRAVELERS
Practice the local language before you hit the road. Available in phrase books, cassette sets, and CD sets.

KAREN BROWN'S GUIDES
Engaging guides—many with easy-to-follow inn-to-inn itineraries—to the most charming inns and B&Bs in the U.S.A. and Europe.

SEE IT GUIDES
Illustrated guidebooks that include the practical information travelers need, in gorgeous full color. Thousands of photos, hundreds of restaurant and hotel reviews, prices, and ratings for attractions all in one indispensable package. Perfect for travelers who want the best value packed in a fresh, easy-to-use, colorful layout.

OTHER GREAT TITLES FROM FODOR'S
Baseball Vacations, The Complete Guide to the National Parks, Family Vacations, Golf Digest's Places to Play, Great American Drives of the East, Great American Drives of the West, Great American Vacations, Healthy Escapes, National Parks of the West, Skiing USA.